Explorations in the Economics of Aging

A National Bureau
of Economic Research
Conference Report

Explorations in the Economics of Aging

Edited by **David A. Wise**

The University of Chicago Press

Chicago and London

DAVID A. WISE is the John F. Stambaugh Professor of Political Economy at the Kennedy School of Government at Harvard University, and the area director for health and retirement programs and the program director for the Economics of Aging at the National Bureau of Economic Research.

The University of Chicago Press, Chicago 60637
The University of Chicago Press, Ltd., London
© 2011 by the National Bureau of Economic Research
All rights reserved. Published 2011.
Printed in the United States of America

20 19 18 17 16 15 14 13 12 11   1 2 3 4 5
ISBN-13: 978-0-226-90337-8 (cloth)
ISBN-10: 0-226-90337-0 (cloth)

Library of Congress Cataloging-in-Publication Data

Explorations in the economics of aging / edited by David A. Wise.
        p. cm.—(National Bureau of Economic Research conference report)
    "This is the thirteenth in a series of NBER volumes on the Economics of Aging"—Introduction.
    ISBN-13: 978-0-226-90337-8 (alk. paper)
    ISBN-10: 0-226-90337-0 (alk. paper)
    1. Aging—Economic aspects. 2. Medical care, Cost of.
3. Medicare. 4. Aging—Religious aspects. I. Wise, David A.
II. Series: National Bureau of Economic Research conference report.
HQ1061.E975 2011
305.26—dc22
                                                2010031519

⊗ The paper used in this publication meets the minimum requirements of the American National Standard for Information Sciences— Permanence of Paper for Printed Library Materials, ANSI Z39.48-1992.

Relation of the Directors to the
Work and Publications of the
National Bureau of Economic Research

1. The object of the NBER is to ascertain and present to the economics profession, and to the public more generally, important economic facts and their interpretation in a scientific manner without policy recommendations. The Board of Directors is charged with the responsibility of ensuring that the work of the NBER is carried on in strict conformity with this object.

2. The President shall establish an internal review process to ensure that book manuscripts proposed for publication DO NOT contain policy recommendations. This shall apply both to the proceedings of conferences and to manuscripts by a single author or by one or more co-authors but shall not apply to authors of comments at NBER conferences who are not NBER affiliates.

3. No book manuscript reporting research shall be published by the NBER until the President has sent to each member of the Board a notice that a manuscript is recommended for publication and that in the President's opinion it is suitable for publication in accordance with the above principles of the NBER. Such notification will include a table of contents and an abstract or summary of the manuscript's content, a list of contributors if applicable, and a response form for use by Directors who desire a copy of the manuscript for review. Each manuscript shall contain a summary drawing attention to the nature and treatment of the problem studied and the main conclusions reached.

4. No volume shall be published until forty-five days have elapsed from the above notification of intention to publish it. During this period a copy shall be sent to any Director requesting it, and if any Director objects to publication on the grounds that the manuscript contains policy recommendations, the objection will be presented to the author(s) or editor(s). In case of dispute, all members of the Board shall be notified, and the President shall appoint an ad hoc committee of the Board to decide the matter; thirty days additional shall be granted for this purpose.

5. The President shall present annually to the Board a report describing the internal manuscript review process, any objections made by Directors before publication or by anyone after publication, any disputes about such matters, and how they were handled.

6. Publications of the NBER issued for informational purposes concerning the work of the Bureau, or issued to inform the public of the activities at the Bureau, including but not limited to the NBER Digest and Reporter, shall be consistent with the object stated in paragraph 1. They shall contain a specific disclaimer noting that they have not passed through the review procedures required in this resolution. The Executive Committee of the Board is charged with the review of all such publications from time to time.

7. NBER working papers and manuscripts distributed on the Bureau's web site are not deemed to be publications for the purpose of this resolution, but they shall be consistent with the object stated in paragraph 1. Working papers shall contain a specific disclaimer noting that they have not passed through the review procedures required in this resolution. The NBER's web site shall contain a similar disclaimer. The President shall establish an internal review process to ensure that the working papers and the web site do not contain policy recommendations, and shall report annually to the Board on this process and any concerns raised in connection with it.

8. Unless otherwise determined by the Board or exempted by the terms of paragraphs 6 and 7, a copy of this resolution shall be printed in each NBER publication as described in paragraph 2 above.

Contents

Preface

This volume consists of papers presented at a conference held in Carefree, Arizona, in May 2009. Most of the research was conducted as part of the program on the Economics of Aging at the National Bureau of Economic Research. The majority of the work was sponsored by the U.S. Department of Health and Human Services, through the National Institute on Aging grants P01-AG005842 and P30-AG012810 to the National Bureau of Economic Research. Any other funding sources are noted in the individual chapters.

Any opinions expressed in this volume are those of the respective authors and do not necessarily reflect the views of the National Bureau of Economic Research or the sponsoring organizations.

Introduction

David A. Wise and Richard Woodbury

The next twenty years mark a new phase in the demographic transition of the United States, as the baby boom generation becomes eligible for Social Security and Medicare. This large population mass, which has been in a prime working and earning phase of their careers, and supporting a comparatively smaller population of older retirees, reaches an age when they too may retire. The social and economic transition inherent in this demographic shift will be shaped to a significant extent by the labor market decisions of this population, how much they will have saved for their retirement, the cost of their health care, and the future evolution of retirement and health policy.

Research in the economics of aging is not limited to the United States, or to changing age demographics, or to studies of the elderly. The field covers aging issues around the world, in both developed and developing countries. It involves research on both health and economic circumstances, for both individuals and populations, and with particular focus on how health and economic circumstances evolve interactively over the life course. It encompasses advances in research methodology, data resources, experimental interventions, and the evolution of public policy in health, work, disability, and retirement.

This is the thirteenth in a series of NBER volumes on the economics of aging. The goal of this series is to present studies that are at the forefront of economics of aging research along multiple dimensions. The topics addressed in each volume have evolved with the science, though some core

David A. Wise is the John F. Stambaugh Professor of Political Economy at the Kennedy School of Government, Harvard University, and director of the program on aging at the National Bureau of Economic Research. Richard Woodbury is a senior administrator with the program on aging at the National Bureau of Economic Research.

themes have persisted. The volumes have generally included work on the evolving financial circumstances of individuals as they age, and the factors that influence financial well-being. They have included work on health and disability, medical practice patterns, health care costs, health care financing, and health policy. They have included work on aging around the world, including an increased focus on aging in developing countries. They have included work on the relationships between health and economic circumstances. And they have included work on research methodology, database development and, most recently, on what can be learned from experimental interventions. Through thirteen volumes, the large majority of this research has been funded by the National Institute on Aging, which has made a long-term commitment to advancing the economics of aging field.

The previous volumes are *The Economics of Aging, Issues in the Economics of Aging, Topics in the Economics of Aging, Studies in the Economics of Aging, Advances in the Economics of Aging, Inquiries in the Economics of Aging, Frontiers in the Economics of Aging, Themes in the Economics of Aging, Perspectives on the Economics of Aging, Analyses in the Economics of Aging, Developments in the Economics of Aging,* and *Research Findings in the Economics of Aging.* This introduction provides an overview of the studies contained in the volume, relying to a significant extent on the authors' own language to summarize their findings.

The volume is organized into four substantive topic areas, not dissimilar from past volumes, though with a continuing evolution of emphasis. The first section contains studies on retirement saving in the private sector. The second deals with trends in health care costs and coverage. The third focuses on relationships between socioeconomic circumstances and health. The fourth looks at issues in aging in less developed countries. There are many issues that cut across this organization. For example, in addition to the health issues addressed in the second and third section, chapter 1 in the first section draws out the important implications of poor health for the post-retirement evolution of assets, and chapter 10 in the fourth section considers a way to fight anemia in India. As noted, the studies are all components of longer-term research themes of the NBER program on aging, and an attempt is made to place these new studies in the context of our larger agenda.

Each chapter also includes comments provided by a discussant. These comments add a depth of perspective on each research topic. In some cases, the discussant comments put the primary study into a larger context. In some cases, they are critical commentary. And in other cases, they are expansions of either the theoretical underpinnings or empirical findings that are reported in the primary studies. The result is a richer treatment of each topic addressed. Because the volume focuses on studies that are at the forefront of economics of aging research, they are by their nature more exploratory or innovative. The discussant comments provide a certain grounding or breadth of perspective that is particularly valuable in assessing these more exploratory and innovative research directions.

Retirement Saving

Each of the thirteen volumes in the NBER's Economics of Aging series has looked at a new dimension in the evolving financial circumstances of individuals as they age. This theme has persisted, first because of the major changes over twenty-five years in how individuals finance their retirement. Studies have documented the changing composition of financial resources available at older ages, projected future changes, and followed cohorts of individuals affected by these changes. The "financial circumstances" theme has also persisted because of a realization that people's behavior is so dramatically influenced by the design of public and private programs and policies. This has opened up an entirely new area of research in understanding how the determinants of financial decision making, as well as behavior, change research—how to induce financial decision making that leads to better outcomes.

Financial support at older ages comes from a combination of Social Security, traditional defined-benefit pension benefits offered by employers, retirement saving, and income from work. The landscape and relative weight of these components has changed dramatically over the past two decades, and will likely change again in the decades ahead. The major change of the last two decades has been the growth in retirement saving programs, and particularly 401(k) plans, and a parallel decline in traditional defined-benefit pension programs. The trends to date suggest that private saving will be far more important and widespread in its implications than employer-provided pensions achieved at their peak. The implications of this saving will play out over time, as new retirees will have spent an increasing portion of their careers contributing and accumulating assets in private retirement accounts. The first two chapters in this volume consider issues in retirement saving.

Chapter 1, on "Family Status Transitions, Latent Health, and the Post-Retirement Evolution of Assets," is the most recent in a series of NBER studies on retirement saving by James M. Poterba, Steven F. Venti, and David A. Wise. In most of our past work, we have focused on the accumulation of assets in retirement saving accounts, and the implications of retirement saving for the financial circumstances of those that will be retiring in the future. As noted already, the implications are profound. In this study, we redirect our attention from the accumulation phase to the use of accumulated assets in later life. This redirection is a natural evolution of our research agenda, as 401(k)-type plans have matured. What is happening as more new retirees have substantial 401(k) balances that few previous retirees had available? How will this growing financial resource affect older households, both now and in the future?

A key question is the extent to which people's accumulated assets are (a) annuitized, thereby assuring that one does not outlive their financial resources, no matter how long they live; (b) drawn down gradually over time, thus providing an ongoing and steady stream of financial support for post-retirement consumption, but without a long-life guarantee; versus (c) "saved for a rainy day," thereby conserving resources for irregular or unanticipated financial needs.

Our initial work on asset drawdown suggests that accumulated assets, including both housing equity and retirement accounts, tend to be conserved for transitional life events, such as adverse health changes, widowhood, or nursing home entry. The aim of chapter 1 is to analyze more carefully these relationships. We focus our analysis on two questions: first, whether the drawdown of assets is triggered by shocks to family status, and second, how the evolution of assets is related to health status. We use longitudinal Health and Retirement Study (HRS) data from 1992 to 2006, following households across two-year intervals between waves, and evaluating how their asset balances change as they age from one survey wave to the next. There are several key results.

First, households without major family status transitions tend to conserve their assets, even allowing them to grow further into older age. For example, among two-person households who were age fifty-six to sixty-one in 1992 (aging to seventy to seventy-five years old in 2006), and who remained two-person households across the survey period, the average wave-to-wave increase in total assets was 6.3 percent. Even for older cohorts, those who were seventy to seventy-five years old in 1993 (aging to eighty-three to eighty-eight years old in 2006), the average wave-to-wave increase in total assets was 4.6 percent. For continuing one-person households, the median estimates are smaller, but assets still tend to increase, except at much older ages, when they are closer to constant across waves.

Second, people in households that experience a family status transition during an interval—by becoming widowed or divorced—often experience a large decline or no increase in total assets. The wave-to-wave change in assets following a family status transition is very different from the continuing asset growth of households without this transition. Substantial declines in asset balances are associated with divorce, and the declines are statistically different from zero. The total assets of persons entering widowhood increase on average but the increase is not significantly different from zero. Households that experience a family status transition also have substantially lower levels of assets than continuing two-person households.

Third, both the level and evolution of household assets is strongly related to health. People in better health have more assets to begin with, and more continuing growth of those assets into older ages. For example, among continuing two-person HRS households age fifty-six to sixty-one in 1992, the ratio of assets of people in the top health quintile to the assets of people in the bottom quintile was 1.7 in 1992, and grew to over 2.2 by 2006. Among continuing one-person HRS households age fifty-six to sixty-one in 1992, the ratio of assets of persons in the top health quintile to the assets of persons in the bottom grew from 2.8 in 1992 to 4.1 in 2006. Similar differences are found for older Asset and Health Dynamics Among the Oldest Old (AHEAD) households.

Our research in chapter 1 is empirical; we analyze data on how asset balances change after certain life events. In his discussant comments, David Laibson introduces a theoretical framework for modeling how individuals use their accumulated assets in later life. It provides a thoughtful theoretical perspective on the empirical findings that we report, and will inform our future work on the topic.

Chapter 2 is also part of a continuing series of studies on retirement saving, in this case by a research team made up of John Beshears, James J. Choi, David Laibson, and Brigitte C. Madrian. Most of their previous work has looked at how the characteristics of 401(k) plans affect the savings decisions of plan participants. The key finding from this work is that plan features like automatic enrollment and the default provisions of the plans have tremendous influence on the likelihood of participation, the amount saved, and the allocation of assets across the investment alternatives in the plan. More recent work has focused more extensively on portfolio allocation and its implications, such as the extent to which fund management fees are considered in investment decisions in 401(k) plans, and how the salience of management fees may impact investment decision making. Chapter 2 is another contribution in this ongoing series, asking in particular, "How Does Simplified Disclosure Affect Individuals' Mutual Fund Choices?" It adds one more piece to our understanding of how people make financial decisions, and how financial decision making might be improved through simple policy changes or interventions.

Motivated by concerns about the complexity of mutual fund prospectus statements, and by evidence that many investors may ignore them, the Securities and Exchange Commission (SEC) recently proposed and subsequently adopted a new simplified disclosure document. Mutual funds now have the option of sending investors this two- to four-page document, dubbed the "Summary Prospectus," instead of the more lengthy statutory prospectus. The Summary Prospectus contains key information about the mutual fund's investment objectives, strategies, risks, costs, and performance. This information can also be found in previously extant fund literature (the statutory prospectus, the Statement of Additional Information [SAI] and the shareholder report). The question explored in the study is whether people's investment behavior changes with the simplified presentation.

The methodology used in the study involves a behavioral experiment. The authors recruited 186 nonfaculty, white-collar Harvard employees to participate. The subjects were asked to allocate two hypothetical savings account portfolios: one among four actively managed equity mutual funds, and one among four actively managed bond mutual funds. The amount of each subject's payment for participation depended on how their chosen portfolios actually performed subsequent to the experimental session.

The subjects were assigned randomly into one of three groups. In the first group, subjects received only the funds' more lengthy statutory prospectuses. In the second group, subjects received only the funds' simplified Summary Prospectuses. In the third group, subjects received the Summary Prospectuses but could additionally request the statutory prospectuses. Subjects were randomly assigned to be paid based on either their subsequent *one-month* portfolio return or their subsequent *one-year* portfolio return. This distinction was important because the funds with initial investment fees, or "loads," should have been viewed as less attractive when the time horizon of the investment was shorter.

The study finds that providing the Summary Prospectus does not alter subjects' investment choices. The dollar-weighted average fees and past returns of mutual fund choices are statistically indistinguishable across the three experimental groups. However, subjects receiving the Summary Prospectus spent less time on their investment decision. Thus the principal welfare gain from the Summary Prospectus appears to come from allowing investors to spend less time and effort to arrive at the same portfolio decision they would have come to after reading only the statutory prospectuses.

It is not clear that the portfolio allocation decisions that people make are good ones, however. Lack of understanding of sales loads, in particular, appears to be widespread. For example, mutual fund purchase fees, or loads, as well as redemption fees at liquidation, should be avoided to a greater degree when the investment horizon is short. Yet even when the subjects in the study had a one-month investment horizon—where minimizing loads is the only sensible strategy—they did not avoid loads. Indeed, they chose portfolios with loads plus redemption fees that were on average 200 basis points higher than the load-minimizing options. This implies that investors are either confused about loads, overlook them, or believe (implausibly) that their chosen portfolio will achieve an annual rate of return that is as much as 24 percentage points higher than the load-minimizing portfolio. The simplified Summary Prospectus developed by the SEC appears not to alleviate these kinds of errors.

As emphasized in the discussant comments by Steven F. Venti, the lack of responsiveness to fees, loads, and expenses in investor decisions could be far more important than other components of the prospectus presentation. Based on the findings from chapter 2, Venti suggests that a great deal of care should be taken in the design of materials provided to investors, such as reframing the prospectus to focus more on fees and loads and less on past returns.

Health Care Costs

Most of the our past NBER volumes on the economics of aging have included new investigations of health, health care, or health policy, and this thirteenth volume is no exception. With continuing advances in medicine, continuing increases in health care costs, and major health policy changes at the national level, health care will almost certainly remain at the forefront of economics of aging research going forward as well. Highlighted in this volume are three topics that have grown in importance to the well-being of the elderly, and that have brought them to the forefront of economics of aging research: growing out-of-pocket medical costs as an increasing risk to financial security, continuing growth of Medicare costs, and implementation of Medicare Part D.

In chapter 3, "The Risk of Out-of-Pocket Health Care Expenditure at the End of Life," Samuel Marshall, Kathleen McGarry, and Jonathan S. Skinner analyze the magnitude, variation, persistence, and composition of out-of-pocket medical expenditures among older households. They are interested in the extent to which high out-of-pocket burdens represent temporary financial shocks, such as from a more sudden acute illness, or persistent financial burdens, such as from a long-term chronic illness. They focus in particular on patterns of out-of-pocket medical spending in the period leading up to death. The study follows up on earlier work on out-of-pocket spending by these investigators, but with a new emphasis on spending variation among households across longer time periods, and in the period before death.

Based on HRS data from 1998 to 2006, the results suggest that out-of-pocket expenditures near death are considerable, averaging over $10,000 per person in the last 1.2 years of life. Not surprisingly, the distribution of out-of-pocket spending is highly skewed, with a median level of spending under $4,800, but a ninety-fifth percentile of nearly $38,000. There is also considerable persistence in out-of-pocket costs over longer time horizons. Mean out-of-pocket expenditures for the last five years (including both single and married households) is about $33,000, with a median of $21,416 and a ninety-fifth percentile of over $100,000. For married couples only, the study finds mean and median estimates of combined spending of $55,672 and $41,693 over the six-year period surrounding the death of a spouse.

The largest components of out-of-pocket spending include nursing home care, hospital care, insurance premiums, and helpers. Combined spending for nursing home and hospital care averages $2,658 per person. (Nursing home care makes up two-thirds of this amount.) The ninety-fifth percentile level of spending for this category is much higher, at $17,499. Insurance premiums are also important components of spending, averaging $1,975. The third major component is helpers, averaging $1,911 in out-of-pocket spending. Spending on helpers is highly concentrated among relatively fewer households; the seventy-fifth percentile of spending is $0, the ninety-fifth percentile is over $13,000.

Out-of-pocket expenditures increase with both income and wealth. For example, the average out-of-pocket spending for the highest-income quartile is $11,469, compared with $7,443 for the lowest income quartile. The bottom wealth quartile spent an average of $5,731, compared with $14,324 in the top wealth quartile. These differences appear to be driven mostly by greater spending in the home on helpers, home health care, and other services to improve the independence of people living at home. Put differently, a large part of the incremental spending by households with greater financial resources is more discretionary spending in the home, buying independence and avoiding institutional care.

In his discussion of the chapter, David R. Weir adds perspective on the broader changes in finances that are likely to affect individuals in the period leading up to death, and that may explain changes in asset holdings that are larger than out-of-pocket spending for health care. He notes transfers to children, charitable donations, perhaps travel, and lost earnings (by self or spouse) as illustrations of how asset profiles might be altered by terminal illness.

Chapter 4 moves from out-of-pocket spending to Medicare spending. In "Cost Growth in Medicare: 1992 to 2006," Amitabh Chandra, Lindsay Sabik, and Jonathan S. Skinner examine trends in Medicare spending from 1992 to 2006 across all hospital referral regions (HRRs) in the United States. They decompose cost growth into changes in the distribution of the population among high- and low-spending HRRs, spending per enrollee, number, or medical encounters, and spending per encounter. They also look at the differences between Part A and Part B spending growth, and between different service categories within Part A and Part B. The study is an updated version of NBER work on Medicare cost trends that was conducted by other investigators in past years of the program, and it identifies some differences in cost trends in more recent years.

The study looks first at aggregate trends in Medicare spending and enrollment. Overall per capita Medicare fee-for-service spending grew at a real rate of 3.8 percent per year between 1992 and 1999, and at a rate of 2.7 percent per year from 1999 to 2006. Throughout both of these periods growth in Part B spending was higher than growth in Part A spending. Among subcategories of Part A and Part B spending, reimbursements for inpatient short stays and skilled nursing facilities had the highest absolute growth during the earlier years, while outpatient hospital services and medical care services had the highest absolute growth during the latter years. Relative growth in reimbursements for hospice services was high across both periods, though baseline spending for this category was low. Per enrollee spending in the highest cost area, hospital short stays, was relatively flat, while per enrollee spending on hospital outpatient services and physician medical care services more than doubled over the fourteen-year period. Reimbursements for home health care services grew quickly from 1992 to 1996, but dropped off after the Balanced Budget Act (BBA) of 1997 changed the reimbursement rules for home care. Patterns of growth in total Medicare spending are similar to per capita patterns, though total spending increases more rapidly in recent years with the acceleration of Medicare enrollment.

Both the number of medical encounters and the amount spent per encounter increase over the study period; though in latter years, the growth comes almost entirely from increased spending per encounter. Of course, within these aggregates, different types of services have different usage trends. For example, there are increases in physician medical care services and diagnostic, lab, and x-ray services. These result from more Medicare enrollees receiving these services, and from increasing frequency of use among those who receive them. For hospital outpatient services, the study finds similar increases in both the percent of enrollees using services and the number of encounters per enrollee. There is also wide variation in growth rates by procedure, with procedures like coronary artery bypass graft (CABG) and hip fracture remaining relatively flat or declining over the study period, while back surgery, hip replacement, knee replacement, and percutaneous coronary intervention (PCI) increase substantially. In general the procedures that experienced the greatest increases in use are those that may be more discretionary, rather than clearly indicated clinically.

Analyzing the data geographically, the large majority of Medicare spending growth is found to result from increased spending within HRRs, rather than from a redistribution of the population into higher spending HRRs. The rate of spending growth, however, varies considerably across HRRs. For Part A spending, the average annual growth rate of the slowest growing quintile of HRRs was 1.9 percent, while the fastest growing quintile had an average growth rate of 2.7 percent. Growth in Part B averaged 4.4 percent in the slowest growing quintile and 6.1 percent in the fastest growing quintile. High growth HRRs can be found with both high and low baseline levels of spending, and in larger and smaller referral regions.

A final section of the study looks at how "financial entrepreneurship" may differ across hospital referral regions. The authors seek to identify financial entrepreneurship by looking at the impact on home health care spending of the regulatory tightening in the Balanced Budget Act of 1997. Those affected more significantly by the regulations may have been more proactive in taking advantage of the looser reimbursement rules when they were in effect before the BBA. Thus the change in home care reimbursement following the BBA may be an indicator of more active financial entrepreneurship. Interestingly, both Part B reimbursements and purchases of durable medical equipment were found to be significantly higher in these more "entrepreneurial" HRR markets.

While chapter 4 analyzes historical spending trends in Medicare Parts A and B, chapter 5 focuses on the new Medicare Part D prescription drug program. Participation in Medicare Part D requires individuals to make active enrollment and plan choice decisions. Active decisions are made initially when first enrolling in the program, and can be revisited periodically during the program's annual open enrollment periods. Whether consumers make wise choices at these decision points is of interest not only for the evaluation of this particular market, but for consumer-directed health care more generally. In chapter 5, "The Demand for Medicare Part D Prescription Drug Coverage: Evidence from Four Waves of the Retirement Perspectives Survey," Florian Heiss, Daniel McFadden, and Joachim Winter explore how people decided among the prescription drug plan options made available through Medicare Part D, based on their prior drug use, self-rated health, and other factors.

To obtain data on health, prescription drug use, and Part D selection, the authors conducted four Internet-based interviews with samples of older Americans. They call their survey the Retirement Perspectives Survey, or RPS. The first wave of the RPS survey was conducted in November 2005, just before enrollment into Part D began. After the initial enrollment period closed on May 15, 2006, the authors reinterviewed the same respondents to elicit their actual Medicare Part D decisions for 2006. Third and fourth waves of the RPS survey were conducted in March/April 2007 and March/April 2009, enabling an expansion of the database to the decision making that occurs during the annual open enrollment periods. The latter waves also contained added measures of decision-making competence, planning horizon, and attitudes toward risk.

The analysis in chapter 5 concentrates on "active" decision making, either by enrolling in a Medicare Part D plan for the first time, or actively switching plans during the eligible open enrollment windows. The aim is to understand whether choices were related to the salient features of the program and the economic incentives they generated. Given the structure of the program, an individual's expected drug costs for the first year should be the most important determinant of plan selection. The results suggest that this is indeed the case. Enrollment in Medicare Part D was found to be driven strongly by the number of drugs used on a regular basis in the previous year. In all RPS waves, respondents who take three or more prescription drugs on a regular basis are much more likely to have stand-alone Part D coverage than those who take fewer drugs. Similarly, respondents whose self-rated health is "excellent" are less likely to have stand-alone Part D coverage.

All other variables, including those measuring decision-making competence, planning horizon, and attitudes toward risk, had little predictive power in explaining plan enrollment. The overall conclusion from the analysis is that consumers respond to the immediate incentives as they relate to their current health status and drug expenditures.

In her discussion of the chapter, Amy Finkelstein highlights the success of the study in identifying adverse selection, as distinct from moral hazard, in Medicare Part D coverage. She notes that it is rare to find situations in panel data where one can use past behavior (in this case prescription drug use) to demonstrate adverse selection in subsequent decision making about insurance. She also provides perspective on whether choice among Medicare Part D coverage options leads to better or worse social outcomes.

Socioeconomic Circumstances and Health

The third section of the volume deals with the relationship between socioeconomic characteristics and health. This too has been a continuing theme through most of the NBER's Economics of Aging books. Measures of well-being in one domain (income, wealth, or education, for example) are highly correlated and causally related to measures of well-being in the other domain (self-reported health, chronic illness rates, disability, or mortality, for example). The range of studies advancing our understanding of this relationship has encompassed a breadth of likely causal pathways, characteristics of the relationship, and implications; and has drawn on both single-country and comparative cross-national investigations.

The next four chapters in this volume address topics that continue to advance our understanding of how socioeconomic circumstances and health interrelate. The issues covered include the implications of differential mortality by income on the progressivity of the Social Security system, cognition and economic outcomes, religion and health, and scale variations in self-reported work disability. Each moves the science forward, either through an incremental substantive question, new data resource, or methodological development. The first two analyze issues in the United States; the latter two are multinational studies.

In chapter 6, "Differential Mortality by Income and Social Security Progressivity," Gopi Shah Goda, John B. Shoven, and Sita Nataraj Slavov assess the implications of differential mortality by income for the lifetime progressivity of the "old-age" or retirement portion of Social Security. It is well known, for example, that Social Security has a highly progressive benefit formula that applies in the determination of the monthly benefit amounts from the program. Workers with low lifetime earnings get a monthly payment stream with a much higher replacement rate than workers with high lifetime earnings. However, because of differential mortality by income, those with low lifetime earnings will on average receive their Social Security benefits for a shorter period of years. Thus, some of the progressivity in the benefit amount is counterbalanced by the longer average lifetimes experienced by higher lifetime income recipients of Social Security. The goal of this study is to quantify these offsetting effects.

The methodology used to study overall lifetime progressivity of age-based Social Security benefits is to calculate internal rates of return (IRRs) and net present values (NPVs) for the program under assumptions of differential mortality, as compared with population-average mortality rates. The study also considers how progressivity has changed from older to younger cohorts of program participants, as differential mortality by income has increased over time. The analyses are conducted using both hypothetical (or illustrative) earnings profiles, and the actual earnings histories of a sample of Social Security participants.

The key finding from the study is that differential mortality can change significantly the distributional characteristics of the program, though its impact varies by gender and cohort. Among older cohorts, differential mortality makes virtually no difference for women and a relatively small difference for men. For these older cohorts, the differences in mortality by income are not strong enough to offset the basic progressivity of the benefit formula. For more recent cohorts, differential mortality makes a substantial difference for men in particular. For example, in the 1938 birth cohort, differential mortality reduces the IRR from 1.51 percent to 1.07 percent for low income men, and raises it from 0.75 percent to 1.28 percent for high-income men. That means that for this cohort, once differential mortality is taken into account, men in the seventy-fifth percentile of income receive a higher rate of return on their payments into the system than men in the twenty-fifth percentile of income. The result is driven by the fact that mortality inequality is much larger for the younger cohorts. At least in terms of rates of return, an apparently progressive system becomes regressive.

Other finds from the study are that women experience higher IRRs and NPVs than men, because women have longer life expectancies than men. Also, for both men and women, later cohorts experience higher IRRs and NPVs than earlier ones, due to increases in overall life expectancy for these later cohorts. Of course this cross-cohort trend could reverse again in the future, depending on how Social Security taxes, benefits, and ages of eligibility for benefits continue to evolve going forward.

The discussion by Michael Hurd compares the results of this chapter with previous findings about Social Security progressivity, and explains some of the differences between them. In doing so, Hurd notes certain flaws in the current analysis, and a more comprehensive perspective from which to evaluate Social Security progressivity. The discussion also offers perspective on the term progressivity, and its relationship to public policy objectives.

Chapter 7 looks at another aspect of the socioeconomic status (SES)-health dynamic, focusing on cognitive skills as potentially influencing economic well-being over the life course. Indeed, the growing participation and saving in 401(k) plans may have created an increased impact of cognition, as individuals must decide for themselves how much to contribute to the plans, and how to invest their accumulated savings among the options available in the plan. In "Cognition and Economic Outcomes in the Health and Retirement Survey," John J. McArdle, James P. Smith, and Robert Willis examine the association of cognitive skills with wealth, wealth growth, and wealth composition for people in their pre- and post-retirement years.

The analysis relies on selected waves of HRS data, supplemented by a cognitive economics survey (CogEcon) that measures cognitive capabilities in more depth. The HRS is well-known for its high-quality measurement of many key SES variables, including income and wealth. In some waves of the HRS, cognitive measures are also assessed, including immediate and delayed memory recall, episodic memory and intact mental status, numeracy, numerical reasoning, and retrieval fluency. The study explores the relationship between these various cognitive measures and wealth outcomes. The study also compares the cognition-wealth relationship for the person in a household who is most responsible for finances with the cognition-wealth relationship for the person who is less financially responsible.

The study finds that "numeracy," as measured by answers to three relatively simple mathematical questions, is by far the most predictive of wealth among all cognitive variables in the HRS sample. The association between numeracy and wealth holds for both the financial and nonfinancial respondents, but the magnitude of the estimated impact is much higher for the financial respondent. In quantitative terms, the estimated effect of the financial respondent answering one of the "numeracy" questions correctly is a roughly $30,000 increase in household wealth; while the estimated effect of the nonfinancial respondent answering a question correctly is a roughly $10,000 increase in household wealth.

Other cognitive measures were also predictive of household wealth, but less powerfully than numeracy. For example, the limited HRS data on number series (as a broader measure of numerical reasoning) showed some impact on wealth. The more complicated and time intensive measurement of number series in the face-to-face component of the CogEcon sample performed much better in predicting wealth. Episodic memory (or word recall) also appears to be related to the total and financial wealth holdings of the family, and applies to both the financial and nonfinancial respondent. The variables on mental status and retrieval fluency had very weak and erratic relationships with the financial outcomes measured.

The authors emphasize that their research is not about the causal pathways underlying the cognition-wealth association, but is more purely exploratory about the existence of the relationship. In his discussion, Finis Welch also highlights the exploratory character of the chapter, and introduces some of the questions one would want to address in follow-up research.

In chapter 8, Angus Deaton explores aging, religion, and health (also the chapter title). He considers both the determinants and consequences of religion. For example, determinants of religiosity and religious practice may include demographic characteristics such as age and gender, economic factors such as income and education, and attitudes of government toward religion. Among the consequences of religion may be health-related behavior and health status, as well as broader measures of well-being. To explore these issues, Deaton relies on data from the Gallup World Poll, which randomly samples individuals from 146 countries around the world.

The chapter works with a model in which religiosity and religious practice are caused by income, education, age, and sex according to a stable set of patterns. Religion in turn is considered as a causal factor influencing health. While Deaton acknowledges substantial uncertainty, multidirectionality, and theoretical ambiguity in the causal relationships between religion and other variables, the study is presented as a largely exploratory first step in learning about these relationships. The study estimates these patterns for each country separately, and then examines similarities and differences across countries. It is a largely descriptive analysis of patterns of aging, religiosity, and health throughout the world.

In the vast majority of countries, women are found to be more religious than men, and the elderly more religious than the young. These two phenomena are related in that the difference in religiosity between men and women is positively and strongly correlated with the difference in religiosity between the young and the old. It is difficult to separate out age from cohort effects, but at least some of the evidence is consistent with pure age effects that are roughly consistent with rational choice theory—that religion should be postponed until late in life, that lower wages promote religiosity, and that the acquisition of religion can be postponed when life is longer. There is no obvious link between long-term income growth and the gap in religiosity between young and old, which is contrary to income-driven secularization.

The study also finds that, at least on average, over all countries, and over countries sorted into income groups, religious people do better on a number of health and health-related indicators. These protective effects appear to be strongest in poorer countries. Deaton emphasizes that none of these results show that the health benefits of religion can be obtained by joining a church, or even by undertaking a serious conversion. People who are religious are almost certainly different from nonreligious people in ways that go beyond their religiosity and beyond the basic educational and demographic controls that are used in the chapter. Even so, some of the correlations identified in the chapter appear remarkably universal across the religions and countries of the world.

Like the previous chapter, this study is highly exploratory; it is a very new area of economics of aging research, using a newly available data resource. Given the novelty of the research topic, and the novelty of the data, a real value in James P. Smith's discussant comments is the companion perspective offered. He interprets the empirical relationships presented in the chapter, and provides a second view, or a second set of observations on the apparent relationships between economic circumstances, religion, and health, and what causes those relationships.

In chapter 9, "Work Disability, Work, and Justification Bias in Europe and the United States," Arie Kapteyn, James P. Smith, and Arthur van Soest look at response scale differences in self-reported health measurement across countries and socioeconomic groups. The study aims to apply an innovative data calibration methodology known as vignettes to interpret self-reported measures.

As motivation for the study, the authors note the significant variation across Western European countries in both the fraction of workers receiving disability insurance benefits and, separately, the fraction that report having a work-limiting disability. But to what extent are differences in disability enrollment a result of differences in functional disability? Or, alternatively, to what extent do differences in program enrollment lead people to self-report differences in health? The complication in trying to make meaningful comparisons across countries is that self-reported disability status (or self-reported health measurement of any kind) may not mean the same thing to different people in different circumstances in different places.

Put another way, the response scales on which people describe their health may be different from one person to the next, and may be systematically related to culture, demographic group (such as age, gender, race, or ethnicity), socioeconomic circumstance (such as income, education, or wealth), public policy, work status, or other characteristic. Self-reported responses to health questions may also be subject to "justification bias"—the greater likelihood of reporting a disabling health condition as justification for not working, for example.

One question explored in the study is the magnitude of the variation in response scale and justification bias across countries. A second question is whether the response scale variations and biases can be corrected in a way that allows for meaningful cross-country comparisons of health. The study seeks to identify justification bias and other systematic response variations across countries and across socioeconomic groups in the United States and Europe, focusing specifically on self-reported work-limiting disability.

The primary methodology used in the chapter is to apply anchoring vignettes. The basic idea behind vignettes is as a calibration tool. A vignette describes the health-related circumstances of a hypothetical individual, and asks the respondent to make an assessment of that person's work-limiting health status on a scale matching the scale used to self-report their own work-limiting health status. For example, is the hypothetical person "not at all limited" in the work they do, "mildly limited," "moderately limited," "severely limited," or "cannot do any work?" The responses to the vignettes help to interpret what the respondent means in describing their own health status; they help calibrate the self-reported disability status measurement to a kind of benchmark response.

The study finds that people's self-reported definition of what constitutes a health-related work limitation is related to the generosity of earnings replacement schemes and employment protection in different countries. In countries with more generous income replacement programs, there is an increased likelihood of reporting a health-related work limitation that is independent of actual health status. The study finds further that the variation in self-reported disabilities across European countries declines substantially when vignettes are used to calibrate responses, and to make the response scales more comparable across countries.

There are also noticeable differences in response scales between the United States and the European countries studied. Americans appear to be less likely to self-report themselves as work disabled than Europeans. The results suggest as well that justification bias plays a larger role in response patterns in the United States; Americans appear to use health-related work disability as a justification for not working, whereas Europeans do not feel the need to do so. The effect of health limitations on employment at older ages is estimated to be about twice as large in the United States as it is in Europe, reflecting at least in part the earlier departure from the labor force that occurs in many European countries regardless of health.

The discussant comments by Angus Deaton provide a critical perspective on the use of vignettes as a data calibration tool. Deaton argues that the use of vignettes rejects the assumption that people's self-reports of disabilities are internationally comparable, and replaces it with an assumption that their capacity for empathy is internationally comparable. Since the two assumptions are very similar, and similarly plausible or implausible, he sees little gained from their use. The ability of vignettes to correct response scales across different languages and cultures is also questioned. Together, the study and the critique provide informative lessons, an illustrative application and analytic perspective on this innovative methodological approach.

Aging in Less Developed Countries

In the last several NBER volumes on the economics of aging, we have added work on aging, health, and living circumstances in less developed countries. These studies have informed our knowledge of the particular challenges of aging in very poor regions of the world. The research has also explored the potential for improving health and economic circumstances, based on public policy changes that have been implemented, and experimental interventions that have been tested. The collection of high-quality data on these poor regions of the world has been a particularly important goal of past work, and several papers have been produced describing household circumstances, based on these new data.

The last two studies in this volume also deal with aging in less developed countries. One involves an experimental health intervention in a very poor region of rural India. The other is a study of how high spending on funerals affects the household finances and life circumstances of families in a very poor region of South Africa. Both studies are extensions of past work on health and economic circumstances in these regions by the respective investigator teams.

In chapter 10, "Is Decentralized Iron Fortification a Feasible Option to Fight Anemia Among the Poorest?," Abhijit Banerjee, Esther Duflo, and Rachel Glennerster describe the impact of a village-level health intervention to fortify locally milled flour. Iron deficiency is believed to be the most common nutrient deficiency in the world today, and is thought to cause reduced productivity, increased susceptibility to illness, and cognitive difficulties in childhood. Iron supplementation of foods is considered an attractive means to reducing anemia, because it requires no additional effort on the part of the consumer, and can be done cheaply in centralized locations. However, for very poor and isolated populations, such as the population in the tribal district of Udaipur, where this study was conducted, centralized food fortification is not a practical solution: most households consume their own grain, and do not purchase any goods that could easily be fortified. The only way to reach these households is to fortify flour at the village level. So for this experimental study, local millers were trained and supplied with simple equipment to fortify flour in a safe and easily implemented way.

The intervention was implemented in 68 villages, randomly chosen out of 134. A first objective of the evaluation was to assess the logistical feasibility of the intervention: is it possible to recruit, train, and monitor millers and to keep them regularly supplied? Will the population accept the program? A second objective was to determine the impact of the program on anemia. To this end, the researchers collected data on hemoglobin levels at baseline, midline, and end line. The third objective was to determine whether the program had any health effect, beyond a possible reduction in anemia. To achieve this, the investigators collected rich data on health at baseline and end line and administered a unique monthly health survey. The final objective was to assess whether there would be any economic impacts of the program, such as through increased work capacity and higher school attendance.

The results were mixed. Program take up increased steeply over the first six months, but subsequently declined. Ultimately take up was quite low (around 30 percent of flour was fortified). The program was effective in reducing anemia as long as the take up was high enough, but ineffective when and where take up was low. It also reduced symptoms of fatigue when take up was sufficiently high. It did not lead to other improvement in health, or to increases in labor supply.

Because the tangible health benefits of the program may have seemed modest to the people receiving the iron supplements, their willingness to pay (or to add even a minor additional inconvenience) appears to be low. For example, the drop in program participation was faster among people whose nearest miller was not fortifying flour as well as for those who had to walk more than 1.5 kilometers to find a fortifying miller. Ultimately, low demand from the households seems to be at the root of the decay of the program. This is despite some positive impact on symptoms of weakness in the program's initial phase.

The discussion of the chapter by Amitabh Chandra and Heidi Williams explores explanations for the mixed success of the experimental intervention, and potential changes or additions to the intervention that could improve its effectiveness.

In chapter 11, "Requiescat in Pace? The Consequences of High-Priced Funerals in South Africa," Anne Case and Alicia Menendez highlight the substantial fraction of a household's economic resources that are expended on funerals in South Africa, and the implications of this spending for economic well-being. According to the authors, funerals in South Africa are generally considered an individual's most important rite of passage. As a result, they tend to be more elaborate and expensive than weddings, graduations, or naming ceremonies for children. Households may spend the equivalent of a year's income for an adult's funeral, borrowing from money lenders if need be to have a funeral that befits the status of the household and of the person who died. The study is an attempt to quantify these costs, and to analyze their impact on the circumstances and functioning of the household.

The study analyzes data that the authors helped to collect in the Agincourt Demographic Surveillance Site in South Africa in 2004. The data describe the economic and health circumstances of about 3,000 individuals in close to 500 households. The authors find that the average amount spent on an adult funeral is 3,400 rand—equivalent to 40 percent of average annual total household expenditures. The implications of this spending for the lives of surviving families appear to be substantial. For example, households that experienced a death in the past five years have significantly lower expenditures per person than do other households. Adults in households that experienced a death report significantly more symptoms of depression and anxiety, and significantly more problems in their households. Children in households that experienced a death in the past five years are significantly less likely to be enrolled in school than are other children their age.

Many of these effects on households appear to result from the amount of money that the household spent on the funeral. In other words, the differences in household circumstances are found to be associated not just from the death itself, but from the amount of financial resources that a household contributes to the funeral. For example, the larger the household's financial contribution to the funeral, the less likely it is that children are enrolled in school, and the more likely it is that adults are depressed and anxious.

The authors find little evidence that households that experienced deaths were different in observable ways from other households. They find no association between the death of family members aged six or older and assets holdings, maximum education of a member, or the type of household dwelling. Drawing on multiple aspects of the database, households that experienced a death appear much like other households in the demographic surveillance area. Thus the occurrence of the death, and the amount spent on the funeral, appear to result in poorer household circumstances along a number of dimensions. The implication is that reigning in the size of funerals may serve to improve post-funeral household circumstances.

The discussion of the study by Esther Duflo notes other countries where funeral spending is high, and where public policy has been used to try to contain it. The discussion also considers the reasons for high funeral spending, such as social and cultural norms, as well as the role of life or burial insurance.

I

Retirement Saving

1

Family Status Transitions, Latent Health, and the Post-Retirement Evolution of Assets

James M. Poterba, Steven F. Venti, and David A. Wise

Personal retirement accounts are one of the primary means of saving for retirement in the United States. Since the advent of these accounts in the early 1980s, a great deal of attention has been directed to the accumulation of retirement assets in these accounts. Much less attention has been directed to the drawdown of assets under a regime in which personal accounts play an increasingly important role. When private retirement saving was dominated by employer-provided defined-benefit plans, benefits were typically dispersed in the form of annuities. Under the personal account regime only a very small fraction of retirement assets are annuitized, and the drawdown of assets is largely self-directed.

The increasing importance of personal retirement accounts raises a number of important questions. One is how the evolution of assets in retirement is related to precipitating "shocks," such as health events, widowhood, divorce, and nursing home entry. All of these shocks may have financial

James M. Poterba is the Mitsui Professor of Economics at the Massachusetts Institute of Technology, and president and chief executive officer of the National Bureau of Economic Research. Steven F. Venti is the DeWalt Ankeny Professor of Economic Policy and professor of economics at Dartmouth College, and a research associate of the National Bureau of Economic Research. David A. Wise is the John F. Stambaugh Professor of Political Economy at the Kennedy School of Government, Harvard University, and director of the program on aging at the National Bureau of Economic Research.

This research was supported by the U.S. Social Security Administration through grant #10-P-98363-1-05 to the National Bureau of Economic Research as part of the SSA Retirement Research Consortium. Funding was also provided through grant number P01-AG005842 from the National Institute on Aging. The findings and conclusions expressed are solely those of the authors and do not represent the views of SSA, any agency of the federal government, or the NBER. We have benefited from the comments of participants in the Conference on the Economics of Aging in May 2009, particularly our discussant David Laibson, and from two reviewers for the University of Chicago Press.

consequences. Another is how the distribution of assets evolves with age. What is the likelihood of a household being unable to cover the cost of health shocks or the cost of a change in family status? A third question is how alternative methods of managing asset drawdown may affect financial well-being. In particular, how does the current largely "self-directed" system compare to a more "managed" system such as one featuring partial or full annuitization of personal account assets? Finally, how do recent and anticipated future developments, such as the recent decline in financial asset values, rising retirement ages, and the anticipated growth in personal retirement assets in future decades, affect the ability of households to meet health and family status shocks?

The principal aim of this chapter is to set out a data framework that can support analysis of these questions. We focus our analysis on the extent to which the drawdown of assets is triggered by shocks to family status and how the evolution of assets is related to health status.

Venti and Wise (2001, 2004) considered the drawdown of home equity in retirement. They found that, on average, home equity increased through age seventy and declined slightly (1.76 percent per year) thereafter. Almost all of this average decline for older retirees could be accounted for by the decline in home equity among households experiencing shocks to family status, like death of a spouse or entry into a nursing home. There was little decline for households that did not experience shocks, which suggested that home equity was typically not used to support general consumption in retirement but instead was conserved for a "rainy day." Megbolugbe, Sa-Aadu, and Shilling (1997, 1999) and Banks et al. (2007) also found that the drawdown of assets was greatest at times of change in family status. Davidoff (2007) concludes that households may preserve their home equity to finance potentially large health expenses, using home equity as an informal source of long-term care insurance.

In Poterba, Venti, and Wise (2008), we found that IRA and 401(k) assets tend to be conserved and that less than one-quarter of all account holders withdraw assets from these accounts before age 70.5, the age at which they become subject to minimum distribution requirements. Even among those who made withdrawals before age 70.5, the amounts averaged less than 2 percent of the balance. Holden and Schrass (2009) found that only 21.4 percent of IRA-owning households age fifty-nine to sixty-nine made a withdrawal in 2008. This evidence suggests that personal retirement plan assets, like home equity, are husbanded in retirement—at least by many households.

Most previous research on retirement saving has focused on asset accumulation, not the drawdown of assets after retirement. A notable exception is the study by Hurd and Rohwedder (2006), which tracks wealth changes and household consumption in panel data. There have also been a number of studies, summarized in Hurst (2008), of household consumption after retirement. But the consumption literature in most cases does not examine changes in asset holdings.

Among the studies that do focus on changes in wealth, there has been limited attention to shocks to family status. Hurd (2002), using Health and Retirement Study (HRS) data, finds that most components of the portfolios of the elderly grow after retirement. The exception, he finds, is that the probability of owning a home declines after age eighty. Coile and Milligan (2009), also studying HRS data, find that holdings of housing and vehicles decline with age but that holdings of financial assets increase. They find that shocks, particularly widowhood, are coincident with asset drawdown, and in particular with a decline in home ownership. They do not compare the age profile of housing and vehicle ownership for those with, and without, shocks to health and family status. Haveman et al. (2005) consider whether assets at retirement are sufficient to maintain for the next ten years the earnings replacement rate at retirement, using the Social Security Administration's (SSA's) New Beneficiary Survey. They find that although the median replacement rate remains constant, there is substantial variation over time. Over a fifth of the households judged to have adequate saving at retirement fell below their retirement-age replacement rate by ten years after retirement. Lupton and Smith (2000) explore the relationship between family status and wealth using the first wave of the HRS and three waves of the Panel Study of Income Dynamics (PSID). Their cross-sectional analysis using the HRS shows that there are large wealth differences by marital status. Their longitudinal analysis using the PSID shows that assets increase for continuously married families, are unchanged for divorced or separated families, and decline for widowed families. The PSID results pertain to households that are younger than the HRS households that we study, and thus the estimated changes in assets reflect differences in pre-retirement saving rather than post-retirement asset drawdown.

In this chapter we ask if the key features of the drawdown of home equity and personal retirement assets are reflected in the drawdown of other assets as well. Our key data source is the HRS. We use eight waves of data from the original HRS cohort who were age fifty-one to sixty-one in 1992, and seven waves of data from the original Asset and Health Dynamics Among the Oldest Old (AHEAD) cohort who were age seventy and older in 1993. The results are based on the observed evolution of the assets of these two cohorts as they age. The HRS cohort is followed from 1992 until 2006 and the AHEAD cohort from 1993 until 2006. Thus, our results do not capture the effect of the recent sharp decline in financial and housing markets.

A key issue confounding our analysis is the high incidence of apparent asset reporting errors and missing data. Details of these data problems are set out in the appendix. We use medians and trimmed means in an attempt to limit the effects of data errors. We are also limited in our analysis because the HRS and AHEAD data do not allow reliable estimation of 401(k) assets, an increasingly important source of retirement saving. This limitation and measurement problems are discussed in section 1.1.

This chapter is divided into eight sections. The first five consider the relationship between family status transitions and the post-retirement evolution of total assets, defined broadly to include financial assets, home equity, and retirement plan assets. We emphasize the drawdown of assets that are controlled directly by the household. Thus we do not include the asset value of annuities received from Social Security or from defined-benefit pension plans. We focus on how asset accumulation patterns vary across households that experience different family status transitions, distinguishing continuing two-person families, families that transition from two-person to one-person families, and continuing one-person families. In section 1.1, we describe how the data are organized for analysis, as well as the limitations of the data. In section 1.2, we consider the evolution of the assets of the HRS cohort between 1992 and 2006. In section 1.3, we consider the evolution of the assets of the older AHEAD cohort between 1993 and 2006. In section 1.4, we look more closely at the assets of individuals in households that experience a family status transition by considering their assets before and after the transition. In section 1.5, we compare the results based on the HRS and AHEAD cohorts with results for the same cohorts based on the Survey of Income and Program Participation (SIPP) data. We also expand the analysis of family status transitions to consider the effect of latent health on the level and the evolution of assets. In section 1.6, we describe the latent health index that we use to index health status. In section 1.7, we describe the relationship between latent health and the level and evolution of assets, within family status transition groups. Section 1.8 is a summary and discussion of future work.

1.1   Family Status Transitions and the Evolution of Assets: Data Limitations and Organization

We begin with analysis of the evolution of total assets based on data from the HRS using both the original HRS cohort and the AHEAD cohort. The analysis, however, is confounded by data limitations and reporting errors that have motivated the analysis and conditioned how the analysis proceeds. Thus we give attention to these issues before explaining how the data is organized for analysis.

The key limitation of the HRS and AHEAD data is the measurement of 401(k) assets. These data sets provide reliable information on assets in IRA and Keogh plans but, as noted before, not on assets in 401(k) accounts. A large proportion of IRA balances (which are included in our measure of total assets) represent rollovers from 401(k) plans, however. But the information on directly held 401(k) balances in the HRS is incomplete and is not used in this analysis. Thus we compare the results based on the HRS and

AHEAD data with results based on the SIPP that does include 401(k) assets. We find that SIPP trends are similar to those based on the HRS and AHEAD data, but the rates of increase are typically higher based on the SIPP data.

Data reporting errors and missing data also pose difficulties for our analysis and condition the approach we have taken. Curtin, Juster, and Morgan (1989); Juster, Smith, and Stafford (1999); Bosworth and Smart (2009); and others have shown that survey estimates of wealth are well-known to be susceptible to underreporting and misreporting. This is true in all large household-level surveys and is a particularly severe problem among wealthy respondents.

A careful examination of the HRS data used in this analysis reveals two sources of apparent error. The first is the misreporting of asset ownership. A household may, for example, report owning a home (or some other major asset) for four waves, then report no ownership for a wave, and then report ownership again in subsequent waves.[1] The second source is the misreporting of the value of an asset. In this case a respondent may report a particular value for several periods, then report a wildly different value for one period, and then report the original value in subsequent periods. In some cases these apparent "errors" may be valid responses—a person may sell a home and not repurchase for another year. If this is the case, then the loss of value in the "misreported" asset should be offset by an increase in value elsewhere on the household balance sheet. This does not happen in the majority of the cases, so misreporting is the most likely explanation for many of the extreme dips and spikes we observe in the data. Smith (1995) provides additional details on inconsistent asset levels in the first two waves of the HRS.

The high frequency of apparent misreporting of asset values leads to volatile estimates of mean assets, especially in small samples. This type of measurement error is particularly serious in longitudinal analyses when the variable of interest is the wave-to-wave *change* in wealth. A single misreport in a panel will result in two incorrect measurements of the change in wealth. For example, failure to report an asset on one wave will lead to a large negative change and a large positive change in two consecutive surveys. Moreover, these spurious changes are likely to be large relative to correctly reported values, so misreports generate a large amount of "noise" relative to signal, thus making it very difficult to obtain reliable estimates of even simple statistics such as the mean rate of wealth accumulation.

We have directed considerable attention to dealing with data problems associated with apparent misreporting. In most instances we do not directly

---

1. This problem is particularly severe for pension assets—a major component of total wealth. Gustman and Steinmeier (2004); Gustman, Steinmeier, and Tabatabai (2008); and Dushi and Honig (2008) show that a large fraction of the population has little knowledge of the features of their pension and often misreport something as basic as pension type (DC vs. DB). In many surveys, including the HRS, a misreported pension type means that the pension balance is not collected.

estimate changes in total assets. Instead we obtain estimates of the change in assets by separately estimating the level of assets at the beginning of the period and the level of assets at the end of the period and then calculating the mean change as the difference between mean levels. We also make extensive use of medians and trimmed means to lessen the influence of outliers that may be the result of misreporting.[2]

There are two additional features of the HRS data that bear on the quality of reported asset information. First, these apparent misreporting errors persist in the data despite the sophisticated bracketing methods employed in the HRS. When a respondent fails to provide an asset value, a follow-up question asks if the value fell in a particular interval. Additional follow-up questions narrow the range. These bracketing methods have been shown to significantly reduce the rate of nonresponse. Second, there are some special issues concerning the collection of data on 401(k) assets. In particular, persons are well-known to misreport the type of pension (defined benefit or defined contribution) they have. When a currently employed person with a DC plan misreports his pension as DB, the person is not queried about the balance. Thus we observe many large wave-to-wave fluctuations in 401(k) assets that appear to be the result of misreporting pension type. There are also difficulties with the collection of 401(k) balances for persons who are retired, but still have a 401(k) balance with their previous employer. In principle, information about pensions with past employers should have been "preloaded" in the HRS survey instruments to prompt questions about these balances. However, in many years this preloading did not occur or was incomplete so complete 401(k) balances were not obtained. Because of these problems we have chosen to exclude all 401(k) balances from the measure of total assets in our analyses using the HRS (we do include IRA and Keogh assets). In section 1.5 we compare HRS data to SIPP data, which contains more complete 401(k) data, to gauge the extent of this problem.

Our analysis uses wealth at the beginning and end of each two-year interval to calculate the change in assets. This change in assets can be separated into two components: withdrawals (or deposits) and capital losses (gains). The distinction is particularly relevant in the current financial crisis because it is important to know if declining wealth reflects active asset spend-down or passive asset repricing. The HRS provides limited information on this distinction. There is very good information on direct withdrawals from IRAs and Keoghs, but the data on withdrawals from 401(k) are subject to the same problems that prevent us from using the data on 401(k) balances. There

---

2. There is, in principle, another approach we could employ—go back to the raw data and "correct" misreported values. This approach would rely in part on an "asset verification" module, described in Hill (2006), that is now part of the biannual HRS survey. Responses in the current survey wave are compared to responses in the previous wave and respondents are asked to reconcile inconsistencies. The data collected by this module have not been used in the present analysis, although we hope to use them in future analyses.

are also very good data on house sales that allow us to distinguish between withdrawals of home equity and falling house values. The data on withdrawals from other asset balances is less complete. Respondents are only asked if they bought or put money in stocks or mutual funds and if they sold or cashed in any stocks or mutual funds since the previous interview. They are also asked the dollar amount of these transactions. There is no information on withdrawal of funds from other assets (e.g., bonds, CDs, money market instruments, etc.) held by households.

We turn now to how we organize the data for analysis. For this analysis the unit of observation is the *person* rather than the household. From the HRS we follow persons first surveyed in 1992 when they were age fifty-one to sixty-one and subsequently resurveyed every other year through 2006 (when they were age sixty-five to seventy-five). We look at asset growth over the two-year intervals between each of the seven survey waves, from 1992 to 1994, 1994 to 1996, and so forth through 2004 to 2006. From the AHEAD cohort, we follow persons aged seventy to eighty first surveyed in 1993 and then resurveyed in 1995, 1998, 2000, 2002, 2004, and 2006. For these persons we consider changes from 1993 to 1995, 1995 to 1998, 1998 to 2000, 2000 to 2002, 2002 to 2004, and 2004 to 2006. In many instances we follow subsets of the HRS and AHEAD age ranges; for example, looking only at persons age fifty-six to sixty-one from the HRS or persons age seventy to seventy-five from the AHEAD. The age groups we consider are summarized in figure 1.1. For each age interval the figure shows the range of ages for the youngest members of the group and for the oldest members of the group. For example, the last row of the figure, labeled "HRS 51–65 in 1992: youngest" shows that the youngest member of this age interval was fifty-one years old when first surveyed in 1992 and sixty-five years old when last surveyed in 2006.

Finally we also use data from three panels of the SIPP. From the 1996 panel of the SIPP we obtain data for 1997, 1998, 1999, and 2000 and thus we calculate asset changes from 1997 to 1998, 1998 to 1999, and 1999 to 2000. From the 2001 panel of the SIPP we have data for 2001, 2002, and 2003, and thus changes from 2001 to 2002, 2002 to 2003, and 2003 to 2004. From the 2004 panel of SIPP we have data for 2004 and 2005, and thus the change from 2004 to 2005. We have six year-to-year changes from the SIPP data, from 1997 to 1998, 1998 to 1999, and so forth to 2004 to 2005. The SIPP data differ in one important way from the HRS data: SIPP collects data for all respondents age fifteen and older (but top-codes age at eighty-five). Thus it is possible to choose a sample from the SIPP that "matches" as closely as possible the age ranges in the two HRS samples.

For each of the three data sources we consider assets at the beginning and end of each interval, although the width of the intervals differ—one year in the SIPP and, with one exception, two years in the HRS and the AHEAD data.

For each person in each survey we categorize family status at the

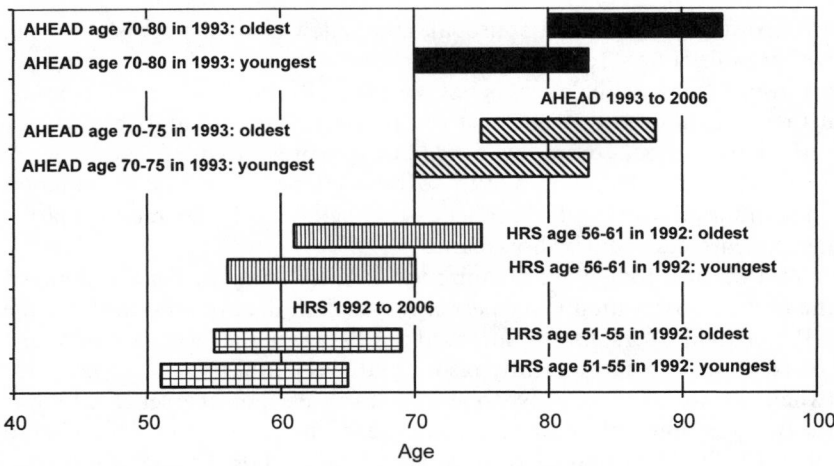

Fig. 1.1   HRS and AHEAD cohorts and age groups followed

beginning of the interval as belonging to either a one-person household or to a two-person household. Over the interval between surveys a person initially in a one-person household may remain in a one-person household. We designate the family status transition for this person as $1 \rightarrow 1$ indicating that the person is in a one-person household in both years. If this person remarried (or partnered) during the two-year interval then the person is classified as $1 \rightarrow 2$. Similarly, we classify persons initially in two-person households as $2 \rightarrow 2$ if the person remains in a two-person household, $2 \rightarrow 1(\text{div})$ if the person divorces or separates by the end of the interval, and $2 \rightarrow 1(\text{wid})$ if the spouse dies by the end of the interval. The sample sizes for persons classified as $1 \rightarrow 2$ are quite small so this group has been excluded from many of the figures presented following.

To illustrate this organization of the data, we show HRS assets by family status in both 1992 and 1994, and the change in assets between the two years. Table 1.1 shows these data for persons aged 51 to 61 in 1992 (in year 2000 dollars). Total assets include equity in owner-occupied housing, IRA and Keogh balances, other financial assets, and the value of vehicles, less debt. The value of business assets and other real estate are excluded. Balances in 401(k) plans are excluded from the HRS and the AHEAD data because, as noted before, a complete 401(k) series cannot be obtained from these sources, but 401(k) assets are included in the SIPP data. We present medians and trimmed means, as well as simple means, because the latter are sensitive to outliers.

The table shows the organization of one of many family status transitions that can be obtained from the HRS, AHEAD, and SIPP surveys. Between 1992 and 1994 the median wealth of persons in continuing two-person

Table 1.1   **Median and mean total assets in 1992 and 1994 for HRS respondents age fifty-one to sixty-one in 1992 by family status**

Family status transition group	Total assets in 1992	Total assets in 1994	Change	Percent change
		Medians		
2 → 2	142,263	157,723	15,460	10.9
2 → 1 (wid)	83,395	72,019	−11,376	−13.6
2 → 1 (div)	95,414	40,010	−55,404	−58.1
1 → 2	75,301	113,593	38,292	50.9
1 → 1	39,239	42,214	2,975	7.6
		Means		
2 → 2	228,693	255,843	27,150	11.9
2 → 1 (wid)	173,759	154,696	−19,063	−11.0
2 → 1 (div)	165,988	114,748	−51,240	−30.9
1 → 2	135,573	194,098	58,525	43.2
1 → 1	99,799	111,079	11,280	11.3

households increased 10.9 percent and the median wealth of persons in continuing one-person households increased 7.6 percent. Among persons experiencing a change in family status, persons becoming widowed experienced a slight increase in assets, those becoming divorced experienced a large decline, and persons marrying saw their assets increase dramatically. The means in the lower panel show a similar pattern. The key results we present in later sections are based on graphical descriptions of the changes by family status for each of the intervals and for each of the data sources. As emphasized earlier, reporting errors can have an important effect on the changes between the beginning and the end of an interval. To mitigate the effect of errors on the results shown in this chapter we emphasize comparisons based on trimmed means and on medians, as explained before.

Before looking at additional results, we show sample sizes for each interval by family status transition in table 1.2. These data draw attention to the effect of selection on the change in assets within and between intervals. For example, consider the change in assets of persons in continuing two-person households (2 → 2) in the 1992 to 1994 interval, which is used to obtain the estimates in the first row of table 1.1. In subsequent sections we report changes in assets for these persons in later intervals as well. These persons will only appear in the 2 → 2 transition group for the next interval, 1994 to 1996, if they remain in a two-person household for the next two years. Those who will lose a spouse during the next two years will be in the 2 → 1 group in 1994 to 1996. Persons who will lose a spouse in a subsequent interval tend to have lower assets than those who will continue in two-person households. The numbers in table 1.2 only give a general indication of the extent of selection. For example, consider the decline in the number of persons in the 2 → 2 group in the HRS sample between the 1992 to 1994 and the 1994 to

Table 1.2 Number of persons in each interval by change in family status transition group

HRS persons age 51 to 61 in 1992

Group	1992–1994	1994–1996	1996–1998	1998–2000	2000–2002	2002–2004	2004–2006
2 → 2	6,365	5,732	5,344	4,978	4,614	4,382	4,017
2 → 1 (wid)	108	111	133	131	127	118	153
2 → 1 (div)	121	69	64	41	38	32	40
1 → 2	88	96	71	65	58	65	44
1 → 1	1,598	1,559	1,535	1,554	1,554	1,630	1,634
Total	8,280	7,567	7,147	6,769	6,391	6,227	5,888

AHEAD persons age 70 to 80 in 1993

Type	1993–1995	1995–1998	1998–2000	2000–2002	2002–2004	2004–2006
2 → 2	2,371	1,813	1,412	1,043	771	551
2 → 1 (wid)	187	213	181	142	118	86
2 → 1 (div)	7	19	7	4	3	
1 → 2	29	29	13	15	12	10
1 → 1	1,778	1,613	1,601	1,468	1,318	1,138
Total	4,372	3,687	3,214	2,672	2,222	1,785

1996 intervals (6,365 to 5,732). Part of the decline in the number of persons occurs because some of the persons in the $2 \to 2$ group in 1992 to 1994 are in one of the $2 \to 1$ groups in 1994 to 1996. This is the key selection. Persons in the $2 \to 1$ group have lower assets than persons in the $2 \to 2$ group. But part of the decline in the number of persons is also due to attrition from the sample. In addition, persons in the $1 \to 2$ group in 1992 to 1994 are in the $2 \to 2$ group in 1994 to 1996 if they remain married for the next two years. Persons who continue in the $1 \to 1$ group also tend to have greater assets than those who leave the sample because of death.

1.2   The HRS Cohort

We next summarize asset changes for the HRS cohort and then for the AHEAD cohort; we also compare the two and compare results based on these surveys with results based on the SIPP. We begin by graphing the "raw" means like those presented in the bottom panel of table 1.1. As the graphs will show, the data are confounded by a large number of reporting errors and missing values. Ultimately, we will need to find a way to "correct" the errors and "fill in" the missing values. For present purposes, we simply show how two alternative estimation procedures—trimming outliers and using medians—can affect the results. To demonstrate the effect of alternative estimation procedures we use data for persons aged fifty-one to fifty-five in 1992 from the HRS cohort.

Figure 1.2 shows the means based on the raw data. Here and in the subsequent analysis all values are in constant year 2000 dollars. These estimates are analogous to those shown in the bottom panel of table 1.1. There appear to be many aberrant within and between interval changes in assets. Closer examination of the data reveals that there are a large number of apparent errors in the raw data. These include cases where balances for major assets (such as housing or retirement accounts) are apparently misreported (the asset total reported in one wave is very different from the total reported in adjacent waves). The effect of outliers is evident in the figure. To address this problem, we show means based on trimmed data in figure 1.3 and estimates of medians in figure 1.4.

To obtain the trimmed means we estimate separate generalized least squares (GLS) regressions for assets at the beginning and end of each interval. Each GLS regression allows the residual variance to differ from interval to interval. For *each family status transition group,* we estimate a specification of this form:

(1)
$$A_{ibj} = \alpha_b + \sum_{j=1}^{J} \delta_{bj} I_j + \varepsilon_{ibj}$$

$$A_{iej} = \alpha_e + \sum_{j=1}^{J} \delta_{ej} I_j + \varepsilon_{iej}.$$

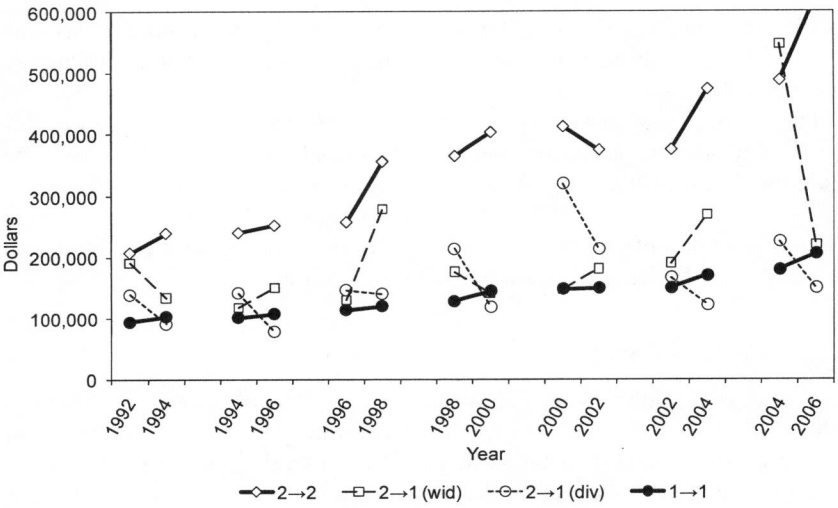

Fig. 1.2   Mean total assets for HRS persons age fifty-one to fifty-five in 1992

In these equations A is the asset level (in constant dollars). The first equation pertains to beginning assets in each interval and the second equation to ending assets; I_j is an indicator variable for the *jth* interval, i indicates person, b indicates the beginning of an interval, and e indicates the end of an interval. As set out, these equations reproduce exactly the results shown in figure 1.1. The key feature of the estimates is that the error variance is allowed to vary by interval. To obtain trimmed means, for each interval and for each family status group we eliminated the observations with the top 1 percent and the bottom 1 percent of residuals. In cases where there are fewer than 100 observations in an interval we exclude the observations with the highest and lowest residuals.

Then we reestimate the same GLS regressions on the trimmed data and predict the mean beginning and ending assets that are graphed in figure 1.3. For illustration, appendix table 1A.1 shows the GLS estimates for beginning assets of $2 \rightarrow 2$ persons based on the raw data and then based on the trimmed data. It can be seen that the standard error of the means based on the trimmed data are for some intervals as little as one-third as large as the standard error based on the raw data. The comparisons are similar for the other transition groups.

Comparing Figures 1.2 and 1.3 suggests that trimming reduces the estimated mean assets, especially for the $2 \rightarrow 2$ and $1 \rightarrow 1$ transitions. For example, the 2006 mean for the $2 \rightarrow 2$ group is reduced from over \$600,000 using the raw data to just over \$400,000. In addition, the within-interval changes are much more consistent from one interval to the next. Some apparently aberrant means for the $2 \rightarrow 1$(widowed) and $2 \rightarrow 1$(divorced) groups remain.

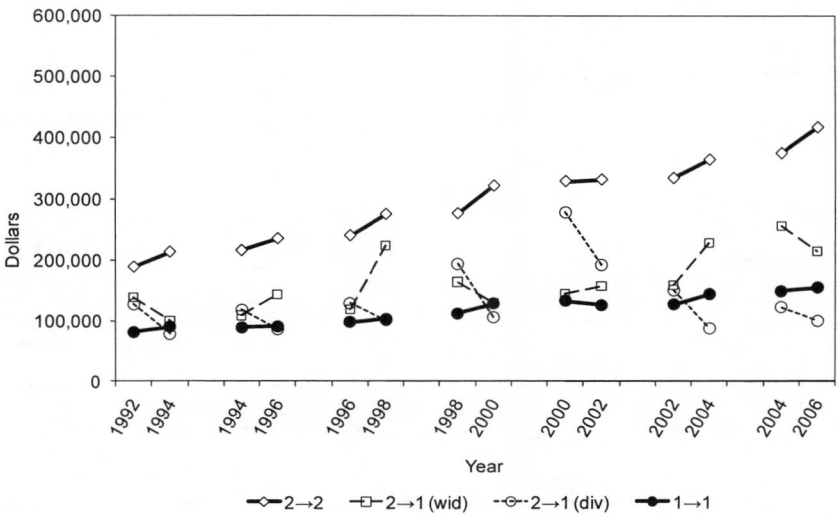

Fig. 1.3   Mean total assets for HRS persons age fifty-one to fifty-five in 1992, trimmed

We also experimented with trimmed data based on the change in assets over each interval. In this case, we estimated a GLS regression like the one before but used the change in assets for each interval (instead of one regression for beginning assets and a second for ending assets) as the dependent variable. Then for each interval, the top and bottom 1 percent of changes were eliminated. In most instances, we report only the trimmed results based on asset levels, but in a few instances we have calculated average asset changes over all intervals based on trimmed change data.

Figure 1.4 shows medians. The medians are much lower than the means, as might be expected, and the apparently aberrant mean values are not reproduced in the medians. For the other age groups and cohorts discussed later, only trimmed mean and median values are shown.

Focusing on the trimmed mean results in figure 1.4, several general features of the data stand out. First, the assets of persons in continuing two-person households ($2 \rightarrow 2$) increase in each interval (all in year 2000 dollars). Second, the assets of continuing $1 \rightarrow 1$ persons in the $1 \rightarrow 1$ group also increase in most intervals; 2000 to 2002 is the only exception. Third, the assets of $1 \rightarrow 1$ families are much lower than the assets of $2 \rightarrow 2$ families in all intervals.

Fourth, the assets of persons in two-person households that will become one-person households during the interval ($2 \rightarrow 1$) are typically much lower at the beginning of an interval than the assets of persons in continuing two-person households ($2 \rightarrow 2$). Also, the assets of $2 \rightarrow 1$(divorced) persons typically decline substantially within each interval. The asset of $2 \rightarrow 1$(widowed)

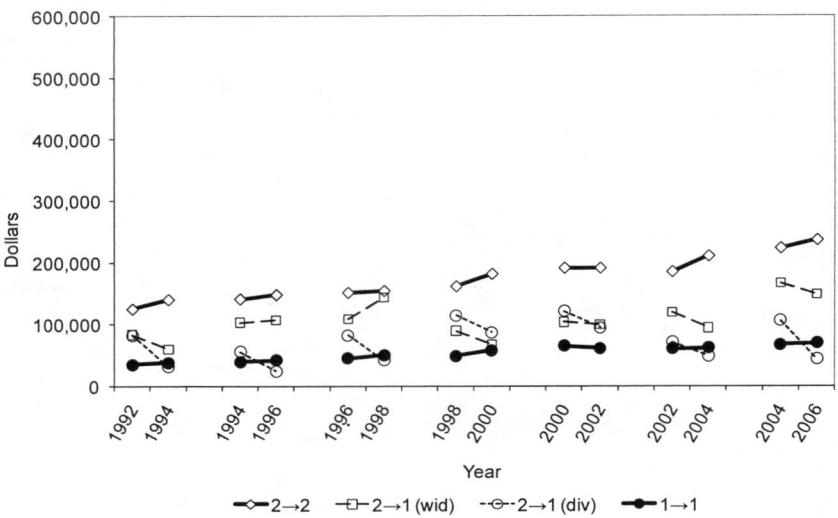

Fig. 1.4   Median total assets for HRS persons age fifty-one to fifty-five in 1992

persons—although also much lower than the assets of $2 \to 2$ persons at the beginning of the period—do not decline in most intervals. The medians in figure 1.4 show much the same pattern.

The average *change* in assets in each interval is summarized in table 1.3 for each of the four family status transition groups and for each of the three estimation procedures. The average increase over the seven intervals is shown in the second column. Recall that beginning assets in each interval differ substantially by family status transition group. To quantify the difference, the first column of this table shows the average (over the seven intervals) of the ratio of the beginning assets of the $2 \to 1$ and $1 \to 1$ groups relative to the beginning assets or the $2 \to 2$ group. For example, based on trimmed means the beginning assets of the $2 \to 1$(widowed) transition groups was about 56 percent of the average of the $2 \to 2$ group; the average of the $2 \to 1$(divorced) group is about 59 percent of the $2 \to 2$ group. Asset changes (in the second column) show that the assets of the $2 \to 2$ group increase on average by close to 11 percent, but the average of the $2 \to 1$(divorced) group fell by about 32 percent based on the trimmed means. The average of the $2 \to 1$(widowed) group increased by about 15 percent. The beginning assets of the $1 \to 1$ group were only about 40 percent of the assets of the $2 \to 2$ group. The mean assets of the $1 \to 1$ persons increased by about 6.5 percent, a little more than half the rate of increase observed for the $2 \to 2$ group.

The medians show somewhat different magnitudes but broadly similar patterns for the most part. The medians show that the beginning assets of

Table 1.3   **Summary of asset changes by family status transition group, HRS persons fifty-one to fifty-five in 1992, in year 2000 dollars**

Group	Average of beginning assets relative to $2 \to 2$	Average % increase over 7 intervals[a]
	Means	
$2 \to 2$	1.000	14.42
$2 \to 1$ (wid)	0.544	26.17
$2 \to 1$ (div)	0.606	−31.23
$1 \to 1$	0.405	8.02
	Trimmed means	
$2 \to 2$	1.000	10.57
$2 \to 1$ (wid)	0.561	15.42
$2 \to 1$ (div)	0.585	−32.18
$1 \to 1$	0.405	6.45
	Medians	
$2 \to 2$	1.000	4.99
$2 \to 1$ (wid)	0.657	0.90
$2 \to 1$ (div)	0.541	−27.03
$1 \to 1$	0.303	0.43

[a]For the trimmed means this is the difference between beginning mean and ending mean assets, as a percent of beginning mean assets, averaged over the seven intervals. For medians this is the median change in assets within an interval as a percent of median beginning assets, averaged over the seven intervals.

the $2 \to 1$(widowed) persons were about 66 percent of $2 \to 2$ persons, the assets of $2 \to 1$(divorced) persons about 54 percent of the assets of the $2 \to 2$ persons, and the assets of $1 \to 1$ persons only about 30 percent of those of the $2 \to 2$ persons. The median increase in the assets of $2 \to 2$ persons was about 5 percent. But the median increase in the assets of the $1 \to 1$ group was only about 0.04 percent. The median decline in the assets of $2 \to 1$(divorced) persons was about 27 percent and the median of the assets of $2 \to 1$(widowed) persons was about 1 percent.

In this section we have presented estimates separately for each family status transition group, thus explicitly accounting for differences in assets held by each family type at the beginning of each interval. If initial asset levels are not distinguished, the wave-to-wave changes in assets within family status transition groups are confounded with differences in initial asset levels. This is illustrated in figure 1.5, which shows beginning and ending assets for hypothetical $2 \to 2$ and $2 \to 1$ groups of equal size (in hundreds of thousands of dollars). The first row shows that assets for the $2 \to 2$ group increase by 50 (from 300 to 350). The next row shows that assets for the $2 \to 1$ group decline by 50 (from 100 to 50). If we do not distinguish the two groups and begin with the average of the assets of the two groups, we overestimate the asset *increase* for the $2 \to 2$ families and overestimate the asset *decrease* for the $2 \to 1$ families as shown in the bottom two rows of the diagram.

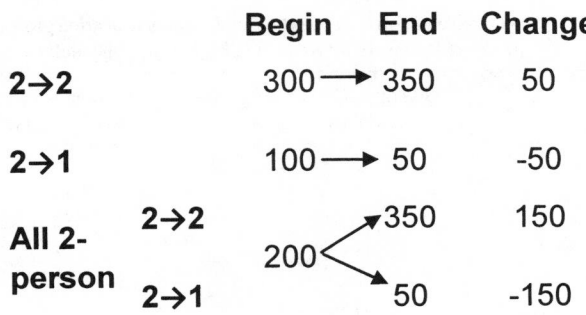

Fig. 1.5   **Illustration**

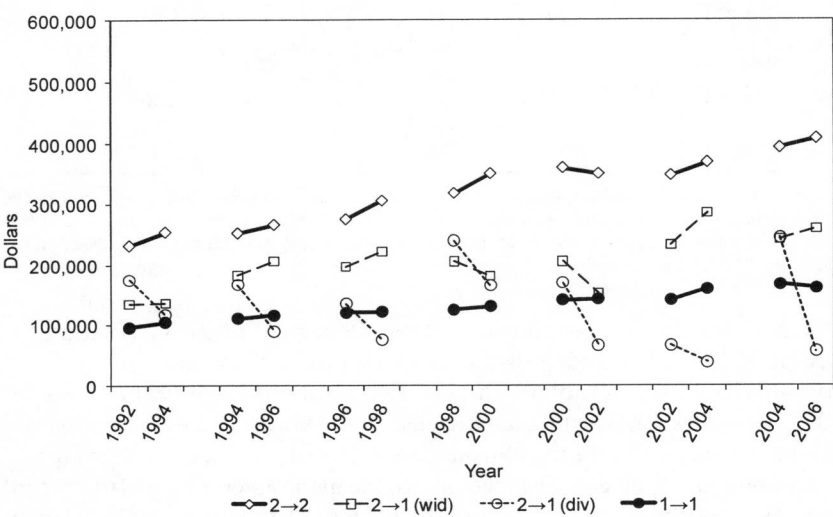

Fig. 1.6   **Mean total assets for HRS persons age fifty-six to sixty-one in 1992, trimmed**

Figures 1.6 and 1.7 and table 1.4 pertain to HRS persons aged fifty-six to sixty-one in 1992. The key difference between this age cohort and the fifty-one to fifty-five cohort is that the younger cohort would have been in the labor force for many of the intervals; they were between the ages of sixty-five to sixty-nine in 2006 and on average retired in about 2000 or 2002. The older age cohort would have been seventy to seventy-five in 2006 and on average may have retired in about 1996.

The general trends for the four transition groups for the fifty-six to sixty-one cohort are much the same as the trends for the fifty-one to fifty-five cohort. There are differences in magnitude, however, and they can best be seen by comparing the averages for the two age cohorts shown in table 1.4. Based on the trimmed means, the average within-interval percent increase

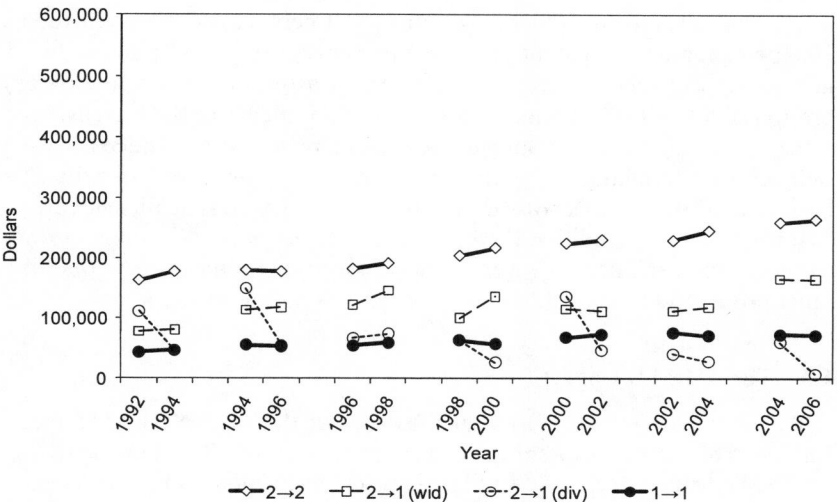

Fig. 1.7   Median total assets for HRS persons age fifty-six to sixty-one in 1992

Table 1.4   **Summary of asset changes by family status transition (group, HRS persons fifty-one to fifty-five and fifty-six to sixty-one in 1992, in year 2000 dollars)**

Family status transition group	Age 51–55		Age 56–61	
	Average of beginning assets relative to 2 → 2	Average % increase over 7 intervals[a]	Average of beginning assets relative to 2 → 2	Average % increase over 7 intervals[a]
	Means			
2 → 2	1.000	14.4	1.000	8.6
2 → 1 (wid)	0.544	26.2	0.654	1.9
2 → 1 (div)	0.606	−31.2	0.656	−35.3
1 → 1	0.405	8.0	0.413	4.8
	Trimmed means			
2 → 2	1.000	10.6	1.000	6.3
2 → 1 (wid)	0.561	15.4	0.648	2.5
2 → 1 (div)	0.585	−32.2	0.565	−47.6
1 → 1	0.405	6.5	0.415	4.2
	Medians			
2 → 2	1.000	5.0	1.000	2.5
2 → 1 (wid)	0.657	0.9	0.558	2.6
2 → 1 (div)	0.541	−27.0	0.459	−22.6
1 → 1	0.303	0.4	0.302	0.0

[a]For the trimmed means this is the difference between beginning mean and ending mean assets, as a percent of beginning mean assets, averaged over the seven intervals. For medians this is the median change in assets within an interval as a percent of median beginning assets, averaged over the seven intervals.

in assets is lower for the older $2 \rightarrow 2$ and $1 \rightarrow 1$ persons—6.3 percent versus 10.6 percent and 4.2 percent versus 6.5 percent for the $2 \rightarrow 2$ and the $1 \rightarrow 1$ groups, respectively. The large reduction in the assets of the $2 \rightarrow 1$(divorced) group is evident for both age cohorts. Based on medians, the increases are close to zero for both the younger and the older age cohorts. Indeed, for the older cohort the change in the median assets of the $1 \rightarrow 1$ group is zero. The large decline in the assets of the $2 \rightarrow 1$(divorced) group is again evident.

It might be expected that the increase in the assets of the younger group would be greater since they were in the labor force for more years than the older group and thus could save out of earning for more years.

1.3   The AHEAD Cohort

We now turn to the evolution of the assets of the older AHEAD cohort. Members of this cohort were aged seventy and over in 1993, when the survey began. They have been followed for six waves until 2006, when they were at least eighty-three years old. Figure 1.8 shows the trimmed mean assets of the respondents aged seventy to eighty in 1993, based on within-interval data that has been trimmed as described in the previous section. Results based on medians are shown in figure 1.9. Rohwedder, Haider, and Hurd (2006) make a compelling case that the increase in assets between 1993 and 1995 is likely exaggerated because of underreporting in the 1993 survey. For completeness, however, we show results for this interval as well as the other intervals.

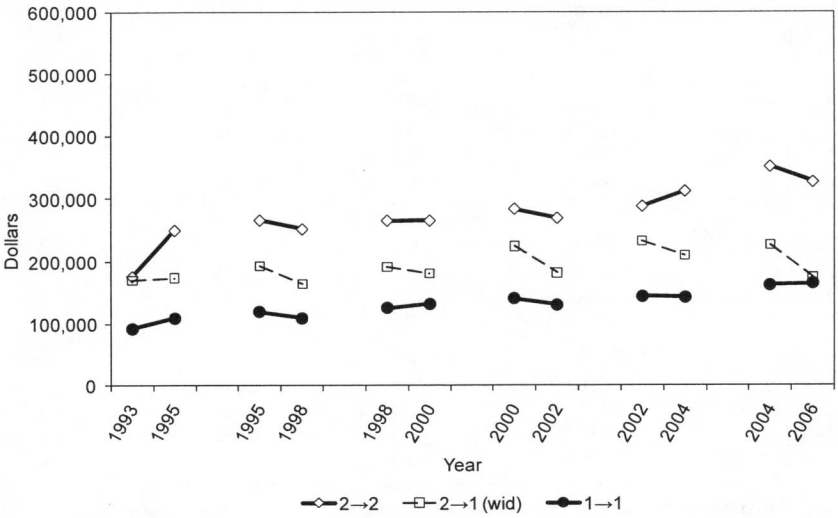

Fig. 1.8   Mean total assets for AHEAD persons age seventy to eighty in 1993, trimmed

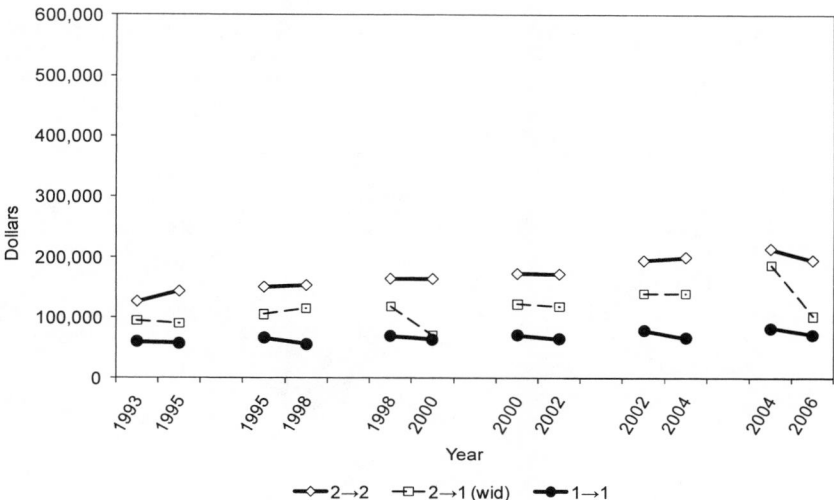

Fig. 1.9   Median total assets for AHEAD persons age seventy to eighty in 1993

Results for both estimation procedures, as well as estimates based on the raw data, are summarized in table 1.5. There are very few divorces in this age group so data are shown only for the $2 \to 1$(widowed) group. Even in this age group, the assets of the $2 \to 2$ transition group increase on average by over 5 percent based on the trimmed means. The assets of the $1 \to 1$ group increase by about 1.5 percent based on the trimmed means. The assets of persons whose partners die decline by almost 11 percent, and the assets of persons who will become widowed in an interval are over 20 percent lower at the beginning of the interval than the assets of the continuing $2 \to 2$ transition group. The median increase in assets of the $2 \to 2$ group is less than 2 percent and the median change in the assets of the $1 \to 1$ group is negative (–0.59 percent).

Recall that households in the HRS cohort were between the ages of fifty-one and sixty-one in 1992 and between seventy-five and eighty-five in 2006. Persons in this older AHEAD cohort were seventy to eighty in 1993 and they were eighty-three to ninety-three in 2006. Thus there is some age overlap between the two cohorts; for example, the original HRS cohort contains households aged seventy to seventy-five in 2006 and the AHEAD cohort contains households aged seventy to seventy-five in 1993. For ease of comparison, figure 1.10 shows, in the same figure, the evolution of assets for HRS respondents age fifty-six to sixty-one in 1992, who were seventy to seventy-five in 2006, and the AHEAD respondents who were seventy to seventy-five in 1993, based on the trimmed mean sample. Analogous results based on medians are presented in figure 1.11.

The difference between the two cohorts—the "cohort effects"—are

Table 1.5 **Summary of asset changes by family status transition (group, AHEAD persons seventy to eighty in 1993, in year 2000 dollars)**

Group	Average of beginning assets relative to 2 → 2	Average % increase over 6 intervals[a]
Means		
2 → 2	1.000	7.10
2 → 1 (wid)	0.829	−18.22
2 → 1 (div)		
1 → 1	0.516	0.68
Trimmed means		
2 → 2	1.000	5.50
2 → 1 (wid)	0.776	−11.74
2 → 1 (div)		
1 → 1	0.483	1.44
Medians		
2 → 2	1.000	1.59
2 → 1 (wid)	0.747	−5.92
2 → 1 (div)		
1 → 1	0.424	−0.59

[a]For the trimmed means this is the difference between beginning mean and ending mean assets, as a percent of beginning mean assets, averaged over the intervals. For medians this is the median change in assets within an interval as a percent of median beginning assets, averaged over the seven intervals.

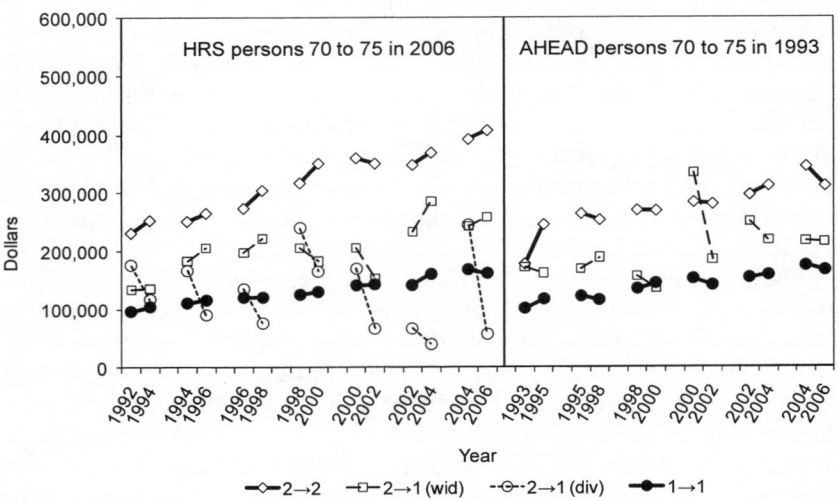

Fig. 1.10 **Mean total assets for HRS persons age fifty-six to sixty-one in 1992, and AHEAD persons seventy to seventy-five in 1993, trimmed**

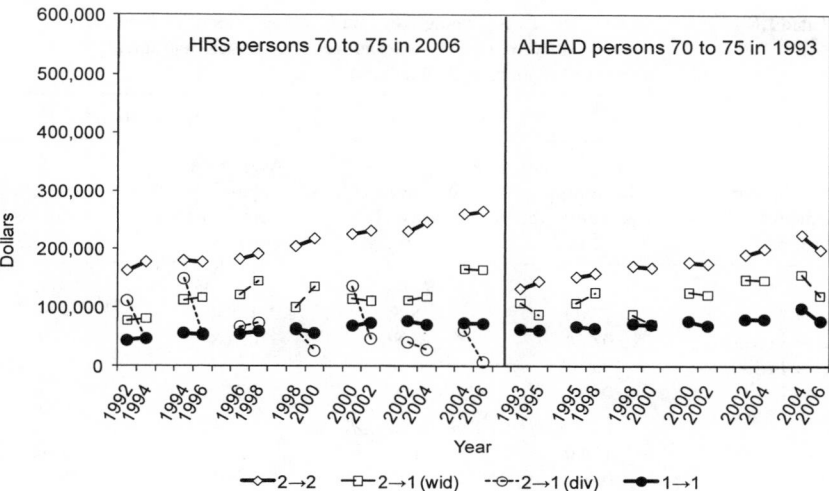

Fig. 1.11   Median total assets for HRS persons age fifty-six to sixty-one in 1992, and AHEAD persons seventy to seventy-five in 1993

evident in the figures as the "seam" between the HRS and AHEAD cohorts. Persons who attained ages between seventy and seventy-five in 2006 had much greater assets (in year 2000 dollars) than persons who had attained ages between seventy to seventy-five in 1993, thirteen years earlier. The cohort effect is particularly large for the 2 → 2 transition group.

The evolution of assets for the two groups is summarized in table 1.6. Several features stand out. First, for persons in both 2 → 2 and 1 → 1 groups the average percent increase in mean assets is substantially lower for the seventy to seventy-five age cohort than for the fifty-six to sixty-one age cohort. There is little difference in the median percent change in the assets of the younger and older 1 → 1 groups, however. Both are close to zero—0.0 percent for the HRS cohort and –0.48 percent for the AHEAD cohort. Second, for both age groups and for each of the estimation procedures persons who will become widows over an interval—the 2 → 1(widow) group—start the interval with lower assets than those who will continue in two-person households. Third, for both estimation procedures, assets of the older 2 → 1(widow) group decline.

Finally, to provide a concise summary of the evolution of assets and to provide an estimate of the statistical significance of our findings for the HRS and AHEAD cohorts, we show estimates of the average within-interval change in assets over all intervals. To do this we have estimated GLS regressions and median regressions of the *change* in assets over all intervals. That is, we combine the seven intervals to obtain a single estimate of the average change over all intervals. The estimates based on trimmed means are

Table 1.6   **Summary of asset changes by family status transition (group, HRS persons fifty-six to sixty-one and AHEAD persons age seventy to seventy-five, in year 2000 dollars)**

Family status transition group	HRS 56 to 61		AHEAD 70 to 75	
	Average of beginning assets relative to 2 → 2	Average % increase over 7 intervals[a]	Average of beginning assets relative to 2 → 2	Average % increase over 6 intervals[a]
	Means			
2 → 2	1.000	8.59	1.000	4.94
2 → 1 (wid)	0.654	1.86	0.768	−6.76
2 → 1 (div)	0.656	−35.30		
1 → 1	0.413	4.84	0.520	2.18
	Trimmed means			
2 → 2	1.000	6.27	1.000	4.62
2 → 1 (wid)	0.648	2.54	0.701	−5.83
2 → 1 (div)	0.565	−47.58		
1 → 1	0.415	4.22	0.514	1.42
	Medians			
2 → 2	1.000	2.48	1.000	1.94
2 → 1 (wid)	0.558	2.57	0.705	−7.94
2 → 1 (div)	0.459	−22.55		
1 → 1	0.302	−0.02	0.440	−0.48

[a]For the trimmed means this is the difference between beginning mean and ending mean assets, as a percent of beginning mean assets, averaged over the intervals. For medians this is the median change in assets within an interval as a percent of median beginning assets, averaged over the intervals.

presented in the first column of table 1.7. The method of trimming is the same as that described before. In this case, we estimate a GLS regression like equation (1), but the dependent variable is the change in assets for each interval. This procedure is in contrast to our earlier approach of estimating one regression for beginning assets and another for ending assets. The median estimates are presented in the second column of table 1.7. Both the trimmed mean and median estimates of the change in assets for 2 → 2 persons are positive for all age groups and all estimates are statistically significantly different from zero. The trimmed mean assets of the 1 → 1 group also increase for all age groups but the estimate for the AHEAD cohort is not statistically different from zero at the 5 percent level. All of the median estimates for the 1 → 1 group are close to, and statistically indistinguishable from, zero. The trimmed mean and median assets for the 2 → 1(wid) group increase for the HRS cohorts but decline for the AHEAD cohort. We cannot reject the null hypothesis that all of these differences are equal to zero at conventional levels of statistical significance. On the other hand, the trimmed mean and median estimates of assets of the 2 → 1(div) group

Table 1.7   **Direct estimate of average within interval change in total assets over all intervals, by family status transition**

Group	Estimated trimmed mean change in assets	z-score for trimmed mean change in assets	Estimated median change in assets	z-score for median change in assets
	HRS age 51 to 55 in 1992			
2 → 2	26,654	20.25	7,830	16.89
2 → 1 (wid)	9,748	1.37	977	0.35
2 → 1 (div)	−43,266	−7.55	−20,718	−3.45
1 → 2	39,134	5.13	14,111	2.44
1 → 1	7,792	6.8	73	0.75
	HRS age 56 to 61 in 1992			
2 → 2	20,040	15.5	4,751	8.62
2 → 1 (wid)	6,543	1.16	2,785	1.22
2 → 1 (div)	−47,611	−6.21	−21,343	−1.97
1 → 2	72,707	7.13	49,857	4.22
1 → 1	6,144	5.39	0	0
	AHEAD age 70 to 75 in 1993			
2 → 2	13,250	3.45	3,888	3.71
2 → 1 (wid)	−8,364	−0.81	−4,521	−1.72
2 → 1 (div)				
1 → 2				
1 → 1	3,763	1.77	−115	−0.91

decline substantially for the HRS cohorts. In contrast, for the 1 → 2 group for the HRS cohorts, the increase in the trimmed mean and median assets is large and statistically significantly different from zero.

1.4   Past and Future Assets

The aforementioned results show the change in total assets that is coincident with a change in family status. We considered, for example, assets at the beginning and end of a two-year interval, as well as the change in assets over the two-year interval, for persons who are in continuing two- or one-person families over the interval, or who transition from a two- to a one-person family during the interval. We now consider the assets of these same persons prior to the beginning of the interval and after the end of the interval in which the family status transition occurs. That is, we want to consider the past and future assets of persons who *experience a transition within a particular interval.* What were asset balances in the years preceding the transition and what were asset balances in the years subsequent to the transition?

Table 1.8 shows total asset data for HRS respondents age fifty-six to sixty-one in 1992 for all seven intervals, identified by the interval in which the

Table 1.8 Median total assets of persons before, during, and after transition, by year of transition, persons age fifty-six to sixty-one in 1992

Year of family status transition	Family status transition	Median total assets (in thousands)					
		1992–1994		In year of family status transition		2004–2006	
		Beginning assets	Ending assets	Beginning assets	Ending assets	Beginning assets	Ending assets
1992–1994	2 → 2	163	177	163	177	238	241
	2 → 1 (wid)	78	81	78	81	94	82
	2 → 1 (div)	112	46	112	46	121	76
	1 → 1	44	47	44	47	67	64
1994–1996	2 → 2	164	181	180	177	244	244
	2 → 1 (wid)	107	113	113	118	86	112
	2 → 1 (div)	102	159	150	55	37	121
	1 → 1	49	56	56	53	68	67
1996–1998	2 → 2	171	186	182	191	247	249
	2 → 1 (wid)	123	139	122	145	138	122
	2 → 1 (div)	90	64	67	74	104	54
	1 → 1	53	58	55	59	68	69
1998–2000	2 → 2	177	191	204	217	254	254
	2 → 1 (wid)	121	110	100	136	144	161
	2 → 1 (div)	215	210	63	27	21	10
	1 → 1	61	65	63	57	71	71
2000–2002	2 → 2	180	195	225	230	257	259
	2 → 1 (wid)	130	152	115	111	98	110
	2 → 1 (div)	93	138	136	46	85	26
	1 → 1	65	71	68	74	72	73
2002–2004	2 → 2	182	195	230	245	257	259
	2 → 1 (wid)	131	124	112	119	159	175
	2 → 1 (div)	26	55	41	28	32	189
	1 → 1	70	76	77	71	72	71
2004–2006	2 → 2	189	203	260	264	260	264
	2 → 1 (wid)	182	165	166	165	166	165
	2 → 1 (div)	114	57	60	7	60	7
	1 → 1	75	78	73	72	73	72

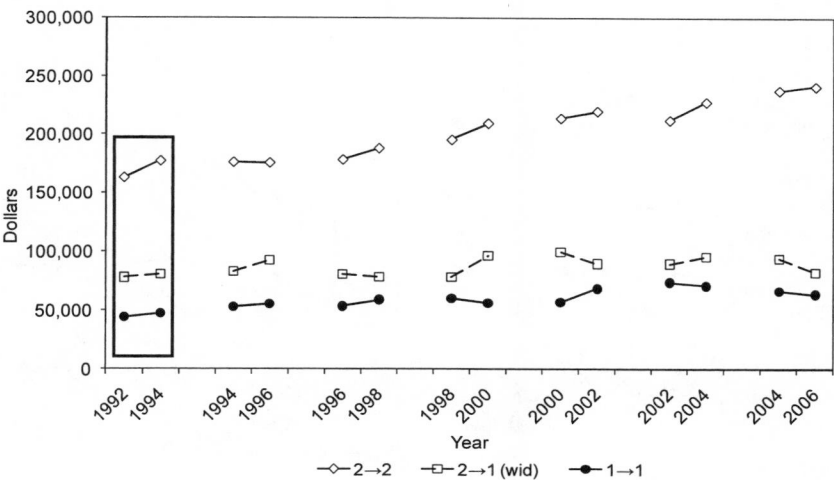

Fig. 1.12   Median total assets by household status change in 1992–1994, persons age fifty-six to sixty-one in 1992

family status change occurred. This transition interval is denoted the *base* interval. The assets of the people who experienced each type of family status transition are reported for intervals before and after the base interval. For example, the first of seven panels of the table shows beginning and ending assets in the first interval and the last interval whose family status changed in the first interval, 1992 to 1994. The fourth panel shows prior and future assets of persons that changed family status in the fourth interval, 1998 to 2000. The seventh panel shows the prior assets of persons whose family status change is reported for the last interval, 2004 to 2006. Each panel shows asset balances for persons in each family status group in the base period. These persons may be in other family status groups in periods other than the base period. Thus, for example, the first row of table 1.8 pertains to persons who remained in two-person households ($2 \rightarrow 2$) for the 1992 to 1994 interval. Some of the persons shown in this row may have divorced or become widowed in future years.

The asset patterns are difficult to distinguish in the table, but are more easily seen in figures. Figures 1.12, 1.13, and 1.14 show assets pertaining to the first, fourth, and seventh panels of the table. In each figure, the year in which the asset change occurred (the base interval) is highlighted in a box. For ease of exposition we show only the assets for three groups, $2 \rightarrow 2$, $2 \rightarrow 1$(wid), and $1 \rightarrow 1$, and emphasize the assets of the $2 \rightarrow 1$(wid) group compared to the $2 \rightarrow 2$ group. The key finding is that two-person households that will experience a $2 \rightarrow 1$(wid) transition during the 1992 to 2006 period had lower assets than continuing $2 \rightarrow 2$ households long before the transition occurred. Thus for the $2 \rightarrow 1$(wid) group the finding that pre- and

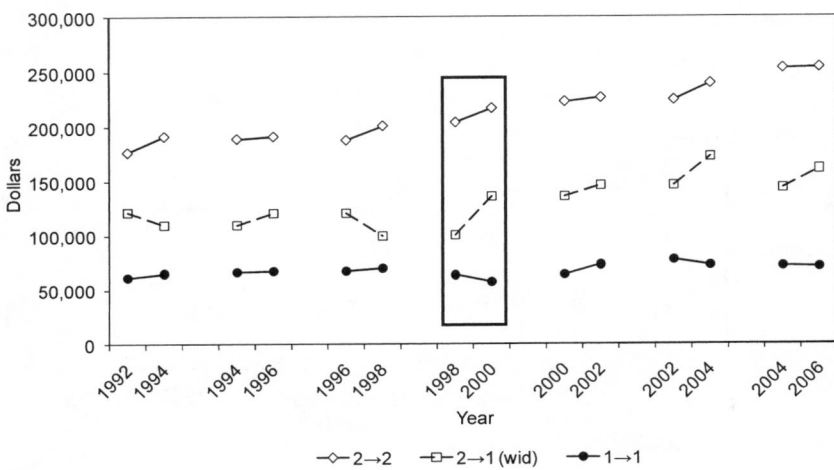

Fig. 1.13   Median total assets by household status change in 1998–2000, persons age fifty-six to sixty-one in 1992

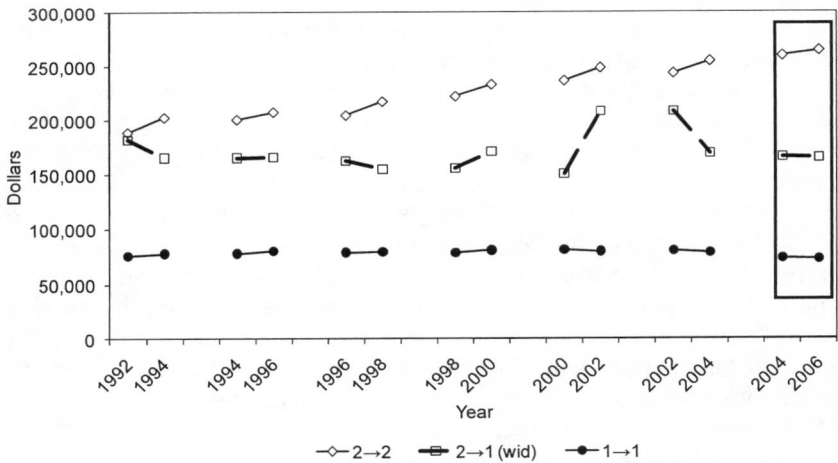

Fig. 1.14   Median total assets by household status change in 2004–2006, persons age fifty-six to sixty-one in 1992

post-transition asset levels are low is an important message that complements that finding of the drop in assets at the time of the transition.

Consider first figure 1.14, which shows the assets in each interval of persons by family status transition group in the last (2004 to 2006) interval. First compare the assets of persons in the 2 → 2 group to the assets of persons in the 2 → 1(wid) group. In the last interval, in which the change in family status occurred, the assets of persons in the 2 → 1(wid) group were much lower than the assets of persons in the 2 → 2 group. But the assets of the 2 → 1(wid) group had been lower for most of the fourteen prior years. In 1992 the assets of these two groups were similar, but over the next fourteen years the assets of the 2 → 2 group increased substantially, while the assets of the 2 → 1(wid) group changed little, on balance. That is, the assets of persons who would experience a 2 → 1(wid) transition many years in the future did not change much in the years prior to the transition, while the assets of the persons who were to experience a 2 → 2 transition in the future increased substantially in prior years. (The relationships for the other base intervals are similar in this respect, but for the other intervals, the assets of the 2 → 1(wid) group were much lower than the assets for the 2 → 2 group.)

Moving on to figure 1.12, we can follow the future assets of persons who changed family status in the first interval (1992 to 1994). We see that the assets of the 2 → 2 group in the first interval continued to increase in all of the later periods. The initial wealth of this group was $177,439 at the end of the first interval in 1994 and $241,431 at the end of 2006 (in year 2000 dollars), an increase of 36.1 percent over the next twelve years. Persons whose spouse died between 1992 and 1994, the 2 → 1(wid) group, had assets about half the level of the 2 → 2 group in the first interval, and the surviving persons in this group had only a small increase in assets over the next fourteen years, about 2.0 percent. The 1 → 1 group in the first interval experienced a 34.0 percent increase in assets over the next twelve years.

Figure 1.13 shows the prior and subsequent assets of persons who changed family status in 1998 to 2000. The assets of the 2 → 2 group were increasing in each of the prior three intervals and continued to increase in each of the three subsequent intervals. The 2 → 1(widowed) group had much lower assets than the 2 → 2 group in the prior three intervals and continued to have much lower assets in the future three intervals. The patterns for the other intervals are much like the patterns revealed in the three intervals discussed.

Finally, we want to emphasize that the sequence of family status transitions can be quite complicated. To demonstrate this feature of the data, we use the prior and future family status transition of persons with base transitions in 1998 to 2000, those represented in figure 1.13. For example, the first panel of table 1.9 shows the percent distribution of the family status transition groups of persons who were in the 2 → 2 group in 1998 to 2000. The entries in bold in the first row show that most of those in the 2 → 2 group in the base year were also in the 2 → 2 group in the prior three intervals and in the subsequent three intervals.

One might suppose that that those in the 2 → 1(wid) group in the base year (in the second panel of the table) would typically be in the 2 → 2 group in prior intervals, as they are. One might also expect that they would be in the 1 → 1 group in subsequent years. But this is not so certain. We see that 10.3 percent are in the 1 → 2 group in the next interval, suggesting that they

Table 1.9 Percent of persons in each family status transition group in each year by family status transition group in 1998–2000, age fifty-six to sixty-one in 1992

Group	1992–1994	1994–1996	1996–1998	1998–2000	2000–2002	2002–2004	2004–2006
			Group 2 → 2 in 1998–2000				
2 → 2	97.1	97.4	98.9	100.0	96.8	93.8	89.5
2 → 1 (wid)	0.3	0.2	0.0	0.0	2.7	2.7	4.0
2 → 1 (div)	0.7	0.2	0.0	0.0	0.5	0.3	0.7
1 → 2	0.7	1.5	1.1	0.0	0.0	0.4	0.5
1 → 1	1.2	0.8	0.0	0.0	0.0	2.8	5.5
			Group 2 → 1 (wid) in 1998–2000				
2 → 2	96.7	97.5	100.0	0.0	0.0	13.7	9.4
2 → 1 (wid)	0.0	0.0	0.0	100.0	0.0	0.0	0.0
2 → 1 (div)	0.0	0.0	0.0	0.0	0.0	0.0	0.0
1 → 2	0.9	2.5	0.0	0.0	10.3	2.3	0.0
1 → 1	2.4	0.0	0.0	0.0	89.7	84.0	90.6
			Group 2 → 1 (div) in 1998–2000				
2 → 2	72.8	65.7	78.6	0.0	0.0	11.6	15.0
2 → 1 (wid)	0.0	0.0	0.0	0.0	0.0	0.0	0.0
2 → 1 (div)	0.0	5.8	0.0	100.0	0.0	0.0	3.6
1 → 2	0.0	13.7	21.4	0.0	25.0	6.9	0.0
1 → 1	27.2	14.8	0.0	0.0	75.0	81.5	81.5
			Group 1 → 2 in 1998–2000				
2 → 2	33.0	25.6	0.0	0.0	91.3	83.7	75.9
2 → 1 (wid)	1.2	5.6	15.1	0.0	4.0	7.4	0.0
2 → 1 (div)	7.8	4.7	13.1	0.0	4.6	6.6	1.9
1 → 2	0.0	0.0	0.0	100.0	0.0	0.0	0.0
1 → 1	58.0	64.1	71.7	0.0	0.0	2.3	22.2
			Group 1 → 1 in 1998–2000				
2 → 2	18.0	10.0	0.0	0.0	0.0	1.1	1.4
2 → 1 (wid)	4.6	5.7	9.2	0.0	0.0	0.2	0.3
2 → 1 (div)	2.3	1.6	1.4	0.0	0.0	0.2	0.0
1 → 2	0.7	0.2	0.0	0.0	1.5	2.1	1.4
1 → 1	74.4	82.4	89.4	100.0	98.5	96.5	96.9

Note: The base for these calculations is all persons in the sample in a given interval.

remarried during the next interval. And by the following interval, 13.7 percent were once again in the $2 \rightarrow 2$ group.

The $2 \rightarrow 1$(div) group (in the third panel) also follow disparate transitions before and after the base transition. For example, 21.4 percent were in the $1 \rightarrow 2$ group in the prior interval, suggesting that they were married in the prior interval. Another 25 percent were in the $1 \rightarrow 2$ group in the following interval, suggesting that they remarried in the interval just after the base interval.

We have emphasized the errors in asset reporting. It may also be that there are errors in reports of family status as well, and we will need to pursue this issue further in future work.

In summary, we conclude that households that continue as two-person households $(2 \rightarrow 2)$ in any of the seven two-year intervals not only increase total assets in that interval, but also typically experience an increase in assets in all prior and subsequent intervals. The same pattern typically holds for continuing one-person $(1 \rightarrow 1)$ households as well. We also find that the asset history of two-person households that experience a change in family status—$2 \rightarrow 1$(wid)—is very different from the history of continuing two-person families. The $2 \rightarrow 1$(wid) group have much lower assets than persons in $2 \rightarrow 2$ households in the interval during which they experienced the transition, but this group also had much lower assets than persons in continuing two-person households long before they experienced the change in family status.

1.5 The SIPP Cohort Estimates

Recall that the total assets based on HRS and AHEAD data exclude 401(k) assets that have not been rolled over into an IRA. To determine whether the general trends seem to be the same when 401(k) assets are included, we now show assets based on SIPP data. For ease of comparison we show figures analogous to figures 1.10 and 1.11 that show trimmed means and medians for persons age fifty-six to sixty-one in 1992 (the HRS cohort) and for persons age seventy to seventy-five in 1993 (the AHEAD cohort). Because the SIPP surveys persons at all ages in each wave, these data can be "matched" to the age groups surveyed in the HRS and AHEAD cohorts. However, the years sampled in SIPP are different from the years sampled in the HRS and AHEAD. Thus, the intervals we show based on the SIPP do not exactly match the HRS and AHEAD intervals. In addition, the SIPP figures are based on one-year intervals in contrast to the two-year intervals for the HRS and AHEAD. Figure 1.15 shows the SIPP data for trimmed means and figure 1.16 shows the SIPP data for medians. Each of the figures shows data for the same two cohorts graphed in figures 1.10 and 1.11, although not for the entire time period shown for the HRS and AHEAD cohorts. Persons who were fifty-six to sixty-one in 1992 are observed six times in the SIPP, first

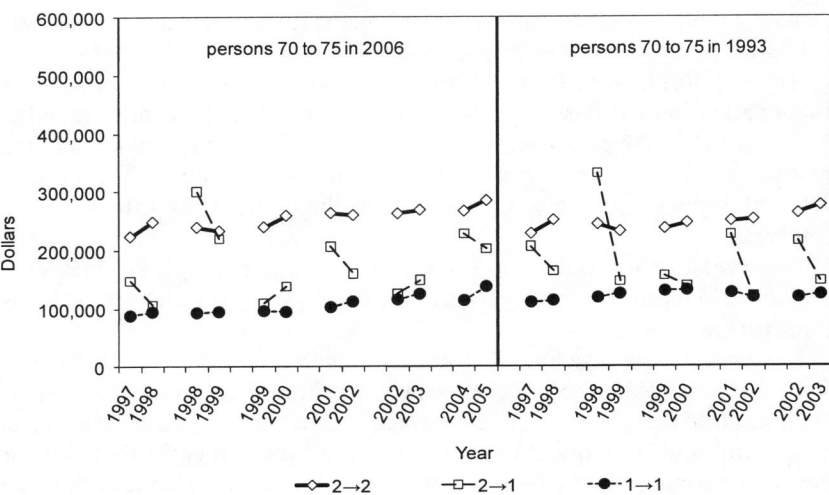

Fig. 1.15   Mean total assets for persons age fifty-six to sixty-one in 1992, and persons seventy to seventy-five in 1993, trimmed SIPP data

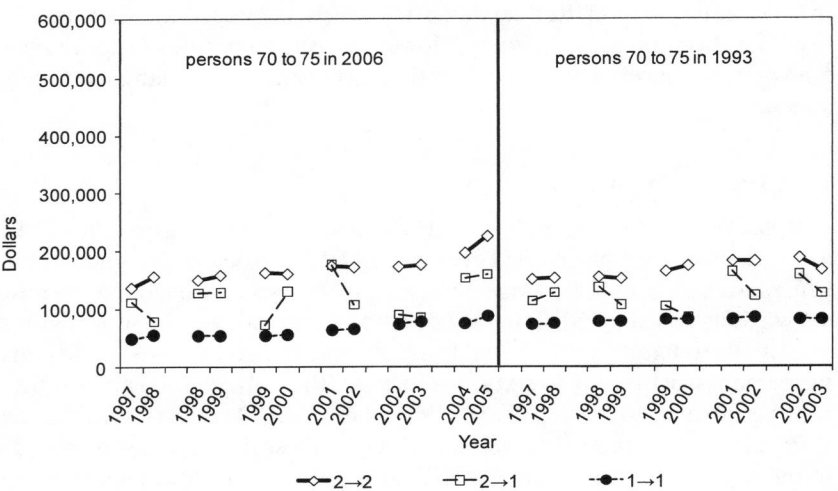

Fig. 1.16   Median total assets for persons age fifty-six to sixty-one in 1992, and persons seventy to seventy-five in 1993, SIPP data

at ages sixty-one to sixty-six in 1997 and last at ages sixty-eight to seventy-three in 2004. Persons who were age seventy to seventy-five in 1993 are first observed in the SIPP at ages seventy-four to seventy-nine in 1997 and last at ages seventy-nine to eighty-four in 2002. Data for 2004 cannot be used for the older cohort because the SIPP top-codes age at eighty-five.

Table 1.10   **Summary of asset changes by family status transition (group, persons fifty-six to sixty-one in 1992 in the HRS and SIPP, in year 2000 dollars)**

	HRS		SIPP	
Family status transition group	Average of beginning assets relative to 2 → 2	Average % increase over 5 two-year intervals[a]	Average of beginning assets relative to 2 → 2	Average % increase over 6 one-year intervals[a]
	Trimmed means			
2 → 2	1.000	5.8	1.000	4.12
2 → 1 (wid)	0.645	0.8		
2 → 1 (div)	0.506	−50.6		
2 → 1 (combined)			0.749	−7.19
1 → 1	0.411	3.2	0.407	7.84
	Medians			
2 → 2	1.000	2.0	1.000	5.52
2 → 1 (wid)	0.560	3.6		
2 → 1 (div)	0.339	−18.6		
2 → 1 (combined)			0.736	1.97
1 → 1	0.306	0.0	0.365	7.85

Notes: The HRS estimates are based on data for the 1996–1998, 1998–2000, 2000–2002, 2002–2004, and 2004–2006 intervals. The SIPP estimates are based on data for the 1997–1998, 1998–1999, 1999–2000, 2001–2002, 2002–2003, and 2004–2005 intervals. Note that the HRS estimates are for two-year intervals and the SIPP estimates are for one-year intervals.

[a]For the trimmed means this is the difference between beginning mean and ending mean assets, as a percent of beginning mean assets, averaged over the intervals. For medians this is the median change in assets within an interval as a percent of median beginning assets, averaged over the intervals.

Because we observe households over a one-year interval in the SIPP, the sample size is not large enough to distinguish between 2 → 1(wid) and 2 → 1(div). We have combined these two transition groups into a single 2 → 1 group, primarily widows for the older group. The trimmed mean estimates for this group are erratic, although the medians are smoother.

The SIPP data for persons in the 1 → 1 and 2 → 2 groups show a pattern of asset change that is similar to the pattern based on the HRS and AHEAD cohorts. For persons age fifty-six to sixty-one in 1992 the asset levels for persons in the 1 → 1 and 2 → 2 groups are lower in the SIPP survey and the upward trend over time is more prominent in the HRS data. This is true for both median and trimmed mean estimates. A similar relationship between the SIPP and AHEAD data is observed for persons aged seventy to seventy-five in 1993.

The differences between estimates based on the SIPP and the HRS-AHEAD data are summarized more clearly in tables 1.10 and 1.11. Table 1.10 pertains to the younger cohort, age fifty-six to sixty-one in 1992. Recall that the HRS intervals are two years in length while the SIPP intervals are

Table 1.11   Summary of asset changes by family status transition (group, persons seventy to seventy-five in 1993 in the AHEAD and SIPP, in year 2000 dollars)

Family status transition group	AHEAD		SIPP	
	Average of beginning assets relative to $2 \to 2$	Average % increase over 4 two-year intervals[a]	Average of beginning assets relative to $2 \to 2$	Average % increase over 6 one-year intervals[a]
	Trimmed means			
$2 \to 2$	1.000	−0.05	1.000	3.09
$2 \to 1$ (wid)	0.678	−6.99		
$2 \to 1$ (div)				
$2 \to 1$ (combined)			0.931	−33.12
$1 \to 1$	0.503	−0.61	0.497	1.46
	Medians			
$2 \to 2$	1.000	1.15	1.000	−1.17
$2 \to 1$ (wid)	0.679	−6.97		
$2 \to 1$ (div)				
$2 \to 1$ (combined)			0.801	−15.03
$1 \to 1$	0.431	−0.26	0.470	0.65

Notes: The AHEAD estimates are based on data for the 1995–1998, 1998–2000, 2000–2002, and the 2002–2004 intervals. The SIPP estimates are based on data for the 1997–1998, 1998–1999, 1999–2000, 2001–2002, 2002–2003 and 2004–2005 intervals. Note that the AHEAD estimates are for two-year intervals (except for the three-year interval for 1995–1998) and the SIPP estimates are for one-year intervals.

[a]For the trimmed means this is the difference between beginning mean and ending mean assets, as a percent of beginning mean assets, averaged over the intervals. For medians this is the median change in assets within an interval as a percent of median beginning assets, averaged over the intervals.

one year. The HRS and SIPP estimates are quite different for the $2 \to 1$ transition groups, although these comparisons are confounded because the SIPP does not distinguish widowhood from divorce. Perhaps the most notable difference between the HRS and the SIPP results is the substantially larger within-interval increase based on the SIPP data, for both the $2 \to 2$ and the $1 \to 1$ groups and for both the trimmed mean and the median estimates. It is possible that this result is due to the inclusion of 401(k) assets in the SIPP but not the HRS data. Households are likely contributing to their 401(k) plans during their working years and thereby increasing their account balances through both account inflows and potential appreciation. Recall that the SIPP increases are over one year and the HRS increases over two years.

Table 1.11 pertains to the cohort aged seventy to seventy-five in 1993. None of the estimates for the $2 \to 2$ or the $1 \to 1$ groups differ greatly. Based on trimmed means, however, the SIPP estimates show somewhat larger percent increases than the HRS estimates for the $2 \to 2$ and the $1 \to 1$ cohorts; both estimates are slightly negative based on the HRS data.

1.6   Health and Asset Accumulation: Latent Health Index

In addition to understanding the relationship between asset evolution and family status transitions, we want to explore the relationships between health and asset evolution. Because family status transitions are likely to be correlated with the health status of the family members, it is possible that our classification of households by transition groups may proxy in part for underlying differences in health status. In this section and the next, we take some preliminary steps to develop an explicit measure of health status, and to investigate its relationship to the asset evolution we have described before. We begin in this section by explaining the "latent" health measure that we use. Then, in the next section, we show how differences in latent health are associated with differences in the levels and rates of change in total assets. Within family status transition groups we find very large relationships between our latent health measure and the evolution of assets.

The HRS collects substantial information on health status and changes in health status. We use this information to calculate a "latent" health index. We assume that latent health is revealed by information about health contained in responses to the health questions over the course of the survey waves. We suppose that persons with poorer "latent" health will report more poor health indicators than persons in better health. The index is used to group persons by latent health status at the beginning of each of the two-year intervals (seven intervals in the HRS and six intervals in the AHEAD) for which we observe a change in assets.

We construct a latent health index as an "evolving" index that uses information up to the beginning of each interval. For example, suppose we are considering the change in assets between the third and fourth waves of the HRS survey (between 1996 and 1998). We group persons by a health index based on health indicators available in the 1992, 1994, and 1996 waves of the HRS. If we consider the change in assets between 1992 and 1994 we construct the index from the 1992 responses. An index for the asset change between 2004 and 2006 can be constructed from the seven survey waves between 1992 and 2004. This is the procedure we follow.

The HRS contains a large number of detailed questions that can be used to construct an index of latent health. The results reported here use a latent health index based on responses to the following questions:

1. Body mass index (BMI) at beginning of period
2. Sum of real out-of-pocket (OOP) medical costs
3. Number of periods: self-reported health fair or poor
4. Number of periods: health worse in previous period
5. Number of hospital stays
6. Number of nursing home stays
7. Number of doctor visits

8. Number of periods: home care
9. Number of periods: health problems limit work
10. Number of periods with back problems
11. Number of periods with some difficulty with an ADL (activities of daily living)
12. Number of periods with difficulty walking several blocks
13. Number of periods with difficulty sitting two hours
14. Number of periods with difficulty getting up from chair
15. Number of periods with difficulty climbing stairs
16. Number of periods with difficulty stoop/kneel/crouch
17. Number of periods with difficulty lift/carry
18. Number of periods with difficulty to pick up a dime
19. Number of periods with difficulty reach/extend arms up
20. Number of periods with difficulty push/pull
21. Ever experience high blood pressure
22. Ever experience diabetes
23. Ever experience cancer
24. Ever experience lung disease
25. Ever experience heart problems
26. Ever experience stroke
27. Ever experience psychological problems
28. Ever experience arthritis

The evolving latent health index is constructed by obtaining the first principal component of all of the health indicators. The first principal component is the weighted average of the health indicators where the weights are chosen to maximize the proportion of the variance of the individual health indicators that can be explained by the first principal component. For presentation purposes we convert the first principal component into percentile scores and group persons by quintile of this score.

1.7   The Relationship between Latent Health and Asset Levels and Evolution

To explore the link between the evolving latent health index, asset levels, and asset evolution, we begin by showing illustrative results based on the raw trimmed data. We then discuss "smoothed" results based on an extension of the trimming procedure to analyze family status transitions in equation (1).

Figure 1.17 shows wave-to-wave changes in mean total assets for continuous two-person households in the HRS cohort by "latent health" quintile. The positive association between latent health and the level of assets is striking. Persons in the lowest (fifth) health quintile have median total assets about half as large as persons in the top (first) quintile in 1992 to 1994 and about one-third as large in 2004 to 2006. Of course, the existence

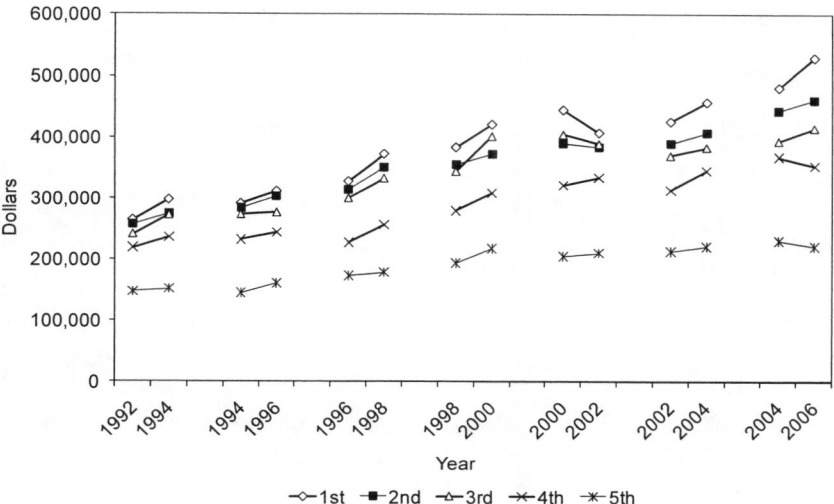

Fig. 1.17   Mean total assets for persons age fifty-six to sixty-one in continuing two-person households in 1992, by evolving health quintile, trimmed

of a health-wealth relationship is well-known. We do not try to explain this relationship, but simply describe the relationship between the evolution of assets as people age and their latent health.

Although the relationship between latent health and asset evolution appears quite systematic in figure 1.17, to smooth out random fluctuations from interval to interval we parameterize the relationship between latent health and asset accumulation within each interval. The idea is not to impose a given structure on the data, but rather to smooth over randomness from interval to interval. We want a procedure that will mimic the results shown for the raw data in figure 1.17. The parameterization is an extension of the specification shown in equation (1). For each family status transition group we estimate a specification of the form:

$$(2) \qquad A_{ibj} = \alpha_b + \sum_{j=1}^{J} (\delta_{bj} + \beta_{bj}h_i) \, I_j + \varepsilon_{ibj}$$

$$A_{iej} = \alpha_e + \sum_{j=1}^{J} (\delta_{ej} + \beta_{ej}h_i) \, I_j + \varepsilon_{iej}.$$

In these equations, A is asset level (in constant dollars), h is latent health (expressed as a percentile score), I_j is an indicator variable for the *j*th interval, and i, b, and e represent, respectively, person, beginning of the interval, and end of the interval. The key feature of the parameterization is that the estimated effect of latent health is linear within each interval, but the relationship is allowed to differ from interval to interval. One restriction

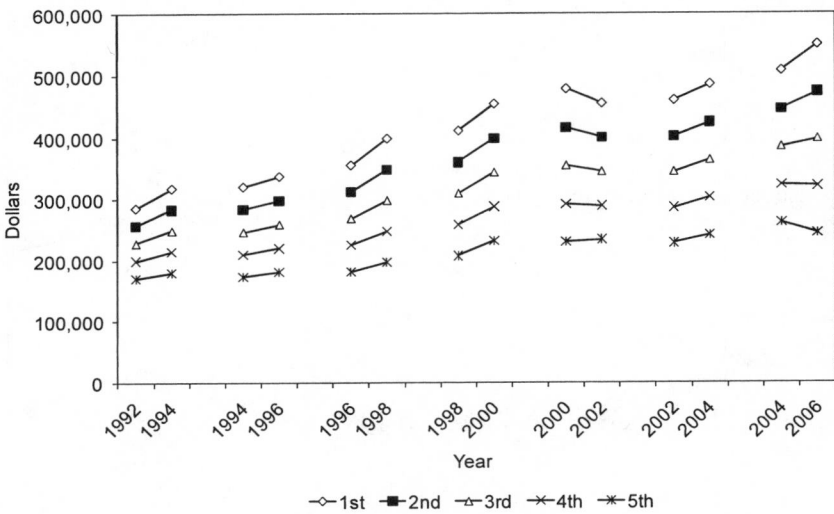

Fig. 1.18   Mean total assets for HRS persons fifty-six to sixty-one in 1992, 2 → 2 households, by evolving health quintile, smoothed

embodied in this specification is that the effect of latent health is linear with the index percentile. The same trimmed data used in the family status transition analysis before is used here. We refer to these estimates as the "smoothed" estimates.

The equations in (2) enable us to predict the beginning and ending asset levels for any latent health level and for any family status transition group. Using estimates from this specification, the estimated *trimmed mean* asset levels for continuing two-person families are shown in figure 1.18—analogous to the trimmed means without parameterizing latent health that were shown in figure 1.17. The prediction for the first quintile (between the eightieth and one-hundredth percentiles) is obtained by setting h (latent health) to 90 percent; the prediction for the second quintile sets h to 70 percent, and so forth. As in figure 1.17, the influence of stock market booms and busts on the accumulation of total assets is evident. These "smoothed" estimates capture very closely the trends based on interval-by-interval estimates but without the random variation from interval to interval in the effect of latent health. The estimates for persons age fifty-six to sixty-one in 1992 in continuing two-person households are shown in appendix table 1A.2.

The effects of latent health are very large. The ratio of assets of persons in the top health quintile to the assets of persons in the bottom quintile is 1.7 in 1992. The assets of persons in the top quintile increased much more between 1992 and 2006 than the assets of persons in the fifth quintile. By the end of 2006 the ratio of assets in the top quintile to assets in the bottom quintile was over 2.2. The estimates for the HRS cohort age fifty-one to

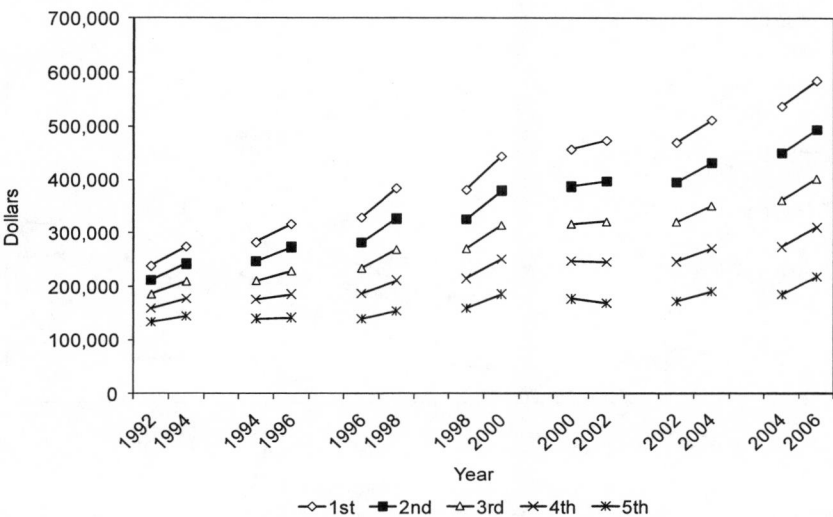

Fig. 1.19   **Mean total assets for persons age fifty-one to fifty-five in continuing two-person households in 1992, by evolving health quintile, smoothed**

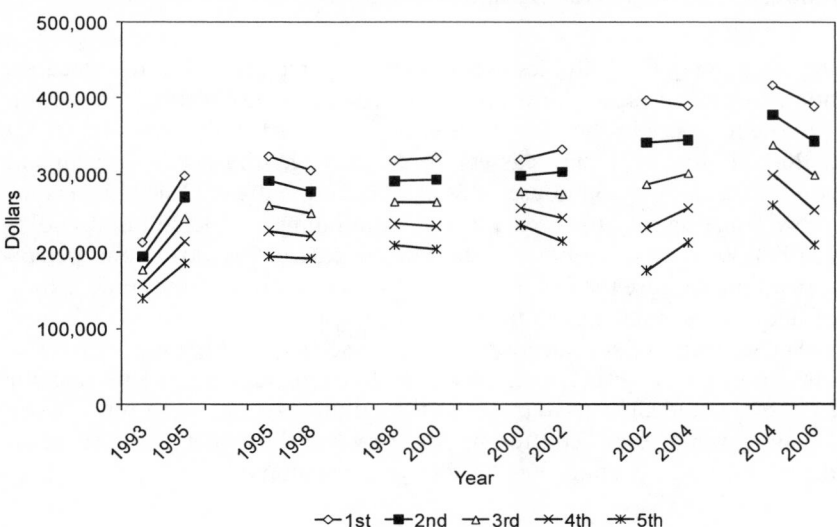

Fig. 1.20   **Mean total assets for AHEAD persons seventy to seventy-five in 1993, 2 → 2 households, by evolving health quintile, smoothed**

fifty-five, shown in figure 1.19, look much the same. In 1992, the ratio of assets in the first quintile to assets in the fifth quintile was almost 1.8. By 2006 this ratio was 2.7.

Figure 1.20 shows estimates for persons in continuing two-person AHEAD households who were age seventy to seventy-five in 1993. Again,

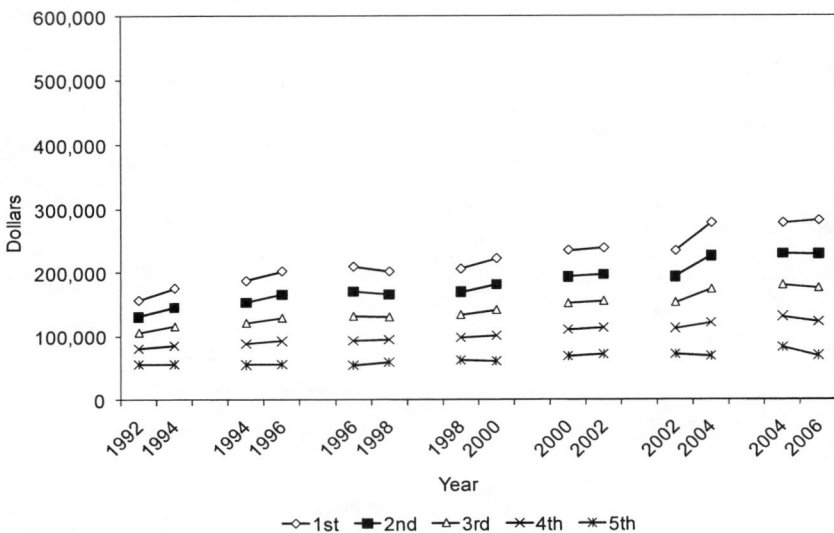

Fig. 1.21   Mean total assets for HRS persons fifty-six to sixty-one in 1992, 1 → 1 households, by evolving health quintile, smoothed

the "fanning out" of profiles occurs as these persons age, but the spread is not as dramatic as for the younger cohorts. The ratio of assets in the top quintile to assets in the bottom quintile increases from 1.5 in 1993 to 1.9 in 2006. Figure 1.21 shows assets for persons age fifty-six to sixty-one in continuing one-person households in 1992 and figure 1.22 show assets for persons age seventy to seventy-five in continuing one-person households in 1993. We have not reported latent health results for two-to-one-person transitions because the small number of observations and the confounding of data errors make the estimates very unstable.

The same sort of specification used in this section could be used to control for additional covariates such as age and gender. Controlling for age, for example, would allow us to trace out the within-interval evolution of assets for any given age. But controlling for age would likely have little effect on the results that we report here for five-year age intervals.

1.8   Summary and Discussion

In this chapter, we consider the post-retirement drawdown of total assets, including housing, retirement accounts, and other financial assets. We ask how total assets evolve after retirement—whether total assets tend to be husbanded and drawn down primarily at the time of precipitating shocks. We give particular attention to the relationship between family status transitions and the evolution of assets, and the relationship between "latent" health status and the evolution of assets.

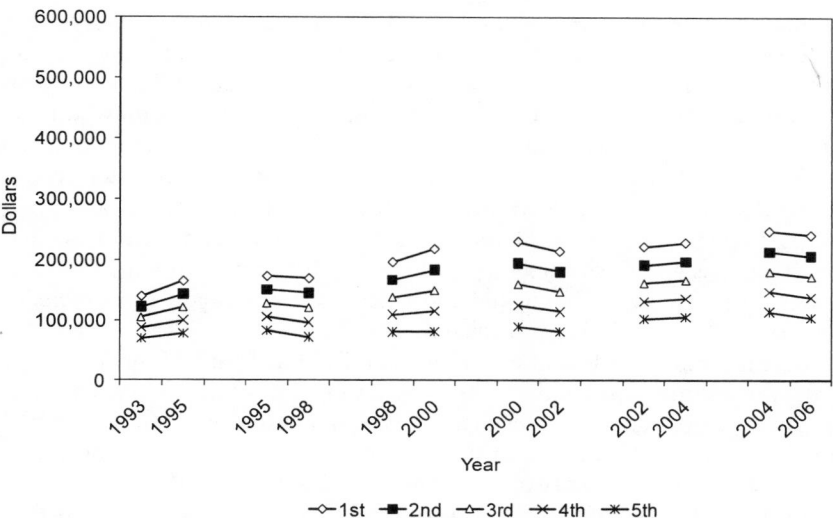

Fig. 1.22   Mean total assets for AHEAD persons seventy to seventy-five in 1993, 1 → 1 households, by evolving health quintile, smoothed

Our analysis is based primarily on HRS and AHEAD data. We organize the data so that we can observe the change in assets between each of the waves of the surveys, and we observe the changes by family status transition. Thus, we can observe the change in assets between waves for persons who continue in two-person or in one-person households between one wave and the next. This allows us to determine how asset evolution is related to family status transition. In particular, we can compare the change in assets for persons who experience a family status transition between waves with the change for persons who continue in two-person or in one-person households. In this way, we emphasize the discontinuous change in assets that accompany shocks to family status, in particular the transition from two- to one-person households.

We find several key regularities in the data. First, that the evolution of assets is strongly related to family status transitions. The total assets of continuing two-person households increase substantially well into old age. For persons aged fifty-six to sixty-one when initially observed in 1992 and aged seventy to seventy-five when last observed in 2006 the average (trimmed) wave-to-wave increase in total assets is 6.3 percent for continuing two-person households. For the older cohort, aged seventy to seventy-five in 1993 and eighty-three to eighty-eight in 2006, the average (trimmed) rate of growth is 4.6 percent for continuing two-person households. For persons aged fifty-six to sixty-one when initially observed in 1992 and seventy to seventy-five when last observed in 2006, the average (trimmed) wave-to-wave increase in total assets is 4.2 percent for continuing one-person households. For the older cohort, aged seventy to seventy-five in 1993 and eighty-three to eighty-eight in 2006, the average (trimmed) rate of growth is 1.4 percent for one-person households. The median estimates tend to be smaller, but still positive with the exception of the older continuous one-person households, for whom the average increase is not significantly different from zero. In contrast, persons in households that experience a family status transition during an interval, either as a result of a divorce or the death of a spouse, often experience a large decline or no increase in total assets. Substantial declines are associated with divorce, and the declines are statistically different from zero. The total assets of persons entering widowhood increase on average but the increase is not significantly different from zero.

Second, households that experience family status transitions during an interval—widowhood or divorce—have lower levels of assets than continuing two-person households. The mean *beginning* assets of persons who will experience a family status transition are approximately 55 to 65 percent of the assets of continuing two-person households. Further, these differences exist not just at the time of the transition, but are also evident long before the family transition and continue long after the transition. This finding underscores the need to account for differences in initial assets when estimating the change in assets at the time of a family status transition. Otherwise, the effects of family status transitions are confounded with prior differences in assets.

Third, the evolution of assets is very strongly related to a latent health index that we construct using principal component analysis and a range of self-reported health status measures in the HRS and AHEAD surveys. For continuing two-person HRS households aged fifty-six to sixty-one, the ratio of assets of households in the top health quintile to the assets of households in the bottom quintile is 1.7 in 1992. The assets of households in the top quintile increased more between 1992 and 2006 than the assets of households in the fifth quintile. By the end of 2006 the ratio of assets in the top quintile to assets in the bottom quintile was over 2.2. For continuing one-person HRS households aged fifty-six to sixty-one the ratio of assets of households in the top health quintile to the assets of households in the bottom quintile is 2.8 in 1992. The assets of households in the top quintile increased more between 1992 and 2006 than the assets of households in the fifth quintile. By the end of 2006 the ratio of assets in the top quintile to assets in the bottom quintile was 4.1. Similar differences are found for older AHEAD households.

Finally, we speculate about possible explanations for our results and how our results are related to recent research on the "adequacy" of saving. Households *on average* seem not to reduce their asset holdings in old age except at the time of changes in family status. While some might argue that this suggests that most households could have spent more before and during retirement, our results do not necessarily suggest oversaving or underspending in retirement. If households accumulate assets to self-insure against uncertain future health shocks, then one might find many households holding stable or even rising assets over most of their retirement period. Such self-insurance was the rationale that Venti and Wise (2004) used to explain their results on the husbanding of home equity. Marshall, McGarry, and Skinner (chapter 3, this volume) make clear that out-of-pocket medical expenditures can be very large—so the potential "loss" that households may be insuring against could warrant holding substantial assets.

For similar reasons our findings do not necessarily support the view that people on average are well prepared for retirement, although they do seem to suggest better preparation than a number of other studies suggest. Hurd and Rohwedder (2009) for example, assess saving adequacy by determining if assets at retirement are sufficient to maintain observed age-consumption profiles throughout the retirement years. Our results, however, suggest that for most types of households, assets are on average greater at age seventy-five than at sixty-five. This implies that if the Hurd-Rohwedder analysis was carried out at an older age, with fewer remaining years of consumption to finance and potentially higher asset levels, the results might be somewhat more encouraging about retirement saving adequacy.

We should also note that our results provide an incomplete analysis of retirement income adequacy because we do not consider alternatives to drawing down assets as a means of financing consumption in retirement. For example, we do not account for other income sources such as earnings or annuities from Social Security or defined-benefit pensions. Annuity wealth is important because it affects how much nonannuity wealth needs to be drawn down in retirement. Much of our analysis focuses on the change in asset holdings over various intervals before and after retirement, and it is possible that some households with very low levels of assets are reporting increases in assets. This could generate a finding of rising asset holdings, but at a level that does not provide a substantial buffer for post-retirement financial or health shocks.

We also emphasize the empirical relationship between latent health and wealth accumulation. A number of previous studies have made formal efforts to integrate health shocks into models designed to assess the adequacy of saving—Hurd and Rohwedder (2009); Scholz, Seshadri, and Khitatrakun (2006); and Scholz, Gale, and Seshadri (2009) are leading examples. But from the presentation of these models it is unclear how important potential future health shocks are as a source of wealth accumulation. Recent work by De Nardi, French, and Jones (2006) is an exception. In their model households are shown to respond to uncertain future health costs by increasing saving. Their study does not, however, ascertain whether observed levels of wealth, though higher than they would otherwise be, are "adequate" to insure households against the financial consequences of health shocks. Laibson, in the discussion comments that follow this chapter, presents a more direct attempt to integrate the empirical patterns presented here with a theoretical model that is capable of determining whether observed levels of wealth are "optimal." We believe there is much promise in this approach.

In future work we will address many of the issues raised in our introduction but that have not been addressed in this chapter. These include an assessment of the likelihood that households will be able to cover the costs of health and family status shocks, the merits of different methods of asset drawdown, and the effect of factors such as the recent asset price decline, rising retirement ages, and the growth of personal retirement accounts on the ability to meet health and family status shocks in the future. The analysis reported here can be viewed as a starting point for these further analyses.

Finally, as emphasized before, missing data, reporting errors, and other data limitations pose serious limitations on the analysis. In this chapter, we have used medians and trimmed means to limit the influence of data errors. As we proceed to further analysis we will give more careful attention to correcting errors and to cross-section-longitudinal methods to check the data and fill in missing observations.

Appendix

Table 1A.1   **Raw and trimmed regressions for beginning assets, age fifty-one to fifty-five in 1992**

	Raw data, $2 \to 2$			Trimmed data, $2 \to 2$		
	Number of observations		17,909	Number of observations		17,550
	Number of groups		7	Number of groups		7
	Obs/grp	min=	2,130	Obs/grp	min=	2,087
		avg=	2,558		avg=	2,507
		max=	3,139		max=	3,076
	Wald chi(13)		282.63	Wald chi(13)		656.8
	prob > chi2		0.0000	prob > chi2		0.0000
Variable	Coefficient	Std. error	z	Coefficient	Std. error	z
I2	33,335	9,646	3.5	27,003	5,950	4.5
I3	50,586	9,109	5.6	51,142	6,481	7.9
I4	157,132	25,194	6.2	87,632	7,665	11.4
I5	205,017	22,872	9.0	140,439	9,274	15.1
I6	167,503	13,925	12.0	145,396	9,451	15.4
I7	280,279	31,712	8.8	185,648	10,498	17.7
inter	207,108	6,182	33.5	188,291	3,827	49.2

Table 1A.1   (continued)

	Raw data, 2 → 1 (wid)			Trimmed data 2 → 1 (wid)		
	Number of observations		348	Number of observations		334
	Number of groups		7	Number of groups		7
	Obs/grp	min=	37	Obs/grp	min=	35
		avg=	50		avg=	48
		max=	62		max=	60
	Wald chi(13)		7.68	Wald chi(13)		16.73
	prob > chi2		0.2628	prob > chi2		0.0103
Variable	Coefficient	Std. error	z	Coefficient	Std. error	z
I2	−73,097	53,848	−1.4	−29,935	29,078	−1.0
I3	−60,280	54,276	−1.1	−20,113	29,805	−0.7
I4	−14,837	72,723	−0.2	25,195	43,331	0.6
I5	−43,288	55,018	−0.8	6,262	31,823	0.2
I6	−779	63,206	0.0	19,588	36,610	0.5
I7	356,384	261,050	1.4	117,354	43,832	2.7
inter	190,788	50,758	3.8	138,587	24,696	5.6

	Raw data, 2 → 1 (div)			Trimmed data, 2 → 1 (div)		
	Number of observations		248	Number of observations		234
	Number of groups		7	Number of groups		7
	Obs/grp	min=	21	Obs/grp	min=	19
		avg=	35		avg=	33
		max=	68		max=	66
	Wald chi(13)		8.15	Wald chi(13)		7.61
	prob > chi2		0.2275	prob > chi2		0.2681
Variable	Coefficient	Std. error	z	Coefficient	Std. error	z
I2	2,083	43,580	0.1	−8,969	32,677	−0.3
I3	7,076	33,730	0.2	1,437	27,421	0.1
I4	74,465	55,713	1.3	66,443	45,943	1.5
I5	180,242	76,209	2.4	150,551	67,768	2.2
I6	27,386	48,419	0.6	23,053	38,667	0.6
I7	85,791	73,686	1.2	−5,226	35,143	−0.2
inter	139,361	20,834	6.7	127,474	16,424	7.8

(*continued*)

Table 1A.1   (continued)

	Raw data, $1 \rightarrow 1$			Trimmed data, $1 \rightarrow 1$		
	Number of observations		4,993	Number of observations		4,894
	Number of groups		7	Number of groups		7
	Obs/grp	min=	681	Obs/grp	min=	668
		avg=	713		avg=	699
		max=	753		max=	738
	Wald chi(13)		53.51	Wald chi(13)		96.71
	prob > chi2		0.0000	prob > chi2		0.0000
Variable	Coefficient	Std. error	z	Coefficient	Std. error	z
I2	7,170	9,964	0.7	7,570	6,696	1.1
I3	19,569	11,685	1.7	16,305	7,020	2.3
I4	34,084	11,549	3.0	31,406	7,922	4.0
I5	53,836	12,329	4.4	51,658	9,060	5.7
I6	55,999	14,109	4.0	45,294	7,970	5.7
I7	85,507	15,776	5.4	67,964	9,014	7.5
inter	94,229	7,194	13.1	80,983	4,388	18.5

Notes: Variables I2 through I7 are indicator variables for each interval. Estimation is by generalized least squares allowing for heteroskedacity across waves.

Table 1A.2   **Trimmed regressions used to produce "smoothed" asset profiles for persons in $2 \rightarrow 2$ households**

	Number of observations		17,009
	Number of groups		7
	Obs per group	min=	1,834
		avg=	2,430
		max=	3,159
	Wald chi(13)		1,223.9
	prob > chi2		0.0000
Variable	Coefficient	Std. error	z
	Beginning assets, age 56–61 in 1992		
I2	38,881	12,198	3.2
I3	77,336	14,265	5.4
I4	137,148	16,087	8.5
I5	209,601	18,820	11.1
I6	189,438	18,199	10.4
I7	238,555	20,357	11.7
I1*h	−1,429	147	−9.7
I2*h	−1,835	166	−11.1
I3*h	−2,168	213	−10.2
I4*h	−2,546	252	−10.1
I5*h	−3,101	308	−10.1
I6*h	−2,898	294	−9.9
I7*h	−3,072	341	−9.0
intercept	299,503	8,121	36.9

Table 1A.2   (continued)

	Number of observations		17,008	
	Number of groups		7	
	Obs per group	min=	1,834	
		avg=	2,430	
		max=	3,159	
	Wald chi(13)		1,133.3	
	prob > chi2		0.0000	

Variable	Coefficient	Std. error	z
Ending assets, age 56–61 in 1992			
I2	21,923	13,771	1.6
I3	89,098	15,782	5.7
I4	147,597	18,291	8.1
I5	148,258	17,827	8.3
I6	181,592	19,420	9.4
I7	252,778	22,223	11.4
I1*h	−1,716	159	−10.8
I2*h	−1,949	194	−10.1
I3*h	−2,518	238	−10.6
I4*h	−2,779	292	−9.5
I5*h	−2,765	281	−9.8
I6*h	−3,057	313	−9.8
I7*h	−3,805	373	−10.2
intercept	334,525	8,757	38.2

Notes: Variables I2 through I7 are indicator variables for each interval; h is latent health expressed as a percentile score. Estimation is by generalized least squares allowing for heteroskedacity across waves.

References

Banks, J., R. Blundell, Z. Oldfield, and J. Smith. 2007. Housing price volatility and downsizing in later life. NBER Working Paper no. 13496. Cambridge, MA: National Bureau of Economic Research, October.

Bosworth, B., and R. Smart. 2009. Evaluating micro-survey estimates of wealth and saving. Center for Retirement Research at Boston College Working Paper no. 2009-4.

Coile, C., and K. Milligan. 2009. How household portfolios evolve after retirement: The effect of aging and health shocks. *Review of Income and Wealth* 55 (2): 226–48.

Curtin, R., F. T. Juster, and J. Morgan. 1989. Survey estimates of wealth: An assessment of quality. In *The measurement of saving, investment and wealth,* ed. R. Lipsey and H. Tice, 473–552. Chicago: University of Chicago Press.

Davidoff, T. 2007. Illiquid housing as self-insurance: The case of long-term care. University of California, Berkeley, Haas School of Business. Working Paper.

De Nardi, M., E. French, and J. B. Jones. 2006. Differential mortality, uncertain medical expenses, and the saving of elderly singles. NBER Working Paper no. 12554. Cambridge, MA: National Bureau of Economic Research, September.

Dushi, I., and M. Honig. 2008. How much do respondents in the Health and Retirement Study know about their tax-deferred contribution plans? A cross-cohort comparison. Michigan Retirement Research Center Working Paper no. 2008-201.

Gustman, A., and T. Steinmeier. 2004. What people don't know about their pension and social security. In *Private pensions and public policies,* ed. W. Gale, J. Shoven, and M. Warshawsky, 57–88. Washington, DC: Brookings Institution.

Gustman, A., T. Steinmeier, and N. Tabatabai. 2008. Do workers know their pension plan type? Comparing workers' and employer's pension information. In *Overcoming the saving slump,* ed. A. Lusardi, 47–81. Chicago: University of Chicago Press.

Haveman, R., K. Holden, B. Wolfe, and A. Romanov. 2005. Assessing the maintenance of saving sufficiency over the first decade of retirement. CESifo Working Paper no. 1567. Munich: Ifo Institute for Economic Research.

Hill, D. 2006. Wealth dynamics: Reducing noise in panel data. *Journal of Applied Econometrics* 21:845–60.

Holden, S., and D. Schrass. 2009. The role of IRAs in U.S. households' saving for retirement, 2008. *Research Fundamentals, Investment Company Institute* 18 (1): 1–20.

Hurd, M. 2002. Portfolios of the elderly. In *Household portfolios,* ed. L. Guiso, M. Haliassos, and T. Jappelli, 431–72. Cambridge, MA: MIT Press.

Hurd, M., and S. Rohwedder. 2006. Life-cycle consumption and wealth paths at older ages. RAND Manuscript, presented at IZA Conference. Bonn, Germany.

———. 2009. The adequacy of resources in retirement, then and now. Presented at the AEA (American Economic Association) Meetings. December, Atlanta, GA.

Hurst, E. 2008. Understanding consumption in retirement: Recent developments. In *Recalibrating retirement spending and saving,* ed. J. Ameriks and O. Mitchell, 29–45. Cambridge: Cambridge University Press, Pension Research Council.

Juster, F. T., J. Smith, and F. Stafford. 1999. The measurement and structure of household wealth. *Labour Economics* 6 (2): 253–75.

Lupton, J., and J. P. Smith. 2000. Marriage, assets, and savings. RAND Corporation Publications Department Working Paper no. 99-12.

Megbolugbe, I., J. Sa-Aadu, and J. Shilling. 1997. Oh yes, the elderly will reduce housing equity under the right circumstances. *Journal of Housing Research* 8 (1): 53–74.

———. 1999. Elderly female-headed households and the decision to trade down. *Journal of Housing Economics* 8:285–300.

Poterba, J., S. Venti, and D. Wise. 2008. *Tapping assets in retirement: Which assets, how, and when?* NBER Retirement Research Center, September.

Rohwedder, S., S. Haider, and M. D. Hurd. 2006. Increases in wealth among the elderly in the early 1990s: How much is due to survey design? *Review of Income and Wealth* 52 (4): 509–24.

Scholz, J. K., W. Gale, and A. Seshadri. 2009. Are all Americans saving optimally for retirement? Presented at the AEA meetings. December, Atlanta, GA.

Scholz, J. K., A. Seshadri, and S. Khitatrakun. 2006. Are Americans saving optimally for retirement? *Journal of Political Economy* 114 (4): 607–43.

Smith, J. 1995. Wealth accumulation between the waves. Paper presented at University of Michigan Workshop on HRS Surveys. November, Ann Arbor.

Venti, S., and D. Wise. 2001. Aging and housing equity. In *Innovations in retirement financing,* ed. O. Mitchell, Z. Bodie, P. B. Hammond, and S. Zeldes, 254–81. Philadelphia: University of Pennsylvania Press.

———. 2004. Aging and housing equity: Another look. In *Perspectives in the economics of aging,* ed. D. Wise, 127–80. Chicago: University of Chicago Press.

Comment   David Laibson

How do households decumulate their retirement savings? This is one of the most important open questions in the retirement savings literature. Poterba, Venti, and Wise (hereafter PVW) establish many interesting and important facts about the decumulation process. After resolving lots of critical technical issues that arise because of measurement errors in the HRS data, PVW show three properties. First, net worth tends to rise robustly throughout old age in both two-person households and one-person households. Second, demographic transitions (e.g., widowhood) tend to slow the growth of wealth, and this wealth reduction begins long before the actual demographic transition occurs. Third, there is a very strong positive association between health and wealth. Healthy households have higher levels of wealth and higher growth rates of wealth.

These facts should lead economists to reevaluate the classical model of life cycle consumption. Figure 1C.1 plots the predictions of the classical model (e.g., the life cycle hypothesis of Modigliani and the permanent income hypothesis of Friedman): a tent-shaped wealth accumulation pattern. Wealth rises smoothly during working life. Then wealth falls smoothly during retirement. However, PVW's evidence supports a more complex wealth decumulation pattern, like the pattern plotted in figure 1C.2. In this figure, wealth continues rising even *after* retirement, until elevated health-related expenses cause a substantial decline in wealth. At the end of this health shock, wealth resumes its rise until another health event occurs. Figure 1C.2 illustrates a case with two (wealth-reducing) health events, but in principle many expensive health events could occur before wealth is completely spent. Moreover, these health events need not be discrete (the discrete case is illustrated in the figure).

In this discussion, I present a tractable model of such complicated decumulation dynamics. The model is in continuous-time, though the model has discrete medical events.

Let μ represent the hazard rate of arrival of one of these discrete medical events. To keep the modeling simple, assume that a medical event is *both* expensive and deadly (e.g., a retiree experiences a stroke, which leads to

David Laibson is a Harvard College Professor and the Robert I. Goldman Professor of Economics at Harvard University, and a research associate of the National Bureau of Economic Research.

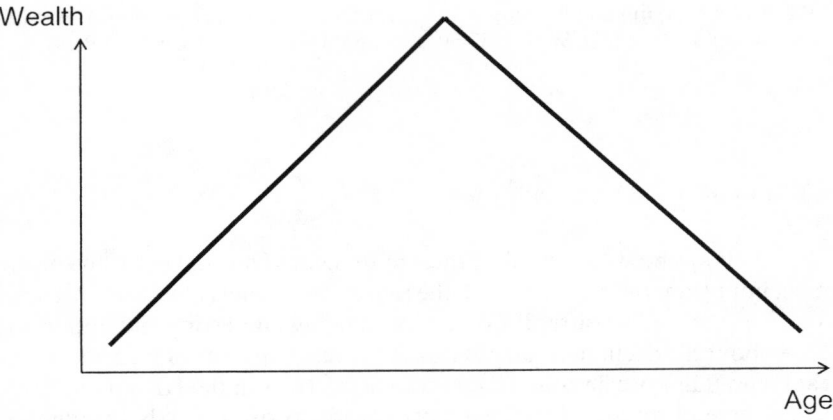

Fig. 1C.1   Life cycle wealth dynamics predicted by classical theories

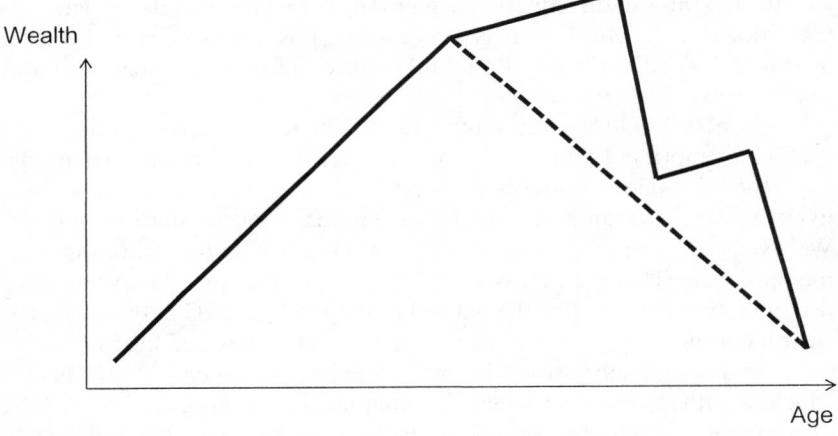

Fig. 1C.2   Stylized empirical patterns of wealth decumulation

hospitalization, long-term care, and mortality). I summarize this by assuming that discrete medical-event utility is given by

$$M(C_M) = \frac{s C_M^{1-\gamma}}{1-\gamma},$$

where C_M is the out-of-pocket expenditure (endogenously chosen) during the medical event.

I assume that there is no bequest motive and no annuity market. Households have a utility function with constant relative risk aversion, γ. The flow utility for a household of size n is given by

$$n \times u\left(\frac{C}{n^\theta}\right) = n \times \frac{(C/n^\theta)^{1-\gamma}}{1 - \gamma}.$$

To gain intuition, consider the following three benchmark cases: (a) no returns to scale, $\theta = 1$; (b) infinite returns to scale, $\theta = 0$; and (c) square-root returns to scale, $\theta = 1/2$. The last case is the leading empirical case.

Outside of medical events, the dynamics for wealth are smooth,

$$dW = rW - C,$$

where r is the real interest rate. During a medical event, the dynamics for W are discrete,

$$\Delta W = W - C_M.$$

With a discount rate of ρ, the continuous-time Bellman equation for a one-person household (e.g., after the death of a spouse), is given by

$$\rho V_1(W) = u(C) + EdV_1$$

$$= u(C) + \frac{\delta V_1}{\delta W}[rW - C] + \mu\left[\zeta \frac{W^{1-\gamma}}{1 - \gamma} - V_1(W)\right].$$

The continuous-time Bellman equation for a two-person household is given by

$$\rho V_2(W) = 2 \times u\left(\frac{C}{2^\theta}\right) + EdV_2$$

$$= 2 \times u\left(\frac{C}{2^\theta}\right) + \frac{\delta V_2}{\delta W}[rW - C]$$

$$+ \mu\left[\frac{\zeta C_M^{1-\gamma}}{1 - \gamma} + V_1(W - C_M) - V_2(W)\right].$$

Using the guess-and-check method, it is easy to show that the value function for the one-person household is given by

$$V_1(W) = \frac{\phi_1 W^{1-\gamma}}{1 - \gamma},$$

where ϕ_1 is a constant to be solved. Applying the envelope theorem yields,

$$C = \phi_1^{-1/\gamma} W.$$

Solving for the marginal propensity to consume (MPC), $\phi_1^{-1/\gamma}$, yields,

$$\rho + \mu = \gamma\phi_1^{-\frac{1}{\gamma}} + (1 - \gamma)r + \phi_1^{-1}\mu\zeta.$$

We now characterize the tractable case of ln utility, which is obtained by letting $\gamma \to 1$. Now

$$\text{MPC} = \phi_1^{-1} = \frac{\rho + \mu}{1 + \mu\zeta}.$$

Hence, the MPC rises with ρ, falls with ζ, and has an ambiguous relationship with μ. For this case, wealth will accumulate even if

$$r = \rho + \mu.$$

We can solve for medical spending during a medical event experienced by the first spouse:

$$\lambda^* = \arg\max \frac{\zeta(\lambda W)^{1-\gamma}}{1 - \gamma} + \frac{\phi_1(W - \lambda W)^{1-\gamma}}{1 - \gamma}$$

$$= \arg\max \frac{\zeta\lambda^{1-\gamma}}{1 - \gamma} + \frac{\phi_1(1 - \lambda)^{1-\gamma}}{1 - \gamma}.$$

The first-order condition (FOC) implies that

$$0 = \zeta\lambda^{-\gamma} - \phi_1(1 - \lambda)^{-\gamma}.$$

Setting $\gamma = 1$ implies

$$\zeta(1 - \lambda) = \phi_1\lambda$$

$$\lambda = \frac{\zeta}{\phi_1 + \zeta}$$

$$= \frac{\zeta}{[(1 + \mu\zeta)/(\rho + \mu)] + \zeta}$$

Finally, we can also solve for two-person household by confirming that the following functional form satisfies the Bellman equation for the two-person household.

$$V_2(W) = \frac{\phi_2 W^{1-\gamma}}{1 - \gamma}.$$

By the envelope theorem:

$$C = 2^{1-\theta(1-\gamma)/\gamma}\,\phi_2^{-1/\lambda} W.$$

Plugging this expression into the Bellman equation, and simplifying, yields,

$$\rho = 2^{1-\theta(1-\gamma)/\gamma}\,\phi_2^{-1/\gamma} + (1 - \gamma)[r - 2^{1-\theta(1-\gamma)/\gamma}\,\phi_2^{-1/\gamma}]$$

$$+ \mu\left[\frac{\zeta\lambda^{1-\gamma}}{\phi_2} + \frac{\phi_1}{\phi_2}(1 - \lambda)^{1-\gamma} - 1\right].$$

Again, we will study the special case, $\gamma = 1$. This implies

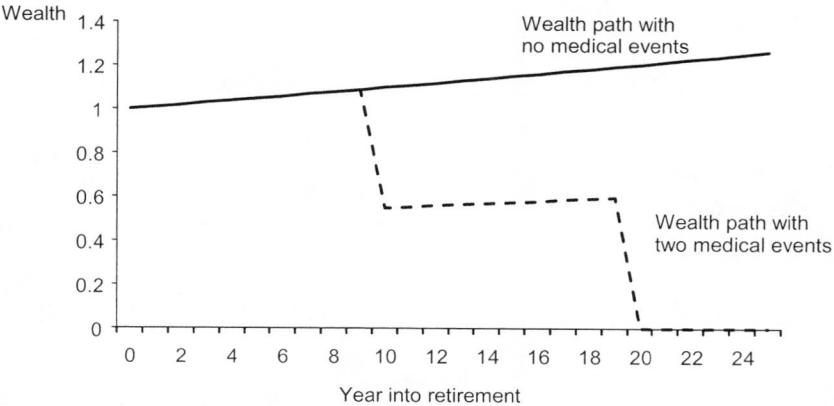

Fig. 1C.3   Predictions of new model with medical events
Note: Calibrated parameters: $\zeta = 50$, $\rho = 0.02$, $\gamma = 1$, $r = 0.03$, $\lambda = 0.5$, $\mu = 0.02$.

$$\mathrm{MPC} = 2\,\phi_2^{-1} = \frac{\rho + \mu}{1 + (\mu/2)(\zeta + [1 + \mu\zeta/\rho + \mu])}.$$

As before, the MPC rises with ρ, falls with ζ, and has an ambiguous relationship with μ. Once again, wealth will accumulate even if

$$r = \rho + \mu.$$

See figure 1C.3 for a calibrated/simulated path of wealth. The model has several implications. An increase in the taste for health expenditure—that is, an increase in ζ—lowers the MPC. Wealth grows in retirement even when the discount rate equals the interest rate. Indeed, wealth grows in retirement even when the discount rate plus the mortality rate ($\rho + \mu$) equals the interest rate. Households choose to make large proportionate reductions in wealth that coincide with medical events. These proportionate reductions in wealth are not a sign of financial distress. Rather, they reflect an optimal decision to spend wealth on health services during a severe medical event. Moreover, even if retirement wealth were much greater, such expenditures would not proportionately change. As our resources rise, the model predicts that we will choose to buy better and better medical services (e.g., private hospital rooms, expensive pharmaceuticals that are not covered by insurance, home nurses, outstanding long-term care facilities, etc.).

This model provides a quantitative framework for studying wealth dynamics after retirement, and explains why households that are not experiencing medical events choose to increase their wealth throughout retirement. The empirical analysis in PVW is critical for the development of models like this that explain the surprising savings behavior of older adults.

2

How Does Simplified Disclosure Affect Individuals' Mutual Fund Choices?

John Beshears, James J. Choi, David Laibson,
and Brigitte C. Madrian

Some regulators believe that the average investor has a hard time reading the statutory prospectuses mutual funds distribute. In the words of the Securities and Exchange Commission (SEC), "Prospectuses are often long . . . Too frequently, the language of prospectuses is complex and legalistic, and the presentation formats make little use of graphic design techniques that would contribute to readability."[1] Partly as a result, two-thirds of investors do not read the prospectus before purchasing mutual fund shares (Investment Company Institute 2006).

John Beshears is assistant professor of finance at the Stanford Graduate School of Business, and a faculty research fellow of the National Bureau of Economic Research. James J. Choi is associate professor of finance at Yale School of Management, and a faculty research fellow of the National Bureau of Economic Research. David Laibson is a Harvard College Professor and the Robert I. Goldman Professor of Economics at Harvard University, and a research associate of the National Bureau of Economic Research. Brigitte C. Madrian is the Aetna Professor of Public Policy and Corporate Management at the John F. Kennedy School of Government at Harvard University, and a research associate and codirector of the working group on household finance at the National Bureau of Economic Research.

This publication was made possible by generous grants from the FINRA Investor Education Foundation and the Social Security Administration through grant #10-P-98363-1-05 to the National Bureau of Economic Research as part of the SSA Retirement Research Consortium. We have benefited from the comments of Annamaria Lusardi and conference participants at the 2009 ASSA Meetings in San Francisco. We appreciate the research assistance of Christina Jenq, Eric Zwick, Anna Blank, Kyle Chauvin, Shaq Chi, Heidi Liu, Will Pan, Logan Pritchard, Akeel Rangwala, Chelsea Zhang, and Christina Zhou. The findings and conclusions expressed are solely those of the authors and do not represent the views of SSA, any agency of the federal government, the NBER, or FINRA. The FINRA Investor Education Foundation, formerly known as the NASD Investor Education Foundation, supports innovative research and educational projects that give investors the tools and information they need to better understand the markets and the basic principles of saving and investing. For details about grant programs and other new initiatives of the Foundation, visit www.finrafoundation.org.

1. SEC Release No. 33-8861.

Motivated by these concerns, the SEC recently proposed and subsequently adopted a new simplified disclosure document. Mutual funds now have the option of sending investors this two- to four-page document, dubbed the "Summary Prospectus," instead of the statutory prospectus. The Summary Prospectus contains key information about the mutual fund's investment objectives, strategies, risks, costs, and performance. This information can also be found in previously extant fund literature (the statutory prospectus, the Statement of Additional Information [SAI], and the shareholder report).

To our knowledge, there has been no direct empirical investigation of how the Summary Prospectus would affect investors' portfolio choices. This chapter contributes toward filling this gap. We recruited 186 Harvard non-faculty, white-collar staff members to participate in a portfolio allocation experiment. All subjects allocated two portfolios: one among four actively managed equity mutual funds, and one among four actively managed bond mutual funds. Subjects' payments depended on how their chosen portfolios actually performed subsequent to the experimental session and were approximately $100 per subject in expectation.

We randomized each subject into one of three information conditions. In the first condition, subjects received only the funds' statutory prospectuses. In the second condition, subjects received only the funds' Summary Prospectuses, which we constructed using the original SEC proposal's specifications. In the third condition, subjects received the Summary Prospectuses but could additionally request the statutory prospectuses (a request that only a few of the subjects in this condition actually made). Subjects were randomly assigned to be paid based on either their subsequent one-month portfolio return or their subsequent one-year portfolio return.

We find that providing the Summary Prospectus does not alter subjects' investment choices. Dollar-weighted average fees and past returns of mutual fund choices are statistically indistinguishable across the three information conditions. However, subjects receiving the Summary Prospectus spent less time on their investment decision. Thus, the principal welfare gain from the Summary Prospectus comes from allowing investors to spend less time and effort to arrive at the same portfolio decision they would have come to after reading only the statutory prospectus. Of course, the shorter Summary Prospectus saves paper, printing, and shipping costs as well.

Our experiment also sheds new light on the scope of investor confusion about sales loads.[2] We find that subjects' portfolio choices do not respond sensibly to loads and redemption fees, whether or not they receive the Summary Prospectus. Loads and redemption fees should be avoided to a greater

---

2. See also Elton, Gruber, and Busse (2004); Barber, Odean, and Zheng (2005); Cronqvist (2006); and Choi, Laibson, and Madrian (2010) for other evidence of irrational investor behavior with respect to mutual fund fees.

degree as the investment horizon shrinks. Nonetheless, subjects with a one-month investment horizon chose portfolios with loads plus redemption fees that are on average 200 basis points higher than the load-minimizing portfolio. This implies that subjects are either confused about loads, overlook them, or believe that their chosen portfolio has an annualized log return (before loads) that is an implausible 24 percentage points higher than the load-minimizing portfolio's.

In a study related to ours, Kozup, Howlett, and Pagano (2008) examine the impact of certain types of summary information on individuals' attitudes toward mutual funds. Contrary to our results, these authors find that summary information increases subjects' sensitivity to past fund performance. However, their experiment differs from ours in a number of respects: (a) their study was conducted before the release of the SEC proposal and therefore does not use the Summary Prospectus format specified in the proposal; (b) their summary information is much briefer and emphasizes comparisons between a fund and the universe of similar funds; (c) the mutual funds in their experiment are fictional; and (d) their subjects did not make incentivized portfolio choices but instead rated their investment intentions, attitudes, and perceptions of future performance and risk with regard to a fund using 7-point scales.

An advantage of using laboratory experiments to evaluate policy proposals is that results can be produced extremely rapidly. We learned of the Summary Prospectus proposal in mid-January 2008, and we were able to finish collecting data and tabulate preliminary results by the end of February 2008, which we sent to the SEC. We believe that in the future, laboratory experiments should become a common part of the policy proposal vetting process.

The chapter proceeds as follows. Section 2.1 provides additional detail on the Summary Prospectus. We describe our experimental design in section 2.2. Section 2.3 discusses the experimental results, and section 2.4 concludes.

2.1 Background on the Summary Prospectus

In Release No. 33-8861, published on December 14, 2007, the SEC describes its Summary Prospectus proposal as follows:

> We are proposing an improved mutual fund disclosure framework that is intended to provide investors with information that is easier to use and more readily accessible, while retaining the comprehensive quality of the information that is available today. The foundation of the proposal is the provision to all investors of streamlined and user-friendly information that is key to an investment decision.

The SEC's aspirations for the Summary Prospectus, as described in Release No. 33-8861, are ambitious:

We anticipate that our proposal will improve investors' ability to make informed investment decisions and, therefore, lead to increased efficiency and competitiveness of the U.S. capital markets. Similarly, the ability of investors to directly locate the information they seek regarding a fund or funds through the use of the Internet may result in more fund investors or existing investors investing in more funds.

Mutual funds now have the option of satisfying their prospectus delivery obligations under the Securities Act of 1933 by sending a Summary Prospectus. In other words, investors going forward are more likely to receive only a two- to four-page document rather than a prospectus that sometimes runs hundreds of pages. Investors receiving the Summary Prospectus can also receive the longer statutory prospectus via mail or Internet upon request.

Appendix A shows the sample Summary Prospectus that the SEC included in its proposal. The document begins with a description of how one can receive the statutory prospectus and other fund documents. It then displays the following information about the fund:

- Investment objective
- Fees and expenses
- Historical portfolio turnover rate
- Principal investment strategies
- Principal risks
- Historical returns
- Top ten portfolio holdings
- Investment advisor
- Portfolio manager
- How to purchase and sell fund shares
- Dividend, capital gain, and tax information
- A disclaimer about payments the fund may make to broker-dealers and other financial intermediaries

All of this information can usually be found in the union of the statutory prospectus, the Statement of Additional Information (SAI), and the shareholder report.

The Summary Prospectus that was finally adopted is similar to the original proposal, and is described in SEC Release No. 33-8998. The amended document eliminates the top ten portfolio holdings and adds the ticker symbol, a slightly revised description of fund expenses,[3] information about where to find additional detail on the fund's front-end load breakpoint discounts (based on investment amount), a description of the adverse tax

---

3. The wording, "expenses that you pay each year as a percentage of the value of your investment" replaces "expenses that are deducted from Fund assets."

consequences of portfolio turnover, and a stronger emphasis that payments from the fund to broker-dealers may create a conflict of interest.

In addition, the SEC now requires that every statutory prospectus begin with a section that replicates the fund's Summary Prospectus. In this chapter, we focus on the effect of introducing the stand-alone Summary Prospectus because it is the more radical change. The summary section added to the statutory prospectus would likely have an effect that is directionally similar to the Summary Prospectus, but attenuated because it is part of a long document that often goes unread.

2.2   Experimental Design

In February 2008, we recruited 186 nonfaculty Harvard employees drawn from the ranks of the administrative, professional, clerical, and technical staff.[4] We paid subjects a $20 participation fee and promised them an additional payment that depended on their investment decisions, as described below.

Upon entering the study, subjects received instructions that they were going to make investment choices for two hypothetical $100,000 portfolios. One portfolio could only be invested in stock mutual funds; the other could only be invested in bond mutual funds. We would then select one portfolio based on whether the high temperature at Logan Airport on a future date was even or odd. We would pay subjects 0.1 percent of the selected portfolio's value at the end of the investment period. For example, if the portfolio's terminal value was $100,000, subjects would receive a $100 portfolio-based payment.

Subjects entered their portfolio allocations onto choice sheets. One sheet listed a menu of four equity mutual funds, and the other listed a menu of four bond mutual funds. Appendix B reproduces an example of a choice sheet.

Each choice sheet was one page long and had three sections. The first section explained the purpose of the experiment—to allocate 100,000 experimental dollars among the four listed equity or bond mutual funds—and described the payment scheme. The second section gave a numerical example of how the portfolio payout would be calculated. The third section contained a matrix in which participants entered their investment allocation. Participants were instructed to allocate their investment across as many or as few funds as they desired, subject to two constraints: (a) they had to allocate exactly $100,000 in total, and (b) they had to satisfy the minimum opening

4. We actually recruited 314 subjects, but we discard the data of 125 subjects because errors in the experimental materials distributed to those subjects make interpreting their choices problematic. We discard an additional three subjects in order to make the frequency of menus in each condition equal. Our results do not qualitatively change if we analyze the larger sample of subjects.

balance requirement for any fund to which they made an allocation. We imposed the latter restriction to mimic the constraints that an investor would face when making a real investment in these funds. The minimum opening balance for each fund was listed next to the column where participants were to write their selected allocation.

We randomly assigned subjects to one of three information conditions. In the "Prospectus" condition, subjects received only the eight funds' statutory prospectuses when making their investment decision. In the "Summary Prospectus" condition, subjects received only Summary Prospectuses, which we constructed for the funds based upon the sample Summary Prospectus provided in the SEC's proposal. (Appendix C describes in more detail how we constructed these Summary Prospectuses.) In the "Summary Prospectus+" condition, subjects initially received only the Summary Prospectuses but could also receive the statutory prospectuses upon request. This latter condition was designed to mimic the SEC proposal, which allows firms to distribute only the Summary Prospectus while giving investors the option to request the statutory prospectus if desired.

Half of subjects made the equity allocation before the bond allocation; the other half made the allocations in reverse order. At any given moment in the experiment, subjects possessed only one investment choice sheet and one set of fund documents. That is, when subjects were making their equity allocation, they only possessed materials relevant to the equity funds available to them. Similarly, subjects only possessed materials relevant to bond funds when making their bond allocation.

We also randomly varied (independently of information condition) the subjects' investment horizon. Half of subjects would receive their portfolio payments based upon what a real-life investor would receive if he bought their selected portfolio at 3:00 p.m. on February 29, 2008 and sold it at 3:00 p.m. on March 31, 2008. The other half would receive their portfolio payments assuming the investor bought their selected portfolio at 3:00 p.m. on February 29, 2008 and sold it at 3:00 p.m. on February 28, 2009.[5] The investment horizon relevant for the subject was displayed on the choice sheet. We promised to pay subjects soon after their investment period ended.

Finally, we randomly assigned subjects (independently of the other two randomization dimensions) to receive one of ten menus of mutual funds. Each of the ten menus consists of four equity funds and four bond funds. To populate the menus, we began by randomly selecting ten equity funds and ten bond funds from the Center for Research in Security Prices (CRSP) mutual fund universe that satisfied the following criteria: (a) they had a share class with a front-end load (Class A) and a share class with no front-end load

5. Because February 28, 2009 is a Saturday, the sale would actually be executed on March 2, 2009. Hence, the investment horizon was slightly over one year. Charging back-end loads assuming that the investment horizon was exactly one year does not qualitatively change our conclusions about how the Summary Prospectus affected fees paid.

(Class C); (b) they were active in 2007; (c) their S&P style code was Equity Large Cap Growth, Equity Large Cap Value, or Equity Large Cap Blend for equity funds and Fixed Income High Yield for bond funds; (d) they were not a "fund of funds" or an index fund; (e) they were available to retail investors; (f) they were open to new investments in 2007; (g) they reported historical return information; and (h) they did not have special characteristics like a religious affiliation, social investment objectives, investments limited to a single sector, or a tax-managed strategy.

We then created ten distinct menus of funds from these ten equity and ten bond funds. The first five menus satisfied the following requirements: (a) each fund appeared in exactly two of the five menus, with one menu offering the Class A shares of the fund, and the second offering the Class C shares of the fund; (b) the same fund did not appear twice in the same menu (e.g., Fund 1's Class A and Fund 1's Class C were not in the same menu); and (c) every menu offered two fund share classes with front-end loads (Class A) and two fund share classes with no front-end loads (Class C). The next five menus were created based on the first five menus by inverting the share classes of each menu. For example, if one menu offered Bond Fund 1 (Class A), Bond Fund 2 (Class C), Bond Fund 3 (Class A), and Bond Fund 4 (Class C), its inverted menu would offer Bond Fund 1 (Class C), Bond Fund 2 (Class A), Bond Fund 3 (Class C), and Bond Fund 4 (Class A).

Unfortunately, there were errors in the Summary Prospectuses we constructed for one equity fund and one bond fund. We therefore drop subjects offered these two funds from our analysis, whether or not they received a Summary Prospectus.[6] Because four out of the ten menus we constructed contained a problematic fund, our sample is reduced by 40 percent. Our results do not qualitatively change if we include subjects who received the problematic menus.

Table 2.1 displays features of the eighteen mutual funds that remain in our sample. Front-end loads for Class A shares range between 1.75 percent and 5.75 percent. There is almost no variation in back-end loads for Class C shares; all the funds except one charge a 1 percent load if the shares are held for less than twelve months, although some funds count the beginning of the calendar month or calendar year of purchase as the start of the holding period, rather than the exact day of purchase. Some funds also charge an additional redemption fee of up to 2 percent if shares are sold within a shorter time frame. (For ease of exposition, we will hereafter refer to loads and redemption fees collectively as "loads.") Expense ratios lie between 0.80 percent and 1.53 percent for Class A shares and between 1.55 percent and 2.18 percent for Class C shares. As expected, there is more cross-sectional variation in the equity fund returns than the bond fund returns.

6. Every subject who was offered one problematic fund was offered the other problematic fund as well.

Table 2.1   Mutual fund shares offered in the experiment

	Share class	Front-end load (%)	Expense ratio (%)	Back-end load (%)	Additional redemption fee (%)	Past 1-year return in prospectus (%)	Longest-horizon return reported in prospectus (%)	Inception date
A Equity funds								
Allegiant Large Cap Growth Fund	A	3.75–5.50	1.17	0	0	7.35	7.23	04/15/1991
	C	0	1.89	1 if held ≤ 18 months[a]	0			01/27/2000
American Century Fundamental Equity	A	3.75–5.50	1.26	0	0	23.88	18.10	11/30/2004
	C	0	2.01	1 if held ≤ 12 months[a]	0			11/30/2004
Dreyfus Premier Core Value Fund	A	3.50–5.75	1.15	0	0	21.00	9.81	02/06/1947
	C	0	1.90	1 if held ≤ 12 months[c]	0			01/16/1998
MFS Emerging Growth Fund	A	3.75–5.75	1.15	0	0	7.54	6.96	09/13/1993
	C	0	1.90	1 if held ≤ 12 months[b]	0			04/01/1996
MFS Value Fund	A	3.75–5.75	1.11	0	0	20.67	13.24	01/02/1996
	C	0	1.76	1 if held ≤ 12 months[b]	0			11/05/1997
Oppenheimer Capital Appreciation	A	3.75–5.75	1.05	0	0	7.51	10.04	01/22/1981
	C	0	1.81	1 if held ≤ 12 months[b]	0			12/01/1993
Sentinel Common Stock Fund	A	3.00–5.00	1.13	0	0	16.00	9.07	01/02/1934
	C	0	2.16	1 if held ≤ 12 months[a]	0			05/04/1998
SunAmerica Growth and Income	A	3.75–5.75	1.53	0	0	14.71	7.68	07/01/1994
	C	0	2.18	1 if held ≤ 12 months[c]	0			02/02/1998
Van Kampen Equity Growth	A	3.75–5.75	1.23	0	2 if held ≤ 7 days	5.76	4.19	05/28/1998
	C	0	1.99	1 if held ≤ 12 months[b]	2 if held ≤ 7 days			05/28/1998

B Bond funds

Fund	Class	Front-end load	Expense ratio	CDSC	CDSC	Return	Date
DWS High Income Fund	A	3.50–4.50	0.94	0	2 if held ≤ 30 days	10.27	01/26/1978
	C	0	1.67	1 if held ≤ 12 months[a]	2 if held ≤ 30 days	5.99	05/31/1994
Eaton Vance Floating-Rate & High Income	A	1.75–2.25	1.01	0	1 if held ≤ 90 days	6.14	05/07/2003
	C	0	1.76	1 if held ≤ 12 months[a]	0	4.21	09/05/2000
Federated High Income Bond Fund	A	3.75–4.50	1.23	0	2 if held ≤ 90 days	10.48	11/30/1977
	C	0	1.98	1 if held ≤ 12 months[a]	2 if held ≤ 90 days	5.71	04/30/1993
Goldman Sachs High Yield	A	3.00–4.50	1.12	0	2 if held ≤ 60 days	11.29	08/01/1997
	C	0	1.87	1 if held ≤ 12 months[b]	2 if held ≤ 60 days	7.12	08/15/1997
HSBC Investor High Yield Fixed Income	A	3.50–4.75	0.80	0	2 if held ≤ 30 days	10.49	11/18/2005
	C	0	1.55	1 if held ≤ 12 months[a]	2 if held ≤ 30 days	10.49	12/14/2005
Loomis Sayles High Income	A	3.50–4.50	1.15	0	2 if held ≤ 60 days	13.86	02/22/1984
	C	0	1.90	1 if held ≤ 12 months[a]	0	3.93	03/02/1998
Oppenheimer Champion Income	A	3.50–4.75	1.11	0	2 if held ≤ 30 days	9.19	11/16/1987
	C	0	1.86	1 if held ≤ 12 months[b]	2 if held ≤ 30 days	5.96	12/01/1993
Pioneer High Yield	A	3.50–4.50	1.10	0	0	10.60	02/12/1998
	C	0	1.81	1 if held ≤ 12 months[c]	0	13.20	02/12/1998
Wells Fargo Advantage Strategic Income	A	3.50–4.50	1.10	0	2 if held ≤ 30 days	11.04	11/30/2000
	C	0	1.85	1 if held ≤ 12 months[a]	2 if held ≤ 30 days	9.96	11/30/2000

[a] Holding period begins on date of purchase.

[b] Holding period begins on first day of purchase calendar month.

[c] Holding period begins on first day of purchase calendar year.

Notes: This table lists characteristics of the mutual fund shares that were offered to subjects in the experiment. For Class A shares, the front-end load varied according to the investment amount. For Class A shares, the front-end load varied according to the investment amount. Expense ratios in the table reflect fee waivers. The prospectuses listed historical returns for only one of each fund's share classes. The table shows the returns for the share class reported in the prospectus. The longest-horizon return reported in the prospectus is either the return since fund inception (if the fund has been in existence for fewer than ten years) or the ten-year return.

The standard deviation of one-year past returns is 6.99 percent across equity funds and 2.03 percent across bond funds. For the longest-horizon past return reported in the prospectus, the standard deviation is 4.06 percent across equity funds and 3.14 percent across bond funds.

In total, there were thirty-six experimental conditions: three information treatments × two investment horizons × six fund menus. There are an equal number of subjects within each cell. In particular, each menu × investment horizon combination appears the same number of times within each information condition. Therefore, we can compare mean allocations across information conditions without worrying that menu or investment horizon effects are confounding these comparisons.

After submitting their portfolio choices, subjects filled out a questionnaire that included demographic and financial literacy questions.

2.3   Results

Table 2.2 shows the characteristics of our subject sample for each information condition. Subjects are thirty-nine years old on average, and 37 percent are male. Almost all subjects are college graduates, and over half have some graduate education. About a fifth are able to correctly identify the types of securities a money market fund holds when asked a multiple-choice question modeled on a question in the John Hancock Eighth Defined Contribution Plan Survey.[7] This compares favorably to the 8 percent of the John Hancock sample who were able to answer the question correctly. Thus, our subjects have higher levels of educational attainment and financial literacy than the overall U.S. population.

Our subjects also understand the concept of diversification. On average, they rate a typical Fortune 500 stock as riskier than a U.S. equity mutual fund on a 5-point scale. In contrast, John Hancock respondents on average thought that the stock of their own company was *less* risky than an equity mutual fund. However, this comparison is potentially confounded by the fact that John Hancock respondents were asked about the stock of their own employer, whereas our subjects were asked about the stock of a typical Fortune 500 company.

Despite being more financially literate than the average American, most of our subjects do not have much confidence in their investment abilities. About half describe themselves as an investor who is "less than knowledgeable" or "not at all knowledgeable." This lack of financial knowledge is a common finding across surveys. For example, Lusardi, Keller, and Keller (2009) surveyed employees at a nonprofit institution, and 38 percent of

---

7. The question text is, "Which of the following types of investments are found in a money market fund? (*You may check more than one type.*)" The possible choices are short-term U.S. government bonds, corporate bonds, stocks, and none of the above.

Table 2.2   **Subject characteristics**

	Prospectus	Summary prospectus	Summary prospectus+
Average age	39.5	38.8	39.7
Percent male	44%	31%	37%
Highest education			
High school or less	2%	2%	3%
Some college	7%	6%	5%
College degree	34%	31%	26%
Some graduate school	10%	26%	23%
Graduate degree	47%	35%	44%
Knows what money market fund holds	21%	18%	24%
Average risk rating (1 to 5; higher = riskier)			
Typical Fortune 500 stock	3.51	3.25	3.37
Large U.S. equity mutual fund	3.00	3.02	2.93
How knowledgeable of an investor do you consider yourself to be?			
Very knowledgeable	0%	2%	0%
Relatively knowledgeable	10%	10%	13%
Somewhat knowledgeable	34%	31%	49%
Less than knowledgeable	39%	43%	17%
Not at all knowledgeable	17%	14%	21%
Sample size	N = 62	N = 62	N = 62

Note: This table shows experimental subject characteristics in each experimental information condition.

respondents reported that insufficient financial knowledge was a problem in their financial decisions.

Comparing across information conditions, the prospectus-only group is slightly more male than the others. Subjects in the prospectus-only group are also more likely to have a graduate degree, although subjects in the other groups are more likely to have at least some graduate school education. Controlling for gender and educational attainment through dummy variables in a regression does not qualitatively change our results.

Table 2.3 shows how the Summary Prospectus affected investment decisions. Because very few of the subjects in the Summary Prospectus+ condition asked to see a statutory prospectus, we pool the Summary Prospectus and Summary Prospectus+ conditions in the remaining analysis. The table reveals no statistically significant differences in average front-end load, back-end load, expense ratio, total fees, past one-year return, or past long-horizon return (defined as the longest-horizon past return reported in the fund's prospectus) when subjects receive the Summary Prospectus instead of the statutory prospectus. The point estimates indicate that in general, subjects receiving the Summary Prospectus pay more in fund fees and choose funds with higher past returns, although the bond portfolios have some point estimates that go in the opposite direction.

Table 2.3 Subjects' investment choices

	One-month investment horizon			One-year investment horizon		
	Prospectus	SP/SP+	Difference	Prospectus	SP/SP+	Difference
	A Equity portfolio					
Front-end load	2.23%	2.56%	0.32%	2.14%	2.58%	0.43%
	(0.24)	(0.15)	(0.27)	(0.24)	(0.15)	(0.27)
Back-end load plus redemption fee	0.55%	0.47%	−0.08%	0.11%	0.06%	−0.05%
	(0.05)	(0.03)	(0.06)	(0.04)	(0.01)	(0.04)
Expense ratio (prorated)	0.13%	0.13%	0.00%	1.64%	1.57%	−0.07%
	(0.00)	(0.00)	(0.00)	(0.04)	(0.03)	(0.05)
Total fees	2.92%	3.16%	0.24%	3.86%	4.18%	0.31%
	(0.19)	(0.11)	(0.21)	(0.20)	(0.13)	(0.23)
Past one-year return	13.61%	13.99%	0.38%	13.68%	14.55%	0.88%
	(0.81)	(0.59)	(1.01)	(0.73)	(0.55)	(0.93)
Longest-horizon past return in prospectus	9.34%	9.51%	0.17%	9.44%	9.71%	0.27%
	(0.38)	(0.34)	(0.55)	(0.45)	(0.32)	(0.56)
	B Bond portfolio					
Front-end load	1.84%	1.81%	−0.03%	2.09%	1.92%	−0.17%
	(0.18)	(0.15)	(0.25)	(0.24)	(0.14)	(0.26)
Back-end load plus redemption fee	1.15%	1.28%	0.13%	0.00%	0.00%	0.00%
	(0.08)	(0.08)	(0.13)	(0.00)	(0.00)	(0.00)
Expense ratio (prorated)	0.12%	0.12%	0.00%	1.47%	1.47%	0.00%
	(0.00)	(0.00)	(0.00)	(0.04)	(0.03)	(0.05)
Total fees	3.11%	3.21%	0.10%	3.54%	3.37%	−0.17%
	(0.17)	(0.15)	(0.25)	(0.19)	(0.11)	(0.21)
Past one-year return	10.50%	10.69%	0.19%	10.79%	10.55%	−0.24%
	(0.20)	(0.12)	(0.22)	(0.18)	(0.12)	(0.21)
Longest-horizon past return in prospectus	7.64%	7.41%	−0.23%	7.26%	7.84%	0.57%
	(0.27)	(0.23)	(0.38)	(0.33)	(0.25)	(0.43)

Notes: Standard errors are in parentheses below the point estimates. Expense ratios in the monthly condition are equal to the reported expense ratio net of waivers divided by twelve. Back-end loads in the yearly condition were not assessed for those funds whose back-end loads expire after twelve months (all but Allegiant Large Cap Growth Fund Class C).

One important test of sensible investment behavior is an increasing avoidance of loads as the investment horizon shrinks. With a one-year investment horizon, a fund with a 2 percent load would be preferred over a no-load fund with an equivalent expense ratio if the ratio of one plus the load fund's annual pre-load return to one plus the no-load fund's annual return is greater than $1/0.98 = 1.02$. With a one-month investment horizon, the ratio would have to be greater than $(1/0.98)^{12} = 1.27$. In other words, the load fund is preferred under a one-month investment horizon if it has an annualized log return that is larger than the no-load fund's annualized log return by at least $\log(1.27) = 24$ percent—an implausibly large amount to rationally expect.

Table 2.3 shows that subjects generally do not avoid loads in the one-month condition. Pooling the equity and bond allocation decisions, subjects chose funds with an average total load of 3.00 percent in the conditions with an investment horizon of one month, which is 200 basis points higher than the lowest available to them. To not minimize loads is to bet that one's chosen portfolio has a log pre-load return that is (implausibly) 24 percentage points per year higher than the load-minimizing portfolio.[8] With a one-month horizon, minimizing loads is the only sensible strategy.

Does the Summary Prospectus affect the relationship between investment horizon and loads paid? Table 2.3 shows that loads are higher in the one-month condition than in the one-year condition, which is to be expected because back-end loads are 0 percent for most funds at the one-year horizon but not the one-month horizon. However, the amount by which loads increase from the one-year horizon to the one-month horizon is unaffected by the Summary Prospectus. For equity portfolios, subjects receiving the Summary Prospectus exhibit a 14 basis point smaller increase than subjects receiving the statutory prospectus; the reverse holds for bond portfolios, where subjects receiving the Summary Prospectus exhibit a 27 basis point *larger* increase than subjects receiving the statutory prospectus. None of these differences are statistically significant.

In summary, there is no evidence that the Summary Prospectus causes subjects to respond to mutual fund fees more optimally.

We can also analyze whether subjects who received Summary Prospectuses instead of statutory prospectuses differed in the extent to which their portfolios were concentrated in certain mutual funds as opposed to evenly spread among four mutual funds, as might be implied by a naïve diversification strategy (Benartzi and Thaler 2001). For our measure of portfolio concentration, we use the Euclidean distance between $(0.25, 0.25, 0.25, 0.25)$ and the portfolio as represented by a point in $\mathbb{R}^4$. This measure ranges from

---

8. This calculation also takes into account expense ratios, assuming that one-twelfth of the annual expense ratio is charged each month. When more than one fund shares the minimum load, we equally weight the load-minimizing portfolio.

0 (portfolio allocated equally across four funds) to $\sqrt{3/4} \approx 0.87$ (portfolio allocated entirely to a single fund). For equity portfolios, the mean concentration measure for subjects receiving Summary Prospectuses was 0.396 (s.e. 0.020), and the mean concentration measure for subjects receiving statutory prospectuses was also 0.396 (s.e. 0.030). The analogous means for bond portfolios were 0.414 (s.e. 0.023) and 0.408 (s.e. 0.031). Neither difference is statistically significant. Thus, it does not seem that the Summary Prospectus led subjects to change the extent to which they deviate from the naïve diversification strategy of equal allocations to four funds.

There is also no strong evidence that the Summary Prospectus made subjects feel better about their investment decision. Table 2.4 shows the distribution of answers to two sets of questions subjects answered after making their portfolio allocations. The first set of questions asked—separately for the equity portfolio and the bond portfolio—how likely subjects were to change their allocation if they consulted a professional investment advisor. The second set asked—again separately for the two portfolios—how confident subjects were that the allocation was the right one for them. None of the answer frequencies differ significantly between the prospectus-only and Summary Prospectus conditions.

Even though the actual quality of portfolio choices appears to be unaffected by the Summary Prospectus, subjects who received the Summary Prospectus spent significantly less time on average making their two portfolio allocations—only 22.5 minutes, versus 31.2 minutes for subjects who received the statutory prospectuses.[9] Therefore, the Summary Prospectus's welfare benefit operates through the time-saving channel, rather than the portfolio-improvement channel.

Table 2.5 shows how participants rated the importance of various factors for their investment choice on a 5-point scale. Fund performance over the past year, fund performance since inception, and investment objectives are ranked as the three most important factors across all information conditions. However, subjects receiving the Summary Prospectus tended to rank past one-year performance as more important and fund performance since inception as a little less important. A desire to diversify across funds and the quality of the documents explaining the mutual fund were also ranked as somewhat important.

2.4   Conclusion

We have evaluated the effect of simplifying mutual fund disclosure by studying the effect of the Summary Prospectus recently adopted by the SEC.

9. The typical amount of time subjects spent on the experimental task is not dramatically dissimilar from the amount of time they might spend choosing a portfolio for their real-world savings. In a survey of nonfaculty employees at the University of Southern California, Benartzi and Thaler (1999) found that the majority of respondents spent an hour or less on the portfolio allocation decision for their defined contribution plan.

Table 2.4   Subjects' confidence in their investment choices

	Equity portfolio			Bond portfolio		
	Prospectus	SP/SP+	Difference	Prospectus	SP/SP+	Difference
How likely is it that you would change your allocation among equity/bond mutual funds if you consulted a professional investment advisor?						
Not at all likely	4.9%	6.5%	1.6%	1.7%	4.0%	2.4%
	(2.8)	(2.2)	(3.7)	(1.7)	(1.8)	(2.8)
Somewhat likely	49.2%	48.0%	-1.2%	50.0%	46.0%	-4.0%
	(6.5)	(4.5)	(7.9)	(6.5)	(4.5)	(7.8)
Very likely	45.9%	45.5%	-0.4%	48.3%	50.0%	1.7%
	(6.4)	(4.5)	(7.8)	(6.5)	(4.5)	(7.8)
How confident are you that the allocation among equity/bond mutual funds you chose is the right allocation for you?						
Very confident	3.3%	4.9%	1.6%	5.0%	1.6%	-3.4%
	(2.3)	(2.0)	(3.2)	(2.8)	(1.1)	(2.6)
Relatively confident	29.5%	29.3%	-0.2%	15.0%	25.0%	10.0%
	(5.9)	(4.1)	(7.2)	(4.6)	(3.9)	(6.5)
Somewhat confident	31.1%	39.0%	7.9%	38.3%	40.3%	2.0%
	(6.0)	(4.4)	(7.6)	(6.3)	(4.4)	(7.7)
Less than confident	31.1%	21.1%	-10.0%	36.7%	25.8%	-10.9%
	(6.0)	(3.7)	(6.7)	(6.3)	(3.9)	(7.2)
Not at all confident	4.9%	5.7%	0.8%	5.0%	7.3%	2.3%
	(2.8)	(2.1)	(3.6)	(2.8)	(2.3)	(3.9)

Notes: Each of the questions above was asked separately for the equity portfolio and the bond portfolio. The top number in each cell is the percent of respondents who gave the corresponding answer. Standard errors are in parentheses below.

Table 2.5   **Importance of various factors in subjects' investment choices**

	Equity portfolio		Bond portfolio	
	Prospectus	SP/SP+	Prospectus	SP/SP+
Quality of document(s) explaining mutual fund	3.21 (4)	3.24 (5)	3.08 (5)	3.16 (5)
Brand recognition	2.16 (8)	2.85 (7)	2.38 (8)	2.74 (8)
Past experience with fund companies	1.98 (9)	2.15 (9)	1.85 (9)	2.15 (9)
Fund fees, expenses, and loads	2.93 (6)	3.14 (6)	2.93 (6)	3.07 (6)
Minimum opening balance requirements	1.50 (11)	1.78 (11)	1.53 (11)	1.84 (11)
Investment objectives	3.64 (3)	3.75 (2)	3.70 (3)	3.83 (2)
Fund performance over the past year	3.67 (2)	3.83 (1)	3.72 (2)	3.84 (1)
Fund performance since inception	3.84 (1)	3.60 (3)	3.77 (1)	3.58 (3)
Fund performance over different horizon	2.90 (7)	2.76 (8)	2.83 (7)	2.84 (7)
Customer service of fund	1.73 (10)	1.99 (10)	1.78 (10)	1.97 (10)
Desire to diversify across funds	3.10 (5)	3.31 (4)	3.10 (4)	3.17 (4)

Notes: Each cell reports the average importance the factor had on the relevant subsample's investment decision, as elicited in the debriefing surveys. There were five possible responses, from "not important at all" to "very important." We assigned integers 1 through 5 to each possible response, with higher integers corresponding to greater importance. Each factor's ordinal rank for the relevant subsample is in parentheses, with lower integers corresponding to greater ordinal importance.

To determine the causal impact of this simplified document, we use randomized trials in which different groups of investors are given different types of prospectuses.

On the positive side, the Summary Prospectus reduces the amount of time spent on the investment decision without adversely affecting portfolio quality. On the negative side, the Summary Prospectus does not change, let alone improve, portfolio choices. Hence, simpler disclosure does not appear to be a useful channel for making mutual fund investors more sophisticated and for creating competitive pricing pressure on mutual fund companies.

Our experiments also shed light on the scope of investor confusion regarding loads. Even when our subjects have a one-month investment horizon—where minimizing loads is the only sensible strategy—they do not avoid loads. In our experiment, subjects chose funds with an average load of 3.00 percent in the conditions with an investment horizon of one month. This choice is like betting that the chosen portfolio has an (implausible) excess log return relative to the load-minimizing portfolio of 24 percentage points per year. We conclude that our subjects either do not understand how loads work or do not take them into account. We also conclude that the Summary Prospectus does nothing to alleviate these kinds of errors.

Appendix A

The SEC's Sample Summary Prospectus (from Release No. 33-8861)

Hypothetical Summary Prospectus – Prepared By SEC Staff – For Illustrative Purposes Only

THE XYZ BALANCED FUND	SUMMARY PROSPECTUS
(Class A and Class B Shares)	November 1, 2007

Before you invest, you may want to review the Fund's prospectus, which contains more information about the Fund and its risks. You can find the Fund's prospectus and other information about the Fund, including the statement of additional information and most recent reports to shareholders, online at [Web address]. You can also get this information at no cost by calling 1-800-000-0000 or by sending an e-mail request to [e-mail address]. The Fund's prospectus and statement of additional information, both dated April 27, 2007, and most recent report to shareholders, dated June 30, 2007, are all incorporated by reference into this Summary Prospectus.

Investment Objective: Income and capital growth consistent with reasonable risks.

Fees and Expenses of the Fund: The tables below describe the fees and expenses that you may pay if you buy and hold shares of the Fund. You may qualify for sales charge discounts if you and your family invest, or agree to invest in the future, at least $25,000 in XYZ Funds.

Shareholder Fees (fees paid directly from your investment)	Class A	Class B
Maximum Sales Charge (Load) Imposed on Purchases (as percentage of offering price)	5.75%	None
Maximum Deferred Sales Charge (Load) (as percentage of the lower of original purchase price or sale proceeds)	None	5.00%

Annual Fund Operating Expenses (ongoing expenses that you pay each year as a percentage of the value of your investment)	Class A	Class B
Management Fees	0.66%	0.66%
Distribution (12b-1) Fees	0.00%	0.75%
Service (12b-1) Fees	0.23%	0.23%
Other Expenses	0.28%	0.46%
Total Annual Fund Operating Expenses	1.17%	2.10%

Example
The Example below is intended to help you compare the cost of investing in the Fund with the cost of investing in other mutual funds. The Example assumes that you invest $10,000 in the Fund for the time periods indicated. The Example also assumes that your investment has a 5% return each year and that the Fund's operating expenses remain the same. Although your actual costs may be higher or lower, based on these assumptions your costs would be:

	1 year	3 years	5 years	10 years
Class A (whether or not shares are redeemed)	$687	$925	$1,182	$1,914
Class B (if shares are redeemed)	$713	$958	$1,329	$1,974
Class B (if shares are not redeemed)	$213	$658	$1,129	$1,974

Portfolio Turnover

The Fund pays transaction costs, such as commissions, when it buys and sells securities (or "turns over" its portfolio). A higher portfolio turnover may indicate higher transaction costs. These costs, which are not reflected in annual fund operating expenses or in the example, affect the Fund's performance. During the most recent fiscal year, the Fund's portfolio turnover rate was 63% of the average value of its whole portfolio.

Principal Investment Strategies: The Fund invests mainly in common stocks, bonds, and notes of U.S. and foreign companies. . . . .

Principal Risks:

- You could lose money by investing in the Fund.

- Risk Number Two – . . . .

- Risk Number Three – . . . .

- Risk Number Four – . . . .

- Risk Number Five – . . . .

Annual Total Return: The following bar chart and table provide some indication of the risks of investing in the Fund. The bar chart shows changes in the Fund's performance from year to year for Class A shares. The table shows how the Fund's average annual returns for 1, 5, and 10 years compared with those of a broad measure of market performance. The Fund's past performance (before and after taxes) is not necessarily an indication of how the Fund will perform in the future.

Sales charges are not reflected in the bar chart, and if those charges were included, returns would be less than those shown.

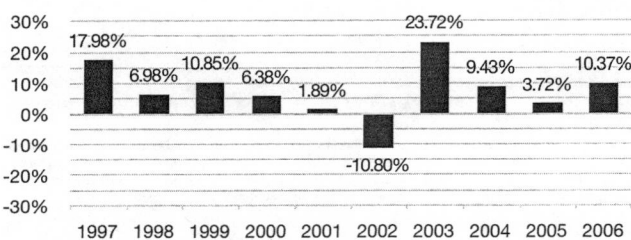

Best Quarter (ended 6/30/03): 12.08%. Worst Quarter (ended 9/30/01): -11.06%. The year-to-date return as of the most recent calendar quarter, which ended September 30, 2007, was 7.03%.

Hypothetical Summary Prospectus – Prepared By SEC Staff – For Illustrative Purposes Only

Average Annual Total Returns for Periods Ended December 31, 2006	1 Year	5 Years	10 Years
Class A (Return Before Taxes)	4.04%	5.72%	7.26%
Class A (Return After Taxes on Distributions)	2.48	4.52	5.05
Class A (Return After Taxes on Distributions and Sale of Fund Shares)	2.30	4.34	4.90
Class B (Return Before Taxes)	4.38	5.62	7.12
S&P 500 Index (reflects no deduction for fees, expenses or taxes)	15.79%	6.19%	8.42%

The after-tax returns are shown only for Class A shares and are calculated using the historical highest individual federal marginal income tax rates and do not reflect the impact of state and local taxes. Actual after-tax returns depend on an investor's tax situation and may differ from those shown. After-tax returns are not relevant to investors who hold their Fund shares through tax-deferred arrangements, such as 401(k) plans or individual retirement accounts.

Top Ten Portfolio Holdings (percent of total net assets) as of September 30, 2007			
Rank	Security	Rank	Security
1	XYZ, Inc. (3.0%)	6	The DEF Co. (1.3%)
2	The ABC Co. (2.3%)	7	The NOP Corp. (1.3%)
3	XYZ Growth, Inc. (1.7%)	8	HIJ Co. (1.1%)
4	The TUV Corp. (1.6%)	9	ABC Corp. (1.0%)
5	QRS Co. (1.4%)	10	OPQ, Inc. (0.9%)

Investment Adviser: XYZ Management Company, LLC

Portfolio Manager: John E. Smith, CFA, Vice President and Equity Portfolio Manager of XYZ Management Company, LLC. Mr. Smith has managed the Fund since 2005.

Purchase and Sale of Fund Shares: You may purchase or redeem shares of the Fund on any business day online or through our Web site at [Web address], by mail (XYZ Funds, Box 1000, Anytown, USA 10000), or by telephone at 800-000-0000. Shares may be purchased by electronic bank transfer, by check, or by wire. You may receive redemption proceeds by electronic bank transfer or by check. You generally buy and redeem shares at the Fund's next-determined net asset value (NAV) after XYZ receives your request in good order. NAVs are determined only on days when the NYSE is open for regular trading. The minimum initial purchase is $2,500. The minimum subsequent investment is $100 (or $50 under an automatic investment plan).

Dividends, Capital Gains, and Taxes: The Fund's distributions are taxable, and will be taxed as ordinary income or capital gains, unless you are investing through a tax-deferred arrangement, such as a 401(k) plan or an individual retirement account.

Payments to Broker-Dealers and Other Financial Intermediaries: If you purchase the Fund through a broker-dealer or other financial intermediary (such as a bank), the Fund and its related companies may pay the intermediary for the sale of Fund shares and related services. These payments may influence the broker-dealer or other intermediary and your salesperson to recommend the Fund over another investment. Ask your salesperson or visit your financial intermediary's Web site for more information.

Appendix B

Sample Experimental Investment Choice Sheet

Subject number: 1

Choose a stock mutual fund portfolio

Please allocate $100,000 among the four **stock** mutual funds listed below. You may choose to allocate all $100,000 to one fund or allocate your investment evenly or unevenly across as many funds as you like.

If your stock portfolio is chosen for payment based on Logan Airport's February 28 temperature, we will calculate how much money a real investor would get back if he or she sent $100,000 to the stock funds below according to the allocation that you choose, assuming that each fund received the investment at 3:00 P.M. on February 29, 2008, and the investments were sold at 3:00 P.M. on March 31, 2008. We will pay you 0.1% of whatever the investment is worth at the end of the investment period.

PAYOFF CALCULATION EXAMPLES

Example #1: Suppose selling your hypothetical investment on March 31, 2008 would give you $110,000. Then we would pay you (in addition to the $20 participation payment you will receive today) $110, which is 0.1% of $110,000.

Example #2: Suppose selling your hypothetical investment on March 31, 2008 would give you $85,000. Then we would pay you (in addition to the $20 participation payment you will receive today) $85, which is 0.1% of $85,000.

Below is the menu of mutual funds from which you may choose.
- Write the dollar amount you would like to allocate to each fund in the last column
- You may invest in as many or as few funds as you choose
- Within each fund, you may only invest in the share class listed after its name below
- Please be careful to allocate a total of exactly $100,000
- If you put money in a fund, that amount must satisfy the minimum opening allocation requirement

Stock Mutual Fund	Symbol	Minimum Opening Allocation if Buying Shares in Fund	Your Allocation in Dollars (column must sum to $100,000)
American Century Fundamental Equity - Class A	AFDAX	$2500	
Dreyfus Premier Core Value Fund - Class C	DCVCX	$1000	
MFS Emerging Growth Fund - Class A	MFEGX	$1000	
Sentinel Common Stock Fund - Class C	SCSCX	$1000	

→ Information about these 4 stock mutual funds is attached ←

Any portfolio allocations which violate minimum opening allocation requirements or which fail to total $100,000 will be ineligible for the investment payout.

Appendix C
Creating the Summary Prospectus

To create the Summary Prospectus documents used in the experiment, we attempted to mimic as closely as possible the sample Summary Prospectus provided by the SEC. In the instances of ambiguity, we made a few decisions and assumptions:

- We limited the number of share classes included in the Summary Prospectus to five due to space limitations. If a fund had more than five share classes, we chose the first five share classes presented in the prospectus, while ensuring that the relevant Class A and Class C shares were included.
- When possible, we used the exact text from the statutory prospectus in the "Investment Objective," "Principal Investment Strategies," "Principal Risks," and "Portfolio Manager" sections of the Summary Prospectus. In instances where the descriptions provided in the statutory prospectus were too long, we extracted the most relevant sentences.
- For the sake of not introducing any new information, we generally did not include any information in the Summary Prospectuses that could not be found in the statutory prospectus, the Statement of Additional Information (SAI), annual report, or most recent shareholder report distributed to subjects. The only exception was the data on top ten portfolio holdings. In instances that funds did not provide this information in their fund literature, we used information from the Google Finance website.
- Below the "Shareholder Fees" table we included a footnote about additional restrictions relevant to the profiled share classes, such as minimum investment amounts and whether share classes were restricted to institutional investors or retirement plans. We did so because fees are often considerably lower for institutions, retirement plans, and large investment amounts. We did not want experimental subjects to think that we were systematically offering them the least attractive share classes available, when in fact we were offering them share classes consistent with their hypothetical principal amount and retail status. Furthermore, we believed that in any final regulation, the SEC would require the Summary Prospectus to disclose these restrictions.
- Some funds did not decompose 12b-1 fees into "Distribution" and "Service" fees. When this occurred, the total amount of 12b-1 fees was listed under "Distribution" fees.

References

Barber, B. M., T. Odean, and L. Zheng. 2005. Out of sight, out of mind: The effects of expenses on mutual fund flows. *Journal of Business* 78 (6): 2095–119.

Benartzi, S., and R. H. Thaler. 1999. Risk aversion or myopia? Choices in repeated gambles and retirement investments. *Management Science* 45:364–81.

———. 2001. Naïve diversification strategies in defined contribution saving plans. *American Economic Review* 90:79–98.

Choi, J. J., D. Laibson, and B. C. Madrian. 2010. Why does the law of one price fail? An experiment on index mutual funds. *Review of Financial Studies* 23: 1405–32.

Cronqvist, H. 2006. Advertising and portfolio choice. Ohio State University. Working Paper.

Elton, E., M. Gruber, and J. Busse. 2004. Are investors rational: Choices among index funds. *Journal of Finance* 59:261–88.

Investment Company Institute. 2006. *Understanding investor preferences for mutual fund information.* Washington, DC: Investment Company Institute.

Kozup, J., E. Howlett, and M. Pagano. 2008. The effects of summary information on consumer perceptions of mutual fund characteristics. *Journal of Consumer Affairs* 42:37–59.

Lusardi, A., P. A. Keller, and A. M. Keller. 2009. New ways to make people save: A social marketing approach. In *Overcoming the saving slump: How to increase the effectiveness of financial education and saving programs,* ed. A. Lusardi, 209–36. Chicago: University of Chicago Press.

Comment   Steven F. Venti

Beshears, Choi, Laibson, and Madrian have produced a series of influential and insightful studies that evaluate how often-neglected features of pension design affect saving and enrollment decisions. This chapter continues that tradition. It provides an experimental evaluation of the effectiveness of the Summary Prospectus (SP), a shortened and simplified document made available to investors. The experiment is well-designed and executed. The results show no direct effect of the SP on portfolio returns, suggesting that the summary prospectus saves time but does not lead to better investment choices. This result may not, for reasons noted later, be unexpected. Perhaps more surprising and of broader interest is what the experimental results say about the information investors consider, how investors use this information, how indecisive investors are, and how sensitive their portfolio choices are to seemingly irrelevant features of the choice environment.

Thirty years ago most workers participating in private pension plans could look forward to receiving benefits in the form of an annuity that depended

Steven F. Venti is the DeWalt Ankeny Professor of Economic Policy and professor of economics at Dartmouth College, and a research associate of the National Bureau of Economic Research.

on their earnings history and years of service. Today over 80 percent of retirement "saving" is through 401(k) and IRA plans. The payout from these plans depends on the investment choices made by the plan participant. There is much concern that participants are not making good choices. Campbell (2006) finds that the poor and less educated often make "significant" mistakes in their portfolio allocations. Mottola and Utkus (2008) find that about 30 percent of all investors make "egregious" portfolio errors that any reasonable financial planner would find objectionable. These include the failure to diversify, overinvestment in company stock, zero investment in equities, and ignoring fees, expenses, and loads when choosing funds.

One possible way to help investors make better choices is to simplify the information they use to make retirement saving decisions. The SEC has done this by adopting a new Summary Prospectus to be distributed by mutual funds. The SP is certainly much shorter than the statutory prospectus and may be simplified, but it is still not simple. It contains investment jargon, numerical examples, and graphs that some readers will surely find demanding. Moreover, some basic knowledge of financial reporting is required to understand whether, for example, the returns reported in the document are net or gross of fees, loads, and other expenses. Nonetheless, the SP is shorter that the other documents available to the investor—which should increase the likelihood that it is read—and the SP pulls together in one place the relevant information that could otherwise only be obtained by consulting multiple documents.

Should we be surprised that this simplified document does not help investors make better (higher return) decisions? I suspect that most real-world investors do not even read the SP. Most are restricted by their retirement plan to select from a single fund family so fund style (identified by fund name) may be all the information they need. If they do read the SP, it is not clear that the information contained in the document can help make better decisions. Information on fees and expenses is clearly helpful, but information on past returns, investment objectives, principal risks, the identity of the fund manager, and so forth, may be of little value. In particular, "returns since inception" is not useful to compare funds with different inception dates.

It could, however, be the case that in the real world the SP is effective but the experiment is incapable of detecting its effect. In the experiment the sample size is small and the participants are more highly educated than the general population. Moreover, investors are playing for very small stakes in the experiment. There is little motivation for investors to acquire financial knowledge when the scale of investment is so small. Also, the menu choices are very similar—all are large cap managed funds in the experiment using equities. Careful study of the SP may improve decisions when the investor has to choose between funds that are highly dissimilar along important dimensions—for example, domestic versus international, large cap versus small cap, or managed versus index.

The most surprising results have to do with investor responses to fees. If

I wanted to design an experiment just to test investor sensitivity to fees and loads, this would be it. The front-end loads vary from 1.75 percent to 5.75 percent, the back-end loads are zero or 1 percent depending on the holding period, and there is considerable variation in fees among funds. Given how little variation there is in fund style and the short time horizon, fees and loads should be the dominant consideration in investor decisions. The most striking finding in this chapter is that fees and loads do not matter. Why this is so is an open question. Are fees and loads just too complicated for investors to understand? Are investors so focused on past performance that they ignore fees and loads? When asked, investors say that past performance is the most important factor in their decision. Fees, expenses, and loads are the *sixth* most important factor—less important than the "quality of documents explaining the mutual fund." I find this behavior fascinating and worthy of further study.

More generally, the experimental results and follow-up interview suggest that even these relatively educated investors have a poor understanding of financial concepts and find financial decision making difficult. Only 20 percent know what securities are held by a money market mutual fund. Fifty percent say they are "less than confident" or "not at all confident" that they have made the right investment choices and 50 percent say they would be "very likely" to change their portfolio allocation if they consulted a financial advisor. These responses paint a picture of the investor as indecisive and loosely committed to his or her investment choices and thus easily influenced by extraneous factors (framing, document design, etc.) that in an ideal world would have little effect on investment choices.

In sum, Beshears, Choi, Laibson, and Madrian have once again provided valuable evidence on how frequently neglected features of the pension system affect the choices investors make. They show that the Summary Prospectus allows retirement plan participants to make faster decisions, but not better decisions. A more striking finding is the puzzling irrelevance of fees, loads, and expenses in investor decisions and how fragile these decisions are. Both results imply that a great deal of care should be taken in the design of materials provided to investors. For example, the findings suggest that reframing the prospectus to focus more on fees and loads and less on past returns may lead to "better" decisions. I will look forward to more experimental evidence on how the design and content of these documents can affect investment choices.

References

Campbell, J. Y. 2006. Household finance. *Journal of Finance* LXI (4): 1553–604.
Mottola, G. R., and S. P. Utkus. 2008. Red, yellow, and green: Measuring the quality of 401(k) portfolio choices. In *Overcoming the saving slump,* ed. A. Lusardi, 119–39. Chicago: University of Chicago Press.

II

Health Care Costs

The Risk of Out-of-Pocket Health Care Expenditure at the End of Life

Samuel Marshall, Kathleen McGarry,
and Jonathan S. Skinner

3.1 Introduction

The financial impact of catastrophic out-of-pocket health care expenditures appears with alarming frequency in the national media (e.g., Trejos 2008; *New York Times* 2008), and there is strong evidence that average out-of-pocket expenditures are growing over time (Paez, Zhao, and Hwang 2009). Most recently, Webb and Zhivan (2010), using the Health and Retirement Study (HRS) data, estimate that 5 percent of households now retiring may face out-of-pocket medical expenses of one-half million dollars or more. The rapid erosion of employer-provided retiree health insurance for current baby boomers and forecasted increases in health care costs will likely make out-of-pocket burdens even larger in the years to come (Fronstin 2006).

However, despite the anecdotal evidence and repeated stories in the popular press, these out-of-pocket expenditures are often elusive and difficult to uncover in survey data. McGarry and Schoeni (2005) reported just $2,500 average spending per year in the HRS for people who were not near death and French and Jones (2004) found that only a very small fraction

Samuel Marshall is a sophomore at Dartmouth College. Kathleen McGarry is professor of economics at the University of California, Los Angeles, and a research associate of the National Bureau of Economic Research. Jonathan S. Skinner is the John Sloan Dickey Third Century Professor in the Social Sciences and professor of community and family medicine at Dartmouth College, and a research associate of the National Bureau of Economic Research.

This research was supported by the U.S. Social Security Administration through grant #10-P98363-1-05 to the National Bureau of Economic Research as part of the SSA Retirement Research Consortium. We are grateful to Michael Hurd and Susann Rohwedder for helpful comments and to Kathy Stroffolino for research assistance. The findings and conclusions expressed are solely those of the author(s) and do not represent the views of SSA, any agency of the federal government, or the NBER. McGarry also acknowledges financial support from the NIA through grant number R01AG16593 and Skinner through P01AG19783.

of households experience catastrophic health care shocks. More recently, De Nardi, French, and Jones (2010) found evidence of high out-of-pocket expenditures, but these arise among single people at very old ages and among high income households.

We return to these issues using data from the HRS from 1998 to 2006 to understand better the distribution and risk of out-of-pocket medical expenses as people approach death. There are several empirical challenges in measuring the risks arising from such costs. First, there are a large number of nonresponses or bracketed responses where proxy respondents—typically children or spouses of the deceased—do not know the exact amount of spending but provide a range (say, nursing home expenses between $2,000 and $10,000, or more than $25,000). Imputations in these cases are clearly necessary, but made difficult by the sparseness of the data in some ranges in a single year. We therefore harness continuous data from all six waves (1998 to 2006) of the HRS to develop more robust imputations.

Second, we adjust for a bias in measuring the variation or "risk" of out-of-pocket spending that arises because of the HRS survey design. Core surveys are fielded every two years and an exit survey is administered to proxies after the death of a respondent. Most questions in the exit interview ask about spending for the period of time elapsed between the last interview and the date of death, so expenditures will vary with the time to death. For people who happen to die soon after their last (core) interview, spending will be relatively low, while for those who survive for nearly the entire two-year window, expenditures will be large. Although measures of average expenditures in the sample may be unbiased, the variable reporting period will tend to overstate the variance and inferences drawn from the tails of the distribution will be invalid. We correct for these biases by normalizing spending quantiles (and means) to a common twelve-month period.[1] We also pay particular attention to the extent to which spending rises in the last few months of life—a period of time often missed in traditional survey questionnaires—and adjust our scaling appropriately.

Third, we quantify the importance of large reported "outlier" measures for out-of-pocket spending, paying considerable attention to potential reporting and coding errors. We walk the fine line between Type 1 error—dropping a large reported spending amount when it is in fact true—and Type 2 error—accepting a large reported value as fact when the respondent (or proxy) misunderstood the question or misreported the response. Rather than exclude individuals who have signaled that they are high-cost, we instead set monthly limits on what costs could reasonably be and cap expenditures at these limits. As well, we consider sensitivity analysis to outliers by capping amounts at different percentiles of spending. We note that the

---

1. Goldman and Zissimopoulos (2004) also use this quantile approach to examine the distribution of spending that controls for observable factors.

correct treatment of these rare and potentially large spending events are particularly important for health care costs, because it is just such high-cost events that are disproportionately important for financial security. We are reassured by finding that our HRS aggregate estimates of out-of-pocket spending for ages sixty-five and over agree well with estimates from the National Medical Expenditures Accounts (Hartman et al. 2008).[2]

Finally, we consider the normative implications of out-of-pocket spending by considering what types of outlays are most closely associated with wealth and income. De Nardi, French, and Jones (2010) have shown that out-of-pocket spending is highly dependent on income and we seek to assess the extent to which this pattern represents spending on consumption above and beyond medical expenditures—say, purchasing plush living arrangements in a high-end assisted care facility—rather than spending for additional medical attention.

The results suggest that out-of-pocket expenditures near death are considerable, with an average of $12,120 (in 2006 dollars) per person in our sample, or $11,618 when scaled to represent the last year of life. However, there is considerable variance, with the twelve-month ninetieth percentile equal to $29,335 and the ninety-ninth percentile equal to $94,310.

Where is all this spending going? The largest single category is nursing home and hospital expenditures, which average $4,731 in the last year of life, of which about two-thirds is for nursing home care. Not surprisingly, the distribution of expenses is highly skewed, with a median of zero, a ninety-fifth percentile of $27,770, and a ninety-ninth percentile of $75,902. Other important sources of spending are for insurance ($1,746), prescription drugs ($1,496), home health care and helpers ($1,966 combined), and "nonmedical" spending to make houses accessible ($721).

Out-of-pocket expenditures are higher for high-income quartiles ($14,269 versus $9,046 for the lowest quartile of income), but the partial impact of income on out-of-pocket spending is diminished considerably in a regression model. Differences in spending by wealth quartile are much larger than income differences, with spending in the top wealth quintile equal to $18,232, compared to $7,173 in the bottom. These differences appear to be driven mostly by greater spending for nursing homes, and for helpers, home health, and other sources of spending that likely help maintain the independence of people living at home.

Our results are therefore consistent with a more nuanced version of the two extreme stories of out-of-pocket spending just noted. Health care expenditures represent a numerically large and potentially important drain on financial resources, particularly for households as time of death nears.

---

2. Hurd and Rohwedder (2009) reach different conclusions, suggesting that the HRS survey may overstate out-of-pocket spending relative to other surveys of health care spending such as the Medical Expenditure Panel Survey (MEPS). We explore this issue later.

However, the large wealth-elasticity (and more modest income-elasticity) suggests that some of this spending may serve to "buy" independence or represent other forms of consumption. This spending is likely to include a health component; evidence presented elsewhere suggests that these additional services could themselves have a positive impact on health outcomes (McCorkle et al. 2000; Mor et al. 2004), suggesting one mechanism by which wealth could buy health.[3]

3.2   Evidence on Out-of-Pocket Health Care Expenditures

There is mixed evidence on how out-of-pocket medical expenditures affect financial security. Perhaps the most publicized study, Himmelstein et al. (2005), was based on a survey of households that had gone through bankruptcy hearings. Roughly half of the sample cited out-of-pocket expenditures as a possible cause of their bankruptcies, suggesting that out-of-pocket medical expenses are extremely burdensome. However, the survey defined relevant expenditures as expenditures of $1,000 or more. And, as Dranove and Millenson (2006) point out, this is not a very high barrier—many households spend more for their annual insurance premiums alone. Using an alternative definition, Dranove and Millenson estimate a more plausible yet still sizeable figure, attributing up to 17 percent of all bankruptcies, at least in part, to out-of-pocket medical expenses. A Commonwealth Fund report (Merlis, Gould, and Mahato 2006) highlighting the "growing strain" of out-of-pocket expenditures on family budgets found that just 11 percent of households had such expenses exceeding 10 percent of income. We note, however, that even many of these "large" expenditures may have little effect on lifetime well-being if they are limited to an isolated year. A large part of the burden is likely to stem from repeatedly high health care costs.

Conversely, several studies have found large amounts of out-of-pocket spending in the Medicare population. Although Medicare provides nearly universal coverage for people sixty-five and over, there are substantial gaps in that coverage. For many, these gaps are filled by privately purchased "Medigap" insurance or by retiree health insurance. While these supplemental plans offer relatively complete coverage of the standard Medicare deductibles and copayments,[4] there are important limitations to the protections provided by such policies, particularly the coverage of long-term care

3. See Smith (1999) for a comprehensive discussion of the relationship between health and economic resources.

4. Medicare requires a modest deductible for doctor visits and a copayment for costs beyond this amount. Medicare does not cover the cost of the first day of hospital care, requires a significant copayment for days sixty-one through ninety and covers nothing for days beyond ninety (after a fixed lifetime "reserve" of sixty days is used). For those with long hospital stays and no other coverage, these costs can be substantial. Perhaps most importantly, Medicare covers neither home health care nor nursing home expenses except for brief periods of medically needed care (rehabilitation) following a hospital stay.

needs. Even for individuals with the most generous Medigap policies, both home health care services and nursing home stays must be paid for out of pocket unless the individual qualifies for benefits from the means-tested Medicaid program or purchases a separate (and expensive) long-term care insurance policy.[5]

Gaps in the coverage of acute medical needs are likely to become increasingly important as the fraction of firms offering retiree health insurance falls. The Kaiser Foundation estimates that among *large* firms the percentage providing retiree coverage has fallen from 66 percent in 1988 to 31 percent in 2008.[6] Among *all* firms, the percentage offering retiree health insurance is substantially lower, with an estimated 13 percent providing retiree coverage in 2002, and likely even less today. Retirees without employer-provided coverage must purchase a Medigap policy on their own, which can cost up to $200 a month for a sixty-five-year-old. Fronstin (2006) estimates that in present-value terms someone retiring at age sixty-five a decade hence could need as much as $400,000 to cover these premiums. These studies suggest that the rise in health care cost growth, coupled with the erosion of retiree insurance from employers, will lead to rapid growth in out-of-pocket expenses even if current costs are not so large.

Finally, even with relatively generous health care coverage and supplemental policies, an individual may incur substantial nonmedical costs associated with a health condition. Items like handicap ramps, grab bars, and food to meet special dietary needs, can be expensive and must typically be borne by the individual himself.

Despite these insurance gaps, previous studies have often failed to find very large health care spending "shocks." For example, Goldman and Zissimopoulos (2003) found median out-of-pocket spending among HRS respondents over a two-year period of just $920, with even the ninety-fifth percentile of out-of-pocket expenditures reaching just $7,000—a significant amount for sure, but less than one might fear for the upper tail of the distribution. However, the Goldman and Zissimopoulus estimates do not include the end-of-life cohorts, and their data are from the 1998 survey when health care generally was less expensive.[7] By contrast, we focus solely on the end-of-life "exit" sample.

Most recently, De Nardi, French, and Jones (2010) quantified expected out-of-pocket expenditures in the HRS for single elderly households and

5. Only 10 percent of the elderly have purchased long-term care insurance (Finkelstein and McGarry 2005).

6. See http://ehbs.kff.org/images/abstract/7814.pdf. The figure of 66 percent is for large firms (200 or more employees) that offer health insurance to those currently working. Ninety-nine percent of large firms offer health insurance.

7. The original cohort samples in the HRS were drawn from the noninstitutionalized population, so that in the early years of the study we would expect the sample to be healthier-than-average. Over time, we expect the HRS cohorts will come to resemble the elderly population more closely as some of the sample transitions into nursing homes.

found elevated spending associated with high levels of income, particularly among the very old (e.g., those age ninety and above). For example, for ninety-five-year olds in the top income quintile, the estimated *average* spending was nearly $16,000. (Expenditures in the lower part of the income distribution are likely to be lower in part because of the important role played by Medicaid in paying for nursing home and home health care for the low-income elderly.) De Nardi, French, and Jones showed further that the risk of high out-of-pocket expenditures helped to explain observed wealth accumulation, particularly among higher-income households who are unlikely to qualify for Medicaid coverage and may want to protect themselves against potentially burdensome long-term care needs.

Webb and Zhivan (2010) consider out-of-pocket risks in a dynamic model. Using the HRS data, they simulate potential spending outcomes for hypothetical sixty-five-year-olds extending out to their (uncertain) deaths, and find very large levels of uninsured risk: their ninety-fifth percentile household faces a present value of $311,000 in health care spending, or $570,000 when adding in the cost of long-term care. However, these estimates likely overstate the true risk for two reasons. First, to capture the true risk of spending absent an insurance safety net, they assume that individuals never receive Medicaid benefits. Yet for many people who simply cannot afford the cost of care, Medicaid represents a feasible if not preferred option (Ameriks et al. 2010). The potential value of Medicaid may also affect lifetime savings and distort the perception of available resources (Hubbard, Skinner, and Zeldes 1995). And second, some of the modeled "risk" may also reflect the income or wealth elasticity of spending on health care, independent of health shocks. That is, the top fifth percentile of spending is likely to include both people who are very sick and people who are very wealthy and who choose to consume a great deal of expensive health services.

Finally, Hurd and Rohwedder (2009) have suggested an alternative reason for why the risk of out-of-pocket expenditures may be overstated in studies using the HRS—that the values reported in the survey itself may be biased upward. They address this concern in two ways. First, they show that for the small group of people who report very high out-of-pocket spending, many do not have enough income or wealth in the household to pay these expenses. The problem of measurement error, however, is endemic in wealth and income and family contributions to medical bills may be poorly captured in the survey. It is thus difficult to determine why the budget constraint appears to be violated—whether it is the medical expenditures that are mismeasured or the resources themselves.

The second objection raised by Hurd and Rohwedder is that aggregate spending in the HRS appears to be too high—as much as 60 percent overstated—relative to other surveys, such as the Medicare Expenditure Panel Survey (MEPS) and the Medicare Current Beneficiary Survey (MCBS). It is true that the MEPS and the MCBS are much better than the HRS in measuring costs paid on behalf of the individual (i.e., both out-of-pocket costs and those insurance payments that would normally be invisible to all but very alert patients who check their insurance company paperwork). However, with respect to out-of-pocket costs in particular, the HRS does ask about specific types of out-of-pocket expenditures in more detail than do these other surveys, and allows people who are unsure about actual dollar amounts to provide a range for the expense—leading to more complete reporting. (For example, the HRS asks who helps the respondent with various tasks and whether and how much helpers are paid, providing a more accurate measure of the cost of in-home assistance than elsewhere.) There is thus the real possibility that the HRS simply does capture expenses not measured in other surveys.

Furthermore, the MEPS and MCBS are both known to miss important components of out-of-pocket spending; after correcting for underreporting, French and Jones (2004) found that HRS out-of-pocket spending was close to aggregate estimates. More recently, Hartman et al. (2007) reported age-specific spending measures using the National Medical Expenditures Accounts (NMEA), which also adjusts for underreported components of out-of-pocket spending from the other survey data. Their estimate for the over-sixty-five population in 2003/2004 was $2,170 on average.[8] Defining the 2004 HRS Core data in an equivalent manner yields a nearly identical annual estimate of $2,151.[9] Including the sample of HRS respondents who died in 2004 (net of insurance payments and nonmedical payments) brings the aggregate to $2,347 per capita, just 8 percent above the NMEA estimate.[10] Based on these figures we do not believe there is evidence of a strong upward bias in the HRS out-of-pocket expenditures, a result similar to that found in Goldman and Zissimopoulos (2010). Still, as Hurd and Rohwedder (personal communication) have pointed out, the national estimates of age-specific spending may themselves be subject to measurement error, thus making it difficult to determine a "gold-standard." Finally, while the aggregates constructed from the HRS data may be approximately correct, the components of spending (in particular nursing home versus nonnursing home spending) may be measured with error (Sing et al. 2006).

8. This estimate interpolates between 2002 and 2004 to estimate 2003 spending, and then averages 2003 and 2004 spending to match up with the two-year horizon of the HRS.

9. This estimate uses similar imputations to those reported later. To adjust for the two-year sample frame, we divide total out-of-pocket spending (net of insurance) by the number of months since the last interview, and then multiply this per-month measure by twelve.

10. While end-of-life spending risk is large at an individual level, it does not add as much to the aggregate estimate both because only a small fraction of the sample dies in any year and because those who do die are alive for (on average) just six months. Our estimate of $2,347 was created by assuming that the 2004 core interview was conducted on December 31, 2004, and included spending in the prior twelve months for those interviewed in the core survey, plus spending for the sample of people who had died in twelve months prior to the interview. There were 517 deaths and their average spending for the calendar year was $6,633.

3.3   Data

Our data for this task come from the Health and Retirement Study (HRS). The HRS is a large panel survey that began in 1992 with a nationally representative sample of the population born between 1931 and 1941. These original respondents have been interviewed biennially ever since, with the most recent data collected in 2008. A separate cohort (the Asset and Health Dynamics Among the Oldest Old [AHEAD] cohort) of those born in 1921 or earlier was interviewed in 1993 and again in 1995. In 1998 these two samples were merged and two additional cohorts were added, making the sample population approximately representative of the U.S. population age fifty or older. A refresher cohort was added in 2004 to maintain representation of the population in their fifties. We restrict our analyses to data from 1998 to 2006 so that we have a full age range of individuals from which to draw and more consistent sets of questions with respect to health care costs.

Another reason for considering just years since 1998 is that, as noted before, the original sample was restricted to the noninstitutionalized population. In the early years of data from any HRS cohort, health care expenditures (both overall and out-of-pocket) are likely to be biased downward because those in nursing homes, who likely have the largest expenses, are excluded.[11] By 1998, however, the bias would have been attenuated somewhat for the original cohorts, as the sample matured and the formerly noninstitutionalized elderly began to enter nursing homes.

The HRS is unusual in that when sample members die, it conducts what is termed an "exit interview." The exit interview is a survey administered to a surviving spouse (if available) or other knowledgeable individual (such as an adult child), and collects information about the deceased individual pertaining to the period of time since the previous "live" survey.[12] Because we are concerned with the cost of health care in the time period near death, these exit interviews are central to our study and we focus our attention on them. However, we rely on the prior core surveys for information about income and wealth of the household.

The HRS collects a great deal of information on financial status, health measures, and out-of-pocket medical expenses, all of which we use in our analyses. In an improvement over past surveys, the HRS used a bracketing method to reduce the number of missing values. If a respondent does not know (or does not wish to provide) an answer to a particular question about the amount of a health care expenditure (or other dollar-denominated question), they are asked a series of questions as to whether the amount is greater

---

11. This problem is likely to be most severe in the older AHEAD cohort and less problematic for cohorts entering the sample in their fifties, when nursing home use is rare.

12. Depending on the year, somewhere in the neighborhood of 35 percent of proxies are the surviving spouse.

than or less than a specific value. This strategy provides us with a specific range of values rather than a missing response. Although the exact amounts are still uncertain and for some uses must be imputed, these brackets are vastly more useful than the missing values that characterize much of survey data, particularly in cases where proxy respondents may not know exact amounts.

We examine nine separate components of spending: insurance premiums (including privately purchased health insurance, Medigap plans, employer-provided insurance, Medicare HMOs, Medicare Part B, and long-term care insurance), prescription drugs, physician payments, hospital and nursing home care,[13] other medical care (including expenses not covered by insurance, such as medications, special food, equipment such as a special bed or chair, visits by doctors or other health professionals—and after 2002, special expenses such as in-home medical care/special facilities or services/in-home medical care), home health care, informal "helper" caregivers at home, nonmedical spending (such as modifying the house with ramps or lifts, hiring help for housekeeping or other household chores or for assisting with personal needs), and hospice care.

Both the bracketed responses and the remaining missing values for individuals who cannot or will not provide even a range of values necessitate the use of an imputation strategy to provide exact values. While the HRS provides imputed values for many other variables in the core interview for the full range of survey years, they ceased imputations for exit interviews in 2000. An important component of our analysis is thus the construction of these values.

The imputation procedures and our methodology for handling outliers are central to our study.[14] Our primary objective was to ensure that the information provided in the survey ends up in the final data set with as little ad hoc restrictions and exclusions as possible. We next consider three of the key issues.

Reasonable caps on spending values. Large reported values for specific spending measures pose a problem for researchers because it is often impossible to discern whether the answer was given in error or whether it represents a rare but very large actual cost. Problems can also arise because of confusion about the appropriate time frame for the question. In the majority of cases respondents are asked to report out-of-pocket expenditures since the previous interview, but for a few expenditure items they are asked about monthly expenses (e.g., for helpers they are asked about payments in the last month and for prescription drugs, about average monthly payments).

13. Nursing home and hospital expenditures were measured jointly in the survey in 1998 and 2000 but separately thereafter. For consistency across waves we combine them in all years but note that where the distinction is made, nursing home expenditures account for the majority of spending.
14. The STATA programs used for the imputation are available on request.

On the one hand, this change in the relevant period can confuse respondents and may lead to falsely overstated medical expenses if, for example, when asked about monthly health expenditures, respondents report the total expense since the last interview, thus raising the prospect of Type 1 error—overstating medical expenses that do not exist. On the other hand, we know that out-of-pocket expenditures are marked by a high degree of skewness, so ad hoc "second-guessing" the respondent might also lead to Type 2 error—rejecting the high reported cost when it is in fact true.

The first column of table 3.1 provides a summary of the caps we use for spending measures that seem unreasonably high.[15] We based the $2,000 cap on monthly health insurance payments for long-term care based on rates provided by the Federal Long Term Care Insurance Program.[16] There are fewer guidelines for pharmaceutical payments, but drug regimens for high-end specialty drugs such as Gleevic alone can run as much as $40,000 annually, and so we set (somewhat arbitrarily) a cap of $5,000 per month in out-of-pocket pharmaceutical spending.[17] (If we were to examine spending beyond 2006, we would want to limit pharmaceutical expenditures further because of the institution of Part D Medicare coverage.) We have much less evidence on private-pay physicians, but choose a maximum payment of twenty visits per month at $250/visit.

Monthly maximum expenditures for helpers and home health care comes from the use of multiple-shift nursing care for people with advanced dementia, for example. We assume a maximum of $15,000 per month ($25 per hour times twenty hours per day times thirty days) for each category. The *average* monthly rate in New York City (the most expensive region) for a private nursing home bed is equal to just under $12,000 per month,[18] so we view a $15,000 fee as a reasonable upper limit on what might be spent in a more expensive facility. Hospital expenditures and other expenses can clearly exceed $15,000 monthly, but for consistency we simply set that as the maximum as well and use a cap of $30,000 when nursing home and hospital expenses were reported together (recall that these are out-of-pocket costs incurred beyond what Medicare or other insurance has covered.)

15. All expenditures are scaled to a monthly amount and capped at that level, then inflated to the appropriate time period.

16. We assumed an eighty-year-old was purchasing long-term care insurance with a $250 maximum daily amount for a five-year maximum benefit period and 4 percent inflation adjustment; the monthly payment was over $1,100 for one person alone; nor does it include other insurance premiums (such as Medicare Part B premiums). See https://www.ltcfeds.com/ltcWeb/do/assessing_your_needs/RateCalcPlanChange. While payments of $2,000 a month are thus possible, it is difficult to imagine valid reports much beyond this amount.

17. Under the 2006 Medicare Part D program, there are limits on out-of-pocket exposure, but even with the Part D plan a recent General Accounting Office study called attention to the rising costs of Gleevic and other drugs arising from the "doughnut hole" in coverage. See http://www.gao.gov/products/GAO-10-529T.

18. See http://www.longtermcare.gov/LTC/Main_Site/Paying_LTC/Costs_Of_Care/Costs_Of_Care.aspx.

Table 3.1   **Monthly caps on expenditures**

Variable	Monthly cap	Fraction affected by cap	Number affected by cap	Unweighted mean prior to cap	Unweighted mean after cap
Health insurance	2,000	.0038	25/6,631	2,063	1,870
Rx	5,000	.0009	6/6,631	1,715	1,628
Doctor	5,000	.0002	1/6,631	390	389
Home care	15,000	.0006	4/6,631	686	652
Helpers	15,000[a]	.0155	103/6,631	1,330	1,173
Other and special	15,000	.0002	1/6,631	388	388
Hospital + nursing home	30,000	.0019	5/2,599	3,840	3,739
Hospital	15,000	.0007	3/4,032	745	667
Nursing home	15,000	.0042	17/4,032	4,807	4,383
Hospice	5,000	.0000	0/6,631	51	51
Nonmedical	5,000	.0003	2/6,631	871	846

[a]Maximum of four months. Total samples may be larger than those used in analysis because of additional selection criteria.

Finally, we set hospice care and nonmedical spending to a monthly limit of $5,000.[19]

One further problem is that questions about helpers and home health care refer to the month prior to death. It seems unreasonable to expect that these expenses were incurred at the same rate stretching back to the previous interview, but it also seems unreasonable to assume these costs were incurred just for one month. Based on a study of (post-1997) median length of stay for home health care Medicare patients (Murkofsky et al. 2003), we assume that both helpers and home health care workers are employed for four months in total.

Table 3.1 further illustrates the impact of these adjustments on specific components of spending.[20] The caps matter the most for helpers (103 people out of 6,631, or 1.6 percent), but the mean difference in the spending measure (between the uncapped and capped values) is just $157 because so few

19. We also inspected many of the outliers more closely, examining, for example, expenditures in relation to the individual's income, wealth, and insurance coverage. We decided that a fixed rule was preferred relative to making ad hoc changes on an individual level. Our inspection of the data and investigations into examples of extremely expensive services available to individuals did, however, serve to demonstrate how difficult it can be to identify true reporting errors.

20. The HRS oversampled a number of specific groups so population weights are necessary in measuring representative points of the distribution (or mean values). In table 3.1 we report unweighted statistics to demonstrate clearly the effect of our caps. These means will therefore not correspond to the weighted means presented in subsequent tables. Population weights are zero in the exit interviews because the individuals are, well, dead. We therefore went back for up to three successive waves of the HRS core interviews to search for the most recent individual weight, which was then assigned to the individual. Still, there were a few individuals (325 of the 6,631 combined sample of decedents) with zero weights. We use these "zero weight" individuals in our imputation procedures but do not include them in the population totals.

individuals report positive values. Other important categories affected by the caps are health insurance (twenty-five people, reducing the average by $193 on average) and nursing home expenses (seventeen people, reducing average expenses by $424).[21] In sum, the caps reduce average spending by less than $1,000 per person, but are likely to scale back the variance by much more. Following, we consider the importance of further capping spending on the ninety-fifth or ninety-ninth percentile.

Sparse imputation values. One of the strengths of the HRS's questioning procedures for health care costs is its use of detailed categories of expenditures. This detailed probing likely captures more expenditure than would a general catch-all question and is useful to an analyst seeking to examine particular forms of spending. However, it also means that the distributions of spending for each of the underlying components are often plagued by small samples, particularly at the upper tails. In any given exit interview there are only 1,200 or so deaths, so for infrequent but important outcomes, such as the out-of-pocket expense associated with a stay in a nursing home or use of hospice care, there are many fewer observations in a given year.

The thinness of the data makes it difficult to impute values using conditional means or a traditional hot-decking procedure. In the case in which a specific bracket is available, say that spending on a particular service was between $10,000 and $25,000, we might be comfortable with imputing a value equal to the midpoint ($17,500) or even the mean over continuous responses in the interval, despite it being based on a small number of continuous responses (i.e., the scope for error is relatively small when bounds are in place). However, there are many cases in which we have opened rather than closed brackets. Individuals could report that they spent more than (say) $25,000 on a health expense but not report an exact amount or any upper limit. Should we impute $26,000? Or double that? With relatively few decedents in any given year, there may not be more than a handful of people who report values above the upper break point for any given component of spending, making it extremely difficult to impute an overall conditional mean, much less one tailored to individual specifics such as age or insurance coverage.

To deal with the sparseness of observations, we impute values based on a distribution constructed from a combined sample of exit interviews for all survey years, a much larger sample of 6,631. We first construct a combined file of exact dollar amounts for each spending category, with all measures adjusted for inflation using the gross domestic product (GDP) deflator and expressed in 2006 dollars. For everyone reporting a bracketed amount, we estimated the conditional mean for that bracket, including open-ended

---

21. Note that the sample size of 4,032 is just for years 2002 to 2006, when nursing home expenditures were reported separately from hospital costs.

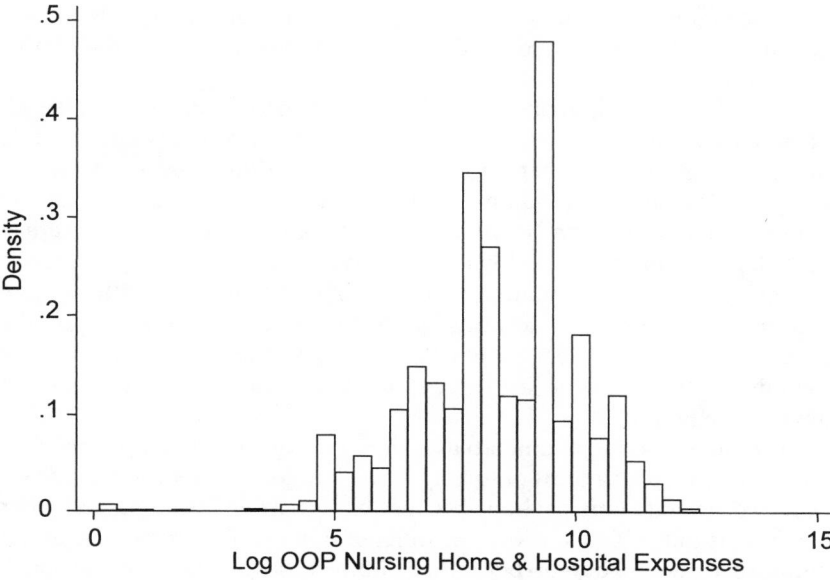

Fig. 3.1   Distribution of nursing home and hospital expenditures: Combined 6 waves

brackets. Because of inflation, the brackets vary over time, and so for each specific set of brackets, a new conditional mean was estimated. We then considered the more complex sets of questions—for example, whether people reported positive amounts (but did not know the amount), in which case they were assigned the mean value conditional on a positive value, or whether people reported not knowing at all, in which case they were assigned the unconditional mean.

An example of the distribution is shown in figure 3.1 for the (log) distribution of hospital and nursing home out-of-pocket expenditures for the entire sample, conditional on a positive amount. These estimates include both imputed and actual estimates, and while there are clear spikes where imputations play a larger part (or reflect rounding by respondents), there is sufficient density of continuously reported variables to suggest a log-normal distribution that is not dominated by outliers.

While we recognize that in stacking data from all years of the survey to conduct our imputation procedure, we are missing any evolution over time in the distribution of expenditures. However, we believe that the potential bias introduced by this method is likely to be less of a problem than any bias introduced by relying on the few continuous data reports in any particular year. We note that this procedure restricts our ability to assess growth in expenditures (other than that stemming from a rise in the number of individuals reporting values in the upper brackets or for those reporting actual expenses)[22] and therefore do not provide a discussion of differences in spending by year.

Time to death. A final data issue that we note here is the differing length of time between interviews, particularly for exit interviews where the date of death might be just a few months after the last interview or as long as two years. If deaths are randomly distributed across a two-year interval, the varying length of time will not affect our population averages. (The average time elapsed, from the respondents' final "live" interviews until their deaths, is approximately fifteen months, with a median of fourteen months.) There will, however, be systematic variation in expenditures with those who die long after their last interview appearing to have higher end-of-life costs than dying soon after the last survey simply because the costs pertain to a longer time period.

There may also be potential biases in reporting patterns as proxies may be more likely to misreport or forget completely about costs when the death occurred several years back, or because of upticks in spending very near death. It is difficult to sort out the difference between forgetfulness and a diminished rate of out-of-pocket expenditures as one goes further back in time prior to the death. And as we show, the flattening out of reported spending beyond a two-year limit is suggestive of a sharp drop-off in recall for these proxies. We present data that has been adjusted for a quartic in the number of months since the last interview, whether for mean expenditures or quantile regressions (to estimate weighted percentiles), where we set the number of months to twelve.

3.4   Results

We use data from the 1998 to 2006 exit interviews, with a combined sample of 6,631 people (6,306 of whom have positive sampling weights). Table 3.2 presents (weighted) summary statistics for the sample of decedents both combined and for individual years. The sample of decedents is, unsurprisingly, quite old. The average age at death is 79.4, with just 12 percent of the decedents under the age of sixty-five. The fraction of men in the sample is somewhat below 50 percent, while average years of schooling is roughly eleven years, with a strong secular trend that rises from 10.6 years (1998) to 11.6 years (2006). The fraction of people who report their race as nonwhite ranges between 11 and 15 percent (depending on the year), while the percent Hispanic is 4.6 percent over the entire period.

Average out-of-pocket expenditures for the entire sample are $12,120.

---

22. We have considered using the stacked sample along with regression equations to control for individual characteristics, but even with the full complement of decedents any regression would be sensitive to outliers.

Table 3.2   Variable means, total and by year 1998 to 2006

	All ($n = 6,631$)	Year of exit interview				
		1998 ($n = 1,253$)	2000 ($n = 1,346$)	2002 ($n = 1,497$)	2004 ($n = 1,227$)	2006 ($n = 1,308$)
Age at death	79.4	81.2	79.3	78.4	80.3	78.2
Sex (1 = male)	0.478	0.458	0.491	0.483	0.457	0.497
Years of schooling	11.1	10.6	10.9	11.1	11.3	11.6
Nonwhite	0.134	0.114	0.130	0.152	0.131	0.140
Hispanic	0.046	0.035	0.038	0.057	0.043	0.053
Birth year	1921.6	1915.5	1919.6	1922.6	1922.8	1926.8
OOP expenditures	12,120	11,183	10,610	11,396	14,451	12,954
Net worth (less house equity) in prior period	178,469	165,669	204,122	178,312	153,664	187,990
Net worth in prior period	281,005	235,321	326,529	283,570	252,988	299,829
Income in prior period	31,713	20,286	34,506	33,726	33,322	35,681

Notes: Sample sizes of specific means for net worth and income are slightly smaller in each year (and for the total) because of missing data. All wealth and income data are for the household in the prior interview wave. OOP = out-of-pocket. Sampling weights are used in the calculations. Unweighted sample sizes are reported.

There is some evidence of a rising trend over time (from $11,183 in 1998 to $14,451 in 2004), but there is a marked decline between 2004 and 2006, to $12,954.[23] This decline is in part the consequence of a modest decline in out-of-pocket drug expenditures (probably more the consequence of a change in how the question is asked than in the introduction of Medicare Part D), but mostly because of an unusually high level of nursing home spending (conditional on admission) in 2004.

Wealth and income from the most recent interview prior to death are reported in table 3.2. Net worth exclusive of housing wealth averages $178,469, and including housing, $281,005. The peak wealth estimates were in 2000, and despite the subsequent downturn there is some hint of a modest positive trend over time. The averages, of course, mask the considerable variation (and skewness) across individuals; the median value of net worth excluding housing is $24,706 (not shown), and for total net worth including housing wealth, the median is $102,000. There is less skewness in income, however; average income is $31,713, while median income is $19,177.

Table 3.3 reports components of out-of-pocket expenditures and their mean, median, ninetieth, ninety-ninth percentiles, and maximum amounts. While mean spending is $12,120, median spending is just $5,175. Indeed, nearly 30 percent of respondents reported less than $100 in any out-of-pocket expenditure. (Whether this is because of underreporting or a true lack of out-of-pocket costs is not entirely clear.) For the ninetieth percentile, spending was $29,790, the ninety-fifth percentile was $49,751, while for the ninety-ninth percentile (not shown) expenditures were $101,581. (The maximum was $331,825.) The impact of extreme outliers on the mean was fairly modest; capping spending at the ninety-ninth percentile amount reduced the mean to $11,690, while capping at the ninety-fifth percentile reduced the mean to $10,400.

As noted previously, nursing home and hospital out-of-pocket expenditures were the single largest category, with a mean of $4,731, and ninety-fifth percentile expenditures equal to $26,136. Expenditures for insurance were less skewed (median, $990, mean $2,096), while drug expenditures were somewhere in the middle; median spending was $448 but the ninety-fifth percentile was $6,000.[24]

Payments to helpers for home-based care can account for substantial expenditures, although it is not a common expenditure category.[25] Fewer than one-quarter of the respondents paid money to someone who helped

23. Note, however, that our imputation method limits our ability to identify trends in expenditures.

24. Note that the maximum values simply reflect our imposition of caps. They may also be a downward biased measure of needed treatment if individuals fail to fill prescriptions because of cost.

25. These values are reported in a section of the survey separately from medical expenditures. One potential concern is that they could therefore overlap with home care expenditures already reported in the main interview. We investigated this issue but it does not appear to be a problem as there was little correlation between the two. There were many cases in which individuals reported paying money to helpers but did not report any formal home health care.

Table 3.3   **Distribution of expenditure by category for exit interviews**

Variable	Mean	Median	p75	p90	p95	Maximum
Total OOP	12,120	5,175	13,681	29,790	49,751	331,825
Insurance	2,096	990	2,633	5,111	7,097	54,503
Drugs	1,761	448	2,400	4,353	6,000	129,998
Physician	353	0	387	1,137	1,211	51,957
Nursing home/hosp.	4,731	0	2,238	11,190	26,136	285,645
Other and special	384	0	0	702	1,624	48,492
Home health	687	0	0	722	2,565	254,997
Nonmedical	790	0	0	604	2,979	115,000
Helpers	1,281	0	0	4,084	8,190	60,000
Hospice	38	0	0	0	0	70,000

Notes: Maximum values are limited due to caps imposed on the data (see table 3.1). Sampling weights are used in the calculations.

with tasks around the home, but the conditional mean was high, adding $1,281 to average expenses near death. Given our assumption that helpers spent no more than four months prior to death with the households, this estimate is likely to underestimate the overall uncertainty arising from such costs. Finally, hospice care is largely covered by Medicare, and thus its contribution to out-of-pocket expenditures was remarkably modest ($38 on average).

The variation across individuals in these expenditures could be overstated given that the sample comprises both people who died more than two years after the prior core survey (and so we are collecting unusually high levels of spending), and people who died within a few months of the survey (so we only pick up modest levels of spending). Figure 3.2 shows the association between total out-of-pocket expenditures and the time since the last core survey. Also presented is the implicit incremental spending—that is, the difference between the current average expenditures for people who died (say) between seven and nine months, minus expenditures for those who died between four to six months. (Thus we assume that the two groups are otherwise identical except for the time since the last interview—perhaps a strong assumption, but not an unreasonable one given the randomness of the interview dates relative to death.)

Figure 3.2 demonstrates that a large fraction of spending in the last two years occurs in the last six months, although spending continues to climb to an average of nearly $20,000 for people whose last interviews were more than two years prior to death. That incremental spending falls off so much in earlier months is suggestive of both recall bias and the attenuation of medical spending further from imminent death. Further modeling would be required to correct for recall bias.

To adjust for these clear differences in expenditures by months since the last interview, we present results that correspond to table 3.3 of the distribution of spending, but adjust for the number of months since the interview by using a quartic in months, and setting the value(s) equal to twelve months

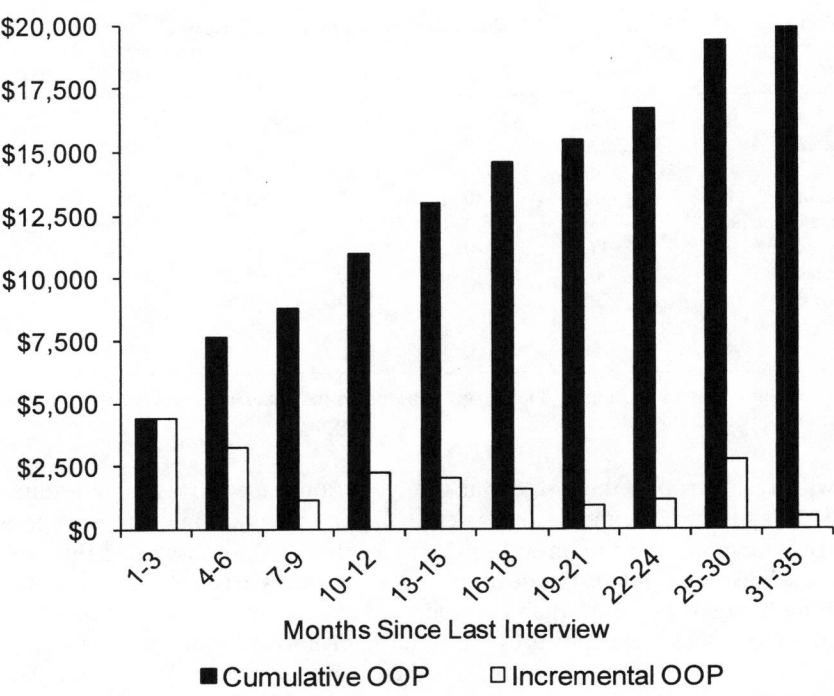

Months Since Last Interview

■ Cumulative OOP   □ Incremental OOP

Fig. 3.2   Average out-of-pocket expenditures by number of months between last interview and time of death

prior to death. Regression results (from both weighted least squares and weighted quantile regressions) are presented in table 3.4. The mean values are similar, and the magnitude of the shrinkage at the ninety-fifth percentile is quite modest or even nonexistent in some cases. The impact of the shrinkage is greatest at the very top of the distribution—for example, as noted previously, the ninety-ninth percentile of unadjusted total out-of-pocket expenditures is $101,581, but the adjusted measure is $94,310. In sum, these twelve-month measures are more accurate estimates of the true distribution of out-of-pocket expenditures, but even after these corrections, the true variation in medical expenditures is still substantial.

We next consider the association between out-of-pocket expenditures and wealth and income quintiles. Table 3.5 presents detailed spending measures by wealth quintile, and table 3.6 shows equivalent measures by income quintile. The mean values are not exactly the same as in the aggregates reported in tables 3.3 and 3.4 because the sample changes somewhat due to missing values for either income (resulting in a sample size of 5,775) or wealth ($N = 6,089$). Total out-of-pocket expenditures for decedents rise from $7,173 in the bottom wealth quintile to $18,233 in the top quintile, an increase of 154 percent. All measures of spending exhibit a positive wealth elasticity,

Table 3.4   **Distribution of expenditure by category for exit interviews, normalized to a twelve-month period**

Variable	Mean	Median	p75	p90	p95	p99
Total OOP	11,618	5,061	12,890	29,335	49,907	94,310
Insurance	1,746	914	2,301	3,274	4,766	21,602
Drugs	1,496	580	2,384	2,811	5,082	11,679
Physician	335	0	462	1,143	1,218	3,120
Nursing home/hosp.	4,975	0	2,303	12,046	27,770	75,902
Other medical	387	0	0	728	2,040	7,382
Home health	617	0	0	742	2,565	9,968
Nonmedical	721	0	0	687	2,761	13,749
Helpers	1,249	0	0	5,009	9,307	20,290
Hospice	51	0	0	0	0	220

Notes: This table reports fitted values for a twelve-month period from the prior interview period using a quartic in months. Definition of categories: Insurance premiums include premiums for Medicare Part B and long-term care insurance as well as Medigap and other privately purchased policies. Physician includes outpatient care in 2002 to 2006 interviews. Nursing home and hospital out-of-pocket expenditures are combined, but are available separately in 2002 to 2006 interviews. Other Medical includes "special" and "other medical" categories. Special being in-home medical care/special facilities or services, and other being "other expenses not covered by insurance, such as medications, special food, equipment such as a special bed or chair, visits by doctors or other health professionals, or other costs." Nonmedical is payments for items "such as modifying the house with ramps or lifts, hiring help for housekeeping or other household chores or for assisting with personal needs." Sampling weights are used in the calculations.

but some are larger in magnitude than others. For example, while nursing home and hospital expenditures are nearly double for the highest quintile compared to the lowest quintile of wealth ($6,521 versus $3,461), the largest proportional differences arise in care provided at home; for example, home care ($1,334 versus $383), nonmedical expenditures ($1,416 versus $335), and helper costs ($2,601 compared to $547).

There are similar associations between spending and income, but as shown in table 3.6, they are much less pronounced. Overall spending rises from $9,046 in the bottom quintile to $14,269 in the top quintile, with patterns similar to those for wealth apparent with respect to spending on home care, nonmedical care, and helper costs. Also of interest are the categories that are *not* associated with income; for example, hospital and nursing home expenses—these are $4,022 for the lowest income level and $4,471 for the highest. In part this is because lower income decedents were more likely to have experienced a nursing home admission than the highest income group (11 percent compared to 7 percent), increasing the unconditional mean. That said, it does not appear that one commonly offered explanation for income-based differences in out-of-pocket spending—the use of "luxury" nursing homes—receives much support in the data.[26]

26. Nursing home admission rates come from the 2002 to 2006 data. There may also be systematic differences in length-of-stay in nursing homes across income groups.

Table 3.5   **Mean values of out-of-pocket expenditures, by wealth quintiles, and by category of payments**

Wealth quintile	Total	Insurance	Drugs	Physician	N. home and hosp.	Other and special	Home care	Nonmedical	Helper costs	Hospice
1	7,173	937	971	217	3,461	306	383	335	547	17
2	9,118	1,453	1,558	256	3,806	252	359	607	813	13
3	11,765	2,360	1,834	406	4,550	366	636	553	978	82
4	14,454	2,591	2,330	422	5,458	424	753	1,028	1,431	18
5	18,233	3,159	2,148	424	6,521	571	1,334	1,416	2,601	60
Total	12,147	2,099	1,768	345	4,759	383	693	788	1,274	38

Notes: Sample sizes are different ($N = 6,089$ for the wealth quintiles and $N = 5,775$ for the income quintiles) owing to missing values for wealth and income; hence the totals do not necessarily correspond to the statistics for the full sample. Sampling weights are used in the calculations.

Table 3.6 **Mean values of out-of-pocket expenditures, by income quintiles, and by category of payments**

Income quintile	Total	Insurance	Drugs	Physician	N. home and hosp.	Other and special	Home care	Nonmedical	Helper costs	Hospice
1	9,046	1,127	1,382	210	4,022	301	371	620	985	28
2	10,347	1,681	1,495	243	4,358	308	494	655	1,100	13
3	14,002	2,261	1,788	336	6,316	339	725	985	1,229	23
4	12,545	2,564	2,200	383	4,092	369	645	1,032	1,227	32
5	14,269	2,832	1,946	527	4,471	600	1,276	680	1,911	26
Total	12,040	2,092	1,762	340	4,651	384	702	794	1,290	25

Note: See notes for table 3.5.

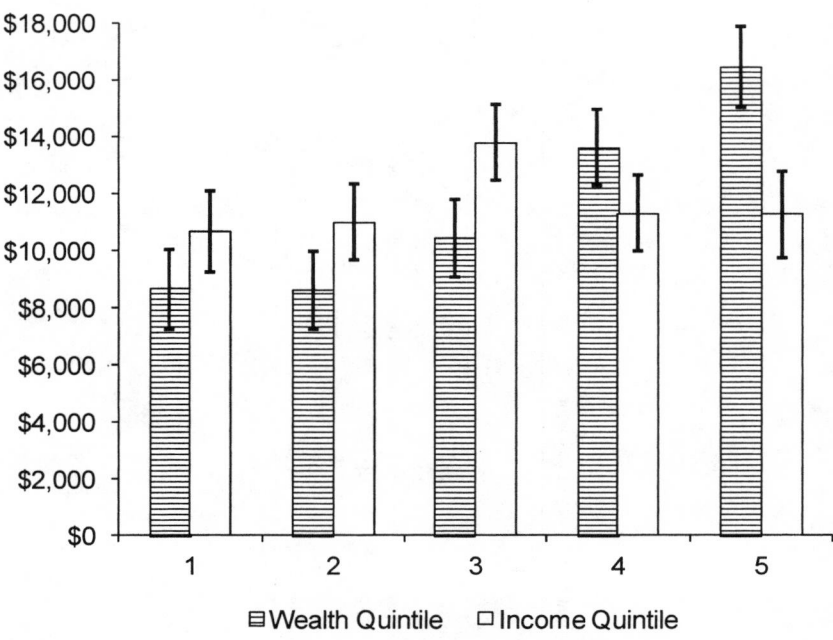

Fig. 3.3   Adjusted out-of-pocket expenditures, by wealth and income quintile

Notes: Estimates are adjusted using mean values of sex, race, Hispanic identification, a quadratic in years of schooling, cubic in age, and quartic in the months between the last interview and the time of death (set to twelve months). Ninety-five percent confidence intervals are included.

We further consider a multiple regression model of spending as a function of observable characteristics to disentangle separate effects of income and wealth on expenditures. We control for sex, race, Hispanic identification, a quadratic in schooling, a cubic in age, and (as before) control for months prior to the previous core interview. Figure 3.3 presents just the predicted measures of out-of-pocket total expenditures, evaluated at the mean values of the explanatory variables and the assumption of a twelve-month value for months since last interview. The regression results indicate that out-of-pocket expenditures are roughly twice as high in the top wealth quintile compared to the bottom wealth quintile (95 percent confidence intervals are shown by the whiskers in the diagram), but that the impact of income is no longer significantly different from zero. In sum, the estimates support the hypothesis that out-of-pocket expenditures are determined primarily by wealth on hand, and not by late-life income flows. This result accords with estimates presented in Smith (1999) that demonstrate a significant positive relationship between wealth and health status in the HRS, but no such relationship between retirement income and health.

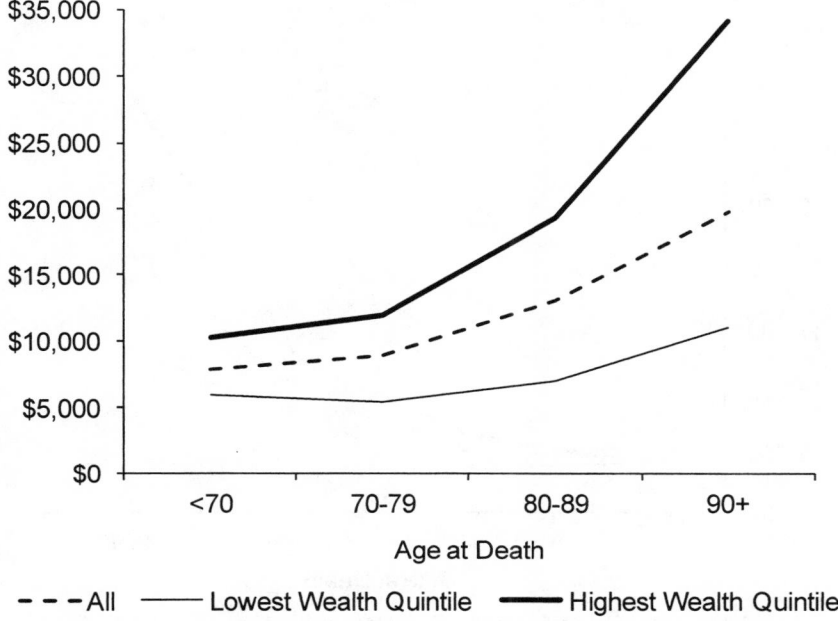

Fig. 3.4   Total out-of-pocket expenditures by age at death and by wealth quintile

Finally, we present raw measures of out-of-pocket expenditures broken down by wealth quintiles and by age group. We find a strong association between spending and age, as also noted by De Nardi, French, and Jones (2010), with a widening distribution of spending with wealth quintile at older ages. In figure 3.4, for example, end-of-life spending for those dying under age seventy is quite modest, but average expenditures rise rapidly so that for the highest wealth quintile, even average spending at age ninety and over is over $30,000 per year. And while this type of pattern is shown also for nursing home and hospital expenditures (figure 3.5), it is most pronounced for home-related services—the sum of home health care, helpers, nonmedical costs, and other medical expenses (figure 3.6). While such spending barely budges with age for the lowest wealth quintile, it rises more than threefold (from an average of $3,448 to $11,594) by age for the highest wealth quintile. This pattern is consistent with a greater likelihood of sudden-onset illnesses for younger decedents, rather than long (and expensive) chronic illnesses among the oldest old.

3.5   Conclusion

Previous studies of out-of-pocket expenditures have generally found low levels of average expenditures but a high degree of skewness in the

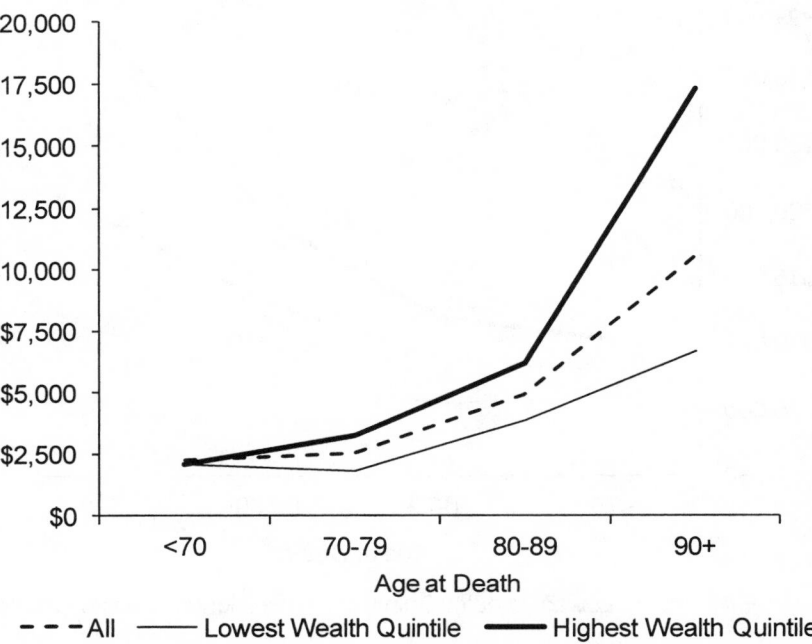

Fig. 3.5   Nursing home and hospital out-of-pocket expenditures by age at death and wealth quintile

distribution (Palumbo 1999; Feenberg and Skinner 1994; French and Jones 2004). In part, the low mean values were the consequence of older data and generally lower health care levels of spending in those years. Our results suggest that, at least for the period 1998 to 2006, out-of-pocket expenditures near the end of life are both pervasive and large, particularly for higher wealth groups and at older ages. Even after adjusting for the variable length of time the decedents are in the sample, average out-of-pocket expenditures in the last twelve months of life are $11,618, with a median of $5,061 and a ninety-fifth percentile measure equal to $49,907. These numbers at least appear to be large relative to the decedent's median nonhousing wealth ($24,706).

We have also found a strong wealth elasticity of spending, which adds some nuance to the notion of health expenditure shocks. Given that our sample consists of recent decedents, it would be hard to argue that the health "shock" experienced by the lowest wealth individual is much different from that shock experienced by the highest wealth group. It may therefore be tempting to view all of these wealth-elastic expenditure choices as "luxury" spending, like purchasing a Lexus rather than a Kia.[27] In this view, the

27. For a model of endogenous out-of-pocket health care expenditures, see De Nardi, French, and Jones (2010).

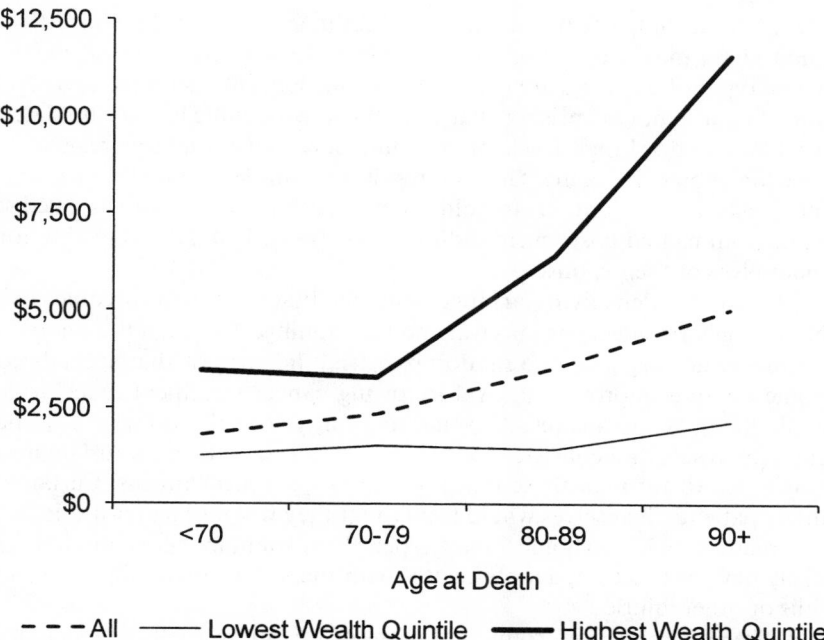

Fig. 3.6   Home-related services (home health care, helpers, nonmedical costs, other medical) by age at death and wealth quintile

low-wealth-quintile spending measure would represent the "true" shock to spending and all the rest is deemed endogenous, and thus perhaps not relevant for coverage under social insurance programs.

However, it may well be that the lowest wealth group is unable to afford uninsured but medically valuable commodities—as one might expect for a group reporting zero median net wealth and an income of less than $10,000—and that no spending is therefore reserved for these needed items. For example, Mor et al. (2004) showed much lower levels of quality—as measured by the prevalence of high-risk pressure ulcers, restraint use, and lack of pain control—in nursing homes catering largely to Medicaid patients.[28] Similarly, those with low income or wealth may only be able to afford low-quality care.

Indeed, the ultimate luxury good appears to be the ability to retain independence and remain in one's house (perhaps altered to permit easy navigation), in association with helpers and home health care assistance. Once admitted to the nursing home, a further benefit of assets is the ability to

28. This finding contrasts with the view of Hurd and Rohwedder (2009), who state that "[b]ecause of Medicaid, amounts spent by a single person on long-term end-of-life stay have practically no value" (3).

eschew Medicaid, which many would prefer to avoid (Ameriks et al. 2010), and to have the ability to purchase more comfortable living arrangements. These types of expenses are generally not amenable to insurance coverage, and thus it is not surprising that only those with sufficient accumulated wealth can afford high levels of spending; levels that are large relative to even high flows of income. Thus our results are consistent with the view that many elderly may continue to hold (or even accumulate) wealth as a hedge against uninsured costs surrounding expensive end-of-life caregiving for themselves or their spouse.

The independent living arrangements facilitated by wealth could also have long-term effects on survival and functioning. Although the evidence on this issue is sparse, one randomized trial did suggest that specialized home nursing improves survival following cancer treatment (McCorkle et al. 2000). While this result applies to a fairly specialized form of home care, the results are consistent with the idea that wealth can translate into better health through these types of (uninsured) mechanisms. Certainly many patients themselves would testify that they will fare better if allowed to remain in their own home. Finally, special food or home accommodations likely have a direct impact on health, with the latter potentially reducing falls or other injuries.

There are several important limitations of this study. First, we recognize the inherent uncertainty surrounding many of the assumptions about limits on spending, whether monthly caps or the length of time we might expect spending to have occurred (e.g., for helpers). That said, we believe that even with conservative imputations, there is strong evidence of substantial pockets of out-of-pocket expenditures in the HRS data, estimates that are not inconsistent with aggregate measures of out-of-pocket spending. Furthermore, large differences exist by ability to pay. Even when we cap total out-of-pocket spending at the ninety-fifth percentile value, to limit the impact of outliers we continue to find dramatic differences in spending by wealth.

Second, we have not adequately captured nonmonetary caregiving by family members that may be provided out of affection, or alternatively motivated by inheritances or other transfers. Past studies suggest that the value of this unpaid care is far greater than that of formal paid care. Furthermore, this unpaid caregiving may well be concentrated in the lower tails of the income and wealth distributions and may offset some of the differences we observe with respect to expenditures on in-home care.

Third, our focus on end-of-life spending does not capture the inherently dynamic process of health care spending that may have been going on for years or even decades, and thus make a greater contribution to lifetime earnings uncertainty (as in Palumbo 1999; Webb and Zhivan 2010; or De Nardi, French, and Jones 2010). Nor do we capture one important source of health risk, which is the likelihood of uncertainty health (or other risks) to jobs for people still working. During a ten-year period for people in their fifties, seven out of ten adults developed health problems, lost their jobs, or lost spouses owing to divorce or death (Johnson, Mermin, and Uccello 2006; also see Smith 2005). Such a loss would lead to much diminished wealth and income just as individuals are approaching retirement age.

Despite these qualifications, we believe that this study sheds important light on the role of medically related expenditures in affecting the resources of the elderly. This issue is of substantial policy in concern, particularly as we consider health care reform, changes in the provision of care, and the much-debated question of whether those retiring today have adequate savings and insurance to cover future health care needs (Skinner 2007). Understanding the nature of risks, and more importantly, the health-based value of these out-of-pocket expenditures—as opposed to their consumption value—is central to designing future social insurance policies to temper their burden.

References

Ameriks, J., A. Caplin, S. Laufer, and S. Van Nieuwerburgh 2010. The joy of giving or assisted living? Using strategic surveys to separate public care aversion from bequest motives. *Journal of Finance,* forthcoming.

De Nardi, M., E. French, and J. B. Jones. 2010. Why do the elderly save? The role of medical expenses. *Journal of Political Economy* 116 (1): 39–75.

Dranove, D., and M. L. Millenson. 2006. Medical bankruptcy: Myth versus fact. *Health Affairs* 25 (2): w74–w83.

Feenberg, D., and J. Skinner. 1994. The risk and duration of catastrophic health care expenditures. *Review of Economics and Statistics* 76 (4): 633–47.

Finkelstein, A., and K. McGarry. 2005. Private information and its effect on market equilibrium: Evidence from the long-term care insurance market. *The American Economic Review* 96 (4): 938–58.

French, E., and J. B. Jones. 2004. On the distribution and dynamics of health care costs. *Journal of Applied Econometrics* 19 (6): 705–21.

Fronstin, P. 2006. Savings needed to fund health insurance and health care expenses in retirement. Employee Benefit Research Institute Issues Brief no. 295, July.

Goldman, D., and J. Zissimopoulos. 2003. High out-of-pocket health care spending by the elderly. *Health Affairs* 22 (3): 194–202. (doi: 10.1377/hlthaff.22.3.194.)

———. 2010. Medical expenditure measures in the Health and Retirement Study. Unpublished Manuscript. Rand Corporation and the University of Southern California.

Hartman, M., A. Catlin, D. Lassman, J. Cylus, and S. Heffler. 2008. U.S. spending by age, selected years through 2004. *Health Affairs* 1:w1–w12. (November 6, 2007, doi: 10.1377/hlthaff.27.1.w1. For data see: http://www.cms.gov/National HealthExpendData/downloads/2004-age-tables.pdf.)

Himmelstein, D. U., E. Warren, D. Thorne, and S. Woolhandler. 2005. Illness and injury as contributors to bankruptcy. *Health Affairs* Web Exclusive, February 2.

Hubbard, R. G., J. Skinner, and S. P. Zeldes. 1995. Precautionary saving and social insurance. *Journal of Political Economy* 103 (2): 360–99.

Hurd, M. D., and S. Rohwedden. 2009. The level and risk of out-of-pocket health care spending. University of Michigan Retirement Research Center, Working Paper no. 2009-218, September.

Johnson, R. W., G. B. T. Mermin, and C. E. Uccello. 2006. How secure are retirement nest eggs? Center for Retirement Research at Boston College Issue Brief 45, April.

McCorkle, R., N. Strumpf, I. Nuamah, D. Adler, M. Cooley, C. Jepson, E. Lusk, and M. Torosian. 2000. A randomized clinical trial of a specialized home care intervention on survival among elderly post-surgical cancer patients. *Journal of the American Geriatrics Society* 48: 1707–13.

McGarry, K., and R. Schoeni. 2005. Medicare gaps and widow poverty. *Social Security Bulletin* 66 (1): 58–74.

Merlis, M., D. Gould, and B. Mahato. 2006. Rising out-of-pocket spending for medical care: A growing strain on family budgets. *The Commonwealth Fund,* February, vol. 10.

Mor, V., J. Zinn, J. Angelelli, J. M. Teno, and S. C. Miller. 2004. Driven to tiers: Socioeconomic and racial disparities in the quality of nursing home care. *Milbank Memorial Fund Quarterly* 82 (2): 227–56.

Murkofsky, R. L., R. S. Phillips, E. P. McCarthy, R. B. Davis, and M. B. Hamel. 2003. Length of stay in home care before and after the 1997 Balanced Budget Act. *Journal of the American Medical Association* 289 (21): 284–48.

New York Times. 2008. The plight of the underinsured. June 12.

Paez, K. A., L. Zhao, and W. Hwang. 2009. Rising out-of-pocket spending for chronic conditions: A ten-year trend. *Health Affairs* 28 (1): 15–25.

Palumbo, M. G. 1999. Uncertain medical expenses and precautionary saving near the end of the life cycle. *Review of Economic Studies* 66 (2): 395–421.

Sing, M., J. S. Banthin, T. M. Selden, C. A. Cowan, and S. P. Keehan. 2006. Reconciling medical expenditure estimates from the MEPS and NHEA. 2002. *Health Care Financing Review* 28 (1): 25–40.

Skinner, J. S. 2007. Are you sure you're saving enough for retirement? *Journal of Economic Perspectives* 21 (3): 59–80.

Smith, J. P. 1999. Healthy bodies and thick wallets: The dual relation between health and economic status. *Journal of Economic Perspectives* 13 (2): 145–66.

———. 2005. Consequences and predictors of new health events. In *Analyses in the economics of aging,* ed. D. A. Wise, 213–40. Chicago: University of Chicago Press and NBER.

Trejos, N. 2008. With out-of-pocket medical expenses rising, it might be time for insurance change. *The Washington Post,* December 7.

Webb, A., and N. Zhivan. 2010. How much is enough? The distribution of lifetime health care costs. Center for Retirement Research at Boston College, Working Paper no. 2010-1, February.

Comment   David R. Weir

The authors join two important themes that have generally been considered separately in prior work, including work by the authors. Out-of-pocket

David R. Weir is director of the Health and Retirement Study at the Institute for Social Research, University of Michigan.

(OOP) medical expenditures are of interest for several reasons. Because of great heterogeneity in health insurance coverage, the distribution of OOP expenditures is wide and unequal. Catastrophic expenditures (relative to the resources of a specific family) can have severe consequences for economic well-being. Out-of-pocket expenditures can also reflect the pricing mechanism of relatively complete health insurance coverage as they capture the deductibles and copay mechanisms that have been strongly pushed by economists as a way to inject some price sensitivity into consumer decisions about health care. Retirement security is also an issue of long-standing importance. Inadequate savings has been a common worry, while recent research has suggested that retirement preparation is generally adequate for most households (Scholz, Sheshadri, and Khitatrakun 2006).

So why join these themes? The primary reason is to ask whether out-of-pocket medical expenditures might threaten the retirement security of households who appear well-prepared for retirement. The primary reason to worry about that is the fiscal imbalance in the Medicare system and the fiscal pressures on the Medicaid system that provide a safety net for nursing home use. Without knowing how those imbalances will be resolved in the future it is impossible to project with certainty what the private burden of health care costs will be and therefore difficult to say whether households are prepared or not.

The authors do not attempt to tackle this difficult problem of political forecasting. Rather, they look at recent trends in out-of-pocket medical expenditures to assess economic risks in the current situation.

They observe fairly consistent increases in out-of-pocket expenditures over the past decade in multiple data sources. The share of persons with any nonzero OOP expenditures has risen considerably. This seems entirely consistent with the growth of deductible and copay mechanisms and the decline of plans offering first-dollar coverage for all services. It is also consistent with the rapid growth in use of prescription drugs. The use of prescription drugs necessarily entails the use of doctors who prescribe them, and, since both drugs and doctor visits are commonly insured with copay systems, these costs will rise as the use of drugs increases, and particularly so as the fraction of people not using any drugs declines.

To address the issue of catastrophic risk, they focus on out-of-pocket expenditures at the end of life. It is well known that total expenditures are very much higher in the last year of life and at least somewhat higher in the two years prior to death. The advantage of this focus for assessing catastrophic risk is that because everyone dies everyone is at risk for this expenditure. However, some people die alone (about 45 percent in the HRS), some while married (41 percent), and others while living with children or other family (14 percent). These arrangements can have important implications for decisions about end-of-life care and about the impact of OOP expenditures on family resources. I would suggest the authors consider estimating some of their models separately by family setting.

To assess OOP spending in the last year of life the authors use data from the Health and Retirement Study (HRS). The data pose two technical challenges: imputation for missing values, and establishing the timing of costs relative to date of death. The first can be somewhat worse for deceased respondents because the proxy reporter who reports on a deceased respondent's medical use between the last live interview and death may not have all the information. The use of linked Medicare claims data, now available for HRS, could be beneficial for both problems. Claims do not report OOP spending but they do provide the amounts and timings of utilization of hospitals and other services, which could help with imputation of OOP expenses and with the timing of when expenses occurred.

The authors use a fairly standard hot-deck approach to imputing OOP expenditures on the different categories of services captured by HRS. The use of unfolding brackets in HRS greatly improves the accuracy of imputation when exact values are not given. However, in the case of exit proxy interviews for deceased respondents, many reporters are unable even to provide a bracket range and so must be fully imputed. I believe the authors could do this better by being less restrictive. The primary cause of high OOP spending in the last year of life is the high rate of utilization, not a different ratio of OOP to covered expenses. Therefore, instead of trying to match a missing report of OOP spending on hospitals by one deceased respondent to a valid report from another deceased respondent, they could match to a live or deceased respondent who had a similar number of nights in hospital, similar chronic conditions, and perhaps similar insurance coverage. Using covariates to guide the imputation will increase precision much more than their approach of conditioning only on survival status. This could even be done as a "cold-deck" imputation, matching to records in the Medical Expenditure Panel Survey, for example, on those variables. Absent these time-consuming extensions to the imputation methods, my interpretation of the hot-deck imputations here is that they will likely not underestimate OOP because large expenditures are more likely to be remembered by family members of the deceased than small ones. The real concern for underestimation is not missing data, it is erroneous report of zero spending when in fact there was spending.

The problem for timing expenditures is that the interval from last live interview to death can be anywhere from a few days to two years or even longer if the respondent missed a wave prior to death. The best solution would be to use the Medicare claims data to establish the timing of total expenditure and to allocate OOP expenditure in the same way within intervals between interviews and between interview and death. A second-best solution would be to attempt to get a total for the two years prior to death by taking the interval from interview to death and adding to it a fraction of the prior interval, where the fraction yields the number of additional months needed to bring the total up to twenty-four months. The approach used by the authors of cumulating costs is sufficient to demonstrate the high level and variability of end-of-life spending but not as easily compared to a two-year interval between live interviews as would be a measure of spending in the twenty-four months before death.

The authors are concerned that several studies indicate larger declines in wealth just before death than can be explained by the estimated amounts of OOP medical expenditure. They note one interpretation, which is that some health care costs are not captured by the survey. Assuming that the entire decline in assets represents health care costs seems to me a very strong assumption. Transfers to children, charitable donations, accelerated consumption (e.g., travel) in anticipation of death, lost work income by self or family, are just a few of the ways asset profiles might be altered by a terminal illness. The HRS asks exit proxy respondents whether the death was "expected." Contrasting sudden to unexpected deaths might provide some leverage for explaining asset rundown.

Finally, to fully realize their proposed "marriage" of out-of-pocket expenditures and retirement security, the authors need a way to translate the metrics of OOP expenditure into a metric comparable to retirement security. One way to do that would be to convert the income and assets of a household into a present value and similarly discount the expected lifetime OOP expenditure stream. Then OOP expenditure can be expressed as a percentage of sustainable consumption, and simulated variation in OOP expenditure as ranges of that percentage. This would tell us how likely it is that OOP expenses could consume a given percent of retirement consumption and thereby how far below pre-retirement consumption the consumption of things other than medical expenditures might fall.

Reference

Scholz, J. K., A. Seshadri, and S. Khitatrakun. 2006. Are Americans saving "optimally" for retirement? *Journal of Political Economy* 114 (4): 607–43.

Cost Growth in Medicare: 1992 to 2006

Amitabh Chandra, Lindsay Sabik, and Jonathan S. Skinner

4.1   Introduction

Expanding health insurance coverage and reducing the trajectory of cost growth are major goals of many health care reform proposals. While the problem of addressing cost growth in health care is often viewed as being separate from efforts to cover the uninsured, it is difficult to sustain a comprehensive insurance expansion when premiums for that program are growing substantially faster than tax receipts and incomes. Cost growth in health care is not a uniquely American phenomenon—Chandra and Skinner (2009) note that every other Organization for Economic Cooperation and Development (OECD) country has experienced substantial expenditure growth—but it has been particularly pronounced in the United States. This observation, combined with a deeper examination of how the United States differs from other OECD countries, led Garber and Skinner (2008) to conclude that U.S. healthcare was "uniquely inefficient."

In this chapter we study the sources of recent cost growth in American health care by focusing on the experience of the fee-for-service (FFS) portion of the Medicare program. Medicare is a social insurance program that covers 45 million Americans over the age of sixty-five and disabled persons

Amitabh Chandra is professor of public policy at the Kennedy School of Government, Harvard University, and a research associate of the National Bureau of Economic Research. Lindsay Sabik is a PhD candidate in health policy at Harvard University. Jonathan S. Skinner is the John Sloan Dickey Third Century Professor in the Social Sciences and professor of community and family medicine at Dartmouth College, and a research associate of the National Bureau of Economic Research.

Paper prepared for the NBER Aging Conference in Boulders, Arizona. Chandra and Skinner acknowledge support from NIA PO1-AG19783. We are grateful to Elliott Fisher and Doug Staiger for comments and collaborations that have greatly influenced this work.

regardless of age if they have received disability Supplemental Security Income (SSI) benefits for two years. It represents 13 percent of the Federal budget and accounts for one in five dollars of national health spending. Thirty percent of all hospital services, 20 percent of all prescription drug spending, and 20 percent of all physician care is paid for by Medicare (Kaiser Family Foundation 2009). Also, cost growth in Medicare is believed by many commentators to be the single largest threat to the long-term federal budget deficit (Orszag 2007; Congressional Budget Office [CBO] 2007). In 2009, Medicare was a $480 billion dollar program and its growth rate exceeded that of national income. The program comprises four parts: Part A (hospital insurance) pays for hospital care, skilled nursing stays, and hospice care; Part B covers physician services and hospital outpatient services; while Medicare Advantage (Part C) accounts for approximately 25 percent of total Medicare spending. Finally, Part D, the recently enacted prescription drug benefit, comprises 11 percent of Medicare spending.[1]

Cost growth in the Medicare program may or may not resemble cost growth in the Medicaid and commercial populations. The Medicare population is older than the general population, and while 20 percent of enrollees are under age sixty-five, they are largely eligible through the Social Security Disability Insurance (SSDI) program and are thus sicker than those covered by private insurance plans. Consequently, Medicare beneficiaries use a different set of services than the general population, leading to some differences in regional patterns of health care between the under-sixty-five and over-sixty-five.[2] On the one hand, Baker, Fisher, and Wennberg (2008) demonstrate that hospital-level resource use is similar between FFS Medicare and commercial insurers for chronically ill individuals in the end of life. On the other hand, there are a number of theoretical reasons to believe that Medicare's administratively set prices cause hospitals and physicians to offset pricing imperfections with increased utilization in the non-Medicare population. The ability of providers to offset the effects of Medicare's reimbursement policy probably varies with the competitiveness of local health care markets.

Regardless of whether Medicare's experience resembles that of other insurers, its size, dependency of general revenues, and role as a social insurance program makes it of interest in its own right. In this chapter we focus on cost-growth in the fee-for-service population (Parts A and B). Within the focus on Medicare, we pay particular attention to drivers of cost *growth* and distinguish these from drivers of the *level* of Medicare spending.

1. This latter percentage does not include prescription drug benefits provided by Medicare Advantage plans.

2. Unfortunately, the state-level data for medical spending in the under-sixty-five population exhibit lower quality than the detailed individual-level clinical data from the Medicare administrative records (Skinner et al. 2009; also see Cooper 2009).

4.2   Data and Methods

Data on Medicare reimbursements for 1992 to 2006 come from the Dartmouth Atlas of Healthcare and include per capita age-, sex-, and race-adjusted reimbursements for each of the 306 Hospital Referral Regions (HRRs) in the United States. They are based on data from the 5 percent Continuous Medicare History Sample (CMHS).[3] These data represent spending on all FFS Medicare beneficiaries over age sixty-five (unless otherwise noted, we exclude disabled beneficiaries under age sixty-five). We do not have claims data for Medicare HMOs, so spending on those enrollees is excluded. All reimbursements are adjusted for inflation using the Consumer Price Index (CPI) and are expressed in 2006 dollars (using the gross domestic product [GDP] deflator gave us similar results).

In addition to total Medicare reimbursements and Part A and Part B reimbursements, spending in the CHMS is broken down into subcategories including inpatient short stays; inpatient long stays; outpatient hospital services; medical and surgical care provided by physicians; diagnostic, lab, and X-ray services; durable medical equipment; home health services; hospice services; and skilled nursing facilities. The majority of payments to hospitals for inpatient care are categorized under hospital short stays. Reimbursements for long stays are generally made to long-term care hospitals, which must have an average Medicare length of stay greater than twenty-five days and are paid under a separate Medicare payment system. The outpatient hospital services category covers reimbursements to hospital emergency rooms and outpatient clinics under Medicare Part B. Since 2000 these have been paid under the outpatient Prospective Payment System (PPS) (as opposed to the physician services in the medical and surgical categories). The medical services category covers most "Evaluation and Management" codes in the Berenson-Eggers Type of Service (BETOS) classification system, including office and hospital visits and specialist visits. The surgical services category covers "Procedures" BETOS codes, although if the procedure was delivered in a hospital outpatient setting these would fall under outpatient hospital services. To clarify, Medicare's payment to a hospital for bypass surgery will be categorized under inpatient short-stay spending, but the physician's time for performing the surgery will be recorded under Part B procedures. The diagnostic, lab, and X-ray services category includes spending on services such as CT scans and MRIs that are not associated with an inpatient admission.

---

3. Reimbursement data for 1998 through 2000 overstated true Medicare spending due to double counting of some claims. After consultation with staff at the Centers for Medicaid and Medicare (CMS) we determined that these data should be deflated by 10 percent to estimate actual spending in those years. All results presented here include this adjustment. It is possible that the "bump" in utilization rates—which were not adjusted—observed during the late 1990s in figure 4.3 may reflect some of the double-counting that our 10 percent deflation is intended to correct.

We supplement this with data from the Area Resource File (ARF) on per capita income. Data from the ARF are available at the county level, so in situations where a county is covered by two HRRs we assign county characteristics by weighting according to the fraction of the HRR population overlapping each county. This is consistent with the strategy followed in Chernew et al. (2009).

First, we examine aggregate trends in Medicare spending, both overall and by category and calculate the cumulative percentage growth, average annual percentage growth, and total increase in per capita reimbursements for 1992 to 2006 and subgroups of this period. We examine changes in the rate at which different procedures and different categories of spending are responsible for cost-growth in Medicare. We consider how utilization, measured by the number of encounters, changes over this period within different service categories. Formally, we perform the following decomposition:

$$(1) \qquad S_1 - S_0 = \sum_R \omega_{r1} S_{r1} - \sum_R \omega_{r0} S_{r0}$$

$$(2) \qquad = \sum_R \omega_{r1}(S_{r1} - S_{r0}) + \sum_R S_{r0}(\omega_{r1} - \omega_{r0})$$

$$(3) \qquad = \sum_R \omega_{r1}\left(\sum_P \eta_{rp1} S_{rp1} - \sum_P \eta_{rp0} S_{rp0}\right) + \sum_R S_{r0}(\omega_{r1} - \omega_{r0})$$

$$(4) \qquad = \sum_R \omega_{r1}\left(\sum_P \eta_{rp1}(S_{rp1} - S_{rp0}) - \sum_P S_{rp0}(\eta_{rp1} - \eta_{rp0})\right)$$
$$+ \sum_R S_{r0}(\omega_{r1} - \omega_{r0})$$

where S_t is average spending in year t; S_{rt} is average spending in region r in year t; ω_{rt} is the proportion of all Medicare FFS enrollees in region r in year t; S_{prt} is average spending for procedure p in region r in year t; and η_{prt} is the number of claims per enrollee for procedure p in region r in year t. This allows us to decompose the change in Medicare spending into two components: (a) between-HRR changes due to changes in where the Medicare population lives, given by the second term in equation (2); and (b) within-HRR changes due to changes in spending per enrollee, given by the first term in equation (2). We can further decompose within-HRR spending changes (the first term in equation [4]) into changes in the number of encounters and changes in spending per encounter. We perform this decomposition for the entire 1992 to 2006 period as well as the 1998 to 2006 period.

That is, the simple accounting framework allows us to determine how much of aggregate spending growth occurs because: (a) high-cost areas experience an expansion in their population ("between" growth), for example, because relatively more elderly people move to Miami, a high-cost area; (b) there are more total procedures or encounters overall per enrollee; and (c) there is greater intensity (whether prices or services) per procedure or encounter. Our approach allows us to distinguish among these three groups, although we caution that there are other decompositions that could yield slightly different results.[4]

Next, we divide HRRs into quintiles based on the level of Medicare spending in 1992 and test for sigma convergence in (log) spending levels by 2006. In other words, we want to know whether the variance of regional spending shrunk over time. We estimate HRR-level regressions of rates of growth in Part A, Part B, and total Medicare spending on HRR-level covariates, including the age distribution of Medicare enrollees, adjusted mortality among FFS Medicare enrollees (a simple measure of illness), and per capita income. (Note that the HRR-level spending measures are already adjusted for age, sex, and race; thus, any impact of age on these measures will capture "spillover" effects; for example, if regions with a higher fraction of the very old practices a different style of care for all age groups.)

These regressions, which should not be given a causal interpretation, are designed to shed light on whether areas where Medicare spending grew faster were areas where mortality (a proxy for illness) or income were growing faster. Our focus on the role of income in predicting Medicare spending is motivated by the insights of Hall and Jones (2007), who argue that diminishing marginal utility from nonhealth consumption in the presence of higher incomes (and consequently, the value of life) will result in a greater share of income being spent on health care. Finding evidence of positive associations between spending, mortality, and income would provide prima facie evidence that there is *some* allocative efficiency behind Medicare spending growth, but would still fall far short of establishing optimality.

4.3   Results

4.3.1   Aggregate Trends in Medicare Enrollment and Spending

The two panels of figure 4.1 demonstrate that the total number of Medicare beneficiaries grew over the 1992 to 2006 period, with the number of enrollees under sixty-five years of age (who receive Medicare after being on the SSDI program for at least two years) experiencing the most enrollment growth. Panel B of figure 4.1 illustrates the share of beneficiaries in FFS versus Medicare managed care (a group for whom we do not have claims). The number of enrollees in traditional FFS Medicare declined through the

---

4. This arises because of an index number issue; $\omega_1 S_1 - \omega_0 S_1$ can also be written $\omega_1(S_1 - S_0) + S_0(\omega_1 - \omega_0)$.

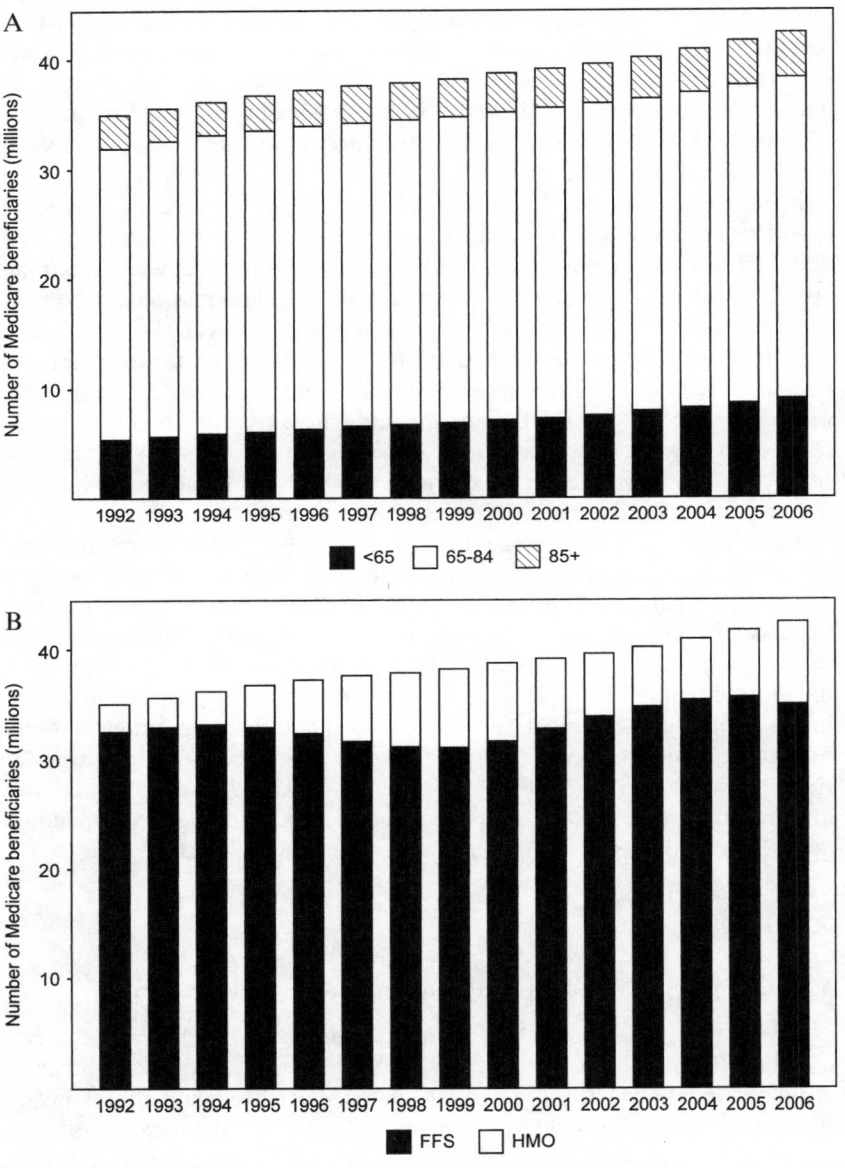

Fig. 4.1 Number of Medicare beneficiaries: *A*, **over time;** *B* **in FFS and Medicare HMOs**

first part of the period as enrollment in Medicare HMOs grew, although the share of beneficiaries in FFS has been growing since 2000. Total enrollment in Medicare will continue to grow in the coming decades as younger baby boomers age into eligibility.

Figure 4.2 illustrates trends in the categories of Medicare spending per enrollee: panel A breaks down growth into key subcategories of Part A spending, panel B does the same for Part B, and panel C for home health spending. We separate home health expenditures because they were charged to Part A prior to the Balanced Budget Act (BBA) of 1997, but have subsequently been charged to Part A or B depending on whether the care is provided in conjunction with a hospitalization. In panel A, the largest component of costs, spending on short stay hospitalizations, has remained relatively flat. In contrast, panel B shows large per enrollee spending growth in the two largest components, hospital outpatient services and physician medical care services, which more than doubled over the fourteen-year period. Reimbursements for home health grew quickly from 1992 to 1996, but rapidly dropped off after the Balanced Budget Act (BBA) of 1997 changed reimbursement rules for home health services.

In table 4.1, panel A, we see that total Medicare FFS spending has grown by approximately $3,000 per beneficiary since 1992, at an average growth rate of 3.2 percent annually (had we used the GDP price deflator the same quantity would have been 3.5 percent), with two-thirds of that increase resulting from the rise in spending on Part B services. The pace of growth varied over this period; overall spending grew at an average real rate of 3.8 percent per year from 1992 to 1999 (a seven-year period) and slowed to 2.7 percent per year from 1999 to 2006 (also seven years).[5] Growth in Part B spending was higher than growth in Part A spending in both periods. Among subcategories of Part A and Part B spending, reimbursements for inpatient short stays and skilled nursing facilities (SNF) had the highest absolute (dollar) growth during the earlier period, while outpatient hospital services and medical care services had the highest absolute growth during the latter period. White (2003) discusses the dramatic role of the new PPS system for SNF, which was adopted in mid-1998, in reducing payments to these facilities. Hospital outpatient services have been reimbursed under PPS from July 1, 2000 but their growth has, if anything, been higher even in the post-PPS era.

Examining percentage growth can be additionally informative, but

5. Both our level and growth numbers are lower than estimates from CBO (2007), since we include only FFS spending for beneficiaries over age sixty-five. The CBO estimates that total Medicare spending was $342 billion in 2005, while our estimate for over-sixty-five FFS enrollees is $225 billion, or about 66 percent of the CBO estimate (CBO 2007). Likewise, they estimate that per capita Medicare spending grew at a real rate of 3.8 percent annually from 1990 to 2005 while we estimate that it grew at an annual rate of 3.2 percent from 1992 to 2006. Thus, it should be noted that our results for FFS enrollees over age sixty-five understate total spending and may slightly understate growth as well.

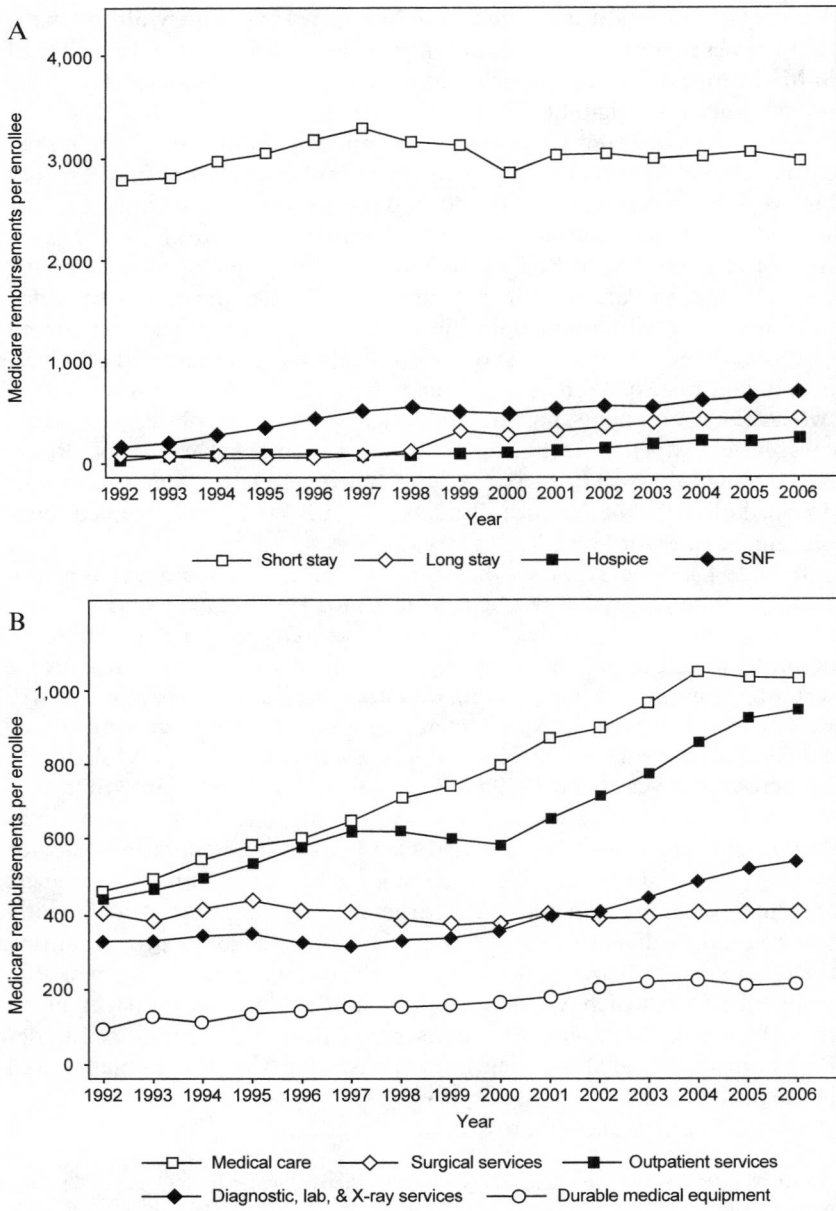

Fig. 4.2   Growth in Medicare spending by type of service: *A*, inpatient; *B*, outpatient and ambulatory care; *C*, home health

Note: All figures in 2006 dollars.

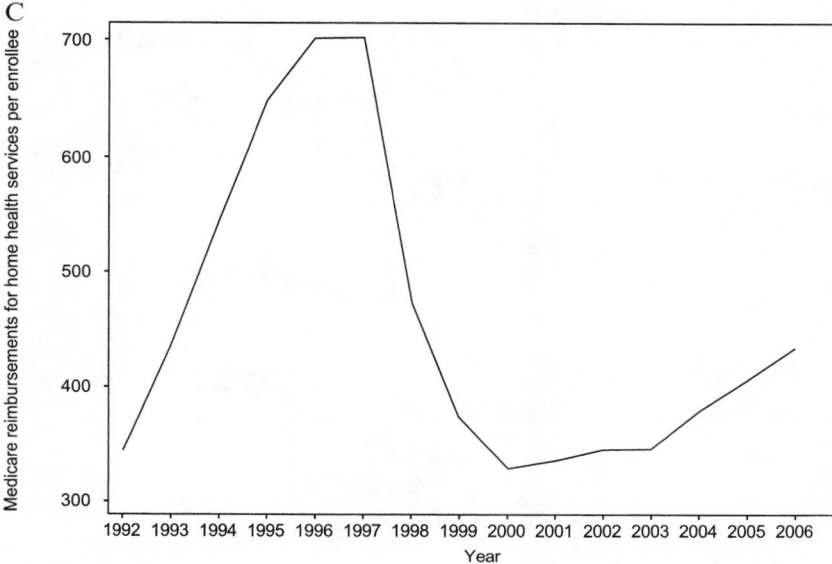

Fig. 4.2   (cont.)

categories with low initial levels of spending often will exhibit higher percentage increases, so categories identified in this way are unlikely to be
lucrative targets for cost-saving policies. The category of durable medical
equipment, which is often the focus of Medicare fraud investigations, shows
considerable percentage growth of 137 percent, but its increase of $125 is
only one-fifth as large as the $565 increase in medical care services, which has
a lower growth rate of 122 percent. Reimbursements for hospice services and
inpatient long stays exhibited the highest growth rates overall, more than
three times the rate of all other categories, but, again, baseline spending for
these categories was low.

Because conversations about the role of Medicare in the federal budget
focus on projections of increases in total expenditures (per beneficiary spending multiplied by the number of beneficiaries), in table 4.1, panel B, we report
growth in total Medicare spending (that is, we account for increases in per
beneficiary spending and the number of Medicare beneficiaries). The reported
patterns of growth in total Medicare spending are similar to per beneficiary
patterns, though overall growth in total spending is naturally higher during
part of the period when Medicare enrollment is increasing more rapidly.

Table 4.2 shows the decomposition of the changes in Medicare spending into within-HRR (spending) changes and between-HRR (population
location) changes, and the further decomposition of within-HRR changes
into changes in spending per encounter and changes in the number of

Table 4.1   Growth in Medicare spending by type of service

	1992	1999	2006	1992–1999			1999–2006			1992–2006		
	Medicare reimbursements per capita			Cumulative percentage growth	Average annual percentage growth	$ increase per capita	Cumulative percentage growth	Average annual percentage growth	$ increase per capita	Cumulative percentage growth	Average annual percentage growth	$ increase per capita
				A Per capita								
Total	5,331	6,854	8,304	29.6	3.8	1,579	20.2	2.7	1,394	55.8	3.2	2,973
Part A	3,404	4,179	4,536	22.9	3.0	780	8.4	1.2	352	33.2	2.1	1,132
Part B	1,927	2,675	3,767	41.4	5.1	799	38.2	4.7	1,041	95.5	4.9	1,840
Inpatient short stays	2,793	3,156	2,979	12.2	1.7	340	-4.9	-0.7	-154	6.7	0.5	186
Inpatient long stays	63	116	442	400.1	25.9	253	39.5	4.9	125	597.7	14.9	379
Outpatient services	436	615	942	37.2	4.6	162	57.3	6.7	343	115.8	5.6	506
Medical care services	465	705	1,030	59.4	6.9	276	39.1	4.8	290	121.7	5.9	565
Surgical services	405	382	410	-7.9	-1.2	-32	9.8	1.3	37	1.1	0.1	5
Diagnostic, lab, and X-ray services	328	332	537	2.2	0.3	7	60.1	7.0	202	63.7	3.6	209
Durable medical equipment	92	153	217	71.3	8.0	65	38.4	4.8	60	137.1	6.4	125
Home health services	345	474	434	8.9	1.2	31	15.5	2.1	58	25.8	1.7	89
Hospice services	34	80	234	148.1	13.9	50	179.1	15.8	150	592.6	14.8	200
Skilled nursing facilities	160	558	690	212.0	17.7	340	37.8	4.7	189	329.9	11.0	530

						B Total						
Total	153.6	183.0	233.0	18.4	2.4	28.3	28.1	3.6	51.1	51.7	3.0	79.4
Part A	98.1	111.6	127.3	12.3	1.7	12.1	15.6	2.1	17.1	29.8	1.9	29.2
Part B	55.5	71.4	105.7	29.2	3.7	16.2	47.3	5.7	33.9	90.4	4.7	50.2
Inpatient short stays	80.5	84.3	83.6	2.5	0.4	2.0	1.3	0.2	1.1	3.9	0.3	3.1
Inpatient long stays	1.8	3.1	12.4	356.9	24.2	6.5	48.7	5.8	4.1	579.5	14.7	10.6
Outpatient services	12.6	16.4	26.4	25.4	3.3	3.2	67.7	7.7	10.7	110.2	5.5	13.9
Medical care services	13.4	18.8	28.9	45.6	5.5	6.1	48.3	5.8	9.4	115.9	5.7	15.5
Surgical services	11.7	10.2	11.5	-15.8	-2.4	-1.9	17.0	2.3	1.7	-1.5	-0.1	-0.2
Diagnostic, lab, and X-ray services	9.5	8.9	15.1	-6.6	-1.0	-0.6	70.7	7.9	6.2	59.4	3.4	5.6
Durable medical equipment	2.6	4.1	6.1	56.5	6.6	1.5	47.5	5.7	2.0	131.0	6.2	3.5
Home health services	9.9	12.6	12.2	-0.5	-0.1	0.0	23.2	3.0	2.3	22.5	1.5	2.2
Hospice services	1.0	2.1	6.6	126.7	12.4	1.2	197.5	16.9	4.4	574.5	14.6	5.6
Skilled nursing facilities	4.6	14.9	19.4	185.1	16.1	8.6	46.9	5.6	6.2	318.7	10.8	14.7

Note: All reimbursement figures in 2006 dollars.

Table 4.2   Medicare spending decompositions

	Within (spending change)			Between (population change)	Total change Within + Between
	Change in spending per encounter	Change in number of encounters	Total within HRR		
A 1992–2006					
Inpatient short stays	72.2	132.1	204.3	-48.7	155.5
Inpatient long stays	-28.9	297.8	268.9	-2.6	266.3
Outpatient services	80.2	365.0	445.2	-2.8	442.3
Medical care services	289.7	255.5	545.2	-11.0	534.2
Surgical services	-163.6	174.9	11.3	-2.9	8.3
Diagnostic, lab, and X-ray services	75.3	112.7	188.0	-4.3	183.7
Durable medical equipment	-45.4	150.7	105.3	-1.0	104.4
Home health services	168.8	-203.4	-34.6	1.0	-33.6
Hospice services	1.5	138.1	139.6	-0.9	138.7
Skilled nursing facilities	209.0	228.0	437.0	-2.0	435.0
Total	658.7	1651.5	2310.2	-75.3	2234.8
B 1998–2006					
Inpatient short stays	336.0	-369.1	-33.0	-5.1	-38.2
Inpatient long stays	62.5	136.7	199.3	0.5	199.8
Outpatient services	282.9	25.2	308.1	-0.9	307.2
Medical care services	160.5	125.8	286.3	3.5	289.8
Surgical services	-6.1	35.7	29.6	1.5	31.1
Diagnostic, lab, and X-ray services	151.6	19.0	170.6	2.7	173.3
Durable medical equipment	17.2	38.6	55.8	0.7	56.4
Home health services	169.0	-154.4	14.7	1.6	16.3
Hospice services	28.6	111.3	139.9	0.6	140.5
Skilled nursing facilities	140.3	-14.9	125.5	2.1	127.6
Total	1342.6	-45.9	1296.7	7.0	1303.7

Notes: The HRRs with missing data on encounters and/or reimbursements are treated as zeros in calculating decomposition (primarily affects HSP, LS; 5 HRRs missing SNF data for 1992 period); population share is 1992, 1998, or 2006 level; baseline spending, number of encounters, and spending per encounter are 1992–1994, 1998–2000, and 2004–2006 averages.

encounters.[6] Over the entire 1992 to 2006 period and the latter part of the period from 1998 onwards, almost all of the increase in spending was driven by within-HRR growth (table 4.2, panel A). That is, not surprisingly, changes in spending resulted from increases in spending per enrollee within HRRs, rather than from the migration of a larger fraction of enrollees into high-spending regions. Considering total Medicare spending over the entire 1992 to 2006 period, about half the growth in per beneficiary spending was due to increases in the number of encounters, and one-fifth was due to greater intensity or reimbursement for a given encounter. However, if we look only at the most recent years, the relative importance of these factors shifts: panel B demonstrates that greater spending per encounter (which may reflect increased treatment intensity as well as higher reimbursement levels for the same services) is the key driver of cost growth from 1998 to 2006. Of particular interest is the recent growth in the use of diagnostic and laboratory services.[7]

To explore these findings in more detail, we were interested in learning whether cost growth (in terms of numbers of encounters) was being driven more by an increased number of beneficiaries receiving services (treatment expansion) or an increase in the amount of services provided to a given beneficiary (treatment intensity). Figure 4.3 reports the trends in the share of enrollees using three services that exhibit rapid cost growth and are covered by the Part B program. Increases in spending on medical care services and diagnostic, lab, or x-ray services are primarily driven by increases in treatment intensity, as the number of encounters per capita is growing more quickly than the percent of beneficiaries using those services. For hospital outpatient services, however, the treatment expansion (percent of enrollees using services) and intensity (number of per capita encounters) are growing at similar rates, suggesting that treatment expansion plays a larger role in the increase in spending on outpatient services.

In addition, we studied hospital discharge data to examine changes in the distribution of conditions being treated. Trends in discharges for major procedures are depicted in the two panels of figure 4.4. We created two panels to provide separate scales for procedures that were relatively more rare. Procedure rates for CABG (bypass), carotid endarterectomy, and hip fracture remained relatively flat or declined, while discharges for back surgery, hip replacement, knee replacement, and PCI (percutaneous coronary interventions, which includes angioplasty) increased substantially. Some of

6. Our total change in spending number is less than the total per beneficiary growth presented in table 4.3 because spending in the categories for which we have data does not account for 100 percent of Medicare spending, so we are unable to account for the entire change over this period through this decomposition. However, we are able to account for the majority of the growth in spending and consider what drives growth within each category.

7. One potential determinant of these services is local malpractice pressure (see Baicker, Fisher, and Chandra 2007).

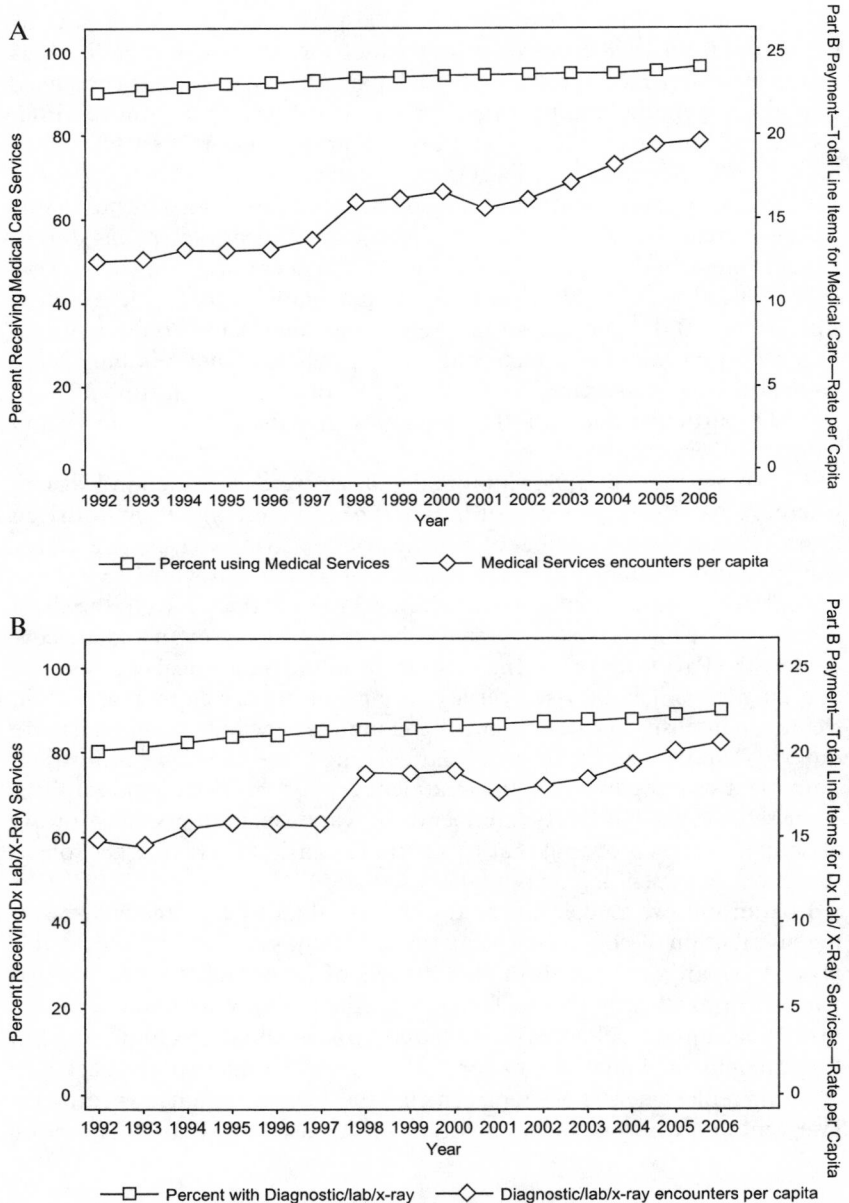

Fig. 4.3 Growth in Medicare utilization by type of service: *A*, **medical care;** *B*, **diagnostics;** *C*, **outpatient**

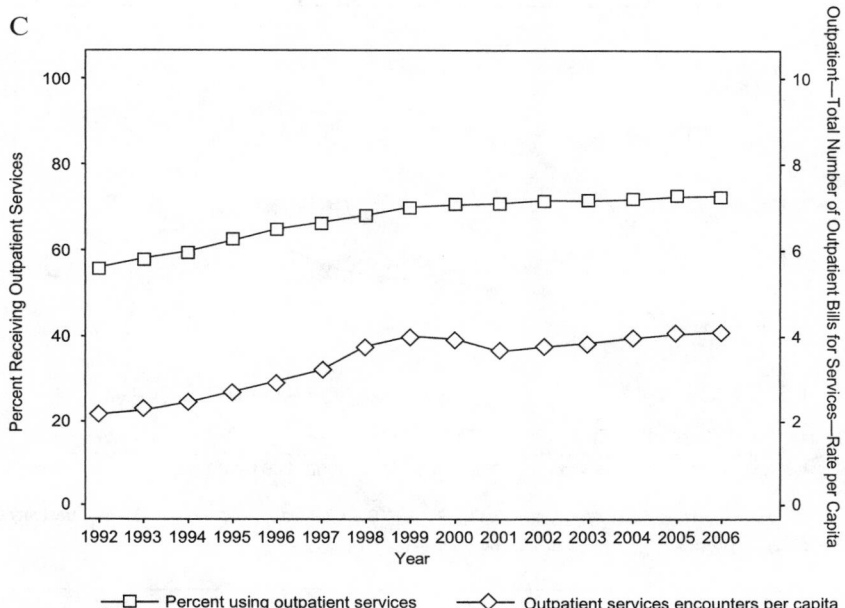

Fig. 4.3   (cont.)

the increase in PCI reflects a substitution away from bypass, but in general, it also reflects the greater use of this procedure in patients with stable coronary disease. We noted a falling incidence of heart attacks in Medicare beneficiaries, probably because younger cohorts of beneficiaries have better management of hypertension and cholesterol, in addition to lower rates of smoking, as noted by Ford et al. (2007).

This suggests that the increase in PCI was largely in patients with stable coronary disease. The Clinical Outcomes Utilizing Revascularization and Aggressive Drug Evaluation (COURAGE) trials examined the benefits from PCI in this population on the margins of both survival and quality of life. Boden and the COURAGE Trial Research Group (2007) did not find that PCI dominated optimal medical therapy as an initial management strategy on the margins of survival and other major cardiovascular events. In subsequent work by Weintraub, Boden, and the COURAGE Trial Research Group (2008) PCI was not found to improve patient outcomes in the domains of angina frequency and treatment satisfaction, but there were small improvements in the quality of life that disappeared by thirty-six months. The increase in PCI can also be interpreted in the context of work by Cutler and Huckman (2003), who note that angioplasty offers lower per unit costs, but can raise total costs because it can be offered to a much larger group of patients than bypass surgery.

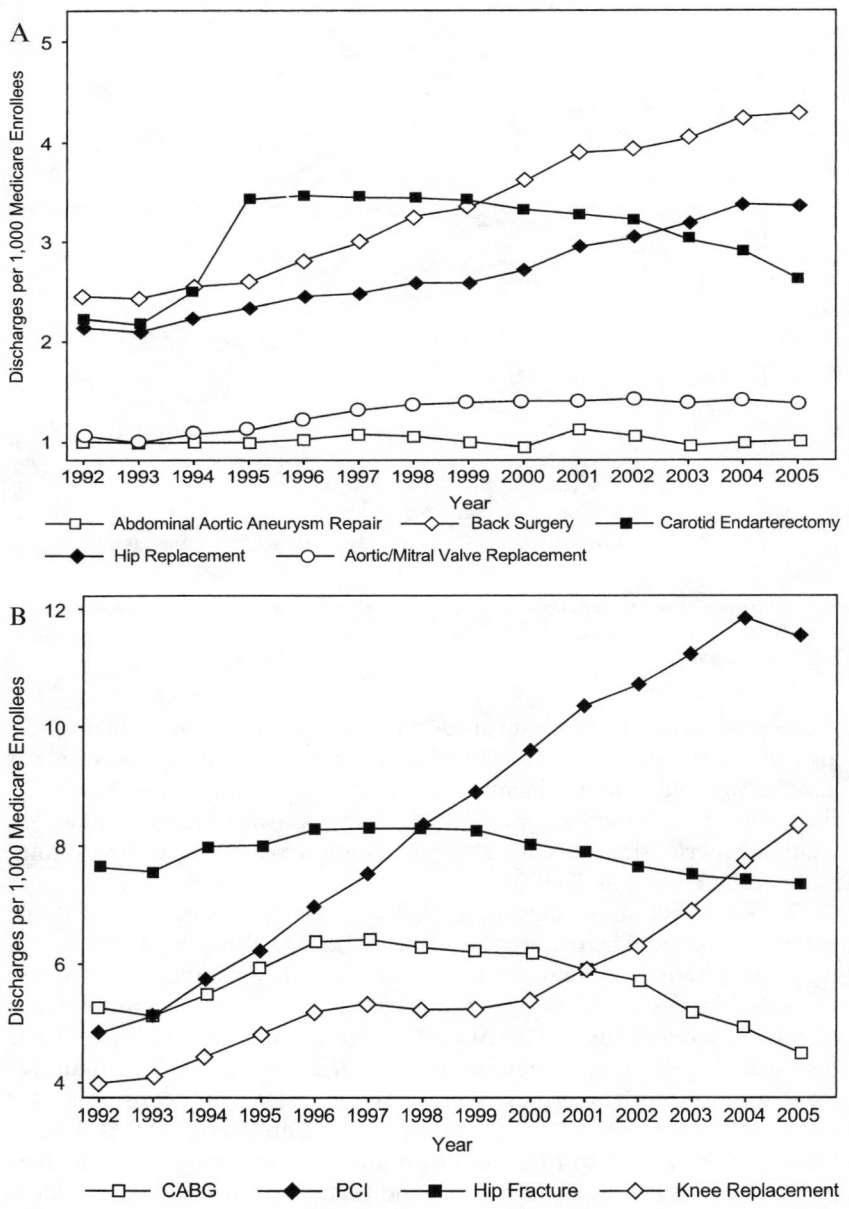

Fig. 4.4   Medicare discharges per 1,000 enrollees, by service category:
A, less common procedures; B, more common procedures

4.3.2   Geographic Variation in Cost Growth

A large literature in medicine and economics notes the presence of large geographic variation in Medicare spending (e.g., Fisher et al. 2003a, 2003b). But with the exception of the work of Fisher, Bynum, and Skinner (2009), less is known about whether high-spending regions are the highest growing ones. In our analysis we find considerable variation in the rates of spending growth across HRRs. For Part A spending, the average annual growth rate was 1.9 percent among the slowest growing 20 percent of HRRs, while the fastest growing quintile grew at an average annual rate of 2.7 percent. Growth in Part B was higher across HRRs than growth in Part A, with the slowest growing quintile experiencing an average annual growth rate of 4.4 percent and the fastest growing quintile growing at an average rate of 6.1 percent. This 2 percentage point-difference in average annual growth rates is economically significant: at 4 percent spending will double in eighteen years, but at 6 percent it will double in only twelve years. Despite these differences in spending growth rates, we note that the dollar increase in spending has been remarkably stable across all levels of initial spending. Figure 4.5 illustrates trends in Medicare reimbursements by quintile of spending in 1992, where quintile 1 had the lowest level of spending in 1992 and quintile 5 the highest. The dollar increases in spending are identical across the quintiles for both Part A and Part B. The high percentage rates of growth among the high growth HRRs are largely driven by their lower baseline spending. As seen in figure 4.5, average annual percent growth rates monotonically decrease across quintiles as baseline spending increases. The pattern of spending growth is very similar across HRRs with different levels of baseline spending, leading us to conclude that high-cost areas do not necessarily experience higher or lower growth in specific characteristics of health care spending.

The implication of equal growth in the dollar amount of Medicare spending should be a compression in relative spending, or a smaller degree of (relative) regional variation across the United States. We can test this hypothesis by comparing the standard deviation of the population-weighted log expenditures in earlier and later time periods. The standard deviation in expenditures for 1992 was 0.19, which grew until reaching a maximum of 0.21 in 1996 (in part because some HRRs experienced much more rapid growth in home health care); since then it has declined, so that in 2006 it is equal to 0.16. (The difference between 1992 and 2006 is significant at the 5 percent level.) Between 1992 and 2006, the standard deviation for Part A spending has fallen from 0.19 to 0.17, and for Part B services it has fallen from 0.21 to 0.17. This result is consistent with the CBO finding that the extent of regional variation has moderated somewhat over time (CBO 2008).

That said, several HRRs are clear outliers in their rates of Medicare cost growth—some are high cost and exhibit high growth rates. Panel A of figure 4.6 shows trends in Part B spending in two HRRs with among the highest

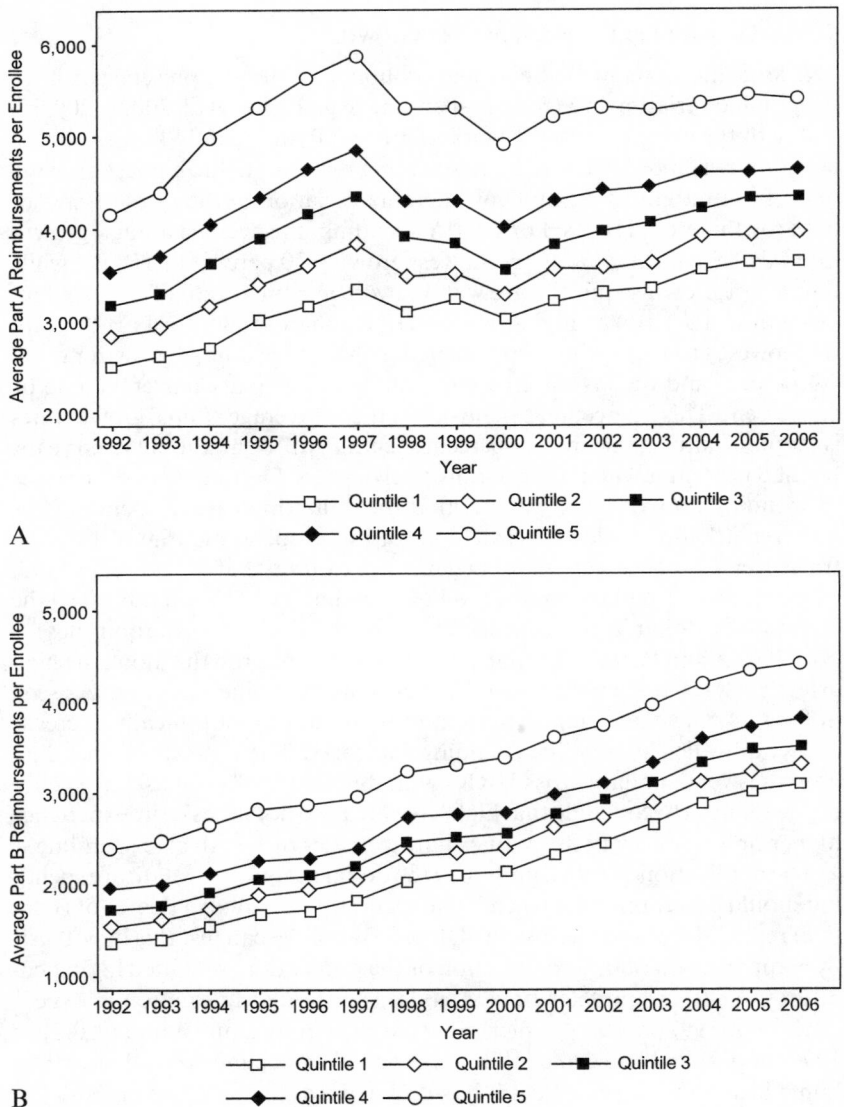

Fig. 4.5 Part A and Part B spending growth by quintile of 1992 spending: A, Part A spending; B, Part B spending

Note: Average growth rates for panel A: Q1 = 2.68, Q2 = 2.42, Q3 = 2.28, Q4 = 1.93, Q5 = 1.90. Average growth rates for panel B: Q1 = 6.06, Q2 = 5.54, Q3 = 5.22, Q4 = 4.83, Q5 = 4.44. All figures in 2006 dollars.

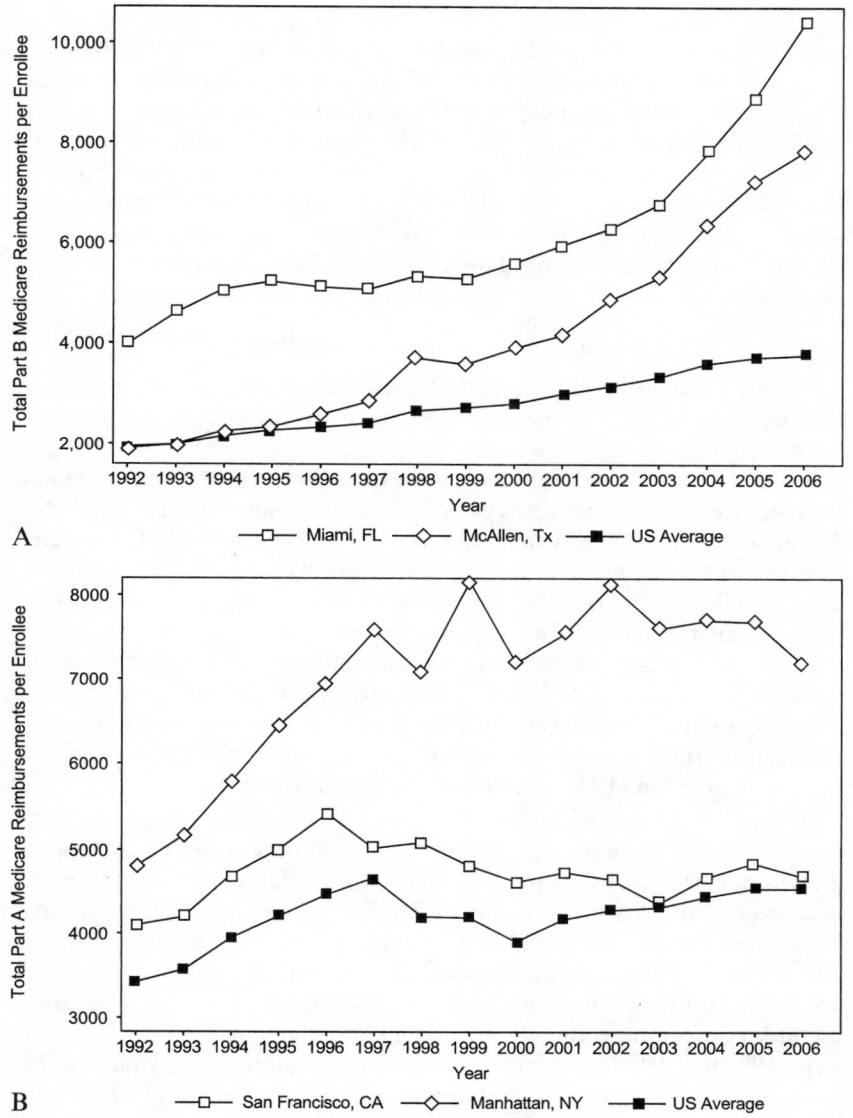

Fig. 4.6   Spending in selected high- and low-growth HRRs:
A, high-growth HRRs; B, low-growth HRRs

Note: All figures in 2006 dollars.

Part B growth rates: Miami, Florida, and McAllen, Texas (we picked these HRRs because their practice style has been discussed at length by commentators such as Gawande [2009]). Miami started the period as one of the highest-cost HRRs and has grown at a considerably higher rate than other HRRs, particularly since 1999. McAllen, on the other hand, was near the U.S. average cost in the early 1990s, but has experienced growth far above the U.S. average and ended the period as one of the highest-cost HRRs. There are also outliers on the side of being low-cost places; as figure 4.6, panel B shows, Manhattan experienced high growth in Part A spending, while San Francisco's rate of growth was significantly below the U.S. average.

4.3.3   Factors Associated with Changes in Spending

Table 4.3 presents results from HRR fixed effects regressions, which are designed to shed light on the determinants of spending increases. The outcome variable, spending growth in each HRR, was measured by the difference in log average per beneficiary reimbursements between the beginning and the end of each time period. Separate regressions were performed for Part A, Part B, and total Medicare reimbursements. The time periods measured were from 1992 to 1993 to 2003 to 2004 (long term) and from 1999 to 2000 to 2003 to 2004 (short term). We pooled data for two years to relieve concerns about mean-reversion. The HRR fixed effects control for all unchanging attributes of these areas, including persistent differences in local price levels and illness. Additionally, the inclusion of HRR fixed effects also implies that differences in the initial level of spending are not confounding the analysis. This is important in light of the previous discussion where higher growth rates were noted in HRRs with low initial spending levels.

In the results reported in table 4.3, we see that higher mortality rates are significantly associated with lower growth in Part A spending and higher growth in Part B spending over the long term (1992 to 2004). A 10 percent increase in mortality rates (within an HRR) is associated with a 5 percent decrease in Part A spending, but a corresponding increase (5.6 percent) in Part B spending. Due to these countervailing effects, changes in mortality are not significantly associated with changes in total Medicare spending. Also, the link between mortality and spending is not significant over the short term (1999 to 2004). Our interpretation of these results is that while changes in patient illness surely predict spending at the individual level, changes in area-level mortality do not predict area-level increases in spending.

In the second column of each set of regressions, we add log per capita income as a regressor. We find that within-HRR changes in income and mortality are largely orthogonal to each other; the coefficients on mortality barely change with the inclusion of income. Over both the long term and the short term, increases in income are associated with decreases in Part A reimbursements (a 10 percent increase in income is associated with a 3 percent decrease in Part A spending). There is no association observed with

| Table 4.3 | | Results from HRR fixed-effects regressions of growth in Part A and Part B reimbursements on HRR mortality and income | | | | |

	ln(Part A reimbursements)		ln(Part B reimbursements)		ln(Total reimbursements)	
	1992/1993–2003/2004					
ln(Mortality)	–0.472***	–0.491***	0.563***	0.567***	–0.0605	–0.0739
	(0.17)	(0.17)	(0.14)	(0.14)	(0.14)	(0.14)
ln(Per capita income)		–0.283**		0.0592		–0.203*
		(0.13)		(0.11)		(0.10)
HRR FE	Yes	Yes	Yes	Yes	Yes	Yes
Age composition	Yes	Yes	Yes	Yes	Yes	Yes
R^2	0.85	0.86	0.98	0.98	0.96	0.96
Average baseline reimbursement	$3,481		$1,953		$5,434	
	1999/2000–2003/2004					
ln(Mortality)	0.201	0.234	0.258*	0.270*	0.289*	0.313*
	(0.21)	(0.21)	(0.15)	(0.15)	(0.16)	(0.16)
ln(Per capita income)		–0.238**		–0.0826		–0.173*
		(0.12)		(0.085)		(0.092)
HRR FE	Yes	Yes	Yes	Yes	Yes	Yes
Age composition	Yes	Yes	Yes	Yes	Yes	Yes
R^2	0.63	0.64	0.96	0.96	0.89	0.89
Average baseline reimbursement	$4,024		$2,742		$6,767	

Notes: Standard errors in parentheses; regressions and means weighted by HRR population.
***Significant at the 1 percent level.
**Significant at the 5 percent level.
*Significant at the 10 percent level.

Part B reimbursements, and the coefficient on total reimbursements is only marginally significant. We do not view this evidence as a definitive rejection of the Hall and Jones (2007) hypothesis—that health care is a luxury good (or more specifically, has higher marginal utility associated with it relative to nonhealth consumption)—but neither do these regressions provide strong support for the hypothesis that health care spending is driven largely by community-level income levels. Note that the HRR fixed effects account for between 74 percent and 96 percent of the variation depending on the time period considered and the spending category. Thus, regional spending patterns exhibit a high degree of stability over time; except for regions like McAllen, high-spending HRRs in 1992 also tend to be high-spending in 2006, and conversely.

Next, we examine the role of one potential explanation for increases in Medicare spending: fraud and its closely related cousin, financial entrepreneurship by hospitals and physicians. Some providers have overstated patients' medical conditions while others have billed for services that were

Table 4.4　　　　Coefficients from regressions of change in Medicare reimbursements on change in home health spending before and after the BBA of 1997

Dependent variable	No covariates	Including covariates
Part A	−0.0962**	−0.102**
	(0.040)	(0.044)
Part B	0.0789***	0.0704***
	(0.016)	(0.015)
Outpatient services	−0.0600***	−0.0738***
	(0.022)	(0.022)
Medical care services	−0.00179	0.0260
	(0.020)	(0.019)
Surgical services	0.154	0.0329
	(0.10)	(0.12)
Diagnostic, lab, and X-ray services	0.00837	0.0231
	(0.038)	(0.037)
Durable medical equipment	0.302***	0.155***
	(0.032)	(0.029)

Notes: Standard errors in parentheses. Each line cell represents coefficient from separate regression, where the dependent variable is ln (change in category 1992–2006) and the independent variable of interest is ln (HH change) = ln(difference between 96–97 (peak) average and 00–01 (trough)). Regressions including covariates control for age distribution, adjusted mortality, and income in the HRR, where values of the covariates are averages for 1992–1993 (baseline).
***Significant at the 1 percent level.
**Significant at the 5 percent level.
*Significant at the 10 percent level.

unnecessary or never delivered in the first place (General Accounting Office [GAO] 1981, 1986, 1996, 2009). One marker of the degree to which financial entrepreneurship occurred in an area is the HRR-level reduction in home health reimbursements after the BBA of 1997 revised rules to reduce wasteful home health reimbursements (McCall et al. 2001). Under this assumption, HRRs with the largest drops in home health spending were also the most likely to be those that had been profiting from the previously loose rules governing home health reimbursement. Panel C of figure 4.2 illustrates this phenomena nationally: 1996 and 2000 represent the peak and trough, respectively, of average home health spending across the United States but there is regional variation in the size of the home health contraction. To investigate the association between financial entrepreneurship among providers and overall changes in Medicare spending within HRRs, we regressed the change in reimbursements for different categories of spending on the change in home health reimbursements from the pre-BBA to the post-BBA years. Table 4.4 presents the coefficients on change in home health spending from separate regressions for each spending category, both with and without adjustments for age, mortality, and income. Part B reimbursements grew significantly more in HRRs that experienced a larger post-BBA drop in home health reimbursements. Each additional 10 percent decrease in home health spending over the BBA period (1996 to 2001) is associated with 0.8 percent greater increase in Part B spending and a 3 percent greater increase in durable medical equipment spending over the long term (1992 to 2006). As previously noted, durable medical equipment is frequently the target of Medicare fraud investigations and is one of the few service categories with little or no risk to the patient from overprovision. Therefore, it seems possible that the boom and bust of home health expenditures provides a useful marker of regions that tend to "innovate" in areas of medicine with high profit margins but uncertain effects on health.

4.4   Discussion

In this analysis we have offered a simple taxonomy of the sources of cost growth in Medicare. Cost growth in this program is largely the consequence of increases in spending on Part B services, mainly medical care and outpatient services. In recent years, growth has been driven more by increases in reimbursement levels for each encounter rather than in the number of encounters. Several expensive treatments—CABG, carotid endarterectomy, and hip fracture—experienced declines in use, while a number of typically discretionary services—back surgery, knee and hip replacement—experienced increases as well. These trends may be due to the entry of younger, healthier cohorts into Medicare, but our trends are robust to controlling for the age composition of the local health care market.

We failed to find an association between changes in income and changes in Medicare reimbursement. It is possible that Medicare's prospective reimbursement structure may introduce a wedge between patients' ability to get the care that they demand as a result of higher incomes, but it should be noted that reimbursement for many services covered by Part B of the Medicare program are not "capped" or subject to any form of capitation. However, even for these Part B services we detected no association between increases in income and increases in use of services. Future work should examine whether non-Medicare spending might reveal an income effect, but that analysis is beyond the scope of this chapter.

Both low and high spending regions (based on initial 1992 level of spending) grew by similar dollar amounts, suggesting that cost growth in health care diffuses in a relatively uniform pattern, and that over time the extent of across-regional variability might decline slightly over time. Still, the degree of persistence in spending levels across regions is high, suggesting that their determination may in part be the consequence of other factors that evolve slowly over time, such as the composition of the physician workforce (Baicker and Chandra 2004) or the organizational structure of hospitals (and hospital beds) in the region. Even within this relative uniformity, we find outliers: costs increased strikingly in McAllen, Texas, and Miami,

Florida, while costs lag behind the average growth rates in San Francisco and San Diego.

One important limitation of our analysis is that we do not measure the benefits of increased spending and emphasize that these may be large relative to the size of the increase in costs. As we discuss, it is very difficult to quantify improvements in health that extend beyond mortality, such as gains in patient satisfaction and reductions in side effects. Because many treatments work on these margins and are expensive does not automatically mean that they are without value. But our focus on costs can help guide the search for where the benefits must be found if the increased spending is viewed as being socially optimal.

References

Baicker, K., and A. Chandra. 2004. Medicare spending, the physician workforce, and beneficiaries' quality of care. *Health Affairs* 23 (4): w184–97.

Baicker, K., E. S. Fisher, and A. Chandra. 2007. Malpractice liability costs and the practice of medicine in the Medicare program. *Health Affairs* 26 (3): 841–52.

Baker, L. C., E. S. Fisher, and J. E. Wennberg. 2008. Variations in hospital resource use for Medicare and privately insured populations in California. *Health Affairs* 27 (2): w123–34.

Boards of Trustees of the Federal Hospital Insurance Trust Fund and the Federal Supplementary Medical Insurance Trust Fund. 2009. *Annual report of the boards of trustees of the Federal Hospital Insurance Trust Fund and the Federal Supplementary Medical Insurance Trust Fund.* Washington, DC: GPO.

Boden, W. E., and the COURAGE Trial Research Group. 2007. Optimal medical therapy with or without PCI for stable coronary disease. *New England Journal of Medicine* 356 (15): 1503–16.

Chandra, A., and J. Skinner. 2009. Technological innovation and expenditure growth in health care. Harvard Kennedy School. Working Paper.

Chernew, M., L. Sabik, A. Chandra, and J. P. Newhouse. 2009. Physician workforce composition and health care spending growth. *Health Affairs* 28 (5): 1327–35.

Cooper, R. A. 2009. States with more health care spending have better-quality health care: Lessons about Medicare. *Health Affairs* 28 (1): w103–15.

Congressional Budget Office (CBO). 2007. The long-term outlook for health care spending. See http://www.cbo.gov/ftpdocs/87xx/doc8758/Frontmatter.2.3.shtml.

———. 2008. Geographic variation in health care spending. See http://www.cbo.gov/ftpdocs/89xx/doc8972/02-15-GeogHealth.pdf.

Cutler, D. M., and R. S. Huckman. 2003. Technological development and medical productivity: The diffusion of angioplasty in New York State. *Journal of Health Economics* 22 (2): 187–217.

Fisher, E. S., J. P. Bynum, and J. S. Skinner. 2009. Slowing the growth of health care costs: Lessons from regional variation. *New England Journal of Medicine* 360 (9): 849–52.

Fisher, E. S., D. E. Wennberg, T. A. Stukel, D. J. Gottlieb, F. L. Lucas, and E. L. Pinder. 2003a. The implications of regional variations in Medicare spending.

Part 1: The content, quality, and accessibility of care. *Annals of Internal Medicine* 138 (4): 273–87.

———. 2003b. The implications of regional variations in Medicare spending. Part 2: Health outcomes and satisfaction with care. *Annals of Internal Medicine* 138 (4): 288–98.

Ford, E. S., U. A. Ajani, J. B. Croft, J. A. Critchley, D. R. Labarthe, T. E. Kottke, W. H. Giles, and S. Capewell. 2007. Explaining the decrease in U.S. deaths from coronary disease, 1980–2000. *New England Journal of Medicine* 356:2388–98.

Garber, A., and J. Skinner. 2008. Is American health care uniquely inefficient? *Journal of Economic Perspectives* 22 (4): 27–50.

Gawande, A. 2009. The cost conundrum—What a Texas town can teach us about health care. *The New Yorker,* June.

General Accounting Office. 1981. *Medicare: Home health services: A difficult program to control,* GAO/HRD-81-155. Washington, DC: GAO.

———. 1986. *Medicare: Need to strengthen home health care payment controls and address unmet needs,* GAO/HRD-87-9. Washington, DC: GAO.

———. 1996. *Medicare: Home health utilization expands while program controls deteriorate,* GAO/HEHS-96-16. Washington, DC: GAO.

———. 2009. *Medicare: Improvements needed to address improper payments in home health,* GAO-09-185. Washington, DC: GAO.

Hall, R. E., and C. I. Jones. 2007. The value of life and the rise in health spending. *Quarterly Journal of Economics* 122 (1): 39–72.

Kaiser Family Foundation. 2009. Medicare spending and financing fact sheet. Available at: http://www.kff.org/medicare/upload/7305-04-2.pdf.

McCall, N., H. L. Komisar, A. Petersons, and S. Moore. 2001. Medicare home health before and after the BBA. *Health Affairs* 20 (3): 189–98.

Orszag, P. R., and P. Ellis. 2007. The challenge of rising health care costs: A view from the Congressional Budget Office. *New England Journal of Medicine* 357 (18): 1793–95.

Skinner, J., A. Chandra, E. Fisher, and D. Goodman. 2009. The elusive connection between health care spending and quality. *Health Affairs* 28 (1): w119–23.

Weintraub, W. S., W. E. Boden, and the COURAGE Trial Research Group. 2008. Effect of PCI on quality of life in patients with stable coronary disease. *New England Journal of Medicine* 359:677–87.

White, C. 2003. Rehabilitation therapy in skilled nursing facilities: Effects of Medicare's new prospective payment system. *Health Affairs* 22 (3): 214–23.

The Demand for Medicare Part D Prescription Drug Coverage
Evidence from Four Waves of the Retirement Perspectives Survey

Florian Heiss, Daniel McFadden, and Joachim Winter

5.1 Introduction

Most developed countries have mixed "universal coverage" health care systems with mandated health insurance financed from some combination of consumer, employer, and government sources. The United States is the only developed country without universal coverage; about 18 percent of the nonelderly population are currently without health insurance (Gruber 2008). The elderly are universally covered under the Medicare program, but historically Medicare did not cover prescription drugs. Before 2006, roughly 25 percent of the elderly population (age sixty-five and above) had little or no insurance coverage for their prescription drugs, and 10 percent had annual pharmacy bills exceeding $5,600 (Winter et al. 2006). According to data from the U.S. Bureau of the Census (Current Population Survey, 2006, Annual Social and Economic Supplement), median per capita income in this population was $15,700 in 2005, and 29 percent of this population had incomes below $10,000. Uninsured prescription drug costs were thus a heavy

Florian Heiss is chair of the Department of Statistics and Econometrics at Johannes Gutenberg University, Mainz. Daniel McFadden is the E. Morris Cox Professor of Economics and director of the Econometrics Laboratory at the University of California, Berkeley, 2000 Nobel Laureate in Economics, and a research associate of the National Bureau of Economic Research. Joachim Winter is chair of Empirical Research in Economics at Ludwig-Maximilians University, Munich.

Paper prepared for the NBER Conference on the Economics of Aging, May 7–10, 2009, Carefree, Arizona. This research was supported by the Behavioral and Social Research program of the National Institute on Aging (grants P01-AG05842-18, P01-AG05842-23, and R56 AG026622-01A1), with additional support from the E. Morris Cox Fund at the University of California, Berkeley. We thank Amy Finkelstein for her insightful discussion. The authors are solely responsible for the results and conclusions offered in this chapter.

burden on unhealthy elderly. This was a major public concern prior to the introduction of Medicare Part D in 2006.

Medicare Part D provides the Medicare-eligible population with universal access to standardized, heavily subsidized prescription drug coverage through government-approved plans sponsored by private insurance companies and health maintenance organizations (HMOs). In addition to providing access to affordable drug coverage to all Medicare beneficiaries (in particular to the chronically ill), a second policy goal was to create a "competitive, transparent marketplace offering a wide array of benefits" (Bach and McClellan 2005, 2733). Overall, the introduction of Medicare Part D has been viewed as a success story (Heiss, McFadden, and Winter 2006, 2010; Goldman and Joyce 2008; Duggan, Healy, and Morton 2008). High enrollment rates have been achieved—in the first year of Medicare Part D, more than 90 percent of the eligible population had prescription drug coverage, either from a Medicare Part D plan or from some other source with comparable coverage (Heiss, McFadden, and Winter 2006). Consumers face a broad menu of plans to choose from, and premiums are at levels lower than anticipated by policymakers and sponsors.

The institutional design of Medicare Part D exemplifies the current trend toward "consumer-directed health care" as it relies on consumer behavior and competition among insurers to attain satisfactory market outcomes with limited government regulation. Policymakers around the world, and particularly in the United States, are increasingly stressing the role of consumer choice and provider competition in the provision of public services.[1] In the case of Medicare Part D, and arguably also in other similar programs, giving consumers more choice also means confronting them with difficult decisions (McFadden, Winter, and Heiss 2008; Kling et al. 2008; Abaluck and Gruber 2009).

The argument for creating markets in which consumers choose among private providers of services depends on consumers' ability to make informed choices. Making optimal, or even just reasonable, decisions in the Part D market is difficult for seniors. They face uncertainty with respect to their future health status and drug costs, a rather complicated benefit schedule with a coverage gap and other peculiar institutional features of the Part D program (to be discussed in detail later), and a large number of available plans with features that vary along several dimensions. The complexity of Medicare Part D was a great source of concern before its introduction (see Heiss, McFadden, and Winter 2006). How seniors decide whether to enroll in Medicare Part D, and what plans they select, is therefore not only of

1. The debate about the effect of high-deductible plans has drawn heavily on a landmark study conducted by the RAND Corporation in the 1970s and 1980s, the Health Insurance Experiment; see Newhouse (2004). Buntin et al. (2006) and Goodman (2006) provide additional discussion of consumer-directed health care.

crucial importance for the success of this particular program, but also for public policies that stress consumer choice more generally.

In this chapter, we study individual decisions made in the initial enrollment period for the Medicare Part D program. In the week before enrollment began in November 2005, we conducted a survey of Americans aged sixty-five and above, termed the Retirement Perspectives Survey (RPS), to study information, perceptions, and preferences regarding prescription drug use, cost, and insurance. After the initial enrollment period closed on May 15, 2006, we reinterviewed the same respondents to elicit their actual Medicare Part D decisions for 2006. Third and fourth waves of our survey were conducted in March/April 2007 and in March/April 2009. Data from RPS-2009 are analyzed in this chapter for the first time.[2] In most of our analysis, we concentrate on "active deciders," the eligible individuals in our sample who did not have prescription drug coverage in November 2005 that was automatically converted to Part D coverage or equivalent in 2006 (e.g., automatic coverage through their current or former employer's health program, the Veterans Administration, or Medicaid). Our aim is to understand whether choices were related to the salient features of the program and the economic incentives they generated. We look at whether active deciders enrolled in Part D or not, at subsequent switching, and at the choice of plans. We stress the role of 2005 prescription drug use, health risks, and subjective factors in the demand for prescription drug insurance. We generally find that seniors' choices respond to the incentives provided by their own health and by the market environment.

The remainder of this chapter is structured as follows. In section 5.2, we review the Medicare Part D program and some of the research on individual decisions that has emerged since its introduction. We describe the Retirement Perspectives Survey project in section 5.3. Our empirical results are reported in section 5.4. In section 5.5, we summarize our findings and discuss avenues for future research.

5.2   A Brief Review of the Medicare Part D Program and Related Research

The Centers for Medicare and Medicaid Services (CMS) within the U.S. Department of Health and Human Services administer health insurance coverage for older Americans via the Medicare program. The Medicare Modernization Act of 2003 (MMA) was enacted to extend coverage for prescription drugs to the Medicare population. Beginning in 2006, the new Medicare Part D benefit reduced the financial burden of prescription drug

---

2. In what follows, the three waves of the Retirement Perspectives Survey are referred to as RPS-2005, RPS-2006, RPS-2007, and RPS-2009, respectively.

spending for beneficiaries, especially those with low incomes or extraordinarily high ("catastrophic") out-of-pocket drug expenses. The CMS administers this program, subsidizing outpatient prescription drug coverage offered by private sponsors of drug plans that give beneficiaries access to a standard prescription drug benefit. In the following, we describe those features of Medicare Part D that are relevant for our subsequent analysis of consumer behavior in this market. More details on the Medicare Part D prescription drug benefit can be found on the CMS website and in Bach and McClellan (2005).

Critical parameters in determining Standard plan benefits are the plan formulary, the beneficiary's annual pharmacy bill for drugs in the plan formulary, the beneficiary's true out-of-pocket (TrOOP) payments for these covered drugs and threshold for catastrophic coverage, and the average monthly premium. In the benefits formula, expenditures for drugs not in the plan formulary are not counted in the pharmacy bill or in TrOOP payments. Part D premiums are also excluded from TrOOP payments. The Standard Medicare Part D plan had the following benefit schedule in 2006:

- The beneficiary has an annual deductible of $250.
- The beneficiary pays 25 percent of drug costs above $250 and up to $2,250. The TrOOP payment is then $750 for a beneficiary whose pharmacy bill has reached $2,250.
- The beneficiary pays 100 percent of drug costs above $2,250 and up to a TrOOP payment of $3,600; this is referred to as the *coverage gap* or *doughnut hole*. The TrOOP threshold of $3,600 is attained at a drug bill of $5,100.
- The beneficiary pays 5 percent of drug costs above a drug cost threshold of $5,100 at which the TrOOP threshold level is achieved; this is referred to as *catastrophic* coverage.

Standard plan coverage in 2007, 2008, and 2009 has the same structure, with parameters being adjusted annually to reflect market base premiums and inflation in drug prices. The combined effect of three annual adjustments can be seen in figure 5.1, which depicts the benefit schedules for 2006 and 2009.

Heiss, McFadden, and Winter (2010) provide a calculation of the actuarial value of Standard Plan benefits, based on a projection by CMS in 2005, the year prior to the introduction of Part D, of the distribution of 2006 drug costs for the full Medicare-eligible population. This calculation shows that the 2006 expected drug cost in this population was $245.03 per month. If enrollment in the Part D Standard Plan had been universal, the expected benefit would have been $128.02 per month, or $91.13 net of the monthly average premium of $37 anticipated in 2005, and the expected TrOOP cost would have been $117.01 per month. The actual monthly average premium of $32.20 in 2006 was lower than anticipated; this may have been the result

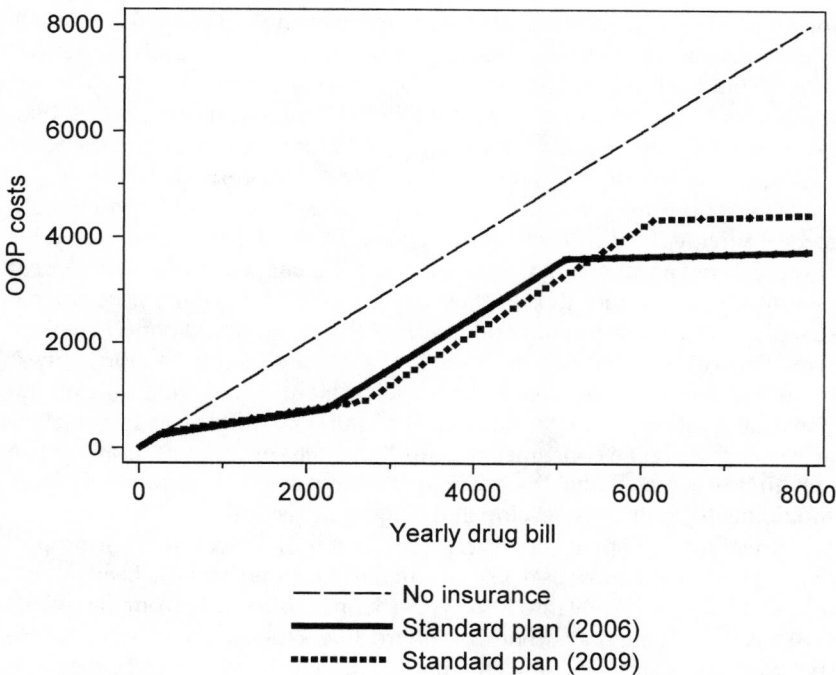

Fig. 5.1   Benefit schedule of the Medicare Part D Standard Plan
Source: CMS data.

of lower drug costs arising from pharmacy benefit management and drug price negotiations by sponsors. Monthly premiums vary with plan sponsor and area, but a national average premium determined by CMS (and used in determining its subsidy) is a publicly available indicator of plan cost to beneficiaries.

The Medicare Part D plans sponsored by private insurance firms may differ from the Standard Plan in their premiums and other plan features, provided that their benefits for any drug cost are on average at least as high as those of the Standard Plan. Enhancements may include coverage for the deductible and for the gap in the Standard Plan. The CMS classifies the stand-alone prescription plans that are available under Medicare Part D in four categories (see Bach and McClellan 2006, 2313). The "standard benefit" is a plan with the statutorily defined coverage, deductible, gap, and cost sharing. An "actuarially equivalent" plan is one that has the same deductible and gap as the Standard Plan, but has different cost sharing (such as copayment tiers for preferred drugs and generic drugs rather than a percentage copayment). Actuarial equivalence to the Standard Plan may be achieved through restrictions in plan formularies, but all approved plans must have formularies that include at least two drugs in each therapeutic category. A "basic alternative" plan is actuarially equivalent to the statutorily defined benefit, but both the deductible and cost sharing can be altered. (Most of these plans have no deductible.) Finally, an "enhanced alternative" plan exceeds the defined standard coverage—for example, by offering coverage in the gap for generic drugs only, or both generic and branded drugs.

One important feature of Medicare Part D is the penalty for late enrollment. Individuals who enroll after May 15, 2006 and do not have creditable coverage from another source face a late enrollment penalty fee of 1 percent a month for every month that they wait to join. The penalty is computed based on the average monthly premium of Part D standard plans in a given year. This rule was put in place to reduce adverse selection. As the analysis of an intertemporal discrete choice model by Heiss, McFadden, and Winter (2010, 2009) shows, the late-enrollment penalty provides a strong monetary incentive for eligible consumers to enroll in 2006 (or more generally, when they first become eligible for Medicare) rather than wait to join only later, should health problems develop and drug costs rise.

The evolution of plan supply in this market is of interest in its own right. Official CMS data allow us to classify all Part D plans that have been offered from 2006 through 2009 into four types (defined differently from the official classification discussed earlier): Standard Plans, plans without deductible (but with a coverage gap), and enhanced plans with gap coverage, either only for generics or for both brand-name drugs and generics. Figure 5.2 shows that while average premiums of plans without gap coverage have remained relatively stable, premiums for plans with gap coverage have increased substantially. The market for the most generous plans with coverage for at least some brand-name drugs in the gap has all but collapsed within the first three years. By 2007, almost half of such plans that had been offered in 2006 had disappeared and the remaining half had dramatically higher average premiums. In 2008, no such plan was offered, and in 2009 there is only one. A plausible interpretation is that sponsors have underestimated the costs of providing a generous plan; for example, due to adverse selection. This issue is investigated further in ongoing parallel research (Heiss, McFadden, and Winter 2009).

The new Medicare Part D prescription drug benefit has received considerable attention in the literature. We do not attempt to provide a comprehensive review of the literature but refer the reader to the paper by Duggan, Healy, and Morton (2008) for a discussion of the Part D drug benefit and the research programs it has generated. In the remainder of this section, we review selected recent papers directly related to the present chapter.

Levy and Weir (2008, 2010) use data from the 2004 and 2006 waves of the Health and Retirement Study (HRS) to estimate the extent of adverse selection into Part D and the impact of Part D on medication use and out-of-pocket spending. They conclude that there was substantial selection into

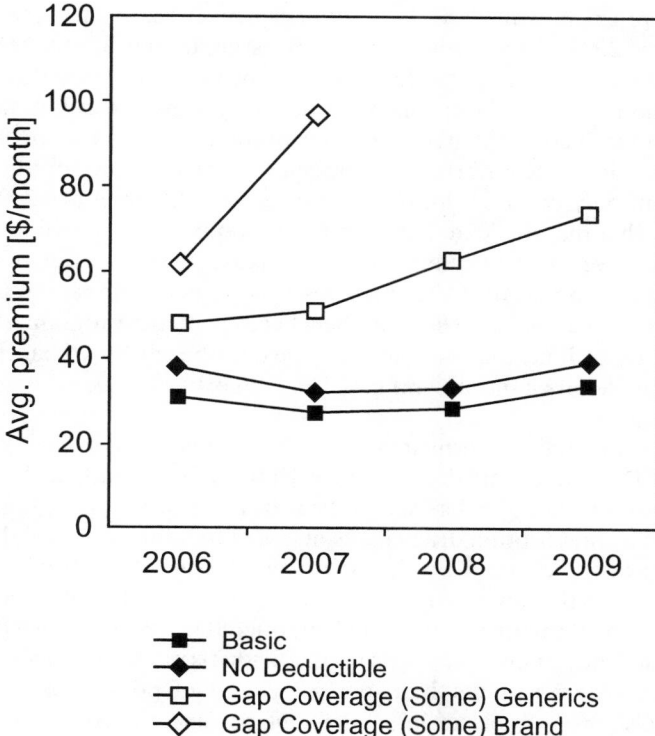

Fig. 5.2   Average premiums of Medicare Part D plans, by type
Source: CMS data (2005–2009 Excel files containing the characteristics of Medicare Part D stand-alone prescription drug plans).

Part D. Among Medicare beneficiaries with no drug coverage in 2004, those with high use and/or spending in 2004 were most likely to be enrolled in Part D in 2006. Many of those who remained without coverage in 2006 reported that they did not use prescription drugs, and the majority had relatively low out-of-pocket spending. In line with the findings by Heiss, McFadden, and Winter (2010), Levy and Weir (2010) conclude that Medicare beneficiaries seem to have been able to make economically rational decisions about Part D enrollment (not necessarily plan choice) despite the complexity of the program. Further, Levy and Weir report that the use of prescription drugs did not change dramatically in response to Medicare Part D. Neither does Part D appear to have reduced the extent of cost-related noncompliance among those who previously had no drug coverage. Levy and Weir conclude that the Part D program has experienced adverse selection but not moral hazard.

Lichtenberg and Sun (2007) also investigate the effect of Medicare Part D on prescription drug use and out-of-pocket costs of eligible seniors. Using data on prescription filled by a large retail pharmacy chain during the period September 2004 to December 2006, they estimate that Medicare Part D reduced user cost among the elderly by 18.4 percent, increased their use of prescription drugs by about 12.8 percent, and increased total U.S. usage by 4.5 percent in 2006. Lichtenberg and Sun estimate that every seven prescriptions paid for by the government crowded out five other prescriptions and resulted in only two additional prescriptions used. Yin et al. (2008) also conclude that the Medicare Part D prescription benefit resulted in modest increases in average drug utilization and decreases in average out-of-pocket expenditures among Part D beneficiaries. Using data from a random sample of pharmacy customers who were beneficiaries of the program after the enrollment deadline, they estimate that the drug benefit saved beneficiaries about nine dollars a month and gave them an extra fourteen days of pills, on average.

Two recent studies investigate the enrollment and plan choices of Medicare Part D-eligible individuals in more detail. Abaluck and Gruber (2009) evaluate the choices of elders across the wide array of Part D options using a data set of prescription drug claims matched to information on the characteristics of choice sets. They document that the vast majority of elders are choosing plans that are not on the "efficient portfolio" of plan choice in the sense that an alternative plan would have offered better risk protection at a lower cost. Their analysis suggests that individuals place much more weight on current plan premiums than on expected out-of-pocket costs. Further, individuals appear to place almost no value on variance reduction.

Kling et al. (2008) investigate suboptimal plan choice from another viewpoint; their analysis is motivated by recent models of individual misperception of prices. They present results from a randomized experiment conducted in the open-enrollment period at the end of 2006, which gave individuals an opportunity to switch plans. One group of seniors enrolled in Medicare drug plans was presented personalized information on the potential cost savings from changing to the lowest cost plan while another group received information about how to access the Medicare website, where this same information was available. The intervention group plan-switching rate was 28 percent, while the comparison group rate was 17 percent. Average predicted costs for 2007 were lower for the intervention group as a whole and lower for those potentially affected by the intervention.

Also related to the issue of whether consumers can make well-informed choices among a large number of plans available to them, Lucarelli, Prince, and Simon (2008) study the welfare impacts of limiting the number of Part D plans based on a joint estimation of plan supply and demand. They assess the effects on equilibrium premiums and welfare of reducing product differentiation and of reducing the maximum number of plans each firm can offer. Lucarelli and colleagues find that implied search costs would have to be at least two-thirds of the average monthly premium in order to justify a regulation that allows only two plans per firm. This number would be substantially lower if the limitation in the number of plans were to be coupled with a decrease in product differentiation (e.g., by removing plans that provide coverage in the gap).

5.3   The Retirement Perspectives Survey, 2005 to 2009

The Retirement Perspectives Survey is a research project conducted by the authors to study the feasibility of using Internet survey designs in elderly populations, and using treatments embedded in surveys to detect and mitigate survey response errors. Beginning in 2005, the continuing methodological research objectives have been combined with a substantive focus on consumer choices and experience in the Medicare Part D prescription drug program. Results from the first three waves of the Retirement Perspectives Study have been reported in a series of papers (Winter et al. 2006; Heiss, McFadden, and Winter 2006, 2009, 2010, McFadden, Winter, and Heiss 2008).

The four waves of the Retirement Perspectives Survey in 2005, 2006, 2007, and 2009 used a panel of individuals maintained by Knowledge Networks (KN), a commercial survey firm. The members of the KN Panel are enrolled using random-digit-dialing sampling to obtain a pool that is representative of the U.S. noninstitutionalized population in terms of demographics and socioeconomic status. Participants are provided with web TV hardware to respond to periodic survey elicitations with content from both commercial and academic clients. The KN Panel members are compensated for participation. The RPS respondents are somewhat younger, more educated, healthier, and computer-literate than the underlying population. For example, about half the panel members use the Internet, compared with about a third in the corresponding population. Sample weighting is used to adjust for attrition in the recruitment and retention process, and for nonresponse to specific surveys. For a detailed discussion of representativeness of the RPS sample and weighting procedures, we refer to Heiss, McFadden, and Winter (2010).

The first wave of our study, RPS-2005, was conducted in November 2005, just before the initial enrollment period for the new Medicare Part D prescription drug benefit began. This survey focused on prescription drug use and intentions to enroll in the new Medicare Part D program. Additional questions concerned long-term care, and a sequence of questions was designed to obtain simple measures of respondents' risk attitudes. In May 2006, after the initial enrollment period had ended, we administered the second wave (RPS-2006). For this survey, we recontacted the Medicare eligible respondents of RPS-2005 and elicited their prescription drug insurance status as well as their Part D decisions, including plan choice. The RPS-2007 and RPS-2009 were conducted in March/April 2007 and

February/March 2009, respectively; their samples consisted of reinterviewed respondents of earlier RPS waves plus refreshment cases. The four RPS interviews required between twenty-five and forty minutes for completion, with variations due to variations in the length of the questionnaire. Most socioeconomic and demographic variables were provided by Knowledge Networks as background on panel members, and were not requested again in the RPS questionnaires.

In table 5.1, we report sample sizes and participation rates for the various RPS waves and segments. Participation rates from the KN panel were generally rather high. For the first wave (RPS-2005), we contacted almost 6,000 KN Panel members aged fifty and older, and 80.6 percent of those invited to participate completed the questionnaire. For RPS-2006, we contacted only KN members who had completed RPS-2005 and were aged sixty-three years or older at the time of the interview (or in a few cases were younger but already on Medicare). The participation rate was again rather high at 82.3 percent. For RPS-2007 two groups were contacted: reinterviews of earlier RPS respondents (i.e., those who had completed either RPS-2005 only or both RPS-2005 and RPS-2006), and a refreshment sample of KN Panel members who had not participated in any prior RPS wave. The participation rate among these groups was the highest for those who had completed both RPS-2005 and RPS-2006 (89.6 percent), and slightly below the other rates for those who had completed RPS-2005 but missed RPS-2006 (76.6 percent). The participation rate for the refreshment sample was 81.5 percent and thus well in line with that in the comparable RPS-2005 sample.

For RPS-2009 we again contacted all previous RPS respondents and a refreshment sample. Since individuals remain on the KN Panel only for a limited time, the number of earlier RPS respondents that were successfully recontacted was relatively small. As consequence, only a fraction of respondents who were interviewed for RPS-2005 also completed all three subsequent interviews. Of the 2,119 RPS-2005 respondents aged sixty-four and older at the time of that interview, 710 (or 33.5 percent) completed all three subsequent interviews; 702 (or 33.1 percent) participated in 2006 and 2007, but not in 2009; 232 (11.0 percent) did not participate in any subsequent interview; and the remaining respondents have holes in their participation pattern over time. Response rates in 2009 were substantially lower than in earlier years, even in the refresher sample, which may indicate that public interest in Medicare Part D has declined relative to earlier years.

These numbers highlight the fact that Internet panels such as the KN Panel are not ideally suited for conducting panel studies over longer time periods since they are not built and administered with the aim of retaining respondents for periods of several years. In private correspondence, KN indicated that among those respondents who were still active in the KN Panel, participation rates achieved for the RPS interviews were higher than those typically observed in other studies that use the KN Panel. The KN

Table 5.1 Sample selection criteria and response rates for the four RPS waves

	RPS-2005	RPS-2006	RPS-2007				RPS-2009				
Age selection rule	50+	63+[a]	64+				64+				
			Subsamples				Subsamples				
Completed RPS-2005		Yes[b]	Yes	Yes	No		Yes	Yes	No	No	
Completed RPS-2006			Yes	No	No		Yes	No	No	No	
Completed RPS-2007							Yes	Yes	Yes	No	
KN members contacted	5,879	2,598	1,704	217	1,250	3,171	1,151	127	789	364	2,430
Completed interviews	4,738	2,137	1,526	165	1,020	2,711	783	77	534	207	1,601
Response rate[c]	80.6%	82.3%	89.6%	76.0%	81.6%	85.5%	68.0%	60.6%	67.7%	56.9%	65.9%

[a]In addition, RPS-2005 respondents younger than sixty-three years were contacted for RPS-2006 if they said that they are on Medicare.

[b]Completion of RPS-2005 was required for this subsample.

[c]The response rate is defined as the number of completed interviews as a proportion of the number of KN Panel members contacted.

attributed this to the highly topical subject of the RPS study. However, high participation rates conditional on still being in the panel cannot compensate for attrition from the panel. Attrition that is selective with respect to observed or unobserved variables would exacerbate these problems.

Table 5.2 contains a comparison of the distributions of key demographic characteristics in the Health and Retirement Study (HRS) 2006 and our analysis samples. For the three interviews in which we observe Medicare Part D enrollment and plan choices (i.e., the 2006, 2007, and 2009 interviews), we define the analysis samples as containing all RPS respondents aged sixty-five or older at the time of the 2006 interview (or at the time of their first interview if they entered the sample in 2007 or 2009 as members of the refreshment sample).[3] Despite the rather complicated structure of the overall RPS panel, the three analysis samples line up well with the HRS sample in terms of these key demographic characteristics; application of the sample weights supplied by Knowledge Networks tends to reduce any differences further. In our subsequent multivariate analysis, we do not use weights; see McFadden et al. (2006) for a discussion.

In our empirical analysis of enrollment decisions and plan choice, we consider the following groups of explanatory variables: socioeconomic characteristics supplied by Knowledge Networks as background variables (age, sex, race, education, and income); measures of current self-rated health status (SRHS) and drug use; and measures of decision-making competence, planning horizon, and attitudes toward risk. We describe these explanatory variables in the remainder of this section. Descriptive statistics are reported in the next section. The dependent variables are also described in section 5.4.

Age, sex, race, and education are naturally defined. The only income variable that is available as part of the KN background variables is total (gross) household income. The KN background data do not contain a measure of wealth.

Current health status is measured using the standard question on self-rated health status as used in the HRS and many other surveys: "How would you describe your current health?" with five response options (excellent, very good, good, fair, poor).

Our measure of current drug use[4] is based on the question, "How many different prescription drugs did you use last year in total (not counting multiple refills)?" We also asked respondents whether they expect their drug use to change: "How do you think the number of prescription drugs that you

---

3. We excluded a small number of observations from the analysis samples that had inconsistencies in key demographic variables.

4. In this chapter, the terms "current drug use" and "drug use in the previous year" are used interchangeably. When we consider enrollment in Medicare Part D for a given year, "current drug use" refers to drug use in the year when the enrollment decision was made (i.e., the "previous year").

Table 5.2   Socioeconomic characteristics, HRS 2006 vs. RPS 2006/2007/2009

	HRS 2006		RPS-2006		RPS-2007		RPS-2009	
	Unweighted (%)	Weighted (%)	Unweighted (%)	Weighted (%)	Unweighted (%)	Weighted (%)	Unweighted (%)	Weighted (%)
Gender								
Female	57.3	56.8	55.8	57.2	55.2	57.2	55.0	56.2
Male	42.7	43.2	44.2	42.8	44.8	42.8	45.0	43.8
Race								
White	83.5	89.3	87.6	83.3	87.0	82.4	84.0	81.5
Nonwhite	16.5	10.7	12.4	16.7	13.0	17.6	16.0	18.5
Age								
61–70	35.8	33.7	39.3	35.9	40.5	36.4	41.6	36.2
71–80	40.3	41.6	46.9	47.9	45.5	45.9	46.1	45.0
81–90	20.4	22.0	12.9	15.1	13.2	16.8	11.5	17.5
>90	3.5	2.7	0.9	1.1	0.9	0.9	0.8	1.2
Education								
Less than HS	31.5	28.3	12.9	26.1	13.1	23.1	12.6	22.4
High school	32.6	33.4	41.5	36.5	39.0	37.3	36.4	37.1
More than HS	36.0	38.4	45.6	37.5	47.9	39.6	51.0	40.5
Income								
<$20K	33.2	31.2	23.4	28.9	21.9	26.2	14.6	21.9
$20K–$60K	46.2	46.9	58.2	52.6	57.9	53.0	54.8	53.3
>$60K	20.6	21.9	18.4	18.5	20.2	20.8	30.6	24.8
SRHS								
Excellent	8.5	9.1	6.1	5.6	5.1	4.6	5.3	5.2
Very good	26.3	27.5	32.2	27.8	30.4	27.9	31.1	27.6
Good	31.6	32.4	39.5	41.8	39.9	41.4	41.0	42.1
Fair	23.3	22.2	18.1	19.8	19.9	20.8	18.3	20.9
Poor	10.3	8.8	4.0	4.9	4.4	5.2	4.1	4.1
Number of observations	11,399		1,666		2,463		1,552	

Notes: The HRS comparison sample consists of respondents aged sixty-five or older at the time of the HRS 2006 interview. The RPS analysis samples consist of respondents aged sixty-five or older at the time of the RPS-2006 interview (or for panel refreshers, at the time of their first RPS interview). A few respondents with inconsistent demographic information were also excluded from the analysis sample.

take on a regular basis will change over the next few years?" Three response options were provided (more, fewer, no change). In earlier RPS waves, we included a probabilistic measure of the subjective expectations with respect to drug use; this measure is not analyzed in this chapter. The RPS-2005, 2007, and 2009 questionnaires contained a series of questions that allows us to impute the respondent's total drug expenditure (evaluated at average pharmacy over-the-counter prices); we do not use this measure in the current version of this chapter (see Winter et al. [2006], and Heiss, McFadden, and Winter [2010], for detailed discussions).

In various RPS waves, we experimented with alternative measures of decision-making competence and preference variables. In the present chapter, we use the "Decision Making Competence" (DMC) scale developed by Bruine de Bruin, Parker, and Fischhoff (2007); an abbreviated version of that instrument was contained in the RPS-2007 questionnaire. For our subsequent analysis, we generated a median-split dummy from the raw DMC measure.

We also use simple measures of the respondent's planning horizon and risk attitudes that were contained in RPS-2009 as explanatory variables. The question on the planning horizon was taken from HRS: "What is your most important period for planning saving and spending?" This question had closed response options (the next few months; the next year; the next few years; the next five to ten years; more than ten years). We construct a dummy variable for responses that imply a planning horizon of more than one year.

The questions on risk attitudes were taken from the German Socio-Economic Panel; they have been used successfully to predict risk-related behavior in various domains (Dohmen et al. 2010). The first question is: "How do you see yourself: Are you generally a person who is fully prepared to take risks or do you try to avoid taking risks?" This question is followed by a series of similar domain-specific questions; in RPS-2009 we used the questions, "How prepared are you to take risks while driving?", ". . . in financial matters?", and ". . . with your health?" All four questions had closed response options on an 11-point scale with extremes labeled as "fully prepared to take risks" and "risk averse." For each measure, we construct a dummy variable for respondents who are prepared to take risks (i.e., who checked a response above the neutral response on the 11-point scale).

5.4   Analysis of Consumers' Medicare Part D Decisions

We begin by reviewing the sources of prescription drug coverage of the RPS respondents in 2006, 2007, and 2009. As noted before, the analysis sample contains respondents aged sixty-five and older who are eligible for Medicare Part D; however, not all eligible individuals had to make an active enrollment decision because of existing coverage from other sources that is comparable to the Medicare Part D standard plan (or better).

In each of the three RPS questionnaires fielded in 2006, 2007, and 2009, we asked a direct question on the source of prescription drug insurance with closed-form response options. While such a question has some potential for producing misclassified responses, our analysis of coverage in 2006 (see Heiss, McFadden, and Winter 2006) showed that RPS responses line up well with official enrollment figures provided by CMS. The top panel of table 5.3 replicates these figures; the bottom panels report comparable figures for 2007 and 2009. About 6 percent of eligible respondents remained without coverage in 2006; the numbers did not change much in 2007 and 2009. Note

Table 5.3   **Prescription drug insurance status, drug use, and self-rated health**

	No coverage	Automatic	Private	Part D	Total	Missing
Source of coverage in 2006						
Observations	94	827	299	349	1,569	97
Row percent	6.0	52.7	19.1	22.2	100.0	
Number of different prescription drugs taken in 2005 (column percent)						
No drugs	38.3	10.5	12.0	9.7	12.3	
1 or 2 drugs	34.0	24.4	30.4	29.2	27.2	
3 or more drugs	27.7	65.1	57.5	61.0	60.5	
Self-reported health status in 2006 (column percent)						
Excellent	14.9	5.4	5.7	5.7	6.1	
Very good or good	69.2	71.2	72.2	73.6	71.8	
Poor or fair	16.0	23.3	22.1	20.6	22.0	
Source of coverage in 2007						
Observations	128	970	707	510	2,315	148
Row percent	5.5	41.9	30.5	22.0	100.0	
Number of different prescription drugs taken in 2006 (column percent)						
No drugs	30.5	6.6	8.2	6.7	8.4	
1 or 2 drugs	36.7	22.5	25.6	22.0	24.1	
3 or more drugs	32.8	70.9	66.2	71.4	67.5	
Self-reported health status in 2007 (column percent)						
Excellent	12.5	5.4	4.7	3.9	5.2	
Very good or good	68.8	70.5	69.2	72.0	70.3	
Poor or fair	18.8	24.2	26.2	24.1	24.4	
Source of coverage in 2009						
Observations	90	599	481	313	1,483	69
Row percent	6.1	40.4	32.4	21.1	100.0	
Number of different prescription drugs taken in 2008 (column percent)						
No drugs	40.0	9.0	9.8	9.0	11.1	
1 or 2 drugs	26.7	21.0	24.3	20.8	22.4	
3 or more drugs	33.3	70.0	65.9	70.3	66.5	
Self-reported health status in 2009 (column percent)						
Excellent	8.9	5.4	4.8	5.1	5.3	
Very good or good	72.2	71.6	70.3	78.0	72.5	
Poor or fair	18.9	23.1	25.0	16.9	22.1	

Notes: "Private" includes prescription drug coverage as part of a Medicare Advantage program. "Part D" includes only Part D stand-alone plans.

Table 5.4   Means of covariates used in reduced-form regressions

	RPS-2006		RPS-2007		RPS-2009	
	Obs	Mean	Obs	Mean	Obs	Mean
Female	1,666	0.56	2,463	0.55	1,552	0.55
Nonwhite	1,666	0.12	2,463	0.13	1,552	0.16
Education: Less than high school	1,666	0.13	2,463	0.13	1,552	0.13
Education: More than high school	1,666	0.46	2,463	0.48	1,552	0.51
Age 70 and younger	1,666	0.47	2,463	0.46	1,552	0.46
Age 81 and older	1,666	0.14	2,463	0.14	1,552	0.12
Income <$20K	1,666	0.23	2,463	0.22	1,552	0.15
Income >$60K	1,666	0.18	2,463	0.20	1,552	0.31
SRHS excellent	1,666	0.22	2,463	0.24	1,552	0.22
SRHS poor or fair	1,666	0.06	2,463	0.05	1,552	0.05
1 or 2 drugs	1,666	0.27	2,463	0.25	1,552	0.22
3 or more drugs	1,666	0.60	2,463	0.66	1,552	0.66
Expects to use more drugs			2,431	0.15	1,538	0.16
DMC scale above median			2,362	0.50		
Planning horizon longer than one year					1,521	0.50
Prepared to take risks (general)					1,539	0.64
Prepared to take risks (health)					1,539	0.27
Prepared to take risks (financial)					1,542	0.42

Notes: All variables are defined as dummy variables.

also that the rates of item nonresponse on this key question were low in all three surveys (6 percent or less).

Table 5.3 also confirms our earlier finding of a strong association of prescription drug coverage and measures of current health. In all three RPS waves, respondents who take three or more prescription drugs on a regular basis are much more likely to have stand-alone Part D coverage than those who take fewer drugs. Similarly, respondents whose self-rated health is "excellent" are less likely to have stand-alone coverage. (We confirm these associations in multivariate regressions reported following). Finally, while table 5.3 shows some stability in responses over time, there are also some variations. For instance, the fractions of "automatic" and "private" coverage change from 2006 to 2007 but are similar in 2007 and 2009. The fractions of "no coverage" and "stand-alone Part D coverage" do not change over time.

Table 5.4 reports descriptive statistics for our explanatory variables. We have converted all variables into dummy variables; the left out categories are naturally defined. We chose to do this to ease interpretation of the regression results; we report the coefficients of logistic regressions as log-odds ratios. Also, the information loss from converting the age variable into a three-category measure turned out to be small, and the only other continuous variable, household income, may suffer from measurement error so that

Table 5.5   Logit regressions—prescription drug coverage from any source (all respondents)

Mean of dependent variable	RPS-2006	RPS-2007		RPS-2009	
	0.940	0.945	0.946	0.939	0.942
Female	0.5984**	0.9473	0.9595	1.1919	1.0972
Nonwhite	1.9583	2.3541**	2.4266**	1.8430	2.0211
Education: Less than high school	0.4654**	0.8546	0.9618	0.7101	0.776
Education: More than high school	1.1794	1.1494	1.145	0.8949	0.8862
Age 70 and younger	0.6480*	0.7182	0.6453*	0.5761**	0.6047*
Age 81 and older	1.2025	0.5948*	0.5610*	0.5440*	0.5368*
Income <$20K	1.4487	0.8838	0.8846	0.9630	1.0291
Income >$60K	2.0077*	1.7923*	1.8392*	2.0905**	1.9667**
SRHS excellent	0.9375	0.7776	0.831	0.8151	0.7129
SRHS poor or fair	0.5148*	0.5806*	0.5453*	1.0218	0.8206
1 or 2 drugs	2.8892***	2.8905***	2.9519***	3.8979***	3.7165***
3 or more drugs	8.3483***	10.110***	10.478***	10.812***	9.8519***
Expects to use more drugs			1.3576		1.3745
DMC scale above median			1.2753		
Planning horizon longer than one year					1.4572
Prepared to take risks (general)					0.9339
Prepared to take risks (health)					0.9005
Prepared to take risks (financial)					1.1251
Constant	6.4693***	4.4951***	3.8892***	3.7363***	3.4718***
Observations	1,569	2,315	2,204	1,483	1,425

Notes: All variables are defined as dummy variables. Coefficients are reported as odds ratios.
***Significant at the 1 percent level.
**Significant at the 5 percent level.
*Significant at the 10 percent level.

using a median split is a conservative approach. As can be seen from table 5.4, rates of item nonresponse are small for the covariates, even for the subjective measures.

In table 5.5, we begin our analysis with a reduced-form regression of whether an eligible respondent has prescription drug coverage from any source. The dependent variable is based on the direct question described earlier. We report a baseline specification with socioeconomic and health variables for 2006, 2007, and 2009; for 2007 and 2009 we also report specifications that add our measure of an expected increase in drug use (which, as we hasten to add, may be endogenous) and either the decision-making

Table 5.6   Logit regressions—Part D prescription drug coverage (active deciders)

	RPS-2006	RPS-2007		RPS-2009	
Mean of dependent variable	0.788	0.799	0.802	0.777	0.788
Female	0.7423	1.2741	1.3556	1.6853*	1.8143*
Nonwhite	1.2946	1.1643	1.2841	0.8646	1.0234
Education: Less than high school	0.4725**	0.7163	0.8406	0.8054	0.8570
Education: More than high school	1.1958	0.9256	0.9069	0.8332	0.7979
Age 70 and younger	0.4930**	0.7624	0.6657	0.6053	0.6031
Age 81 and older	1.0496	0.5449*	0.5399*	0.6577	0.7404
Income <$20K	1.6273	0.8746	0.8741	0.8810	0.9351
Income >$60K	1.5748	1.3768	1.4373	1.4639	1.2535
SRHS excellent	0.7197	0.6815	0.7585	0.5608	0.5774
SRHS poor or fair	0.5034	0.4723*	0.4514*	1.3835	1.1077
1 or 2 drugs	3.3766***	2.7943***	2.7018***	3.7034***	3.5037***
3 or more drugs	9.1045***	10.981***	10.774***	11.823***	11.699***
Expects to use more drugs			1.8346*		1.4768
DMC scale above median			1.3002		
Planning horizon longer than one year					2.4231***
Prepared to take risks (general)					1.0581
Prepared to take risks (health)					1.0209
Prepared to take risks (financial)					1.0261
Constant	1.5404	1.0856	0.8869	0.7989	0.467
Observations	443	638	605	403	387

Notes: All variables are defined as dummy variables. Coefficients are reported as odds ratios.
***Significant at the 1 percent level.
**Significant at the 5 percent level.
*Significant at the 10 percent level.

measure based on the DMC scale (2007 only) or the planning horizon and risk attitude measures (2009 only). The most striking result is that the number of drugs used in the previous year has the strongest effect as a predictor of drug coverage. Some socioeconomic variables are significant; the result that nonwhites were more likely to have coverage in 2007 is curious. Less surprising is the result that high-income respondents are more likely to have coverage—many of them have existing coverage via their (current or former) employer's health insurance.

The structure of table 5.6 is identical to that of table 5.5. The sample is restricted to "active deciders" (i.e., respondents without prior coverage from another source), and the dependent variable is whether they have a stand-alone Part D plan or remain without coverage. Most of these active deciders will have made their enrollment decision during the initial enrollment period in 2005/06; the reason why we report results also for 2007 and 2009 is that we want to test whether the additional "soft" variables obtained in those years have predictive power. As in table 5.5, current drug use remains a strong predictor of Part D coverage among the active deciders. Socioeconomic variables have little predictive power (as we reported in Heiss, McFadden, and Winter [2010]). Expecting to use more drugs has some predictive power in 2007; the planning horizon variable is significant and relatively strong in 2009. Measures of risk attitudes and decision-making competence are not significant in these regressions. This is somewhat surprising since these measures had predictive power for economic decisions in other studies; one reason for the lack of significance may be the relatively small sample of active deciders. In any case, these results confirm what we and others have found in other studies: current drug use is the strongest predictor of Medicare Part D enrollment among active deciders.

Also for active deciders, we looked at potential determinants of plan switching. This was first possible at the end of 2006 for 2007. Table 5.7 therefore reports results from RPS-2007 and 2009. The dependent variable is based on a direct question of whether the respondent was enrolled in the same stand-alone Part D plan in the previous year. The fraction of switchers was slightly below 14 percent in 2006 (for 2007) and close to 18 percent in 2008 (for 2009). The regressions show no variable with strong effects other than being nonwhite in the 2009 data. At this level of analysis, we cannot explain plan switching well with a small set of sociodemographic and health variables. The additional "soft" variables obtained in 2007 and 2009 also show no clear pattern.

Finally, we investigate plan type choice. Specifically, the dependent variable in the following set of regressions is whether a prescription drug plan has coverage in the gap (in most cases, this will be for generic drugs). We constructed this variable using the responses to a direct question that was asked to all respondents with prescription drug coverage from any source. Table 5.8, panel A, reports results for all these respondents, panel B only for active deciders. When we look at all respondents with coverage, the coefficients of the income variables suggest that the probability of having gap coverage increases with income. Using (more) drugs also increases the probability of having gap coverage. Females are less likely to have gap coverage, and nonwhites are more likely. These findings are in line with the fact that many of those with "automatic" enrollment (say, via their employer's health insurance) have gap coverage. When we look only at the active deciders, the coefficients of the income variable change—in this sample, respondents with lower incomes are more likely to have gap coverage (even though we control

Table 5.7   **Logit regressions—Part D plan switching (active deciders)**

	RPS 2007		RPS 2009	
Mean of dependent variable	0.134	0.139	0.176	0.177
Female	0.9653	0.964	0.7462	0.7289
Nonwhite	0.6612	0.6299	5.6205***	5.6288***
Education: Less than high school	1.0573	0.8166	0.5216	0.352
Education: More than high school	1.7903*	1.9129*	1.6731	1.7942
Age 70 and younger	1.3526	1.3948	0.6827	
Age 81 and older	0.7543	0.6261	0.6609	0.928
Income <$20K	0.5608	0.5865	0.9666	1.0872
Income >$60K	0.7111	0.6777	1.1222	1.1166
SRHS excellent	1.0965	1.1787	0.6608	0.7002
SRHS poor or fair	2.5675	2.5594	0.2448	0.2541
1 or 2 drugs	1.0739	1.1181	6.6095*	5.4491*
3 or more drugs	2.0942	1.8233	5.1503*	5.0242*
Expects to use more drugs		0.3094**		0.6447
DMC scale above median		1.1352		
Planning horizon longer than one year				1.184
Prepared to take risks (general)				0.3183*
Prepared to take risks (health)				1.9755
Prepared to take risks (financial)				1.4737
Constant	0.0699***	0.0864***	0.0433***	0.0472***
Observations	418	395	250	243

Notes: All variables are defined as dummy variables. Coefficients are reported as odds ratios.
***Significant at the 1 percent level.
**Significant at the 5 percent level.
*Significant at the 10 percent level.

for current drug use). As before, our measures of decision-making competence, planning horizon, and risk attitudes are not statistically significant as predictors of having gap coverage.

5.5   Conclusions

In this chapter, we investigated how older Americans made their decisions in the enrollment periods for the first four years of the new Medicare Part D prescription drug benefit. We analyzed data from four waves of the Retirement Perspectives Survey (RPS), which we designed specifically to obtain information on older Americans' health status and expenditures, their preferences, and their prescription drug insurance choices before and after the introduction of Medicare Part D. The main purpose of our analysis was to understand how consumers react to the economic incentives embedded in Medicare Part D. This is an important research question that goes far beyond the more pressing public policy issue of how successful the program was in terms of its stated goals. It is our view that understanding

Table 5.8 **Logit regressions—gap coverage**

A *All respondents with coverage from any source*

	RPS-2007		RPS-2009	
Mean of dependent variable	0.488	0.490	0.451	0.454
Female	0.7252***	0.7303***	0.7724**	0.7201***
Nonwhite	1.3710**	1.3555**	2.0925***	2.0367***
Education: Less than high school	1.0955	1.0831	0.9665	0.9835
Education: More than high school	1.1938*	1.2226**	0.8756	0.915
Age 70 and younger	0.9639	0.9419	0.931	0.9215
Age 81 and older	0.7334**	0.7269**	1.148	1.1382
Income <$20K	0.7466***	0.7752**	0.9331	0.9487
Income >$60K	1.3480***	1.3479**	1.3808**	1.3555**
SRHS excellent	0.8367*	0.8605	0.9532	0.974
SRHS poor or fair	0.8296	0.8566	1.4683	1.4628
1 or 2 drugs	1.5620**	1.4120*	1.4679*	1.4927*
3 or more drugs	1.5502**	1.3919*	1.5461**	1.5438**
Expects to use more drugs		0.7493**		1.0118
DMC scale above median		0.916		
Planning horizon longer than one year				1.0325
Prepared to take risks (general)				0.9144
Prepared to take risks (health)				0.8631
Prepared to take risks (financial)				0.9012
Constant	0.7399	0.88	0.5662**	0.6587
Observations	2,190	2,087	1,387	1,337

B *Active deciders*

Mean of dependent variable	0.125	0.124	0.107	0.108
Female	1.0534	1.0457	1.5672	1.5956
Nonwhite	1.834	1.5598	5.2845***	5.6204***
Education: Less than high school	1.5386	1.5436	0.2610*	0.1645**
Education: More than high school	1.0135	0.8863	0.3157***	0.3297***
Age 70 and younger	0.9987	0.9325	0.6866	0.764
Age 81 and older	0.8468	0.7497	1.8317	1.8744
Income <$20K	1.9645**	2.1019***	3.5823***	3.6767***
Income >$60K	1.2013	1.4106	1.4012	1.2763
SRHS excellent	0.7032	0.7854	0.6358	0.577
SRHS poor or fair	0.4223	0.4543	3.2805*	3.8187*
1 or 2 drugs	4.1067**	4.0492**	2.9162	2.3096
3 or more drugs	3.7745**	3.4656**	2.9982*	2.7202
Expects to use more drugs		0.5825		1.0072
DMC scale above median		0.8221		
Planning horizon longer than one year				0.8805
Prepared to take risks (general)				1.0065
Prepared to take risks (health)				1.0999
Prepared to take risks (financial)				0.6532
Constant	0.0319***	0.0414***	0.0339***	0.0440***
Observations	638	605	403	387

Notes: All variables are defined as dummy variables. Coefficients are reported as odds ratios.

***Significant at the 1 percent level.

**Significant at the 5 percent level.

*Significant at the 10 percent level.

whether and how consumers react to economic incentives in complex health insurance markets is an important part of the process of optimally designing social insurance programs such as Medicare Part D. This chapter can be interpreted as a first step in that direction.

Specifically, we asked whether eligible consumers without prescription drug coverage from other sources enrolled in Medicare Part D. Given the structure of the program, expected drug costs for the first year should be by far the most important determinant of those decisions. Our analysis confirmed this: enrollment seems to be driven strongly by the number of drugs used on a regular basis in 2005 (which should be a good predictor of 2006 drug use) and very little by other variables. This result is important since the introduction of Medicare Part D allows us to observe individual risk before any insurance decision: moral hazard cannot have affected drug use of those without coverage prior to the introduction of Medicare Part D. Our data therefore confirm (adverse) selection into this insurance program. In earlier research, we found a similar result when we used an imputed measure of drug costs rather than the number of drugs (Heiss, McFadden, and Winter 2010). This chapter adds to our earlier work by using data from the RPS waves 2007 and 2009, which also contained measures of decision-making competence, planning horizon, and risk attitudes. When we added those measures to our reduced-form regressions, they had little additional predictive power, however.

The overall conclusion from the empirical analysis presented in this chapter is that consumers respond to the *immediate* incentives that are induced by their current health status and drug expenditures combined with the salient, widely publicized features of the Medicare Part D program. To the extent that our measures approximate subjective factors well, they seem to have little effect. This result is, however, subject to further scrutiny.

We end by mentioning directions for future research on Medicare Part D and on consumer-directed health care, and on insurance markets more generally. One issue that deserves more attention is whether consumers' decisions are rational. We did not consider this issue in this chapter but refer to our earlier results (Heiss, McFadden, and Winter 2010) and ongoing research (Heiss, McFadden, and Winter 2009). The latter paper takes into account the intertemporal aspects of the enrollment decision that arise because of the late enrollment penalty (and that may be exacerbated by psychological switching costs). In that paper, we model enrollment and plan choice in stylized environment as a discrete dynamic decision process and confront the predictions from our behavioral model with data on individual enrollment and plan choice from the first three years of Medicare Part D. We view that more structural approach as complementary to the reduced-form analysis presented in this chapter.

References

Abaluck, J. T., and J. Gruber. 2009. Choice inconsistencies among the elderly: Evidence from plan choice in the Medicare Part D program. NBER Working Paper no. 14759. Cambridge, MA: National Bureau of Economic Research, February.

Bach, P. B., and M. B. McClellan. 2005. A prescription of a modern Medicare program. *New England Journal of Medicine* 353: 2733–35.

———. 2006. The first months of the prescription-drug benefit: A CMS update. *New England Journal of Medicine* 354:2312–14.

Bruine de Bruin, W., A. M. Parker, and B. Fischhoff. 2007. Individual differences in adult decision-making competence (A-DMC). *Journal of Personality and Social Psychology* 92:938–56.

Buntin, M. B., C. Damberg, A. Haviland, K. Kapur, N. Lurie, R. McDevitt, and M. S. Marquis. 2006. Consumer-directed health care: Early evidence about effects on cost and quality. *Health Affairs* 25:w516–30.

Dohmen, T., A. Falk, D. Huffman, U. Sunde, J. Schupp, and G. Wagner. Individual risk attitudes: Measurement, determinants, and behavioral consequences. *Journal of the European Economic Association* (forthcoming).

Duggan, M., P. Healy, and F. S. Morton. 2008. Providing prescription drug coverage to the elderly: America's experiment with Medicare Part D. *Journal of Economic Perspectives* 22 (4): 69–92.

Goldman, D. P., and G. F. Joyce. 2008. Medicare Part D: A successful start with room for improvement. *Journal of the American Medical Association* 299 (16): 1954–55.

Goodman, J. 2006. Consumer directed health care. Policy Brief 2006-PB-20, Networks Financial Institute, Indiana State University.

Gruber, J. 2008. Covering the uninsured in the U.S. NBER Working Paper no. 13758. Cambridge, MA: National Bureau of Economic Research, January.

Heiss, F., D. McFadden, and J. Winter. 2006. Who failed to enroll in Medicare Part D, and why? Early results. *Health Affairs* 25:w344–54.

———. 2009. Regulation of health insurance markets: Lessons from enrollment, plan choice, and adverse selection in Medicare Part D. NBER Working Paper no. 15392. Cambridge, MA: National Bureau of Economic Research, October.

———. 2010. Mind the gap! Consumer perceptions and choices of Medicare Part D prescription drug plans. In *Research findings in the economics of aging,* ed. D. A. Wise, 413–81. Chicago: University of Chicago Press.

Kling, J. R., S. Mullainathan, E. Shafir, L. Vermeulen, and M. V. Wrobel. 2008. Misperceptions in choosing Medicare drug plans. Unpublished Manuscript.

Levy, H., and D. Weir. 2008. The impact of Medicare Part D on drug utilization and out-of-pocket spending: Evidence from the Health and Retirement Study. Unpublished Manuscript.

———. 2010. Take-up of Medicare Part D: Results from the Health and Retirement Study. *Journal of Gerontology: Social Sciences* 65B (4): 492–501.

Lichtenberg, F. R., and S. X. Sun. 2007. The impact of Medicare Part D on prescription drug use by the elderly. *Health Affairs* 26 (6): 1735–44.

Lucarelli, C., J. Prince, and K. I. Simon. 2008. Measuring welfare and the effects of regulation in a government-created market: The case of Medicare Part D plans. NBER Working Paper no. 14296. Cambridge, MA: National Bureau of Economic Research, September.

McFadden, D., F. Heiss, B. Jun, and J. Winter. 2006. On testing for independence in weighted contingency tables. *Medium for Econometric Applications* 14 (2): 11–18.

McFadden, D., J. Winter, and F. Heiss. 2008. Consumer-directed health care: Can consumers look after themselves? *Swiss Journal of Economics and Statistics* 144 (3): 285–307.

Newhouse, J. P. 2004. Consumer-directed health plans and the RAND health insurance experiment. *Health Affairs* 23 (6): 107–13.

Winter, J., R. Balza, F. Caro, F. Heiss, B. Jun, R. Matzkin, and D. McFadden. 2006. Medicare prescription drug coverage: Consumer information and preferences. *Proceedings of the National Academy of Sciences of the United States of America* 103 (20): 7929–34.

Yin, W., A. Basu, J. X. Zhang, A. Rabbani, D. O. Meltzer, and G. C. Alexander. 2008. The effect of the Medicare Part D prescription benefit on drug utilization and expenditures. *Annals of Internal Medicine* 148: 169–77.

Comment   Amy Finkelstein

This is an excellent installment in a fruitful and fascinating line of ongoing work by this research team on the Medicare Part D program. This research program is motivated by two important and complementary goals. The first is evaluating the impact of the introduction of Medicare Part D. This was arguably the largest single expansion in social insurance in the United States since 1965. It is therefore an extremely important program to understand in its own right. The second goal, however, goes beyond this important policy evaluation to use the introduction of Medicare Part D as a tool for gaining insight more generally in consumer responsiveness to the economic incentives in social insurance programs. I am going to confine my comments to the second goal, but of course the importance of the application makes the analysis and results all the more interesting.

The current chapter examines the determinants of individual enrollment decisions and plan choices. It examines in particular the role of past drug use, self-rated health, and measures of the individual's time horizon (discount rate), risk attitudes, and decision-making competence. The main findings are twofold. First, prior drug use is a strong (positive) predictor of both whether the individual enrolls and the comprehensiveness of the plan chosen. Second, the other factors examined do not seem to have much explanatory power.

These results are fascinating for several reasons. The first finding—regarding the positive correlation between prior drug use and plan enrollment and comprehensiveness—provides clear evidence of a role for private information about risk type in influencing insurance decisions. Because adverse selection offers a canonical economic rationale for the existence of social

Amy Finkelstein is professor of economics at the Massachusetts Institute of Technology, and a research associate and codirector of the public economics program at the National Bureau of Economic Research.

insurance programs such as Medicare Part D, it is important and interesting to document its existence in this setting.

Moreover, although it might not be apparent from reading the chapter and seeing the seeming effortlessness by which the authors document adverse selection, doing so is in general quite challenging empirically. The widely-used "bivariate probit" test for asymmetric information pioneered by Chiappori and Salanié (2000) is the current industry standard. It rejects the null of symmetric information if there is a positive correlation between insurance coverage and ex post risk occurrence (among individuals who face the same option of contracts). A typical application would be to examine whether those with drug coverage (or those with more comprehensive drug coverage) use more drugs than those without drug coverage (or those with less comprehensive drug coverage). However, a long-recognized limitation of such analysis is that it is a joint test for the presence of either adverse selection or moral hazard. A finding that those with more drug coverage use more drugs may reflect either adverse selection (individuals who ex ante knew that they were higher risk for drug use selected more drug insurance) or moral hazard (ex post those who have more coverage have an incentive to consume more drugs). Since these are two very different forms of asymmetric information and since they have potentially very different public policy implications—the government may have a comparative advantage in ameliorating the welfare costs of adverse selection but does not generally have any comparative advantage in addressing the inefficiencies caused by moral hazard—distinguishing between them is of critical interest and importance.

The authors manage to do this by exploiting the panel nature of their data—and the fact that, prior to 2006, no one in their sample had drug coverage. As a result, their measure of "past drug use" (in 2005) is a pure measure of ex ante expected risk type, not contaminated by contract effects arising from differential insurance coverage (i.e., moral hazard). Their examination of whether drug use in 2005 among the then-uninsured predicts enrollment and plan choice when Medicare Part D opens in 2006 is thus a direct test for adverse selection. It is relatively rare to be able to exploit panel data to distinguish selection from moral hazard; for another example and more discussion of the uses of panel data for this purpose see Abbring and Chiappori (2003) and Abbring et al. (2003).

Their second main finding—that other than prior drug use (i.e., expected risk type) the other measured factors such as individual discount rates, risk attitudes, and decision-making competence do not appear to be important in explaining drug insurance choices—is also of note. In stands in contrast to several recent empirical papers in other insurance markets that have found that preference heterogeneity or heterogeneity in cognitive ability is as or more important than heterogeneity in privately known risk type in explaining insurance choices; these papers include applications to the U.S. long-term care insurance market (Finkelstein and McGarry 2006), the Israeli automobile insurance market (Cohen and Einav 2007), and—closest to the application in this chapter—the U.S. Medigap market for private insurance to supplement Medicare (Fang, Keane, and Silverman 2008). This evidence of heterogeneity in dimensions other than risk type (which influences insurance choices) is important because it suggests that the standard bivariate probit test of asymmetric information may fail to detect asymmetric information in the presence of multiple forms of heterogeneity (Finkelstein and McGarry 2006). It also suggests that the welfare consequences of imposing mandatory coverage in adversely selected markets may be more ambiguous than theories of unidimensional private information suggest (Einav, Finkelstein, and Schrimpf 2007).

The results in the current chapter that find no evidence for other forms of heterogeneity in determining insurance coverage are intriguing. One plausible explanation is that in this market the unidimensional models are a reasonable approximation. Another possibility is that other individual characteristics—such as risk aversion—do in fact affect insurance demand but are very hard to measure. The authors' work leaves open the interesting and important question of which explanation is correct; since these have different implications for—among other things—the value of mandatory insurance coverage, more work on this question would be greatly valuable.

In particular, given the authors' finding of adverse selection in this market, a natural question concerns the value of offering choice in Medicare Part D. A distinguishing feature of the design of Medicare Part D—relative to traditional Medicare Parts A and B—is that it allows the beneficiaries choice in the nature of their insurance benefit. This opens up scope for adverse selection (as the authors demonstrate indeed appears to be the case) and the resulting allocative inefficiency that adverse selection produces.

Their documentation of adverse selection raises the question of whether a mandatory (uniform) drug coverage plan would be socially optimal. This is conceptually ambiguous. When individuals differ in their preferences as well as their risk type, mandatory uniform coverage involves a trade-off: it can redress the allocative inefficiency induced by adverse selection, but at the cost of potentially imposing allocative inefficiency by requiring individuals whose first-best (symmetric information) insurance allocation may differ to all have the same coverage. Which source of inefficiency is larger—and therefore whether or not the gains from allowing choice in insurance exceed the costs—is an empirical question (see Einav, Finkelstein, and Cullen [2008] for an empirical approach to examining this question). In the context of Medicare Part D, it is also a very important policy question and one that I hope future work in this area will address.

References

Abbring, J. H., and P. Chiappori 2003. Moral hazard and dynamic insurance data. *Journal of the European Economic Association* 1:767–820.

Abbring, J. H., P. Chiappori, J. J. Heckman, and J. Pinquet. 2003. Adverse selection and moral hazard in insurance data: Can dynamic data help to distinguish? *Journal of the European Economic Association* 1 (Papers and Proceedings): 512–21.

Chiappori, P., and B. Salanié. 2000. Testing for asymmetric information in insurance markets. *Journal of Political Economy* 108 (1): 56–78.

Cohen, A., and L. Einav. 2007. Estimating risk preferences from deductible choice. *American Economic Review* 97 (3): 745–88.

Einav, L., A. Finkelstein, and M. R. Cullen. 2008. Estimating welfare in insurance markets using variation in prices. NBER Working Paper no. 14414. Cambridge, MA: National Bureau of Economic Research, October.

Einav, L., A. Finkelstein, and P. Schrimpf. 2007. The welfare cost of asymmetric information: Evidence from the U.K. annuity market. NBER Working Paper no. 13228. Cambridge, MA: National Bureau of Economic Research, July.

Fang, H., M. P. Keane, and D. Silverman. 2008. Sources of advantageous selection: Evidence from the Medigap insurance market. *Journal of Political Economy* 116 (2): 303–50.

Finkelstein, A., and K. McGarry. 2006. Multiple dimensions of private information: Evidence from the long-term care insurance market. *American Economic Review* 96 (4): 938–58.

III

Socioeconomic Circumstances and Health

Differential Mortality by Income and Social Security Progressivity

Gopi Shah Goda, John B. Shoven,
and Sita Nataraj Slavov

6.1   Introduction

There is a widespread belief that people with low lifetime labor income have higher age-specific mortality and lower remaining life expectancies at age sixty or sixty-five than those with middle or high lifetime earnings. Historically, there was very little evidence to either support or undermine this belief. The evidence that did exist found mortality differences by current labor income that could not be easily translated to measures based on lifetime income due to reverse causality issues: someone with poor health status is likely to have low current earnings as well as high mortality. Recently, however, new estimates of the mortality gap by lifetime income and its trend over time have been produced.

In this chapter, we assess the implications of differential mortality by lifetime income for the progressivity of the "old-age" or retirement portion of Social Security. Social Security has a highly progressive benefit formula to determine monthly payments in that those with low lifetime earnings get a much higher replacement rate than those with high lifetime earnings. For example, Social Security might replace 70 percent of earnings for someone with a full-length career in the bottom quartile of the earnings distribution,

Gopi Shah Goda is the Postdoctoral Fellow Program coordinator and research scholar at the Stanford Institute for Economic Policy Research. John B. Shoven is the Charles R. Schwab Professor of Economics at Stanford University, and a research associate of the National Bureau of Economic Research. Sita Nataraj Slavov is associate professor of economics at Occidental College.

This research was supported by the National Institute of Aging through grant #P30-AG012810 to the National Bureau of Economic Research. The opinions and conclusions expressed are solely those of the authors and do not represent the opinions or policy of NIA or any agency of the federal government. The authors would like to thank Andrew Hung and Mod Lueprasitsakul for superb research assistance.

but only 30 percent of earnings for someone in the top quartile. The rationale for this pattern is that those in the higher earnings brackets presumably have more opportunities to accumulate pensions and private saving to help finance their retirement.

However, the recent studies on the mortality gap by lifetime income suggest that at least some of this progressivity is counterbalanced by the longer average lifetimes experienced by higher lifetime income recipients of Social Security. Because the old-age benefits of Social Security benefits are paid as a life annuity, groups with higher life expectancies have higher returns than those with lower life expectancies. We do not examine the disability portion of Social Security in this study. Disability benefits are presumably progressive in that those with lower lifetime earnings are more likely to have experienced partial or total disabilities.

The recent literature on differential mortality by lifetime income allow us to reassess the progressivity of the retirement portion of Social Security by calculating internal rates of return and net present values for the program under assumptions of differential mortality. We compare these measures of progressivity to the same measures calculated, assuming all individuals experience average population mortality rates. Under the assumption of constant mortality across lifetime income subgroups, the Social Security system is progressive regardless of the measure shown. However, a good deal of the progressivity is undone or even reversed when differential mortality is taken into account. The results are similar for both stylized earners at different points of the earnings distribution and actual workers' earnings histories.

The chapter proceeds as follows. Section 6.2 discusses the literature on Social Security progressivity and differential mortality by income. Section 6.3 describes the earnings and mortality data used, as well as the way that earnings histories and differential mortality estimates were developed from these data sources. The methodology used to calculate internal rates of return and net present values is described in section 6.4, and results are presented in section 6.5. Section 6.6 concludes.

6.2   Literature Review

A handful of studies have analyzed the relationship between mortality and Social Security progressivity. Early studies include Aaron (1977), Steuerle and Bakija (1994), and Garrett (1995). These studies calculate returns to Social Security for hypothetical workers and suggest that differential mortality reduces the amount of progressivity in Social Security. More recent studies, including Coronado, Fullerton, and Glass (2000) and Liebman (2001), examine the redistribution in the old-age portion of Social Security more generally. Coronado, Fullerton, and Glass (2000) proceed in several steps, reclassifying Social Security recipients by different measures of income and incorporating mortality probabilities that differ by income. They conclude that the system is far less progressive than it first appears, and may even be regressive under certain assumptions. Liebman (2001) uses a microsimulation model to show that Social Security becomes less redistributive when mortality is assumed to differ by race and education. Both of these more recent studies perform calculations for a data set of individual earning histories based on a combination of survey, administrative, and imputed data. The Congressional Budget Office (CBO 2006) makes the point that when disability and survivor benefits are taken into account, Social Security is more progressive than when only retirement benefits are considered.

Many of these studies use estimates of differential mortality from several decades ago. Garrett (1995) uses stylized earnings histories and mortality differentials estimated in the 1960s and 1970s in Kitagawa and Hauser (1973). Coronado, Fullerton, and Glass (2000) apply a crude adjustment to mortality ratios based on mortality differentials by annual income. The authors acknowledge that annual income may be lower due to illness preceding death, and that their estimates may be biased as a result of reverse causality. However, the estimates they use from Rogot, Sorlie, and Johnson (1992) were the best available estimates of differential mortality by income available at the time.

Recent research has produced new estimates of how mortality differs by lifetime income, as well as suggestive evidence that the mortality inequality by income has been growing over time (Singh and Siahpush 2006; Cristia 2007; Waldron 2007; CBO 2008; Jemal et al. 2008; Duggan, Gillingham, and Greenlees 2006). These studies are broadly consistent in their conclusions, and are based on richer and more recent data than previous estimates of differential mortality. In this study, we rely on estimates in Cristia (2007) and Waldron (2007), as described in the following section, to generate mortality probabilities that differ by measures of lifetime income.

6.3   Data

6.3.1   Mortality

We begin with mortality data obtained by request from the Social Security Administration. The data consists of cohort life tables that underlie the 2007 Trustees Report. For cohorts born in 1925 and later, Social Security provides projected mortality rates under three different alternatives (I, II, III). The intermediate scenario, or Alternative II, is used in our analysis for cohorts born after 1925.

Waldron (2007) provides estimates of odds ratios (the mortality rate of the bottom half of the income distribution relative to the mortality rate of the top half of the income distribution) for men in five cohorts, broken down into five-year age groups between sixty and eighty-nine. The measure of income used in Waldron (2007) is average nonzero earnings from age

Table 6.1   Mortality of bottom half relative to top half of lifetime income distribution (males)

Year of birth	Age					
	60–64	65–69	70–74	75–79	80–84	85–89
1912–1915	**1.27**	**1.24**	**1.20**	**1.13**	**1.09**	**0.94**
1916–1919	**1.51**	**1.36**	**1.34**	**1.20**	**1.05**	0.90
1920–1923	**1.50**	**1.40**	**1.34**	**1.31**	*1.22*	*1.07*
1924–1927	**1.51**	**1.53**	**1.48**	*1.40*	*1.31*	*1.16*
1928–1931	**1.71**	**1.61**	*1.57*	*1.49*	*1.39*	*1.24*
1932–1935	**1.75**	**1.73**	*1.69*	*1.61*	*1.51*	*1.36*
1936–1938	**1.84**	*1.78*	*1.73*	*1.65*	*1.56*	*1.41*

forty-five to fifty-five. Waldron's estimates are shown in bold in table 6.1. The first cell, for example, indicates that an individual between the ages of sixty and sixty-four in the bottom half of the lifetime income distribution has a probability of dying that is 1.27 times higher than an individual in the top half of the distribution. Note that for all cohorts, these odds ratios decline as individuals age. In fact, mortality inequality disappears by the time the 1912 to 1915 birth cohort reaches ages eighty-five to eighty-nine (the bottom half is even estimated as having a slightly lower mortality rate).

Waldron's estimates end at the last observed age for each cohort—for example, while estimates are available through age eighty-nine for the 1912 to 1915 cohort, they are only available through age sixty-four for the 1936 to 1938 cohort. We perform a back-of-the-envelope calculation to estimate odds ratios for the remaining unobserved cohort/age group combinations. First, for each cohort, we compute the difference in the observed odds ratio when moving from one age group to the next. For example, for the 1912 to 1915 cohort, the odds ratio decreases by 0.03 when moving from the sixty to sixty-four age group to the sixty-five to sixty-nine age group; it falls by 0.04 when moving from sixty-five to sixty-nine to seventy to seventy-four. For each age group, we then compute the average difference across cohorts. For example, when moving from the sixty to sixty-four age group to the sixty-five to sixty-nine age group, the average decline (across the six cohorts for which we have observed odds ratios) in the odds ratio is 0.06. We use the average decreases in the odds ratios to estimate odds ratios for the missing cohort/age groups. In the case of the 1936 to 1938 cohort, the odds ratio is assumed to fall by 0.06 (from 1.84 to 1.78). Thus, we assume that mortality inequality declines with age in a similar way for each cohort. Our estimates are shown in italic.

We develop a similar table for women by incorporating estimates from Cristia (2007), which suggest that there is less mortality inequality among women. Cristia's estimates suggest that a male aged sixty-five to seventy-five in the second quintile (which includes the twenty-fifth percentile) has a mortality rate that is 1.14 times the average (for males in that age group), while a

Table 6.2   **Mortality of bottom half relative to top half of lifetime income distribution (females)**

| | Age | | | | | |
Year of birth	60–64	65–69	70–74	75–79	80–84	85–89
1912–1915	1.13	1.10	1.07	1.00	0.97	0.84
1916–1919	1.34	1.21	1.19	1.07	0.93	0.80
1920–1923	1.33	1.24	1.19	1.16	1.08	0.95
1924–1927	1.34	1.36	1.32	1.24	1.16	1.03
1928–1931	1.52	1.43	1.39	1.32	1.24	1.10
1932–1935	1.56	1.54	1.50	1.43	1.34	1.21
1936–1938	1.64	1.58	1.54	1.47	1.39	1.25

male aged sixty-five to seventy-five in the fourth quintile (which includes the seventy-fifth percentile) has a mortality rate that is 0.94 times the average. Thus, the odds ratio for the second quintile relative to the fourth is 1.21. Similarly, a woman aged sixty-five to seventy-five in the second quintile has a mortality rate that is 1.11 times the average, while a woman aged sixty-five to seventy-five in the fourth quintile has a mortality rate that is 1.03 times the average. The implied odds ratio for the second to fourth quintiles is 1.08. The second/fourth quintile odds ratio for women is 88.9 percent of the second/fourth quintile odds ratio for men. We assume the top half/bottom half odds ratios for women are 88.9 percent of the corresponding male odds ratios—these are shown in table 6.2.

In our simulations, we consider the mortality experience of four cohorts: 1915, 1923, 1931, and 1939. For these cohorts, we model inequality by using the odds ratios associated with the 1912 to 1915, 1920 to 1923, 1928 to 1931, and 1936 to 1938 birth cohorts, respectively. We construct age-specific mortality rates for the bottom half and top half in such a way that their ratio is equal to the relevant odds ratio from tables 6.1 and 6.2, and their average is equal to the overall mortality rate from the Social Security Administration's cohort life table. For individuals above age eighty-nine, we apply the odds ratios for ages eighty-five to eighty-nine. For individuals aged twenty to fifty-nine, we apply the odds ratios for the sixty to sixty-four age group. Cristia's (2007) results suggest that mortality inequality is even higher among age groups below the age of sixty. Thus, applying the sixty to sixty-four odds ratios to younger age groups biases the results in the direction of less mortality inequality.

We calculate several measures of life expectancy and mortality risk from the resulting mortality tables. The results are summarized in table 6.3. They show that the bottom half has shorter life expectancies and lower survival rates than median income workers, and the top half has longer life expectancies and higher rates of survival. In addition, the tables show that the projected differences in mortality are widening: while the differential of the

Table 6.3   Projected mortality measures by gender, cohort, and lifetime income

	Males			Females		
Cohort	Top half	Med income	Bottom half	Top half	Med income	Bottom half
	Cohort life expectancy at age 20					
1915	52.25	50.91	49.65	57.93	57.63	57.35
1923	54.86	52.55	50.48	59.94	58.87	57.84
1931	57.34	54.18	51.49	61.61	59.79	58.11
1939	59.35	55.65	52.63	63.06	60.72	58.67
	Cohort life expectancy at age 60					
1915	18.95	18.26	17.60	22.99	23.00	23.03
1923	20.56	19.28	18.13	23.78	23.25	22.73
1931	22.16	20.22	18.59	24.74	23.56	22.49
1939	23.58	21.89	19.91	25.72	24.03	22.58
	Cohort life expectancy at age 65					
1915	15.72	15.20	14.70	19.13	19.21	19.32
1923	17.07	16.05	15.13	19.80	19.41	19.04
1931	18.47	16.83	15.45	20.65	19.66	18.75
1939	19.69	18.25	16.52	21.56	20.05	18.77
	Probability of survival to age 65 conditional on survival to age 20					
1915	0.708	0.676	0.645	0.817	0.807	0.796
1923	0.762	0.712	0.665	0.853	0.831	0.809
1931	0.805	0.745	0.689	0.878	0.848	0.820
1939	0.838	0.791	0.738	0.896	0.865	0.835

cohort life expectancy at age twenty between high income and low income men born in 1915 was 0.58 years, it is projected to grow to 4.4 years for the 1939 cohort. Differentials are smaller for women (by construction) and have the same increasing pattern.

We believe that the income-specific mortality information of Waldron and Cristia is superior to previous estimates. Still, the data are limited. Rather than analyzing the mortality differences between those in the top and bottom halves of the lifetime earnings distributions, we would have liked to have the information by lifetime income decile so that we could examine the mortality experience of the genuinely poor versus those at other parts of the distribution. It seems likely that the extent of mortality inequality is even greater than reflected in the top half/bottom half analysis.

6.3.2   Earnings

We analyze measures of progressivity calculated for stylized workers with earnings at the twenty-fifth, fiftieth, and seventy-fifth percentiles as well as for a large sample of actual earnings histories. The earnings data we use are based on the Benefits and Earnings Public-Use File, 2004. This data source contains earnings histories and other administrative data for a 1 percent random sample of Social Security beneficiaries in December 2004. Because

Social Security did not record annual earnings until 1951 but did record aggregated earnings over the period 1937 to 1950, we omit individuals who had nonzero earnings prior to 1951 so that our final sample contains complete earnings histories. We also limit the sample to those individuals who are receiving Social Security retirement benefits based on their own earnings history, as the data do not contain any way to link married couples. The remaining sample contains 125,829 observations.

We develop earnings to match the cohorts for whom we have estimates of differential mortality. The youngest cohort we examine is the cohort born in 1936 to 1939. We pool the cohorts in the Benefits and Earnings Public-Use file born in these years (33,632 men and 20,429 women), and calculate each individual's average nonzero earnings from age forty-five to fifty-five, denoted by $\overline{EARN}_{45-55}$. This figure is used to classify earners into the bottom half and the top half of the earnings distribution, consistent with Waldron (2007). The classification is done separately by year of birth and by gender. In our subsequent analysis under the assumption of differential mortality, the individuals classified into the "top half" category are assumed to experience mortality rates developed for the top half of the earnings distribution, and individuals classified into the "bottom half" category are assumed to experience the less favorable mortality rates developed for the bottom half of the earnings distribution. The mortality rates are based on Waldron (2007), as described previously.

After individuals are classified into these two earnings groups, we generate six stylized earnings histories: for the twenty-fifth, fiftieth, and seventy-fifth percentile male worker as determined by $EARN_{45-55}$, and a similar set for women. To construct earnings histories for earlier cohorts, we scale back earnings appropriately using Social Security's average wage index.[1]

The earnings profiles for the stylized workers for the 1936 to 1939 birth cohorts are shown in figure 6.1. The earnings are reported in nominal dollars in the year they were earned. The stylized workers at the seventy-fifth percentile experience the steepest increases by age. The last year of earnings observed in the data is 2003, and we assume that 2003 marks the final year of work for this sample.

While examining the progressivity of the stylized workers illustrates the impact differential mortality can have on the distribution of retirement benefits and allows comparison to earlier literature, the stylized earnings histories are unrealistic because the position of actual workers in the earnings distribution moves from one year to the next and people do not stay at the twenty-fifth or seventy-fifth percentile of the income distribution for their entire career. Therefore, we also supplement our analysis with measures of progressivity computed for each worker in our original sample.

---

1. This method is used instead of generating each cohort's earnings histories directly from the sample because of the lack of annual earnings data from 1937 to 1950.

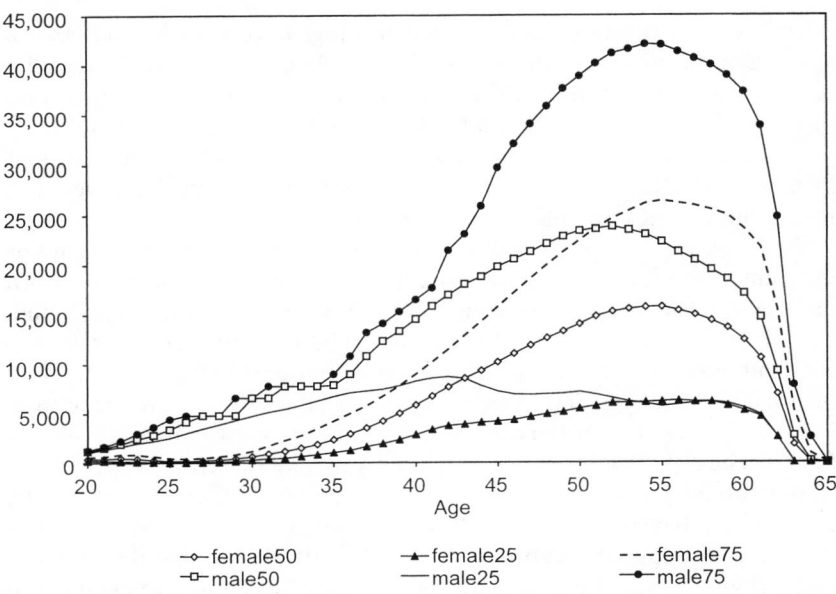

Fig. 6.1   Stylized earnings profiles, birth cohorts 1936–1939

6.4   Measures of Progressivity

We derive measures of the progressivity of Social Security for both the stylized earnings profiles described in the previous section, as well as the sample of earnings histories used to generate the stylized profiles. First, we calculate each worker's Social Security benefits under current law using the worker's whole series of earnings. Each year of earnings is first indexed forward to age sixty of the worker using Social Security's average wage index series. From these indexed earnings, the highest thirty-five values are then added up and divided by 420 to arrive at the Average Indexed Monthly Earnings, or AIME. The AIME includes zeroes if an individual worked less than thirty-five years.

Next we determine each individual's Primary Insurance Amount (PIA) by using the current (2008) nonlinear PIA formula, which encompasses the progressivity in the Social Security system. For retirees turning sixty-two in 2008, the PIA is equal to 90 percent of the first $711 of AIME, plus 32 percent of AIME above $711 and less than $4,288, plus 15 percent of AIME above $4,288. For retirees in earlier cohorts, the thresholds (commonly referred to as bend points) are adjusted with the average wage index. Through this formula, workers with lower levels of AIME receive higher replacement rates from Social Security. The full PIA is payable to workers who retire at the designated normal retirement age for their cohort. The PIA is paid as an inflation-indexed life annuity, which ends at death. We assume the worker claims benefits at his or her normal retirement age, and the stream of benefits represents the cash outflows from the program.

The Social Security payroll tax is 12.4 percent, paid equally by the employee and the employer; however, it is commonly assumed that the employee bears the full amount of this tax. The portion used to fund retirement and survivor benefits is 10.6 percent, and the remaining 1.8 percent is used to fund disability benefits. We therefore use 10.6 percent of earnings in each year to represent the cash inflows to the program corresponding to the Social Security retirement benefits calculated for each worker.

We convert these nominal cash flows to real cash flows using the Consumer Price Index (CPI), and finally adjust the stream of cash flows for mortality using the tables described in the previous section. Each set of cash flows is subject to two different sets of mortality assumptions. Under homogenous mortality, all cash flows are adjusted using population-average mortality appropriate for the worker's birth cohort. Under differential mortality, all cash flows are adjusted using the income-specific mortality table applicable to the worker. For the stylized workers, the twenty-fifth percentile worker is the median of the bottom half and is therefore assumed to experience the mortality rates constructed for the bottom half. Similarly, the seventy-fifth percentile worker is assigned top half mortality, and the median worker uses the average mortality rates of the population. For the actual worker's earnings histories, we classify workers by calculating $\overline{EARN}_{45-55}$ and apply top half mortality to those with $\overline{EARN}_{45-55}$ above the median and bottom half mortality to those with $\overline{EARN}_{45-55}$ below the median.

Under both sets of mortality assumptions, we present two measures of Social Security progressivity: the internal rate of return (IRR), and the net present value (NPV). The IRR is the rate of return that equates the present value of cash inflows to the present value of cash outflows. We compute the IRRs of the expected cash flows from Social Security (as just described). Thus, our IRR measure can be interpreted as the return earned in the aggregate by individuals with the same earnings history within a particular cohort.[2] A rate of return of 2 percent indicates that Social Security is comparable to a safe investment that earns 2 percent each year. The NPV is simply the difference between the discounted present value of all expected cash inflows and outflows, calculated using a safe real rate of return of 2 percent. The NPV is reported in constant 2008 dollars.

---

2. Because the IRR is nonlinear, this is different from the expected IRR earned by an individual with that earnings profile. To find the expected IRR for an individual, we would have to compute the IRRs conditional on survival to every possible age, and then calculate the expected value using the relevant mortality profile. The difficulty in performing this calculation is that if the individual dies before reaching retirement age, the IRR is negative infinity. This distinction is not important for our other measure, the net present value (NPV). Because the NPV is linear, the NPV for a group in the aggregate is the same as the expected NPV for a member of the group.

It is important to emphasize that we are not calculating the rates of return to Social Security actually experienced by people born in 1915, 1923, 1931, and 1938. Rather, what we are analyzing is how they would have done if the 2008 structure of Social Security (adjusted backwards for changes in average wages) had been in effect for their entire lifetimes. By assuming workers in all cohorts receive benefits based on current law, we are ignoring the large start-up gains that older cohorts received because of the growth of Social Security in the 1950s and 1960s and its pay-as-you-go nature. This assumption allows us to isolate the changes in progressivity due solely to changes in mortality and mortality inequality. In reality, older cohorts earned far higher internal rates of return as they paid Social Security taxes during times of relatively low tax rates, but received benefits based on more generous benefit formulas.

6.5   Results

We begin by computing internal rates of return and net present values (as described earlier) for our stylized workers. These results are shown in table 6.4. In each case the "unadjusted" column contains the results obtained using homogeneous mortality. The "adjusted" columns use differential mortality. That is, we use the mortality profile of the bottom half for the twenty-fifth percentile, the mortality profile of the top half for the seventy-fifth percentile, and the average mortality profile for the fiftieth percentile.

Overall, women experience higher IRRs and NPVs compared to men because of their longer life expectancies. Men at all income levels have IRRs that are below the 2 percent level that would be obtained from a safe investment; correspondingly, their NPVs are always negative. In all cohorts, women at the median income and below obtain IRRs that are above 2 percent (and therefore have positive NPVs). In the 1915 and 1923 cohorts, women at the seventy-fifth percentile obtain IRRs that are below 2 percent (and negative NPVs); in later cohorts, these high-income women also obtain IRRs that are above 2 percent. In general, for both men and women, later cohorts experience higher IRRs and NPVs than earlier ones. This is attributable to increases in life expectancy for these later cohorts.

For the 1915 cohort, differential mortality makes virtually no difference to the IRRs earned by women, and a relatively small difference to the IRRs earned by men (it lowers the IRR by 0.21 percentage points for low-income men, and raises it by 0.24 percentage points for high-income men). The changes in the NPVs for women are in the $100 to $200 range (with the NPV of the twenty-fifth percentile falling, and the NPV of the seventy-fifth percentile rising), while the changes in the NPVs for men are in the $1,000 to $2,000 range. For younger cohorts, however, differential mortality has a significantly larger effect, reflecting the fact that mortality inequality is much larger for the younger cohorts. For example, in the 1938 cohort,

Table 6.4   **Results for stylized workers**

	Internal Rate of Return			Net Present Value (at age 20, 2008 dollars)		
	Unadjusted (%)	Adjusted (%)	Difference (%)	Unadjusted	Adjusted	Difference
1915						
Female 25th	3.09	3.06	−0.02	4,283.05	4,179.22	−103.82
Female 50th	2.09	2.09		692.89	692.89	
Female 75th	1.24	1.26	0.02	−9,083.35	−8,897.23	186.12
Male 25th	0.35	0.14	−0.21	−17,602.32	−18,967.45	−1,365.13
Male 50th	−0.53	−0.53		−39,099.20	−39,099.20	
Male 75th	−0.99	−0.75	0.24	−56,917.35	−54,783.07	2,134.29
1923						
Female 25th	3.77	3.64	−0.13	8,826.74	7,936.54	−890.21
Female 50th	2.64	2.64		6,313.99	6,313.99	
Female 75th	1.86	2.00	0.13	−1,984.42	−63.21	1,921.21
Male 25th	1.03	0.71	−0.33	−12,629.79	−15,707.69	−3,077.90
Male 50th	0.29	0.29		−32,843.89	−32,843.89	
Male 75th	−0.05	0.33	0.38	−48,684.20	−42,905.36	5,778.84
1931						
Female 25th	4.01	3.79	−0.22	11,287.51	9,493.64	−1,793.87
Female 50th	2.81	2.81		8,773.85	8,773.85	
Female 75th	2.06	2.30	0.24	967.94	5,105.37	4,137.43
Male 25th	1.19	0.78	−0.42	−12,334.26	−17,010.02	−4,675.75
Male 50th	0.58	0.58		−31,813.90	−31,813.90	
Male 75th	0.33	0.81	0.49	−46,426.82	−36,513.17	9,913.65
1938						
Female 25th	4.41	4.14	−0.27	15,994.82	13,224.33	−2,770.49
Female 50th	3.15	3.15		14,632.08	14,632.08	
Female 75th	2.41	2.71	0.30	7,805.31	14,528.04	6,722.73
Male 25th	1.51	1.07	−0.44	−9,156.76	−15,636.60	−6,479.83
Male 50th	1.00	1.00		−27,309.54	−27,309.54	
Male 75th	0.75	1.28	0.53	−41,733.36	−27,131.87	14,601.48

differential mortality reduces the IRR from 1.51 percent to 1.07 percent for low-income men, and raises it from 0.75 percent to 1.28 percent for high-income men. In fact, once differential mortality is taken into account, males in the seventy-fifth percentile in the two later cohorts receive higher rates of return than males in the twenty-fifth percentile. At least in terms of rates of return, an apparently progressive system becomes regressive. For men in earlier cohorts, and for women in all the cohorts, Social Security remains progressive, although the progressivity is reduced when differential mortality is taken into account.

Our results for stylized workers are comparable to those reported in Garrett (1995), who computes IRRs and NPVs for stylized men, women, and couples in the 1925 birth cohort at different income levels. There are a few significant differences between Garrett's computation and ours. As discussed in the literature review, Garrett uses mortality differentials based on current income that were estimated in the 1960s and 1970s in Kitagawa and Hauser

(1973). Garrett also does not adjust for age in computing wage profiles—for example, in each year, a fiftieth percentile worker earns the income of the median family. (However, he reports in a footnote that adjusting for age does not change his results substantially.) Finally, Garrett allows mortality to vary according to whether a worker is in the bottom quintile or the top four quintiles. Thus, differential mortality lowers the IRRs for the twentieth percentile and below and raises the IRRs for all others. Moving from homogeneous to differential mortality reduces the IRR earned by twentieth percentile males from 1.62 percent to 0.47 percent, raises the IRR earned by the fiftieth percentile male from 0.85 percent to 1.06 percent, and raises the IRR earned by the seventy-fifth percentile male from 0.53 percent to 0.74 percent. Thus, differential mortality makes Social Security regressive. Our comparable results for the 1923 cohort are somewhat more modest. After adjusting for differential mortality, the twenty-fifth percentile male still earns the highest IRR. While the seventy-fifth percentile male earns a slightly higher return than the fiftieth percentile male, the difference is small. This is probably because the correlation between lifetime income and mortality is weaker than the correlation between current income and mortality (which is confounded by reverse causality).

Our next step is to compute IRRs and NPVs for the actual workers in our sample of Social Security beneficiaries. These results are summarized in figures 6.2 to 6.5. Figures 6.2 and 6.3 show the average IRRs for men and women, respectively, for different levels of AIME (where the AIME for each cohort is given in current dollars for the year that workers in that cohort turned sixty). Averages are calculated over $100 intervals. The two series labeled "homogeneous" and "differential" show the average IRR earned by workers at each level of AIME under the assumptions of homogeneous and differential mortality, respectively. The two straight lines on the graphs represent linear approximations of these average IRR curves.

Under differential mortality, a worker's mortality profile depends only on whether he or she is in the top half or bottom half of the lifetime earnings distribution. As discussed before, we classify workers into the top half and bottom half of the earnings distribution based on their nonzero earnings between the ages of forty-five and fifty-five—this classification was chosen to be consistent with Waldron (2007). This measure of lifetime income appears to be highly correlated with AIME and therefore creates a break in the "differential" line at roughly the fiftieth percentile of AIME—workers below the fiftieth percentile see a decline in their IRR, while workers above the fiftieth percentile see an increase in their IRR. As a result, the average IRR initially falls with AIME, then rises briefly, and falls again. It is likely that, had differential mortality data been available for finer income groups, mortality inequality would affect the average IRR in a more continuous way.

These results are consistent with the results for the stylized workers. Across cohorts, all but the lowest income men earn IRRs that are below 2 percent.

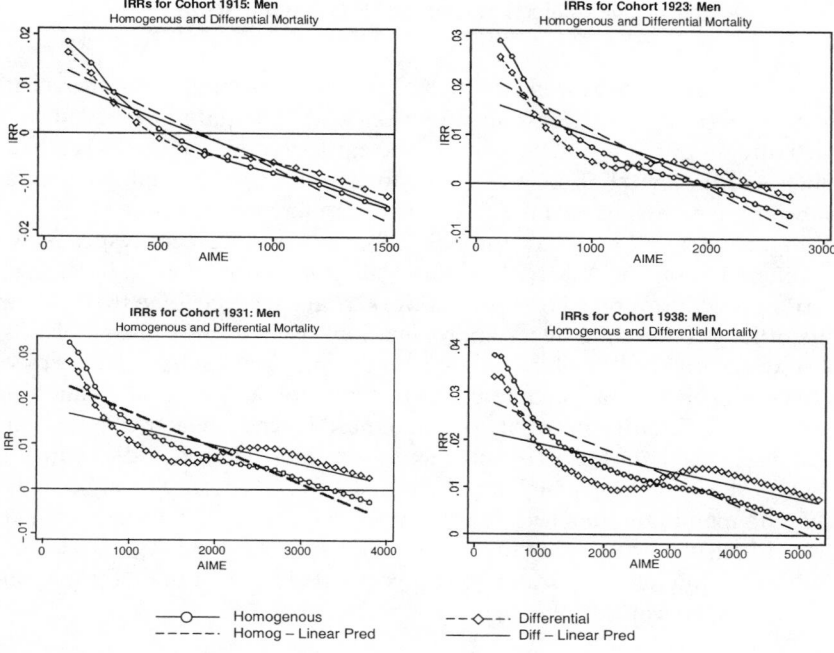

Fig. 6.2   Internal rates of return for men

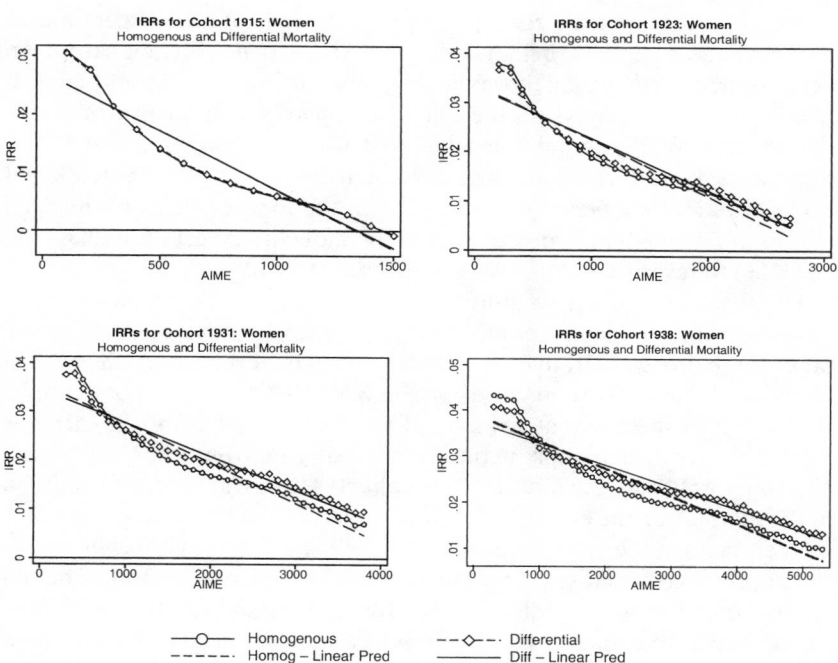

Fig. 6.3   Internal rates of return for women

At each level of AIME, women earn higher IRRs than men, and more recent cohorts earn higher IRRs than earlier ones. Differential mortality makes virtually no difference for women in the earlier cohorts and only a small difference for men. For more recent cohorts, differential mortality makes a substantial difference for men and a modest difference for women.

Figures 6.4 and 6.5 show the NPVs for men and women, respectively, at different levels of AIME. Again, the "homogeneous" and "differential" series show the average NPVs for all workers at each level of AIME, while the other two lines are linear approximations. Men at most income levels receive negative NPVs, while lower-income women generally receive positive NPVs. The NPVs at all income levels are higher for later cohorts. Again, the impact of differential mortality is pronounced for men in later cohorts. For instance, note in the fourth panel of figure 6.4 that men born in 1938 with an AIME of $3,500 have a higher (albeit negative) NPV from Social Security than do men in the same cohort with an AIME of $2,000. Once again, at least in particular income ranges, the program has turned regressive. The impact on differential mortality on progressivity is more modest for women and for men in earlier cohorts.

6.6   Conclusion

Social Security is the largest program of the federal government and is thought to be progressive in that it offers workers with low lifetime earnings a better retirement deal than those with high lifetime earnings. The mechanism to achieve this progressivity is the highly nonlinear benefit (PIA) formula. In this chapter, we incorporate the latest evidence on mortality differences of those with above-median and below-median lifetime earnings. Since Social Security retirement benefits are paid out in the form of inflation-indexed life annuities, differential mortality, and therefore life expectancies, have the potential to reverse the progressive impact of the PIA formula.

The Waldron and Cristia studies published in 2007 indicate that there is more mortality inequality for men than for women and that the level of mortality inequality grew from birth cohort to birth cohort between those born between 1912 and 1915 and those born between 1936 and 1938. For example, the extra life expectancy at age sixty of men in the top half of the earnings distribution relative to those in the bottom half grew from 1.35 years for the 1915 birth cohort to 3.67 for the 1939 cohort. The extra lifetime for women in the top half of the earnings distribution relative to those in bottom half grew from nil in the 1915 birth cohort to 2.79 years in the 1939 cohort.

The growing mortality inequality has the straightforward effect of reducing the progressivity of Social Security. By the 1931 and 1939 birth cohorts, it is no longer true that the retirement portion of the Social Security system offers a better deal for those in the twenty-fifth percentile of the earnings distribution than those in the seventy-fifth percentile, at least in terms of

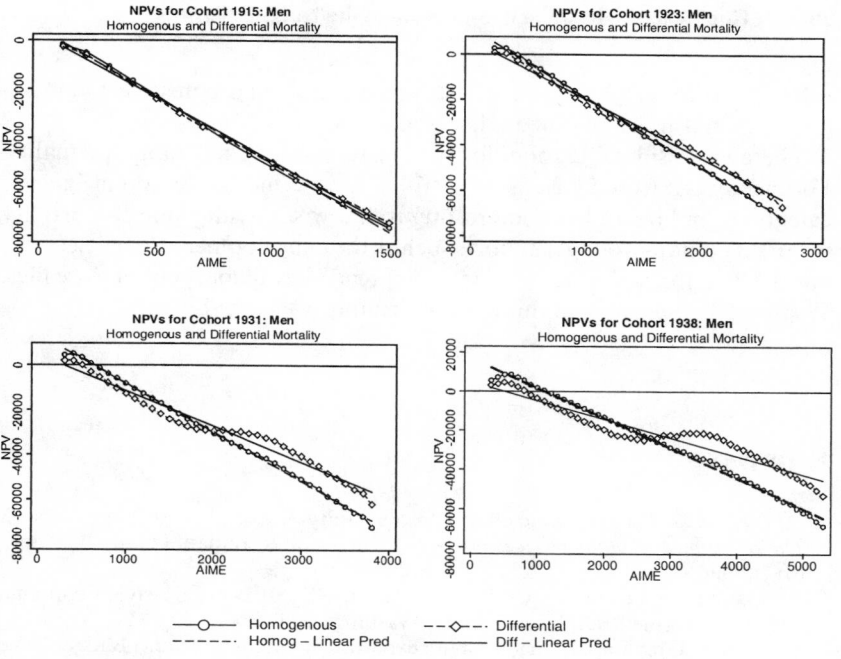

Fig. 6.4   Net present value for men

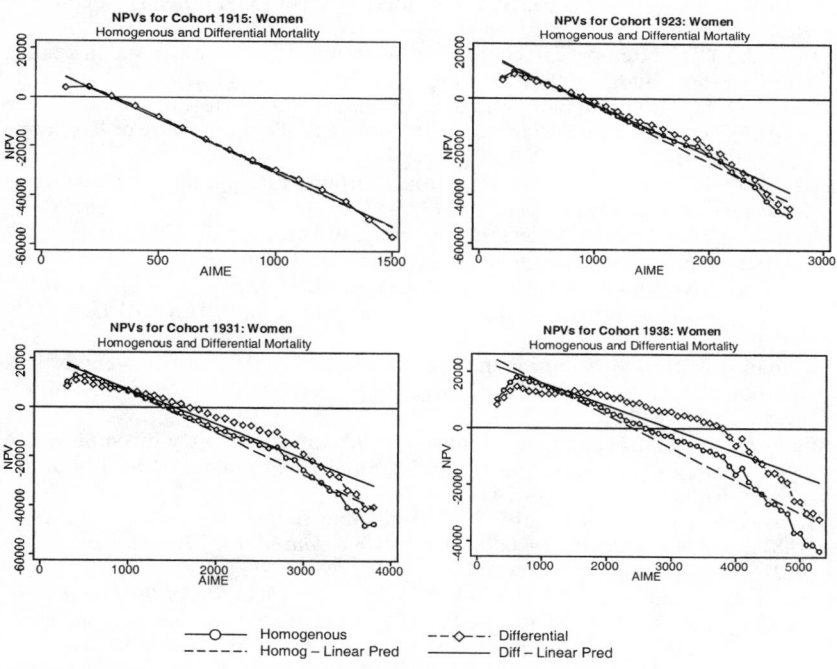

Fig. 6.5   Net present value for women

rates of return. For women, the system has remained progressive, but much less so than if mortality inequality is ignored.

There is considerable room for further research on mortality inequality. For instance, it would have been useful to have a finer gradation of income categories and it would be interesting to know something about mortality inequality among younger cohorts such as the baby boomers. Social Security has the data for such studies, but it is not readily available in public use files. We think further work in this area is certainly warranted.

References

Aaron, H. 1977. Demographic effects on the equity of Social Security benefits. In *The economics of public services,* ed. M. Feldstein and R. Inman, 151–73. London: Macmillan Press.
Congressional Budget Office (CBO). 2006. Is Social Security progressive? Economic and Budget Issue Brief, December 15. Washington, DC: GPO.
———. 2008. Growing disparities in life expectancies. Economic and Budget Issue Brief, July 16. Washington, DC: GPO.
Coronado, J., D. Fullerton, and T. Glass. 2000. The progressivity of Social Security. NBER Working Paper no. 7520. Cambridge, MA: National Bureau of Economic Research, February.
Cristia, J. 2007. The empirical relationship between lifetime earnings and mortality. Congressional Budget Office Working Paper 2007-11, August.
Duggan, J. E., R. Gillingham, and J. S. Greenlees. 2006. Mortality and lifetime income: Evidence from Social Security records. U.S. Treasury Office of Economic Policy Research Paper no. 2007-01.
Garrett, D. 1995. The effects of differential mortality rates on the progressivity of Social Security. *Economic Inquiry* 33 (3): 457–75.
Jemal, A., E. Ward, R. N. Anderson, T. Murray, and M. J. Thun. 2008. Widening of socioeconomic inequalities in U.S. death rates, 1993–2001. *PLoS* 3 (5): e2181.
Kitagawa, E. M., and P. M. Hauser. 1973. *Differential mortality in the United States: A study in socioeconomic epidemiology.* Cambridge, MA: Harvard University Press.
Liebman, J. 2001. Redistribution in the current U.S. Social Security system. NBER Working Paper no. 8625. Cambridge, MA: National Bureau of Economic Research, December.
Rogot, E., P. D. Sorlie, and N. J. Johnson. 1992. Life expectancy by employment status, income, and education in the National Longitudinal Mortality Study. *Public Health Reports* 107 (4): 457–61.
Singh, G. K., and M. Siahpush. 2006. Widening socioeconomic inequalities in U.S. life expectancy, 1980–2000. *International Journal of Epidemiology* 35 (4): 969–79.
Steuerle, C. E., and J. M. Bakija. 1994. *Retooling Social Security for the 21st century.* Washington, DC: Urban Institute Press.
Waldron, H. 2007. Trends in mortality differentials and life expectancy for male Social Security–covered workers, by socioeconomic status. *Social Security Bulletin* 67 (3): 1–28.

Comment   Michael D. Hurd

The actual progressivity of Social Security has become an important topic in connection with proposals to replace some of the existing system with private accounts. Opponents of these proposals argue that an important component of the existing system is progressivity, whereby benefits are related in a redistributive manner to a measure of lifetime earnings. However, it has long been recognized that individuals with higher socioeconomic status, whether measured by education, income, or wealth, live longer than individuals with lower socioeconomic status. Because Social Security is an annuity, a longer life means that total expected lifetime Social Security benefits will be higher among high lifetime earning individuals than would be the case if they survived according to a population life table. These higher payouts may reduce progressivity when measured in this way and could even reverse progressivity. This possibility has noted previously and the effect on progressivity has been estimated with varying results depending on the assumptions made by different authors. For example, Gustman and Steinmeier (2001) use actual Social Security earnings histories linked to the Health and Retirement Study and find that indeed there is significant redistribution from high lifetime earning individuals to low lifetime earning individuals when measured by the expected present value of Social Security benefits. But much of that redistribution disappears when the calculations are put in a household basis due to spouse benefits and survivor benefits. The main contribution of Goda, Shoven, and Slavov is to use more contemporary life tables in these types of calculations. To the extent that there has been a drift in differential mortality it is informative to find how these measures of redistribution are affected. Their findings are more or less in line with those of Gustman and Steinmeier: the greater life expectancy of high earning individuals offsets the concavity of the function relating lifetime earnings to Primary Insurance Amount reducing or eliminating progressivity.

My comments will be about two subjects. First, this lack of progressivity is not found by all researchers. I will give a prominent example of differing results and point out some possible reasons for the difference. Second, I will ask about the use of the word "progressivity" in this context, and will argue that the implications of a lack of progressivity, as measured here, are much less clear than in traditional discussions about tax policy.

The Congressional Budget Office (CBO) has released several studies about the progressivity of the Social Security system (Harris and Sabelhaus 2005; CBO 2006). Their estimates are based on actual work histories of a large sample of workers and projections of lifetime Social Security

Michael D. Hurd is a senior principal researcher and director of the Center for the Study of Aging at RAND, and a research associate of the National Bureau of Economic Research benefits using life tables that account for differential mortality. They differ from Goda, Shoven, and Slavov, who use stylized workers from the twenty-fifth, fiftieth, and seventy-fifth percentiles of lifetime earnings distribution. The main findings from the CBO reports are that Social Security is quite progressive when measured by the variation across lifetime earnings quintiles in the ratio of lifetime Social Security benefits to lifetime taxes. For example, individuals from the lowest earnings quintile can expect to receive about twice as much in benefits as taxes, and this ratio is fairly constant across the birth cohorts from the 1940s to the 1990s (CBO 2006). Those in the highest earnings quintile have a ratio of benefits to earnings of about 60 percent. These numbers indicate a strong progressive system.

What accounts for the difference between these results and those of Goda, Shoven, and Slavov? First, and most importantly, the CBO estimates account for the entire Social Security system: retired worker benefits, disability benefits, and auxiliary benefits (surviving spouse and underaged children of a decreased or retired worker). The disabled worker part of the program is particularly progressive. Auxiliary benefits are also progressive: Social Security provides what is essentially a rather generous life insurance benefit. Obviously, those who die early will have had lower lifetime earnings and so the life insurance program will be progressive; but also because lower socioeconomic status (SES) individuals as measured by, say, education are expected to die earlier, the program is progressive ex ante.

However, the difference between the CBO estimates and Goda, Shoven, and Slavov are not due solely to the fact that Goda, Shoven, and Slavov confine themselves to the retired worker part of the program. Indeed, again measuring progressivity by the variation in the ratio of lifetime Social Security benefits to lifetime earnings, the CBO finds that this ratio varies by a factor of about 1.65. Some reasons for the difference include the rather coarse classification by Goda, Shoven, and Slavov of lifetime earnings into just three groups. The CBO results show that most progressivity is at the lower end of the earnings distribution, where progressivity increases rather sharply as lifetime earnings decrease from about the thirtieth percentile to about the fifth percentile. This variation would be obscured by the coarse Goda, Shoven, and Slavov classification. That cannot be the entire explanation, however, because CBO shows progressivity throughout the entire earnings distribution. Another difference is that CBO is based on household earnings rather than stylized earnings of an individual. Again, that cannot be the explanation because progressivity is higher when only individual workers are considered rather than households (Harris and Sablehaus 2005, table 1). Other differences include the measure of income that is used in the classification both for economic status (to determine progressivity) and for differential mortality. Consider, as an extreme hypothetical example, a wealthy person with high lifetime income (from dividends and interest) but low lifetime earnings (because she worked just enough to qualify for Social

Security benefits). Such a person is likely to have elevated survival. Classifying by lifetime Social Security earnings would reduce differential mortality and increase progressivity because a low lifetime earner would have a very high ratio of lifetime benefits to contributions; classifying by lifetime income would have an uncertain effect on progressivity relative to the first classification because a high income person would both survive longer and have a high ratio of lifetime benefits to contributions.

One aspect that is partially but not completely outside of the Social Security system is the taxation of Social Security benefits. There is a complex interaction between the Federal income tax system and the level of Social Security benefits. A concise summary is that low income people who nevertheless face a positive marginal tax rate on earnings may face a zero marginal (and average) tax rate on Social Security benefits, whereas high income people pay taxes on up to 85 percent of Social Security benefits. Thus, for example, single persons aged sixty-five to sixty-nine in the Health and Retirement Study who lack a high school education will pay about 2 percent of their Social Security benefits in income taxes, whereas single college graduates will pay about 14 percent of their benefits in taxes.[1]

One conclusion about the progressivity of the retired worker part of the Social Security system is that there are unexplained differences between the results of Goda, Shoven, and Slavov and the results of CBO and Harris and Sabelhaus. It would be useful to understand the sources of the differences. In addition, however, because of the special treatment of Social Security under the income tax, some additional progressivity should be attributed in addition to that induced by the concave benefit schedule. Although there is value in considering the retired worker part of the system in isolation because we would like to know the consequences of modifying that part of the program only, the program should be viewed as a social program that has a number of insurance components, which taken together have considerable progressivity.

My second topic is how to think about progressivity in a multiperiod setting and how the policy implications might differ from those in a static setting. The basic statement about the progressivity of the Social Security system is based on the comparison of two measures: economic position as measured by lifetime income or a close approximation, and economic benefits as measured by pension wealth. Pension wealth increases in economic position both because of increases in lifetime contributions and because of differential mortality. If survival increases rapidly enough, pension wealth relative to lifetime contributions could be an increasing function of lifetime income, leading to a regressive system according to this measure. However, the language of "progressive" and "regressive" comes from a simpler situation, one associated with taxation. In that setting consider two people

---

1. Author's calculations based on HRS income data.

with the same utility function. One person is more wealthy than the other. Under standard and reasonable assumptions of declining marginal utility of consumption, redistribution from the wealthy person to the poor person increases total utility, and we would call the tax progressive. Redistributing from poor to wealthy would decrease total utility and it would be regressive.

Now consider two periods with two people that have the same within-period utility function. Person A lives one period and has no wealth; person B lives two periods and has some wealth. The interest rate is zero and the subjective time rate of discount is also zero so that person B consumes the same amount each period. If their pension flows are the same, person B has twice the pension wealth as person A. If, to make pension wealth the same for the two people, the pension of B were reduced and the pension of A were increased so as to keep total pension payments constant, the effect on total utility is uncertain. For example, if the initial wealth of B is small relative to pension level, following the redistribution consumption by person B in the first period could be substantially lower than consumption by person A in the first period. Then, because of declining marginal utility, the total utility of person B could decline more than the increase in utility of person A. That is, total utility would be decreased by the apparently progressive redistribution. Unlike the simple within-period example, redistribution to offset mortality differentials could reduce total utility. Of course, under different initial conditions total utility could increase from the redistribution. But, the situation is very different from the simple one-period case where progressive taxation always increases total utility under reasonable assumptions.

The authors do not advocate policies to increase progressivity in the Social Security system based on differential mortality. We do not understand the causal mechanisms behind the correlation between income and survival, but understanding those mechanisms would be an important input when considering policy options. Furthermore, the relationship between income and mortality is not stable across countries, within countries by age, or within countries over time. Thus, any policy aiming to achieve a more equal expected present value of Social Security benefits may require constant adjustment as the relationship between income and mortality changes.

References

Congressional Budget Office (CBO). 2006. Is Social Security progressive? Economic and Budget Issue Brief, December 15. Washington, DC: GPO.

Gustman, A. L., and T. L. Steinmeier. 2001. How effective is redistribution under the Social Security benefit formula? *Journal of Public Economics* 82 (Oct): 1–28.

Harris, A. R., and J. Sabelhaus. 2005. How does differential mortality affect Social Security finances and progressivity? Congressional Budget Office Working Paper no. 2005-5.

7
Cognition and Economic Outcomes in the Health and Retirement Survey

John J. McArdle, James P. Smith, and Robert Willis

Dimensions of cognitive skills are potentially important but often neglected determinants of the central economic outcomes that shape overall well-being over the life course. There exists enormous variation among households in their rates of wealth accumulation, their holdings of financial assets, and the relative risk in their chosen asset portfolios that have proven difficult to explain by conventional demographic factors, the amount of bequests they receive or anticipating giving (Smith 1999), and the level of economic resources of the household (Smith 1995). The premium on cognitive skills in economic decision making may also be increasing, as individuals are increasingly asked to take greater control of or to adjust prior decisions relating to their household wealth, their pensions, and their health care. These may be cognitively demanding decisions at any age but especially so at older ages.

This research will examine the association of cognitive skills with wealth, wealth growth, and wealth composition for people in their pre- and post-retirement years. Our analysis will rely on selective waves of the Health and Retirement Survey (HRS), a nationally representative panel survey of Americans who are at least fifty years old. This analysis will be supplemented

John J. McArdle is senior professor of psychology at the University of Southern California. James P. Smith is a senior economist and holds the Distinguished Chair in Labor Markets and Demographic Studies at RAND Corporation. Robert Willis is professor of economics at the University of Michigan.

We would like to thank Iva MacLennan and David Rumpel for excellent programming assistance and Finis Welch and Ian Walker for their insightful comments on earlier drafts. This research was supported by grants (AG025529 and AG008291) from the National Institute of Aging to the RAND Corporation, to the University of Southern California (AG07137) and to the University of Michigan (AG026571). This chapter was presented at the NBER conference on economics of aging in Carefree, Arizona, May 2009.

by a cognitive economics survey (CogEcon) that measured several dimensions of cognition in more depth.

The HRS is well-known for its high-quality measurement of many key socioeconomic status (SES) outcomes, including income and wealth (see Juster and Smith [1997] and Juster, Smith, and Stafford [1999]). In addition, HRS includes in some waves several salient dimensions of cognitive skills. These cognition constructs start with immediate and delayed memory recall and the Telephone Interview of Cognitive Status (TICS) battery, as these have been established psychometrically to capture cognitive constructs of episodic memory and intact mental status (see McArdle, Fisher, and Kadlec 2007). Another key aspect of cognition included in recent HRS waves is numeracy, a simple summary measure of respondents' numerical ability. We also present data on two additional measures of numerical reasoning and retrieval fluency, both recently introduced into the HRS as experimental modules, to examine if these dimensions of cognition are associated with significant improvements in the ability of cognition to predict economic outcomes.

The chapter is organized into five sections. The next section presents the main conceptual components of cognition that may potentially influence economic outcomes. The following section describes the main data that we will use and the cognition variables available in the HRS. The third section highlights results that are obtained relating individual attributes, including their cognitive ability, to their total wealth, total financial wealth, and the fraction of wealth held in stock. The next section contains complementary results obtained from the cognitive economics survey (CogEcon), which has a more expansive list of cognitive variables. The final section highlights our main conclusions.

7.1   Cognition and Economics

The mechanisms responsible for cognitive development over the life course that are related to economic outcomes may be the long-term result of many individual and group factors. It is established that children exposed to very serious environmental deprivation show markedly reduced cognitive abilities (Rutter 1985), but detectable effects of normal-range environments on cognitive ability are typically smaller. This is not surprising, given the large number of environmental risk factors and the small effect expected for any particular factor, and that the genetic contributions vary as well (Harden, Turkheimer, and Loehlin 2007). Specific factors associated with lower cognitive performance include low socioeconomic status, birth complications, poor early nutrition, family conflict, and many others (Conger et al. 1994; Ramey et al. 2000).

In a classic analysis of data from the Berkeley Studies, Elder (1974) found that effects of economic deprivation on adult functioning varied with gender and birth cohort. For males in the older cohort (OGS, born 1920 to 1922), being reared in a family with low SES during the Great Depression was associated with higher resilience in adulthood compared to males reared in more favorable circumstances. In contrast, for boys in the younger cohorts (BGS and GS, born 1928 to 1930) being reared in economic adversity was associated with lower psychological functioning in adulthood. These processes applied equally well to behavior of mothers and fathers, as well as sons and daughters. Lee et al. (2003) investigated the relation of educational attainment, husband's education, household income, and childhood socioeconomic status to cognitive function and decline among community-dwelling women aged seventy to seventy-nine years. Among well-educated women, educational attainment predicted cognitive function and decline, although other measures of socioeconomic status had little relation.

Whatever the origin of adult cognitive skills, financial matters are often not straightforward for most individuals and may depend in part on their ability to invoke several dimensions of cognitive skills. One needs to be interested in economic problems and feel comfortable in understanding the choices that are available amidst a wide array of options and feel confident about the computations involved in contrasting alternative rates of return of different assets often calculated over different time dimensions (Banks and Oldfield 2007). This may involve aspects of (a) retrieving relevant prior financial information from *memory;* (b) using one's accumulated knowledge and skills (*crystallized* intelligence [Gc]); and (c) the ability to draw inferences about what is the best solution to a novel problem (*fluid* intelligence [Gf]). (For details, see Cattell [1987]; Horn and McArdle [2007]; McArdle and Woodcock [1998]).

A useful shorthand division of the principal dimensions of intelligence is to separate them into fluid intelligence (Gf) and crystallized intelligence (Gc). Fluid intelligence is the thinking part—memory, abstract reasoning, and executive function. In contrast, crystallized intelligence is the knowing part—the main accumulation of influence from education and lifetime experience (for more details, see McArdle et al. [2002]).

A parallel has been drawn between the psychological theory of fluid and crystallized intelligence and economic theories of investment in human capital. In the formulation of Willis (2007), based on the Ben-Porath human capital production function, fluid intelligence can be thought of as the ability parameter and crystallized intelligence as the accumulated stock of human capital. To be more concrete, the conceptual relationship between these aspects of cognition and human capital knowledge might be summarized as

(1) $$Q_t = B_0(s_t K_t)^{B_1} D_t^{B_2}.$$

In this model a production function relates the amount of learning or increments in human capital (Q_t) to ability (B_0), investments from existing stock of human capital (K_t), and purchased market inputs (D_t). Given its emphasis on ability to think and execute, fluid intelligence (Gf) most closely corresponds to the ability parameter B_0. In this production function the crystallized intelligence (Gc) role as a surrogate for accumulated knowledge is a close parallel to the existing stock of human capital or knowledge (K_t). If we think of the output in equation (1) as increments in knowledge about financial matters, elements of cognition that mimic Gf and Gc will both affect this accumulation and affect financial outcomes. Of course, most everyday cognitive tasks have elements of both fluid and crystallized intelligence so there is not yet an established tight connection between cognitive measures and underlying parameters of the production process.

In an insightful application, Delevande, Rohwedder, and Willis (2008) consider an individual's knowledge of finance to be a component of human capital—or crystallized intelligence—that allows people to achieve a higher expected return on their assets, holding risk constant. They assume that an individual produces additional financial knowledge by combining his or her fluid intelligence or ability, crystallized intelligence, and effort according to a human capital production function (Ben Porath 1967; Cunha and Heckman 2007). The motivation to acquire financial knowledge depends on an important scale economy in this investment process. While increased knowledge raises the feasible expected return per dollar, the total value of the investment depends on the number of dollars to which the improved return is applied.

Thus, other things equal, the value of acquiring financial knowledge is higher for persons who desire higher levels of retirement wealth because of a higher lifetime income, a lower rate of time preference, or lower defined-benefit pension wealth. Similarly, investment will be greater among persons who have lower costs or greater efficiency in acquiring additional knowledge because of greater fluid intelligence or because they have more financial knowledge obtained in their formal education or on the job.

Moreover, these issues may become increasingly salient as the population ages because many aspects of these basic cognitive skills are known to begin to deteriorate from different levels and at varying rates for individuals, starting in middle age and often at even earlier ages. Figure 7.1 plots a simple summary of these age patterns, separating out life cycle paths of intelligence, as well as its fluid and crystallized intelligence components. As in other forms of human capital, crystallized intelligence is believed by cognitive psychologists to grow rapidly with age, but at a decreasing rate plateauing somewhere in the age fifty range. In contrast, elements of fluid intelligence are believed to peak relatively early in life (during adolescence) and then steadily decline with age thereafter.

Problems associated with declines in fluid intelligence with age may be compounded if older individuals are asked to take more personal control of their accounts and the financial decisions about their wealth holdings

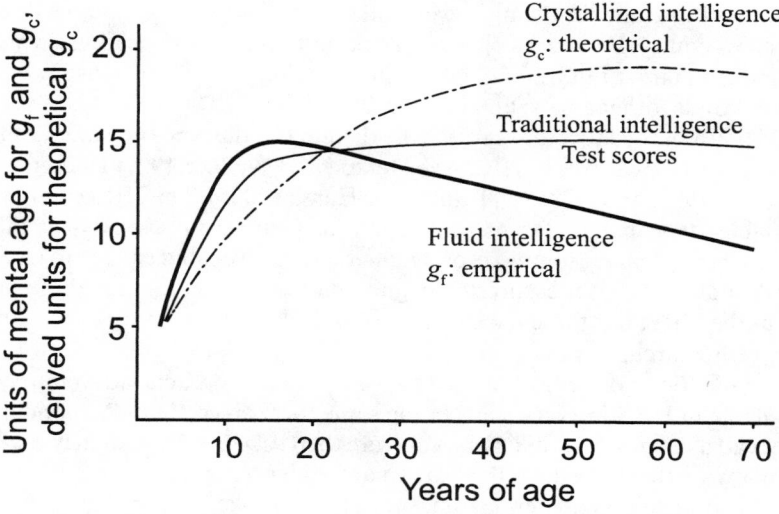

Fig. 7.1   Life cycle pattern of fluid and crystallized intelligence
Source: Cattell (1987, 206): Figure 1. A theoretical description of life span curves of intellectual abilities. (Reprinted with permission.)

and its future trajectory (Hershey et al. 2007). It is possible that the recent financial collapse may place even greater demands on the ability of individuals to make good financial decisions about their wealth holdings in order to maintain income security during their retirement years. For many of these individuals there was little reason to acquire financial knowledge beforehand and they may now be left in a situation of relatively low levels of Gc coupled with rapidly declining levels of Gf.

7.2   Data and Measures of Cognition in the Health and Retirement Survey

This research will rely on a subset of surveys from the Health and Retirement Study (HRS), a nationally representative longitudinal survey of the population of the United States who are over fifty years old. The overall objective of the HRS is to monitor economic transitions in work, income, and wealth, as well as changes in many dimensions of health status among those over fifty years old. The current version of HRS is representative of all birth cohorts born in 1947 or earlier. Follow-ups of all surveys have taken place at approximately two-year intervals.

In HRS, questions were included in each core interview on demographics, income and wealth, family structure, health, and employment. An important advantage of these surveys is that they all contain high-quality wealth modules. In HRS, a very comprehensive and detailed set of questions was asked to measure household wealth. In addition to housing equity, assets were separated into the following eleven categories: other real estate; vehicles; business equity; IRA or Keogh; stocks or mutual funds; checking, savings, or money market funds; CDs, government savings bonds, or treasury bills; other bonds; other assets; and other debt.

The subsets of HRS that we used are dictated by the types and availability of cognition measures in HRS (see Herzog and Wallace 1997; Herzog and Rodgers 1999; and Ofstedal, Fisher, and Herzog 2005). The HRS cognition variables were intended to measure episodic memory, intactness of mental status, numerical reasoning, broad numeracy, and vocabulary. More recent work indicates that measures of cognitive speed can be obtained directly from the HRS, but these measures are relatively new and not yet available for this research.

We rely on two memory measures—immediate and delayed *word recall* available in HRS in every wave in the same form since 1995. Respondents are read a list of ten simple nouns and are then asked to immediately repeat as many of these words as they can in any order. After a five-minute measurement of self-rated depression, they are then asked to recall as many of the original words as possible.[1] Following the analysis of McArdle, Fisher, and Kadlec (2007), we form an episodic memory measure as the average of immediate and delayed recalled results. *Episodic memory* may be a necessary component of reasoning (both *fluid and crystallized intelligence*).

Our second cognitive measure is the mental status questions of the Telephone Interview of Cognitive Status (TICS) battery, established to capture intactness or mental status of individuals. The TICS questions consist of the following items—serial 7 subtraction from 100 (up to five times), backwards counting (from 20 to 1), naming today's date (month, day, year), and naming the president and vice president of the United States. Answers to these questions are aggregated into a single *mental status* score that ranges from 0 to 10. The same form of mental status scores have been available since Asset and Health Dynamics Among the Oldest Old (AHEAD) 95 and HRS 96 (Herzog and Rodgers 1999).

The third cognition measure available is a *number series* test adapted from the Woodcock-Johnson (WJ-R) battery of tests for *fluid reasoning* (McArdle, Fisher, and Kadlec 2007). This test was administered in a 2004 experimental module to a random sample of over 1,200 respondents. This represented an attempt to achieve test scores from a subset of items from the *number series* test of WJ III using an adaptive testing methodology. Each respondent was asked no more than six items where the subsequent sequence of items at each point was determined by correctness of each answer. This test was administered again in a 2006 experimental module where roughly

---

1. In HRS 92 and 94, the original set consisted of twenty words. The same word list is not repeated in the next three subsequent rounds and husbands and wives were given a different list (see Ofstedal, Fisher, and Herzog 2005).

half of respondents who were tested in 2004 were tested again. Fifty percent of those given the test in the 2006 experimental module had not been tested previously. For each respondent, a score was created on the W-scale (logit metric) where higher scores indicate better performance. Because this numerical reasoning test has not yet been placed in the HRS core, sample size is smaller and statistical power may be fairly low. To mitigate these problems, we maximized number of observations with a score by taking an available score from either the 2004 or 2006 experimental module if available. If respondents were tested twice, scores were averaged.

The fourth measure deals with a WJ form of *retrieval fluency,* which was administered in an experimental module in HRS 2006. Respondents were given a category and asked to mention as many items as they could within a forty-five second time frame (shorter than the typical WJ format). The number of correct and incorrect answers was counted by the interviewer.

Starting with HRS 2002 and then asked in alternative waves for repeat interviews, three questions were added to the core interview to measure *numeracy* (respondents' numerical ability). These questions involve the computation of three mathematical computations and one is scored as either correct or incorrect on each of them.[2] Four scores are possible, running from zero to three depending on the number of correct answers.

Thus there are five different measures of cognition available in the HRS that we use in this analysis. While the *episodic memory, mental status,* and *numeracy* are available in multiple core waves in the same form, the other two measures are in an experimental module in a specific wave (*number series* and *retrieval fluency*). This form of availability determines the types of analysis that are possible with the full cognition measures.

A very simple schematic of the translation of these HRS cognition measures into the Gf and Gc components of intelligence is provided following. *Episodic memory* is a very general measure of an important aspect of fluid intelligence since access to memory is basic to any type of cognitive ability. Most of the HRS variation in this measure is picking out the low end—people with bad memory. Similarly, fluid reasoning, as captured by the *number series,* is perhaps our best measure of Gf for numerical ability skills most relevant for financial decision making. *Numeracy,* the actual ability to perform numerical skills mostly learned in schools, represents our preferred measure of Gc for numbers. *Retrieval fluency* is possibly another proxy for Gc since it measures our retrieval of elements of accumulated knowledge, although in this application it captures the retrieval of verbal knowledge (e.g., the number of animals one can name in forty-five seconds) and not

2. Another cognition measure is only available for the original cohort of HRS (those fifty-one to sixty-one years old in 1992) and was a onetime measure. In HRS 92, a modified version of the similarities subscale of the Wechsler Adult Intelligence Scale was revised (*WAIS-R*). This was used to access higher level abstract reasoning by comparing a list of seven pairs of words and then describing how they were alike.

financial knowledge. We will deal with the ability to retrieve financial knowledge, a broader measure of math achievement, and general intelligence when we discuss the cognitive economics survey (CogEcon) later. Finally, the TICS score contains elements of both Gf and Gc—cognitive skills needed for everything but specific to nothing. The types of questions asked are not specific to the financial domains of life.

Types of Cognition Measures Available in the Expanded HRS

- Episodic memory—*short-term memory*
- Telephone Interview of Intact Cognitive Status (TICS—Gf and Gc—needed for everything but specific to nothing
- Number series—Fluid Reasoning close to Gf for numerical ability
- Retrieval fluency—Gc—ability to retrieve long-term storage
- Numeracy—Gc for numbers or quantitative ability—Gq

Additional Measures in CogEcon

- Calculation—Gc—math achievement or general quantitative ability Gq
- Matrix reasoning—Gf—nonverbal reasoning and general intelligence
- Financial literacy—Gc—knowledge of financial matters, especially at the high end

The cognitive measures listed above are intended to indicate different aspects of the adult cognitive profile (see McArdle et al. 2002). Prior research has suggested strong normative age declines in most of these cognitive functions, but a hierarchy of cognitive strengths and weakness of any individual are indicated in many aspects of adult daily functioning. At a most basic level, the need for an intact neurocognitive system is thought to be necessary to deal with everyday issues in communication and learning in the simple judgments needed for survival (e.g., gathering food and water). At another step up in everyday complexity, the ability to remember to complete tasks, to be able to react to simple stimuli, and the ability to deal with simple numerical problems are important skills in the consideration in successfully dealing with everyday challenges (see Farias et al. 2008) Higher order aspects of cognitive skills, such as having expertise in a specific area (i.e., *crystallized intelligence*), or in reasoning in novel situations (i.e., *fluid intelligence*), will be necessary fundamentals in the ability to deal with more complex economic challenges (Hershey et al. 2007; McArdle, Fisher, and Kadlec 2007).

As pointed out by Banks and Oldfield (2007), there are several credible reasons why numeracy, a score representing knowledge about numerical problems, may be related to financial outcomes. More numerate individuals may be more adept at complex decision making, including those involved in financial decisions (Peters et al. 2006). More numerate individuals also appear to be more patient and thus are more likely to have saved and invested in the past (Parker and Fischhoff 2005) and perhaps less risk averse (Benjamin, Brown, and Shapiro 2006).[3]

The use of more abstract reasoning with numbers, as in the simple *number series* puzzles, is intended to represent a different form of cognition (i.e., fluid intelligence), and it is not clear how these abilities are useful in the accumulation of wealth). Examining results from a twenty-five-item test of financial knowledge on the Cognitive Economics Survey, Delevande, Rohwedder, and Willis (2008) find that the *number series* score has a strong and significant effect on the test score, as does educational attainment and number of economics courses the respondent has had.[4] In addition, they find that women, especially older women, have considerably lower test scores than men, probably reflecting a household division of labor about household financial decisions that was especially sharp in earlier cohorts. These ideas about the independent impact of different forms of cognition are directly examined in this research.

7.3   Individual-Level Analysis in the HRS

In this section, we report our main empirical results describing the relation of these dimensions of cognition to wealth accumulation among middle-aged and older adults. Table 7.1 lists means, medians, and standard deviations of variables that enter into the statistical analysis. Mean household wealth in this sample is about $500,000, but wealth has its well-known features of high variability and skewness as the median is just under $200,000. Similarly, total financial wealth is around $313,000 and is even more highly skewed as the median financial household wealth is only $56,000. On average, 9 percent of all financial wealth is held in stock. Mean household income is about $62,000, but income is also very unequal across these individuals (but not as much as wealth is).

Two-thirds of these individuals live as couples, 59 percent are female, and the average age is sixty-eight years old. In these birth cohorts, the typical sample member is a high school graduate. Nine percent of the sample is Latino and 16 percent are African American, reflecting oversamples of both groups in the HRS.

On average, HRS respondents remembered half of the ten words spoken to them in immediate and delayed recall with two-thirds of the sample being able to recall between three and seven words. The HRS respondents were able to correctly compute only a bit more than one answer correctly in

3. Reverse causality is possible where greater involvement in complex financial decisions improves numerical ability.

4. The Cognitive Economics Survey, designed by a team of economists led by Willis, was administered during 2008 to a national sample of 1,222 persons, age fifty-one and older (and their spouses regardless of age), who are participants in the National Change and Growth Survey, a cognition survey designed by McArdle and colleagues (2002).

Table 7.1   **Means and standard deviations**

Variable	Mean	Median	Standard dev.
Total household wealth[a]	498.9	198.0	1,228.83
Total financial wealth[a]	312.7	55.9	1,039.9
Percent of financial wealth in stocks	8.96	0.0	20.86
Percent couples	0.65	n.a.	0.487
Total income[a]	62.18	37.00	173.22
Female	0.589	n.a.	0.492
Hispanic	0.093	n.a.	0.290
Nonwhite	0.163	n.a.	0.369
Education	12.31	12.00	3.40
Age	68.0	68.0	11.1
Cognition variables[b]			
Number series (W-scale)	498.8	507.5	40.2
TICS mental status (0–10)	8.85	10.00	2.16
Word recall (0–10)	4.85	5.00	1.73
Numeracy	1.19	1.00	0.90
Retrieval fluency (W-scale)	496.0	499.6	12.05

Note: n.a. = not applicable.
[a]Thousands of dollars.
[b]Defined over cases asked the cognition questions.

the three question *numeracy* sequence. The experimental HRS measures of *number series* and *retrieval fluency* are both calculated as W scores (McArdle and Woodcock 1998). Each W score is artificially centered at 500 based on the ten-year-olds in the norming sample. The W scoring metric is used so that the change in the probability of getting an item right increases by 25 percent for every 10-point change in the W score. In this W score metric, the resulting average of *number series* and *retrieval fluency* are slightly below 500 and distribution in scores are approximately normal.

We estimate models for three financial outcomes at the individual level: total household wealth, total financial wealth, and the fraction of financial wealth held in stocks. These models are estimated both in level form (in 2006) in table 7.2 and as changes from a year 2000 base in table 7.3. The estimated coefficients and associated t statistics based on robust standard errors are also listed in these tables. Noncognition variables included in these models are standard: gender of the respondent (1 = female), race (1 = African American), Hispanic (1 = Latino), a quadratic in age, marital status (married = 1), a quadratic in household income, and years of schooling. The only nonstandard demographic variable is an indicator variable for whether the respondent was the financial respondent—the partner who was most knowledgeable about financial matters and who answered all household-level financial questions in the HRS survey.

The full set of available cognition variables is included in all models. As described before, some cognition variables such as *number series* and

Table 7.2   **Relationship of household wealth holdings to cognition**
2006 individual sample—robust regression (wealth in thousands of dollars)

	Total wealth		Total financial wealth		Percent in stock	
	Coef.	t	Coef.	t	Coef.	t
Female	5.04	1.39	−0.69	0.46	0.63	1.72
Hispanic	−7.44	1.21	−16.48	6.46	−1.61	2.43
Nonwhite	−60.23	12.86	−24.71	12.71	−3.36	6.68
Age	18.13	11.21	6.13	9.13	−0.59	3.47
Age squared	−0.10	9.16	−0.03	7.22	0.01	5.54
Couple	52.01	11.96	14.38	7.97	−0.16	0.36
Education	10.94	18.08	3.86	15.35	1.00	15.71
Fin. resp.	−20.74	5.02	−7.96	4.64	−1.24	3.01
Total income	2.20	109.0	0.76	90.06	0.01	5.47
Income squared	−0.000	66.63	−0.000	58.55	−1.02e−06	5.83
Cognition variables						
Number series W	0.14	1.19	0.03	0.67	0.02	1.26
TICS mental status	2.41	2.26	0.34	0.77	−0.02	0.14
Word recall	7.63	6.67	3.77	7.92	0.17	1.47
Numeracy	20.09	8.92	7.38	7.89	1.65	7.23
Retrieval fluency W	0.59	1.18	0.42	1.99	−0.07	1.33
Total wealth					0.002	15.39
Cons	−1206.59	4.62	−512.56	4.73	28.83	1.09
N	18,382		18,382		16,220	

retrieval fluency are only present in experimental modules and administered to about 1,000 respondents in each wave. Other cognition variables such as *memory recall, mental status (TICS items),* and *numeracy* were given to all HRS respondents. Missing value indicators are included in all models for people who either did not answer or who were not asked specific questions involved in the construction of the right-hand side variables. By design, the large proportion of missing values for the *number series* and *retrieval fluency* measures in the experimental modules are missing at random.

Results obtained in the 2006 level analysis for noncognitive variables, presented in table 7.2, are consistent with those widely reported in the literature (Smith 1995). Wealth levels, both total and financial, are higher for couples than for single-person households, are lower for minorities, increase at a decreasing rate with age, rise steeply with education and with family income, but with the latter at a decreasing rate. Individuals with higher education, income, and wealth hold more of their financial wealth in stock while minorities hold less in this more risky asset even at the same age, income, and wealth.

Our main interest in this chapter centers on estimated impacts of cognitive variables. The strongest and most consistent results obtained were for the *numeracy* and *memory recall* cognition measures. Answering each

Table 7.3   Relationship of change in household wealth holdings (2000–2006) to cognition 2006 individual sample—robust regression (wealth in thousands of dollars)

	Total wealth		Total financial wealth		Percent in stock	
	Coef.	t	Coef.	t	Coef.	t
Female	−5.80	1.93	−2.09	1.45	0.27	0.52
Hispanic	24.67	4.62	−5.02	1.96	1.57	1.53
Nonwhite	−3.26	0.83	−10.34	5.47	0.32	0.42
Age	3.74	2.34	2.44	3.21	−0.32	1.10
Age squared	−0.27	2.34	−0.17	3.00	0.00	1.15
Couple	20.75	25.16	8.78	5.03	−1.04	1.63
Education	3.10	6.24	1.34	1.59	−0.65	0.72
Fin. resp.	−7.21	2.12	−4.28	2.62	−0.12	0.20
Total income	0.72	25.16	0.15	10.87	−0.01	2.39
Income squared	−0.00	9.96	0.00	53.62	−6.48e−06	1.61
Cognition variables						
Number series W	0.16	0.17	−0.02	0.44	−0.02	0.89
TICS mental status	−0.68	0.74	−1.19	2.69	−0.00	0.02
Word recall	4.84	5.17	3.05	6.80	−0.41	0.25
Numeracy	8.26	4.46	6.05	6.80	0.49	1.55
Retrieval fluency W	0.21	0.52	0.49	2.48	−0.05	0.79
Total wealth—2000	−0.24	147.2	n.a.		−0.00	1.65
Total fin. wealth—2000	n.a.		−0.53	558.51		
Cons	−275.93	4.62	−326.63	3.17	28.83	1.09
N	14,270		14,270		12,058	

Note: n.a. = not applicable.

question correctly in the three question numeracy sequence is associated with a $20,000 increase in total household wealth and about a $7,000 increase in total financial wealth. Enhanced *numeracy* is also associated with a larger fraction on the financial portfolio held in stocks. All these results are strongly statistically significant.

Similarly, improved *episodic memory* is associated with higher levels of household and financial wealth but not with how risky (stock intensive) the financial asset portfolio is. While it is difficult to compare units across cognitive measures, these results imply that remembering three additional words in the *word recall* is associated with total household wealth equivalent to answering one additional question correctly in the *numeracy* sequence. Our three other cognitive measures—*number series, TICS mental status,* and *retrieval fluency*—are not consistently related to these financial outcomes. Part of the lack of statistical significance for *number series* and *retrieval fluency* may well be due to the lower effective sample size for those measures.

The extreme degree of heterogeneity and right skewness in financial outcomes implies that estimated mean effects may not characterize many individuals in the sample. With that caution in mind, table 7.4 (for total

Table 7.4 Relationship of total household wealth holdings to cognition 2006 individual sample—quantile models (wealth in thousands of dollars)

	25th quantile		Median		75th quantile		90th quantile	
	Coef.	t	Coef.	t	Coef.	t	Coef.	t
Female	6.130	2.65	6.794	1.79	12.043	1.52	14.393	0.92
Hispanic	-2.244	0.56	-3.970	0.62	5.199	0.40	-40.208	1.66
Nonwhite	-23.415	7.62	-50.352	10.25	-92.724	9.37	-182.266	9.81
Age	13.050	13.53	20.016	11.81	30.426	7.88	32.186	4.08
Age squared	-0.075	11.11	-0.113	9.54	-0.171	6.40	-0.173	3.18
Married	31.281	11.16	44.719	9.81	40.073	4.19	59.891	3.17
Education	4.530	12.30	9.621	15.15	16.019	11.22	23.883	8.00
Financial respondent	-10.263	3.87	-22.722	5.24	-41.095	4.57	-58.543	3.30
Income	1.914	127.99	3.542	167.89	7.107	160.26	12.093	148.76
Income squared	-0.000	87.63	-0.000	127.14	-0.000	140.75	-0.001	136.52
Number Series W	0.093	1.27	0.211	1.70	0.233	0.89	0.453	0.82
TICS mental status	0.497	0.75	0.686	0.61	0.475	0.19	4.614	0.93
Word recall	4.758	6.64	5.956	4.96	8.243	3.21	6.892	1.36
Numeracy	12.078	8.49	27.235	11.52	48.547	9.62	76.988	7.72
Retrieval fluency W	0.571	1.84	0.572	1.09	2.541	2.23	1.935	0.89
Cons	-951.354	5.90	-1319.679	4.83	-2720.457	4.55	-2613.225	2.28
N	18,382		18,382		18,382		18,382	

household wealth) and table 7.6 (for total financial wealth) lists estimates from quantile regressions, estimated for the first and third quartile, the median and the ninetieth percentile. As expected, estimated effects of most of the noncognitive variables increase as we move up toward higher quantiles in the total wealth and nonfinancial wealth distribution.

Numeracy, the key cognitive variable identified in table 7.2, behaves precisely this way—estimated impacts of numeracy increase as we move up the total wealth quantiles, from an estimated impact of $2.6K at the first quartile, to almost $12K for the median household, and $52K at the ninetieth percentile. A similar pattern is found in table 7.6 when the outcome is total financial wealth. The other key variable, *episodic memory,* does the same but at a far less dramatic rate. Especially for total financial wealth, the estimated impacts of *episodic memory* are fairly uniform across these percentiles. Compared to *Numeracy, episodic memory* may be relatively more important at lower values in the wealth distribution.

The results summarized thus far pertain to wealth levels and composition in calendar year 2006. The panel nature of HRS allows us to examine the association of these cognition measures with changes in wealth observed for individuals in the panel. Tables 7.3, 7.5, and 7.7 list results obtained from models where the outcome is the change between years 2006 and 2000 in total wealth, total financial wealth, and the fraction of financial wealth held as stocks. All right-hand side variables are the same as in the level analysis, but a control is added for year 2000 total household wealth or financial wealth depending upon the financial outcome under investigation.

Not surprisingly, estimated effects of all noncognitive variables are similar to those obtained from the 2006 level analysis but are much smaller in magnitude since now we are predicting changes between the 2006 and 2000 HRS waves. In particular, numeracy and word recall are consistently related to wealth increases over this six-year period, while the estimated impacts of the other cognitive variables are quite weak. Answering each numeracy question correctly is associated with an $8,000 increase in total household wealth.

7.4   Individual-Level Analysis in CogEcon

The data used in this section are the result of collaboration between the National Growth and Change Study (NGCS)+HRS Cognition Study and the Cognitive Economics Survey (CogEcon).[5] A goal of NGCS+HRS is to conduct detailed measurement, through telephone and personal interviewing, of cognitive abilities of a sample of older Americans in the same fifty-plus age range of the HRS by developing data to help understand the

5. The NCGS+HRS was led by McArdle and CogEcon was led by Willis. The design, contents, and field outcomes of CogEcon and NCGS+HRS surveys are described in detail in Fisher and Helppie (2009).

Table 7.5   Relationship of changes in total household wealth holdings (2000–2006) to cognition 2006 individual sample—quantile models (wealth in thousands of dollars)

	25th quantile		Median		75th quantile		90th quantile	
	Coef.	t	Coef.	t	Coef.	t	Coef.	t
Female	0.183	0.09	-1.247	0.59	-2.272	0.60	-4.452	0.54
Hispanic	3.803	1.01	13.139	3.49	21.113	3.09	66.162	4.50
Nonwhite	-4.677	1.66	-0.840	0.30	2.445	0.49	7.984	0.75
Age	6.472	6.05	3.763	3.38	-1.466	0.72	-7.326	1.60
Age squared	-0.046	5.86	-0.025	3.06	0.010	0.71	-0.057	1.72
Married	17.408	6.67	7.999	3.12	11.760	2.56	29.766	2.97
Education	1.210	3.57	1.216	3.47	2.466	3.70	6.974	4.54
Financial respondent	-4.9940	2.07	-5.494	2.29	-2.105	0.49	-3.660	0.38
Income	0.881	43.44	1.515	76.45	2.394	69.93	3.404	45.14
Income squared	-0.000	14.76	-0.001	28.93	-0.001	32.14	-0.002	27.38
Number series W	0.024	0.37	-0.000	0.01	-0.050	0.42	0.102	0.40
TICS mental status	-0.905	1.43	-0.901	1.39	-1.370	1.19	-5.912	2.36
Word recall	3.257	4.99	3.221	4.88	2.218	1.86	2.149	0.84
Numeracy	7.968	6.15	8.770	6.71	12.939	5.41	24.624	4.71
Retrieval fluency W	0.342	1.29	0.281	0.98	1.020	1.87	3.352	2.69
Wealth 2000	-0.573	414.48	-0.285	301.56	0.031	23.24	0.401	139.79
Cons	-439.476	3.14	-302.051	2.00	-450.567	1.58	-1447.415	2.23
N	14,272		14,272		14,272		14,272	

Table 7.6 Relationship of total financial wealth holdings to cognition
2006 individual sample—quantile models (wealth in thousands of dollars)

	25th quantile		Median		75th quantile		90th quantile	
	Coef.	t	Coef.	t	Coef.	t	Coef	t
Female	0.894	1.27	2.208	1.28	4.510	1.02	5.737	0.57
Hispanic	-3.196	2.58	-6.898	2.35	-18.900	2.67	-47.886	3.14
Nonwhite	-7.863	8.39	-19.616	8.76	-53.412	9.86	-114.563	9.65
Age	4.422	15.15	8.884	11.48	14.514	6.88	19.143	3.85
Age squared	-0.026	12.88	-0.051	9.43	-0.081	5.58	-0.099	2.87
Married	-0.213	0.25	0.508	0.24	-0.566	0.11	6.725	0.55
Education	0.739	6.48	2.762	9.54	5.803	7.45	13.375	7.05
Financial respondent	-2.649	3.28	-7.915	4.00	-18.973	3.82	-39.262	3.44
Income	0.825	207.93	2.234	232.18	5.432	217.38	9.898	173.15
Income squared	-0.000	160.79	-0.000	195.68	-0.000	202.25	-0.001	165.84
Number series W	0.005	0.21	0.102	1.81	0.222	1.50	0.173	0.50
TICS mental status	-0.179	0.89	-0.668	1.31	-0.127	0.09	0.015	0.00
Word recall	0.906	4.15	2.069	3.78	1.399	0.99	2.350	0.73
Numeracy	2.605	6.00	11.847	10.99	27.192	9.78	52.309	8.13
Retrieval fluency W	0.179	1.95	0.696	2.91	1.630	2.60	2.356	1.63
Cons	-285.730	5.95	-798.977	6.41	-1558.952	4.76	-2105.232	2.77
N	18,382		18,382		18,382		18,382	

Table 7.7   Relationship of changes (2000–2006) in total financial wealth holdings to cognition 2006 individual sample—quantile models (wealth in thousands of dollars)

	25th quantile		Median		75th quantile		90th quantile	
	Coef.	t	Coef.	t	Coef.	t	Coef.	t
Female	-0.186	0.307	0.525	0.66	-0.810	0.64	2.887	0.55
Hispanic	0.348	0.31	0.678	0.485	1.972	0.89	1.092	0.12
Nonwhite	-4.119	4.99	-2.935	2.81	-2.652	1.64	-14.561	2.29
Age	1.361	4.29	1.343	3.20	0.200	0.30	-3.735	1.37
Age squared	-0.010	4.26	-0.009	3.00	-0.001	0.24	0.033	1.65
Married	1.484	1.95	0.151	0.16	-1.023	0.68	14.807	2.39
Education	0.214	2.13	0.281	2.14	0.738	3.42	3.354	3.55
Financial respondent	-0.835	1.19	-0.851	0.94	-2.094	1.46	-2.229	0.38
Income	0.249	38.60	0.652	87.16	1.459	126.89	2.771	59.78
Income squared	0.000	17.81	-0.000	23.76	-0.000	18.28	-0.001	30.78
Number series W	0.007	0.35	0.030	1.18	-0.014	0.35	0.105	0.62
TICS mental status	-0.531	2.87	-0.977	4.01	-1.078	2.85	-2.018	1.30
Word recall	0.741	3.88	0.755	3.04	0.446	1.13	0.610	0.37
Numeracy	1.743	4.60	2.879	5.85	4.484	5.71	10.426	3.16
Retrieval fluency W	0.162	2.08	0.226	2.09	0.841	4.66	2.243	2.98
Financial wealth-2000	-0.708	1530.60	-0.385	867.41	-0.040	67.39	0.359	142.31
Cons	-134.091	3.25	-176.743	3.12	-419.487	4.47	-1046.97	2.67
N	14,272		14,272		14,272		14,272	

cognitive bases of economic decision making. To do so, a detailed questionnaire containing measures of wealth and portfolio allocation, self-rated and objective measures of financial knowledge, measures of risk tolerance, use of financial advice, and other variables were administered by mail and Internet survey to participants in the NGCS+HRS.

The combined NGCS+HRS/CogEcon data set provides a combination of psychological and economic measurements on the same people with greater detail than any other data set. The CogEcon survey invited 1,222 individual members of the NGCS+HRS sample whose cognitive ability were assessed in face-to-face interviews to participate in the CogEcon mail/Internet survey. Of these, 985 returned surveys, implying a final response rate of 80.6 percent, including age-ineligible spouses. The CogEcon sample consists of individuals who range in age from thirty-eight to ninety-six years, with a mean age of 64.0 years.

The telephone component of NGCS+HRS repeats HRS cognition measures (episodic memory, mental status, numeracy, and adaptive number series measure) used before. The personal interview is an intensive three-hour cognitive measurement of a large number of ability components. These include number series, retrieval fluency, verbal analogies, spatial relations, picture vocabulary, auditory working memory, visual matching, incomplete words, concept formation, calculation, word attack from WJ III (Woodcock, McGrew, and Mather 2001); vocabulary, block design, similarities, and matrix reasoning from the *Wechsler Adult Intelligence Scale* (WAIS) (plus a switching task), and a vigilance task (McArdle and Woodcock 1998).

There are advantages and disadvantages of the CogEcon survey. The principal disadvantage is that sample sizes are much lower than in the core HRS, and with outcomes as heterogeneous as wealth, which may lead to results that are less robust. The principal advantage is that CogEcon is able to measure in far greater depth dimensions of cognition than may be relevant to economic decision making, including wealth accumulation. We view the HRS and CogEcon as complementary sources of relevant information.

Tables 7.8 and 7.9 present results for three regression prediction models of ln current wealth based on data from the CogEcon survey ($n = 942$). In all models, the same demographics as in the core HRS analysis—age (quadratic), education, couple status, and income (quadratic)—are included. These results uniformly show significant positive differences in wealth for persons with increased income (up to a point; $t > 8$), and for persons in intact couples, but no statistically significant independent increments based on age or education. Education does increase wealth in models where we delete all cognition variables.

In the first model in table 7.8, these predictions are estimated in tandem with five cognitive variables derived from the telephone testing alone, which also correspond to cognition variables available in the core HRS. In these data, the five cognitive variables improved the prediction with significant

Table 7.8   **Total wealth model in the CogEcon sample**

	Coef.	t	Coef.	t	Coef.	t
			A. Log wealth			
Age	.052	0.45	.047	0.41	.062	0.50
Age squared	.000	0.22	.000	0.31	.000	0.22
Couple	.979	4.14	.949	4.01	.758	3.07
Education	.053	1.02	.017	0.32	−.083	1.41
Income	.000	8.43	.000	8.26	.000	7.78
Income squared	−1.93e−11	7.32	−1.87e−11	7.08	−1.80e−11	6.82
Cognition variables						
Telephone number series W	.004	1.02				
Face-to-face num series			.019	3.00	−.007	0.81
Episodic memory	.017	2.49	.017	2.53	.012	1.59
TICS mental status	.023	2.00	.018	1.48	.008	0.59
Numeracy	.315	2.20	.199	1.34	.207	1.33
Retrieval fluency	−.037	1.46	−.036	1.44	−.036	1.36
Calculation					.015	1.62
Matrix reasoning					.082	3.43
Mean financial literacy score					.280	2.83
Cons	17.980	1.40	10.860	0.82	14.399	0.98

Table 7.9   **Predicting financial literacy**

	Coef.	t
Age	.1067	2.32
Age squared	−.0007	2.05
Couple	.1493	1.64
Education	.0640	2.98
Income[a]	.0033	3.78
Income squared[a]	−0.330e−07	3.42
Cognition variables		
Face-to-face num series	.0082	2.72
Episodic memory	.0048	1.75
TICS mental status	.0024	0.51
Numeracy	.1318	2.31
Retrieval fluency	.0058	0.59
Calculation	.0065	1.91
Matrix reasoning	.0067	0.77
Cons	−8.048	1.49

[a]Income measured in thousands of dollars.

positive independent contributions of episodic memory ($t > 2$), numeracy ($t > 2$), and mental status ($t > 2$), but neither retrieval fluency nor number series. These results parallel reasonably well those found for the same set of cognitive constructs using the HRS in table 7.2.

The *Number Series WJ-III test* (WJ III) used to measure numerical reasoning was administered in two different forms. The face-to-face test is the standard WJ III forty-seven item version presented using standard WJ rules, with an expected internal consistency reliability of $r_{ic} > .95$ (Woodcock, McGrew, and Mather 2003). The telephone version is a much shorter adaptive form of the same test, where up to six items are presented in three to five minutes (McArdle 2008). The items chosen are selected based on prior performances on earlier items (i.e., harder items are selected if the participant has given correct answers earlier), with an expected internal consistency reliability of $r_{ic} > .85$. In the CogEcon study (NGCS + HRS) the participants were administered the telephone test first and then administered the face-to-face test in standard testing conditions from one to fourteen days later. After taking into account some expected differences due to time-lags, the average test-retest correlation was $r_{tr} > 0.72$ (McArdle et al. 2009).

The second model in table 7.8 substitutes the longer (and more reliable) face-to-face number series test for the telephone version used in the first model. The face-to-face version of the number series score now offers a strong incremental prediction ($t > 3$), and reduces—but does not eliminate—the estimated effects of *numeracy* and *episodic memory.*

In the third model of table 7.8 three new cognitive tests are added—calculation, matrix reasoning, and mean financial literacy score. These tests are not currently available in the HRS. *WJ-III Calculation* is a test of math achievement measuring the ability to perform mathematical computations from Woodcock-Johnson Scales (Woodcock, McGrew, and Mather 2003) with an expected internal consistency reliability of $r_{ic} > .95$. Initial items in calculation require an individual to write single numbers. The remaining items require a person to perform addition, subtraction, multiplication, division, and combinations of these basic operations, as well as some geometric, trigonometric, logarithmic, and calculus operations. The calculations involve negative numbers, percents, decimals, fractions, and whole numbers. Because calculations are presented in a traditional problem format in the test record form, the person is not required to make any decisions about what operations to use or what data to include. *Calculation* is similar to *numeracy* in intent in that they both attempt to measure aspects of Gc applied to numbers.

WASI Matrix Reasoning measures nonverbal fluid reasoning and general intellectual ability from the abbreviated form of the Weschler Adult Intelligence Scale (WAIS III, Wechsler 1997). These twenty items require participants to look at each set of symbols (arrayed in a vector or matrix) with one missing location, and then they are asked to fill in "the best option for the missing piece." The person is not asked or required to make any decisions about reasons why this choice is best. Given its use of abstract and spatial symbols, *matrix reasoning* can be thought of as a dimension of Gf.

CogEcon Financial Literacy/Financial Sophistication are twenty-four items (true/false and confidence). These measures signify the belief that these questions have more sensitivity at the "high" end of the scale (when compared to measures in HRS and many other surveys). These questions have two versions each, one which is "true" and one which is "false," but ask a very similar question. True/false measures of financial sophistication are on a scale ranging from 100 percent to 50 percent confidence that the statement is "false," and 50 percent to 100 percent confidence that the statement is "true." For example, the "true" version (Q17) is: "An investment advisor tells a 30-year-old couple that $1,000 in an investment that pays a certain, constant interest rate would double in value to $2,000 after 20 years. If so, that investment *would* be worth $4,000 *in less than* 45 years." The "false" version reads: "An investment advisor tells a 30-year-old couple that $1,000 in an investment that pays a certain, constant interest rate would double in value to $2,000 after 20 years. If so, that investment *would not* be worth $4,000 *for at least* 45 years." The italics are added to indicate parts of questions that differ. The respondent is instructed to decide whether the statement is "true" or "false," and to indicate their confidence in this answer.

In the third model in table 7.8, when these additional cognitive tests are added as predictions, matrix reasoning is the strongest independent predictor ($t > 3$), and financial literacy is next ($t > 2$), but the calculation test is not a statistically significant predictor. All statements about tests of significance must contain the caveat of relatively small sample sizes in CogEcon.

Including measures of financial literacy in models of wealth accumulation is a bit odd. Financial literacy is not manna from heaven enabling one to successfully navigate the complicated and dangerous waters of financial success. Those with more of an interest or opportunity to invest in financial markets have more of an incentive to invest in acquiring the knowledge of how to successfully operate in these markets or to become financially literate. This view argues that models in table 7.8 have it all wrong and that financial literacy is an outcome that should be studied. Table 7.9 does just that by predicting levels of financial literacy with the same set of personal attributes and set of cognitive variables discussed earlier.

Financial literacy increases with age and with income, but at a decreasing rate, and increases with years of schooling. All these predictive effects are statistically significant. Once again, intact mental status (the TICS score) and retrieval fluency appear to be aspects of cognition that are not related to financial decision making. In contrast, all aspects of cognition related to numerical ability—number series, numeracy, and calculation—are all strongly predictive of better financial literacy. These results point to one possible pathway through which cognitive ability related to numbers may promote wealth accumulation, making it easier to acquire relevant financial knowledge. It also suggests that we may be overcontrolling by including financial literacy in the models in table 7.8, as this may suppress the effects of cognition. The final model in table 7.8 removes the financial literacy variable. Estimated effects of both the number series and calculation are increased by its removal.

These new results broadly highlight the fact that the individual cognition tests can add to the individual-level descriptive predictions of our basic understanding of differences in wealth. There appear to be independent benefits of having both higher financial literacy (i.e., Gc) and higher ability to reason in a nonquantitative fashion (i.e., Gf).

7.5   Conclusions

Inclusion of individual cognitive measures in prediction of economic outcomes has turned out to be useful. While the importance and the pattern of effects needs to consider the specific sources of information (i.e., the entire HRS, individual modules, or CogEcon), these cognitive measures appear to meet minimal standards of being descriptively informative.

Numeracy, as measured by answers to three simple mathematical questions, is by far the most predictive of wealth among all cognitive variables in the HRS sample. This is thought by cognitive psychologists to be a direct measure of a specific and practical form of numerical knowledge (i.e., a form of *crystallized intelligence*). We found independent impacts that were statistically significant for all three financial outcomes. *Numeracy* had more of a problem maintaining statistical significance in the CogEcon sample when tested against other more complex and time intensive measures (*number series* and *calculation*) that in part attempt to measure similar things. Still, one has to be impressed with the ability of the three simple questions in the numeracy sequence to capture the core elements in predicting wealth accumulation.

The independent impact of *number series* has similar characteristics in its relationship to the financial outcomes, but these relationships are not as important with the strong qualification that there currently exists more limited data on this measure in the HRS. The number series is not simply a measure of numerical knowledge, but is a broader measure of numerical reasoning (i.e., an indicator of *fluid intelligence*), and this is not a pure indicator of the acquisition of wealth. The more complicated and time intensive measurement of number series in the face-to-face component of the CogEcon sample does considerably better in predicting wealth.

Episodic memory (or *word recall*) also appears to be related to the total and financial wealth holdings of the family. The remaining two cognitive measures—*mental status* and *retrieval fluency*—have very weak and erratic relationships with these financial outcomes. *Mental status* is statistically significant in only two of six cases and *retrieval fluency* in only one of six cases.[6]

Although these specific cognitive measures were useful in predictions of

6. Remember that retrieval fluency is only available in an experimental module in the 2006 wave, so that statistical significance is a more difficult hurdle for this variable.

measures of accumulated wealth, it is certainly possible that other financial outcomes will be better predicted by different indicators of cognitive functions. Additional analyses of HRS data and other data can be conducted using this basic approach, including cognitive speed measures, and all available cognitive measures for different outcomes.

The type of unabashedly exploratory and descriptive analysis in this chapter cannot establish causal pathways for these associations. There is no randomization in the cognitive ability of HRS respondents and one can easily think of correlates of these cognitive measures that may offer plausible reasons for these associations. Nor can it be easily dismissed that a history of lifetime interests and investments in the stock market, for example, could lead to improved numerical ability. Yet, the presence of these estimated effects of numeracy on total and financial wealth at lower wealth quartiles where levels of commitment of investors is relatively modest should caution at least against a purely reverse pathway from investments to cognitive ability. For some cognitive functions, such as numerical ability, the cognitive training of these skills seem to be readily attainable by most persons, and the returns seem high. At a minimum, the type of strong associations in descriptive analysis in this chapter is a signal that one may want to pursue studies that may offer more discriminating tests of whether these associations can be thought of as plausibly causal.

References

Banks, J., and Z. Oldfield. 2007. Understanding pensions: Cognitive function, numerical ability and retirement saving. *Fiscal Studies* 28 (2): 143–70.

Benjamin, D. J., S. A. Brown, and J. M. Shapiro. 2006. Who is "behavioural"? Cognitive ability and anomalous preferences. Available at: http://ssrn.com/.

Ben-Porath, Y. 1967. The production of human capital and the life cycle of earnings. *The Journal of Political Economy* 75 (4): 352–65.

Cattell, R. B. 1987. The natural history of ability: Distribution and relation to sex and age. In *Intelligence: Its structure, growth, and action, Advances in Psychology* 35:206. New York: Elsevier Science.

Conger, R. D., X. Ge, G. Elder, F. Lorenz, and R. Simons. 1994. Economic stress, coercive family process, and developmental problems of adolescents. *Child Development* 65:541–61.

Cunha, F., and J. Heckman. 2007. The technology of skill formation. *American Economic Review* 97 (2): 31–47.

Delevande, A., S. Rohwedder, and R. J. Willis. 2008. Preparation for retirement, financial literacy and cognitive resources. Michigan Retirement Research Center Working Paper no. 2008-190.

Elder, G. H., Jr. 1974. *Children of the Great Depression.* Chicago: University of Chicago Press.

Farias, S. T., D. Mungas, B. R. Reed, D. Cahn-Weiner, W. Jagust, K. Baynes, and

C. DeCarli. 2008. The measurement of everyday cognition (ECog): Scale development and psychometric properties. *Neuropsychology* 22 (4): 531–44.

Fisher, G. G., and F. Helppie. 2009. Cognitive economics survey study and data documentation. Survey Research Center, University of Michigan, January 9. Working Paper.

Harden, K. P., E. Turkheimer, and J. C. Loehlin. 2007. Genotype by environment interaction in adolescents' cognitive aptitude. *Behavior Genetics* 37:273–83.

Hershey, D. A., J. M. Jacobs-Lawson, J. J. McArdle, and F. Hamagami. 2007. Psychological foundations of financial planning. *Journal of Adult Development* 14:26–36.

Herzog, A. R., and W. L. Rodgers. 1999. Cognitive performance measures in survey research on older adults. In *Aging, cognition, and self-reports,* ed. N. Schwarz, D. Park, B. Knauper, and S. Sudman, 327–40. Philadelphia, PA: Psychology Press.

Herzog, A. R., and R. B. Wallace. 1997. Measures of cognitive functioning in the AHEAD study [Special Issue]. *Journal of Gerontology Series B: Psychological Sciences and Social Sciences 52B:*37–48.

Horn, J. L., and J. J. McArdle. 2007. Understanding human intelligence since Spearman. In *Factor analysis at 100 years,* ed. R. Cudeck and R. MacCallum, 205–47. Mahwah, NJ: Lawrence Erlbaum Associates, Inc.

Juster, F. T., and J. P. Smith. 1997. Improving the quality of economic data: Lessons from HRS and AHEAD. *Journal of the American Statistical Association* 92 (440): 1268–78.

Juster, F. T., J. P. Smith, and F. Stafford. 1999. The measurement and structure of household wealth. *Labour Economics* 6 (2): 253–75.

Lee, S., I. Kawachi, L. F. Berkman, and F. Grodstein. 2003. Education, other socioeconomic indicators, and cognitive function. *American Journal of Epidemiology* 157 (8): 712–20.

McArdle, J. J. 2008. Latent variable modeling of longitudinal data. *Annual Review of Psychology* 60:577–605.

McArdle, J. J., E. Ferrer-Caja, F. Hamagami, and R. W. Woodcock. 2002. Comparative longitudinal structural analyses of the growth and decline of multiple intellectual abilities over the life span. *Developmental Psychology* 38 (1): 115–42.

McArdle, J. J., G. G. Fisher, and K. M. Kadlec. 2007. Latent variable analysis of age trends in tests of cognitive ability in the Health and Retirement Survey, 1992–2004. *Psychology and Aging* 22 (3): 525–45.

McArdle, J. J., and R. W. Woodcock, (Eds.). 1998. *Human abilities in theory and practice.* Mahwah, NJ: Erlbaum.

Ofstedal, M. B., G. G. Fisher, and A. R. Herzog. 2005. Documentation of cognitive functioning measures in the Health and Retirement Study. HRS Documentation Report DR-006, March.

Parker, A. M., and B. Fischhoff. 2005. Decision-making competence: External validation through an individual-differences approach. *Journal of Behavioral Decision Making* 18: 1–27.

Peters, E., D. Västfjäll, P. Slovic, C. K. Mertz, K. Mazzocco, and S. Dickert. 2006. Numeracy and decision making. *Psychological Science* 17: 407–13.

Ramey, S. L., and G. P. Sackett, 2000. The early caregiving environment: Expanding views on nonparental care and cumulative life experiences. In *Handbook of developmental psychopathology (2nd ed.),* ed. A. J. Sameroff, M. Lewis, and S. M. Miller, 365–80. Dordrecht, Netherlands: Kluwer Academic Publishers.

Rutter, M. 1985. Family and school influences on cognitive development. *Journal of Child Psychology and Psychiatry* 26:683–704.

Smith, J. P. 1995. Racial and ethnic differences in wealth in the Health and Retirement Study. *Journal of Human Resources* 30 (December): S158–83.

———. 1999. Inheritances and bequests. In *Wealth, work, and health: Innovations in measurement in the social sciences,* ed. J. P. Smith and R. Willis, 121–49. Ann Arbor: University of Michigan Press.

Wechsler, D. 1997. *Wechsler adult intelligence scale-III.* San Antonio, TX: The Psychological Corporation.

Willis, R. J. 2007. Cognitive economics and human capital. Presidential Address to Society of Labor Economists, Chicago, May 4–5.

Woodcock, R. W., K. McGrew, and N. Mather. 2001. *Woodcock-Johnson tests of cognitive abilities and tests of achievement (3rd edition).* Rolling Meadows, IL: Riverside Publishing.

———. 2003. *Woodcock-Johnson III Normative Update (NU) tests of cognitive abilities.* Chicago, IL: Riverside Publishing Company.

Comment   Finis Welch

I should begin by saying to Mr. McArdle that while I do not know you, I know your coauthors. Someone should have warned you!

Actually this chapter follows a series of papers by Jim Smith that concentrate on wealth. I believe he has done more in this area than any other, especially in studying inequality and in validating the sequential series of questions HRS uses to elicit responses and in comparing the wealth levels in HRS to those of other sources. When Jim talks about wealth (aside from his own) we all listen. When he talks about his own, you should listen, but should not believe.[1] The chapter's innovation is the addition of the cognitive measures as they relate to the levels of wealth in HRS. To someone as old as I am, that is a scary issue. When I saw the title I expected the chapter to begin with a profile of cognitive measures across age that showed physical skills are not the only things that recede with age.

In fact, my main criticism of the chapter is that there are too few descriptive tables. I would love to have seen an age profile of wealth levels as well as one for the 2000 to 2006 changes that, along with 2006 levels of wealth, are analyzed in the chapter. Although I assume that there is a substantial literature on spending down, nothing would be lost if it were addressed here. We understand that the cross-sectional age profiles confuse age and cohort, but we ought to see what we are to be confused about. More important, it would be very nice to see the age profiles of test scores. In this case there would be no confusion between age and cohort.

If scores for older respondents are lower, it is cohort. If scores are higher

Finis Welch is president of Welch Consulting, distinguished professor emeritus of economics at Texas A&M University, and professor emeritus of economics at the University of California, Los Angeles.

1. I have known Jim for almost forty years. If he says "up" it is probably "down."

for older respondents, it is age, and if scores do not change, I will not worry. It would also be illuminating to explore the relation between test scores and education, holding age constant. If education proxies the skills acquired in school, including the ability to learn, then the test scores addressed here are alternative measures of these skills. As such, controlling for the test scores will dilute the linkage between wealth and education just as controlling for education will dilute the linkage between test scores and wealth. It would be interesting to see some of the calculations repeated when education is omitted, perhaps in an appendix, so that the cognitive measures are allowed to assume all of the correlated effects.

There is a lot here for one chapter. It is hard to keep track of the various tests. Not the statistical test, the alternative measures of cognitive skill. The descriptions of the tests and their relation to the concepts of flow and crystallized knowledge are interesting but they seem to have little to do with the empirical work to follow. The chapter's main objective is to see how cognitive ability affects wealth accumulation and maintenance. One wonders vis-à-vis wealth if there is a way of synthesizing the tests into a single measure. Since numeracy seems to have most of the predictive power, I wonder what would be lost if it were used alone? Personally, I would prefer to have the description of the tests and their relation to the flow and crystallized notions in an appendix.

More than any other thing, this chapter is exploratory. It simply searches for links between the various cognitive measures and levels of wealth at advanced ages. The unfortunate part of the story is that in these data we are unable to ask the most interesting questions. Since there is a positive relation between measured cognitive ability and wealth, those questions are:

1. Does the association only reflect the fact that those with greater cognitive ability (henceforth, "smarter people") earn higher incomes?

2. Does it reflect higher saving rates among smarter people (for given income)?

3. Do smarter people invest more productively (for given savings)?

If it is only the first, no one cares. The second would be interesting, but the third would be more so.

Unfortunately, to answer the fundamental questions we would have to have younger people than those found in the HRS.

Despite the inability to address these questions, specification searches can provide some insight. Compare table 7.2 to table 7.4. The ordinary least squares (OLS) estimates in 7.2 provide means of wealth conditional on the test scores and the other controls while the quantile estimates in 7.4 provide the twenty-fifth, median, seventy-fifth, and ninetieth centiles of the wealth distribution, conditional on the same controls.

The text of the chapter points to the estimates in 7.4 and notes that the coefficient on the score on numerical ability increases as one moves from lower to higher quantiles. Since the coefficient on numerical ability in the mean regressions (table 7.2) is positive, the authors point out that this is exactly what one would expect. In fact, at the conference where this chapter was presented, Smith skipped the quantile regressions altogether saying that they provided nothing new. Wrong!

I personally believe that the contrast between the mean and quantile estimates provide the most interesting feature of the empirical work.

As background, think of the classic bivariant regression where the right-hand side (RHS) variable, x, is distributed on the real line and the left-hand side (LHS) variable, y given x, is normal with i.i.d. residuals. If the line is $y = a + bx + u$, then the mean regression (OLS) provides best linear unbiased estimator (BLUE) estimates of a and b. In this case the quantile lines are exactly parallel to the mean, which is $a + bx$. The first quartile is 0.67 standard deviations of the residual, u, below the mean, the median is also the mean since the distribution of y given x is symmetric and the third quartile line has gradient b with intercept $a + .67$ sigma(u). Actually, for the classic case with i.i.d. residuals, the easiest way to calculate the quantile regressions is to run the OLS regression and then use the empirical residuals to calculate shifts in the intercept for the various quantiles. Now consider a case of heteroskedastic residuals.

For simplicity assume that the mean line has zero gradient, that residuals are independent and symmetric, and that the standard deviation of the residuals is increasing in x. In this case the quantiles show increased spread as we move to progressively higher levels of x. All quantiles below the median will have negative gradients and the gradient will be lower at lower quantiles. The gradients for the quantiles above the median will be the exact mirror image of those below. For equal absolute differences of quantiles from the median, the absolute values of the gradients will also be equal. If the mean line has a positive (negative) gradient then that positive (negative) number will simply be added to each of the quantile gradients. With this in mind, return to the contrast between tables 7.2 and 7.4.

Here, in table 7.4, the increasing gradient for the score on the test of numerical ability in the quantile regressions as we move to higher quantiles shows that the variance of wealth increases as the numerical score increases. That, to my mind, suggests that the numerically proficient take more risks. Table 7.2 shows higher average levels of wealth for higher scores on the numerical ability test so it appears that there is a trade—higher risk for higher expected return. This may be pushing the results too far (i.e., taking them too literally), but the two results are at least suggestive. This, of course, is only a small part of the chapter.

The analysis of couples is particularly interesting. Even if dumb husbands say they make the investment decisions, their wealth seems to be higher if they are married to a smart wife. While you may think this is because the dumb guys listen to their wives, it may only be that the smart wives earn more.

It is a fun chapter. I recommend it.

Aging, Religion, and Health

Angus Deaton

8.1 Introduction

In this chapter, I use Gallup World Poll data from random national samples of individuals from 146 countries to investigate both the determinants of religion and its effects on health. These issues are especially relevant for the analysis of aging because, in almost all countries of the world, the elderly are more likely to report that religion is important in their lives. That the elderly should be more religious is predicted both by secularization theory, which argues that successive cohorts become less religious, at least under some circumstances, as well as by the economic theory of intertemporal choice and capital formation, which predicts that people become more religious as they grow older (Azzi and Ehrenberg 1975). One of the aims of this chapter is to document international patterns of how religiosity varies with age and gender, and to produce evidence on the secularization versus aging stories. The second aim is to explore the relationship between religiosity and health. In this, I follow a large contemporaneous empirical literature that documents that religious people typically have better health outcomes (see Koenig, McCullough, and Larson [2000] and McCullough and Smith [2003], who summarize many hundreds of studies). Most of these studies use community data, although a few use large national samples, as in

Angus Deaton is the Dwight D. Eisenhower Professor of International Affairs and professor of economics and international affairs at the Woodrow Wilson School of Public and International Affairs and the Economics Department at Princeton University, and a research associate of the National Bureau of Economic Research.

I am grateful to the Gallup Organization for access to the data in their World Poll. I thank Danny Kahneman and Raksha Arora for their help and collaboration on a related project and Anne Case, Jim Smith, and John Haaga for helpful comments on an earlier draft.

the Hummer et al. (1999) analysis of religious attendance and mortality in the United States. I am aware of no analysis of within-country effects for a large number of countries, nor for the comparison of those effects between countries.

I shall work with a simple triangular causal structure, in which religiosity and religious practice are caused by income, education, age, and sex, and in which health is caused by religion, income, education, age, and sex. I estimate these relationships separately for each country, and then examine similarities and differences across countries, both in the national averages—essentially cross-country regressions of religiosity and health on national characteristics—and in the coefficients from the within-country relationships. It is easy to think of reasons why this causal framework might be wrong—poor health might cause people to turn to religion, or there could be third factors, such as rates of time preference, that affect both religiosity and health. However, I do not believe that there is currently any credible way of distinguishing causality. So I shall simply follow the large majority of the literature, assuming the causal structure and examining the plausibility and interest of what I get within it. As we shall see, there are some startling differences in health outcomes and health behaviors by religiosity, and these patterns are worth describing and thinking about. The mechanisms that have been postulated in the literature—that religion is a superstition that is undermined by education, that wage rates or risk preferences affect religiosity and so help explain differences between men and women, and that the religious have healthier lives—have implications for the patterns of correlation in the data, and those I can examine.

The Gallup data cover more countries—particularly poor countries in Africa—and are nationally representative for more countries than previous international data such as the World Values Surveys, which have been widely used in previous examinations of religion in the world; for example, by Miller and Stark (2002), Norris and Inglehart (2004), and Inglehart (2010).

The chapter is organized as follows. I begin in section 8.2 with a brief summary of the literature that is relevant to the hypotheses that we examine here, the various versions of the secularization hypothesis, of aging, gender, and religion, as well as accounts of the ways in which religion might be good for health. Section 8.3 contains a brief summary of the survey, including the countries covered and the questions that we use. A major exclusion is China, which is included in the World Poll, but without the questions on religiosity and religious attendance. Section 8.4 looks at the links between income, education, age, and religion; consonant with previous research, the World Poll provides some support for the secularization story—older people are more religious, and more educated better-off people are less likely to be religious. Yet there is also evidence for pure age effects predicted by economic theory. Section 8.5 looks at the links between religion and health—conditional on variables such as age, sex, and education—that are linked with both.

8.2   Religiosity, Age, and Other Factors

One of the dominant themes in the literature is the secularization hypothesis, the idea that religious belief and practice will decline over time with economic development, particularly with rising levels of income and education. In one form or another, the argument was made by David Hume, John Stuart Mill, Karl Marx, Max Weber, Sigmund Freud, and many others (see Norris and Inglehart [2004] and McCleary and Barro [2006] for reviews). One extreme version of the hypothesis is that religious belief is a superstition that is dispelled by education. A more economic argument is given in Mill's *Utility of Religion.* Secularism, Mill argues, can provide all of the benefits of religion save one, the promise of eternal life. But as people become better-off in this life, they will substitute current for future utility, and will have less need of religion, an early argument for the importance of the intertemporal elasticity of substitution. Ingelhart (2008) provides an argument related to Mill's, that there are two routes to the good life, a traditional one through religion, with its emphasis on future bliss over present suffering, and a modern one, through education, higher incomes, social tolerance, and political freedom. As countries become richer, better educated, more democratic, and freer, the need for religion will fall. By this argument, economic development can be expected to cause a decline in religious belief, but only beyond the point where "the public of a given society has experienced relatively high levels of economic and physical security" (Norris and Inglehart 2004, 27).

The secularization hypothesis has implications for the age structure of religiosity at any moment of time. If people's religious beliefs are established early in life and do not change, secularization implies that, in the cross-section, religiosity be higher among the elderly, and more so in countries where education, lifetime incomes, or political freedoms have been rapidly expanding. Countries that have had rapid economic growth should show larger gaps in religiosity between young and old, though if Norris and Inglehart are right, this will only be true among the better-off, more secure nations.

Religiosity may also change with age, and in particular, religion may become more important to people as they grow older, and their minds turn to the contemplation of the hereafter. Specific predictions are derived in the important paper by Azzi and Ehrenberg (1975), who model religious practice as a time-intensive accumulation of religious or sacral capital that is valuable only after death. In contrast to the accumulation of human capital, which pays off throughout life, so that the optimal strategy is for people to acquire education when they are young, the accumulation of religious capital is optimally postponed, with the prediction that religious practice will rise with age. Since wages are lower for women than for men, and are lower for blacks than for whites, women and blacks should be more religious than white men, and they should accumulate religious capital earlier with a subsequently flatter profile than for white males. Azzi and Ehrenburg find support for these predictions using American data, and their model provides a useful lens to interpret patterns of religious activity throughout the world, both within countries and between them.

Azzi and Ehrenberg's prediction that women should be more religious than men has been widely observed to be true, although there is no general agreement on the mechanisms involved. Miller and Hoffmann (1995) and Miller and Stark (2002) propose that the decision not to believe in religion is a form of risk-taking behavior—if religion is true, such a decision has extremely unfortunate long-term consequences—and like most such behaviors, is more common among men, especially young men. Although this account does not explain where risk attitudes come from, it provides a unified way of thinking about religiosity, aging, and gender. It also predicts that in religions that do not threaten eternal punishment for nonbelievers—reformed Judaism, Shintoism, Hinduism, and Bhuddism, in contrast to Christian, Orthodox Jewish, and Muslim religions—there will be a smaller gender gap in religiosity, as well as a less pronounced age gradient. This last is also consistent with Azzi and Ehrenberg's model, since there is less need for "sacral capital" to fend off the fires of hell.

In his discussion of this paper, Jim Smith argues that women's religiosity may be linked to the fact that they have the primary responsibility for child-rearing in most countries of the world. David Sloan Wilson (2002) has argued that religion evolved to confer a survival advantage to groups of believers, in which case women would have responsibility for passing on beliefs from one generation to the next. If so, the gender gap might be expected to diminish as fertility falls, which falls foul of the evidence that the gender gap is largest in the richer, nontraditional societies where women have many options other than childbearing (Miller and Stark 2002).

Another important line of inquiry into secularization focuses on the role of the state, and on the hypothesis that state provision of social welfare and social insurance is a substitute for provision by organized religion, so that the latter are displaced by the former as the state grows over time. This line of thought leads to the examination of state welfare spending and religious practice, as well as to the possibility that religion is more important in places where risk is high—for example, in agriculture—or in places where social safety nets are weak—for example, in the U.S. South as opposed to the U.S. North. It is also possible that social security in the form of state pensions, or state-provided health insurance—in the United States focused on the elderly through Medicare—might reduce levels of religious participation throughout life.

There is also a literature on the *consequences* of religion, particularly the extent to which religious people have healthier lives. Idler and Kasl (1997) distinguish three types of mechanisms that they trace back to Durkheim and to Weber. These are "regulative"—religions typically impose rules that cover not only ethical behavior, but also eating, drinking, and sexual activities, rules that usually promote health; "integrative"—religions provide networks that connect people to others who provide tangible economic and psychological support and in some cases, healthcare; and "interpretative"—religion provides meaning and understanding to life that is likely to be especially useful in times of suffering or stress. The empirical literature has found positive health effects of religion for a wide range of conditions and diseases, for both morbidity and mortality. Much of the association with mortality works through the better health behaviors of the religious, but there is also evidence of effects even conditional on a range of social and health behaviors, as in Hummer et al. (2009). A recent review by Michael McCullough and Brian Willoughby (2009) argues that religion enhances self-control; that is, churches promote behaviors and beliefs that support self-regulation. Religious people absorb religious values into their own lives, imbuing their own long-term goals with a sacredness that makes them easier to attain in the face of present temptation. Of course, people who are born with low rates of time-preference and high self-control will also downweight the present relative to the future, including possibly an eternal future, and thus be more likely to join religions that emphasize eternal rewards in exchange for present sacrifice and self-control. Even here, religions may reinforce innate or early-developed dispositions.

The literature in economics has emphasized those aspects of religion that are favorable or unfavorable to economic efficiency and growth, a tradition that goes back at least to Weber. The promotion of self-control is clearly relevant for economic behavior as well as for well-being, as also are the promotion of trust, honesty, and thrift (McCleary and Barro 2006). From its roots in Weber, this literature has also inquired into whether different religions are more or less favorable to economic development; for example, through attitudes to usury (Guiso, Sapienza, and Zingales 2003), or through the promotion of social trust by developing relationships between coreligionists—Protestantism—or less so by emphasizing relationships between worshippers and priests—Catholicism (see Helliwell and Putnam 2004).

8.3 The Gallup World Poll

The World Poll is designed to be a continuing survey of all of the world's citizens. It began in 2006, and I use the data from the first three waves, 2006, 2007, and 2008, by which time 145 countries have been included, of which seventy-eight are in all three waves. The 145 countries contained a total of 6.45 billion people in 2006, more than 98 percent of the population of the world. In each wave and in each country, the poll samples around 1,000 individuals aged fifteen and over, though in some cases the samples are smaller or larger. With only a few exceptions, the samples are random national samples of the target population. The poll uses an identical core questionnaire in all countries. Here I use two questions about religion ("Is religion an important part of your daily life?") and religious observance ("Have you attended a place of worship or religious service within the last seven days?"). The second of these questions is potentially more problematic for religions (such as Buddhism) where attendance at places of worship is relatively unimportant. To simplify, I shall refer to these two questions here as religiosity and worship.

Gallup was unable to ask any of the religion questions in China, which is therefore excluded from the analysis.

The poll also collects information on health and on a number of health-related behaviors. Among the former, I look at self-reported health status, disability status, physical pain, and energy level. All of these are asked as yes or no questions. The wordings are: (a) Are you satisfied or dissatisfied with your personal health? (b) Do you have any health problems that prevent you from doing any of the things that people your age can normally do? (c) Did you experience the following feelings during a lot of the day yesterday? How about physical pain? (d) Did you have enough energy to get things done yesterday? (There are also a number of questions on life evaluation, and on positive and negative affect, and these are the topics of a companion paper.) Among the social and personal health-related behaviors, I look at marital status, time spent with friends, whether the respondent has a friend who would provide support in time of trouble, and whether the respondent smoked yesterday. Finally, I look for links between religion and whether people have confidence in their country's health and medical system; although this is neither a behavior nor an outcome, it is a health-related component of well-being. It may also reflect the provision of health care by religious institutions.

The poll also collects data on a set of socioeconomic and demographic variables, including education (coded into three categories—elementary education or less, secondary or up to three years of tertiary education, and four years or more of tertiary education) and a single question on income. The accuracy and meaningfulness of the income question is doubtful in much of the world and, unsurprisingly, there are a large number of missing values; even so, the question clearly contains some information, and we make some use of it, while also acknowledging its problems.

Excluding China, and combining data from all waves, our sample contains 351,250 observations from 144 countries; the sample size for each country ranges from (at the high end) 7,286 observations for India, 6,979 for Russia, and 5,238 for Germany to (at the low end) Puerto Rico (500), Guyana (501), and Belize (502). Only eight countries have less than a thousand observations. The poll includes countries that rarely appear in international surveys of any kind, including Afghanistan, Cuba, Iraq, and Myanmar, as well as thirty-two countries in Africa, including those such as Togo, Sierra Leone, and Zimbabwe, which have the dubious distinction of having the lowest levels of life evaluation on the planet (Deaton 2008). Apart from the loss of China, the key religion variables are reported by nearly all of the respondents in the survey, so that we have 335,005 valid observations to the worship question and 332,712 to the religiosity question.

8.4   Aging, Income, Education, and Religiosity

I begin with the cross-country patterns of religiosity summarized in the top panel of table 8.1. The first columns for each measure show that religiosity and worship vary greatly across the regions of the world. Africa is the base region in the table, and the average African country (not weighted by population) has 93 percent of its population religious, and 71 percent worshiping in the last week. South Asian and Middle Eastern countries are almost as religious, while the countries of non-English-speaking Northern Europe and East Asia are the least religious, followed by the former communist countries of Eastern Europe. These patterns are only very partially explained by differences in national income; for example, East Asia and Northern Europe are the least religious places, but have very different income levels. In the second column for each measure income is included. Regional effects are not much changed, though income is important, at least for religiosity. The practice of religion, as measured through the worship variable, is not significantly affected by income, conditional on regional effects.

The history and spread of world religions gives good reason to suppose that the regional effects are fundamental, at least in part, and are unlikely to be readily explained by other standard variables. In fact, and apart from income, none of the other country variables that I consider significantly predict religion, conditional on the regions. Of course, the regions have very different levels of education and income, so that conditioning on regions absorbs much of the effect of income and education, and biases against finding evidence for the cross-country version of the secularization hypotheses. The bottom panel of the table shows what happens when the regional effects are excluded. Here, income is a great deal more important, both for religiosity and worship, though the coefficient on the latter is smaller. Average levels of education—as measured in the World Poll—are also associated with lower religiosity and lower worship, and in this case, the effects are stronger for worship. I have also included a set of dummies for whether the majority religion in each country is Catholic, other Christian, or Muslim—the base category is other religion (data taken from Fox and Sandler's [2004] Religion and the State Project). These show that, conditional on national income educational levels, people in majority Muslim countries are more likely to report themselves to be religious, while people in majority Catholic countries are more likely to have worshiped in the last seven days.

Table 8.2 turns to within-country analysis of the importance of religion. For each of up to 142 countries, I ran regressions of religiosity (as a 1/0

Table 8.1 Between-country regressions of religiosity and worship

	Importance of religion				Recent worship			
	Coef.	t-value	Coef.	t-value	Coef.	t-value	Coef.	t-value
Constant	0.93	(38.8)	1.28	(10.7)	0.71	(31.5)	0.906	(8.0)
Africa	—		—		—		—	
South Asia	-0.03	(0.7)	0.00	(0.8)	-0.13	(3.1)	-0.12	(2.7)
East Asia	-0.56	(9.3)	-0.44	(5.1)	-0.45	(8.0)	-0.37	(5.0)
Latin America	-0.14	(4.0)	-0.05	(1.1)	-0.20	(5.8)	-0.14	(3.2)
Middle East	-0.01	(0.3)	0.06	(1.3)	-0.12	(3.2)	-0.11	(2.5)
Ex-communist	-0.40	(11.6)	-0.32	(6.9)	-0.44	(13.6)	-0.40	(8.9)
S. Europe	-0.29	(4.9)	-0.14	(2.1)	-0.31	(5.5)	-0.23	(3.2)
N. Europe	-0.61	(12.4)	-0.44	(6.1)	-0.49	(10.7)	-0.40	(5.8)
Anglo	-0.48	(8.0)	-0.32	(4.0)	-0.37	(6.6)	-0.28	(3.7)
log y	—		-0.049	(3.0)	—		-0.028	(1.8)
obs.	144		133		144		133	
R^2	0.725		0.760		0.676		0.693	
Constant	1.680	(13.8)	1.567	(12.6)	1.192	(11.2)	1.160	(10.4)
log y	-0.093	(5.5)	-0.087	(5.1)	-0.060	(4.1)	-0.063	(4.2)
High school	-0.169	(1.7)	-0.149	(1.5)	-0.228	(2.5)	-0.230	(2.6)
College	-0.717	(2.7)	-0.744	(2.8)	-0.798	(3.4)	-0.800	(3.4)
Catholic	—		0.091	(1.9)	—		0.114	(2.7)
Other Christian	—		-0.003	(0.1)	—		0.036	(0.8)
Muslim	—		0.117	(2.5)	—		0.070	(1.7)
obs.	131		127		131		127	
R^2	0.522		0.570		0.507		0.541	

Notes: The dependent variables in these regressions are the fractions of people in each country who report that religion is important in their lives and the fraction of people who attended a place of worship in the last week. In the top panel, the first regression contains only regional dummies, the second contains regional dummies plus the logarithm of GDP per capita. In the bottom panel, regional dummies are excluded. For education, high school is the proportion of the population who have more than elementary education but less than or equal to three years of college, college is the fraction with more than three years of tertiary education, and the omitted category is the fraction who completed elementary education or less. The education variables are calculated from the World Poll. The last three variables come from the Fox-Sandler religion and the state project and are dummies for majority religion Catholic, other Christian, Muslim, and other, which is the omitted category. Dashed cells = not applicable.

Table 8.2   Averages of estimated coefficients from country by country regressions

	Model 1		Model 2		Model 3		Model 4	
Age 15–19	-0.115	(0.005)	-0.092	(0.007)	-0.110	(0.007)	-0.128	(0.006)
Age 20s	-0.110	(0.005)	-0.094	(0.007)	-0.105	(0.006)	-0.121	(0.005)
Age 30s	-0.090	(0.005)	-0.071	(0.007)	-0.086	(0.006)	-0.100	(0.005)
Age 40s	-0.080	(0.005)	-0.065	(0.007)	-0.072	(0.006)	-0.090	(0.005)
Age 50s	-0.063	(0.005)	-0.054	(0.007)	-0.058	(0.006)	-0.069	(0.006)
Age 60s	-0.029	(0.005)	-0.024	(0.008)	-0.030	(0.007)	-0.033	(0.006)
Age 15*fem	—		-0.039	(0.011)	—		—	
Age 20s*fem	—		-0.026	(0.010)	—		—	
Age 30s*fem	—		-0.029	(0.010)	—		—	
Age 40s*fem	—		-0.022	(0.010)	—		—	
Age 50s*fem	—		-0.010	(0.010)	—		—	
Age 60s*fem	—		-0.004	(0.011)	—		—	
Female	0.065	(0.002)	0.085	(0.009)	0.062	(0.002)	0.069	(0.002)
High school	-0.021	(0.002)	-0.020	(0.002)	-0.020	(0.003)	-0.019	(0.003)
College	-0.049	(0.007)	-0.047	(0.007)	-0.047	(0.008)	-0.048	(0.008)
log income	—		—		-0.014	(0.001)	—	
rural	—		—		—		0.028	(0.004)
village	—		—		—		0.015	(0.003)
suburb	—		—		—		-0.004	(0.006)
obs.	142		142		134		125	

Notes: These numbers are based on individual-level regressions for up to 142 countries. The dependent variable is a 1/0 depending on whether the individual reports that religion is important in their lives. The right-hand side variables are a set of age dummies, as shown, with the omitted category people aged seventy or above; a dummy for gender; the logarithm of family income; dummies for education, where the omitted category indicates that the individual completed elementary education or less; and dummies for location, which are (a) rural or on a farm, (b) in a village or small town, (c) in the suburbs of a city, and (d) in a large city, which is the omitted category. In Model 2, the age dummies are interacted with the gender dummy. Not all countries have all categories so the number of countries, shown in the last row, varies from model to model. Dashed cells = not applicable.

dichotomous variable for each individual) on a standard set of sociodemo-graphic variables including, in all specifications, age, sex, and education. The country by country results are then averaged, without weights—so that each country is treated as an equally relevant observation—to give the numbers shown in the table. The standard errors are computed from the estimated variances for each country, under the assumption of independence over countries. I also included the logarithm of income and indicators of the individual's place of residence along a spectrum from rural to large city; because these variables are not available for all countries, we consider them as variants of the baseline specification. Because of the predictions about the different religiosity of men and women, one of the specifications, Model 2, interacts the age effects with sex.

The baseline specification, Model 1, shows that religiosity increases with age, that women are more religious than men, and that more educated people are less likely to be less religious. Model 3 shows, averaged over eight fewer countries, that people with higher incomes tend to be less religious, and that the income effect appears to operate in addition to the education effect, and largely independently of it, in the sense that the coefficients on education in Model 3 are very similar to those in Model 1. Model 4 shows that, as the religion as insurance theory suggests, rural or farming people are 2.8 percentage points more likely to be religious, with people who live in villages or small towns intermediate between them and people who live in large cities or their suburbs.

The sex and age patterns in the averages hold for most countries of the world. Women are more religious than men in all but 14 of the 142 countries, and in only two of these, India and Guinea, is the negative coefficient on the female dummy more than twice its estimated standard error. Similarly, young people (the fifteen- to nineteen-year-old group) are less religious than the elderly (seventy and over) in all but 16 of the 142 countries, and the only cases where a positive coefficient is more than twice its standard error are Israel, Georgia, the Central African Republic, and Liberia. The Israeli case is particularly remarkable; controlling for sex and education, fifteen- to nineteen-year-olds are 33 percentage points more likely to be religious than elderly Israelis, presumably because so many Israelis are immigrants, and because the younger immigrants are different than older immigrants.

Model 2 allows the age profiles of religiosity to be different for men and women. Table 8.2 shows that the age profiles of religiosity for women are typically *steeper* so that the gap in religiosity between women and men, which is always positive, becomes more pronounced with age. Figure 8.1 looks at this phenomenon in more detail, showing age profiles of religiosity for women and men for each of the World Bank's four broad income group-ings of countries: low income, low middle income, high middle income, and high income. Women are more religious than men at all ages in all four regions, but the gap is largest in the high and high-middle income countries,

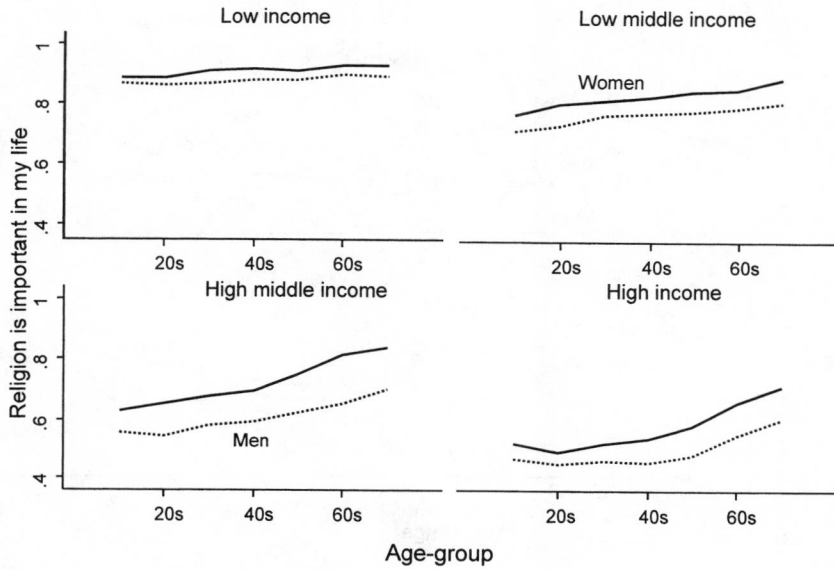

Fig. 8.1   Religiosity and age by sex and income group

and smallest in the low income countries, many of which are in Africa. As we move from poor countries to rich countries, religiosity declines, and does so more for men than for women, so that the gap becomes larger. The religiosity gap between men and women *increases* with age, a finding that is much more pronounced in the richer countries.

I have also drawn the counterpart of figure 8.1 but with worship (attended a religious service in the last seven days) replacing religiosity. Because the results are similar to figure 8.1, the graphs are not shown here. The major differences are first, that worship, unlike religiosity, falls slightly in the highest age group—presumably because of the effect of infirmity on the ability to attend; second, that in the high income group, there is no difference in rates of worship for men and women under age fifty; and third, the biggest gap between men and women is now much more clearly in the upper-middle income countries.

Another way of looking at patterns of religiosity by age and sex is to divide the world, not by income groups, but by the majority religious grouping. This shows that the female male religion gap is confined to majority Christian countries—of course, these are also the richest countries in figure 8.1—particularly majority Catholic countries (see figure 8.2). These findings are broadly consistent with the Miller and Hoffman risky behavior theory. The gender gap is largest in Christian countries, where there is a threat of damnation, and lower in the "other" group, which contains

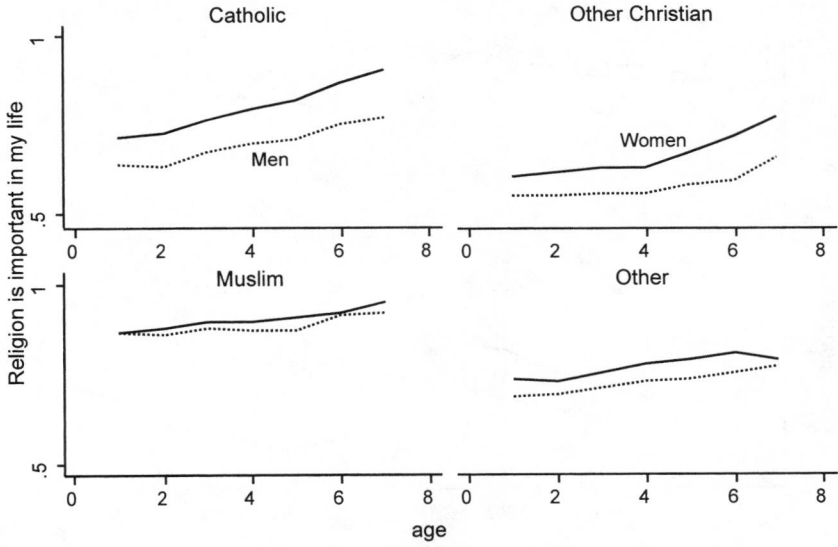

Fig. 8.2   Religiosity and age by sex and major religion

Buddhist, Hindu, and Shinto countries, as well as Israel, where there is no such threat. The accumulation of sacral capital with age is also less rapid in those countries. The majority Muslim countries are something of an exception, but these are countries where very few people are not religious. Indeed, it is not entirely clear how to measure the size of the gap—as an absolute difference, as the ratio of religious men to religious women, or as the ratio of nonreligious men to nonreligious women.

Because we are working with what is essentially a single cross-section, we cannot tell whether the patterns in figure 8.1 are age, cohort, or period effects, though we can try to interpret them according to each. The leading theory of age and gender effects is the wage theory of Azzi and Ehrenberg (1975), and this is consistent with most, although not all, of the evidence in the figure. The gender gap in religiosity is attributed to the wage gap, which is almost certainly lower in the poorest countries, particularly in Africa where women are often the main earners and providers. Religiosity is predicted to fall with rising wages, which is consistent with the pattern across regions. That religious capital should be accumulated at the end of life is predicted by the theory, and holds true for men and women in all four regions. The higher life expectancy in the richer countries is also consistent with the pronounced postponement of religiosity in the high income countries, and I investigate this further later. Particularly for men, religiosity is almost constant with age, picking up only after age fifty. What is *not* consistent with the theory is the steeper age profile for men; if men's wages are higher than women's wages, women should begin their process of accumulation earlier in life, and the gap between women and men should diminish with age, which is the opposite of what we see in these figures.

Rising religiosity with age is also consistent with secularization, which would predict, even in the absence of age effects, that older people—who were born in an earlier, more religious time—will be more religious, even if their religiosity has not changed throughout their lives. In this sense, and as noted by Norris and Inglehart (2004) in their work with the World Values Survey, the age effects in the figure are consistent with secularization, simply as a function of time. One possible model of secularization is that religiosity decreases steadily over time in each country, but at different rates, and that the rate of secularization is slower for women than for men, say a fixed fraction less than unity of the rate of secularization for men. This predicts that women are uniformly more religious than men, and that religiosity increases with age in the cross-section for both men and women. It also predicts that the religiosity gap between the old and the young should be positively correlated with the religiosity gap between women and men, because both are driven by the same process of secularization, and by its different rates in each country. This prediction is strikingly evident in the data; the cross-country correlation between the religiosity gap between old and young (minus the coefficient on the youngest age group in Model 1 in table 8.2) and the gap between women and men (the coefficient on female in Model 1) is 0.5, with a p-value of zero. Even so, this simple model is inconsistent with the rising age gaps in religiosity that we see in figure 8.1, especially in the two richest groups of countries. The slower rate of secularization among women implies that the religiosity gap between men and women in the cross section should *narrow* with age, not widen, as in the data. Put another way, widening with age implies that the religiosity gap was once larger than it is now, which seems implausible, particularly if the poorer countries now are any guide to what the richer countries once were. So neither the wage-based age-effect model nor the simple secularization model is consistent with all of the evidence. In terms of the wage model, our results seem to imply that women attach a higher value to the afterlife than do men.

Another problem with the simple secularization story is that it appears to work *too* well, in the sense that there are too few exceptions. As noted before, it is only for Israel, the Central African Republic, Georgia, and Liberia that the old are significantly less religious than the young. Yet there are many countries in the world where religiosity has risen over time, certainly in terms of the growing involvement of religion in politics, the greater religious orientation of many states, and the replacement of once-secular states by states in which religion plays a greater role (see Shah and Toft [2009], who argue that "God is winning" in global politics, or Micklethwait and Wooldridge's (2009) *God is Back*). It is not only in the former communist countries that state hostility to religion has diminished. Shah and Toft note that the secularism of Ataturk's Turkey, Nehru's India, Nasser's Egypt, and the Shah's Iran, not to mention Saddam Hussein's Iraq, have weakened in favor of states where religion's role in politics is much larger, and they note that in other countries, the liberalization and democratization of politics has brought increases in the importance of religion in public life. They cite Mexico, Nigeria, Turkey, Indonesia, India, and the United States as examples. Of the four countries with a significantly negative age gradient, only Georgia obviously fits this pattern. In the United States, fifteen- to nineteen-year-olds are more than 37 percentage points less likely to be religious than those aged seventy and older (controlling for sex, sex-age interactions, and education). In Iran, the fifteen- to nineteen-year-olds are 15 percentage points less likely to be religious than the seventy-plus group, and those in their twenties are more than 25 percentage points less religious. In Mexico, the youngest group is 40 points less religious than the oldest group. In Egypt, the age profile is essentially flat, and the same is true in Turkey, India, Indonesia, and Nigeria. In Iraq, the young are more religious, and almost significantly so. Of course, the greater involvement of religion in politics could occur without people becoming more religious; for example, if greater democracy leads to a fuller expression of preexisting views in public life.

Risk-taking theory offers a partial account of the high cross-country correlation between the age and gender gaps in religiosity. Suppose that, for some unspecified reason, there are international differences in the degree of risk-taking by young men. Countries with high risk-taking would then have both a large gender gap and a large age gap. If true, this would yield a single explanation for both phenomena.

In an effort to explain the age and gender gaps in religiosity, I have run a series of "upper-stage" cross-country regressions using the within-country estimated coefficients as dependent variables. The first column of table 8.3 show a regression of the age religiosity gap, estimated from Model 1 in table 8.2, on indicators for the World Bank income groups, on indicators for the major religion of each country, on the average rate of gross domestic product (GDP) growth of the country (measured over as many years as are available in the Penn World Table), on life expectancy at birth in 2000, and on the fertility rate in 2006. This age religiosity gap is the coefficient on the dummy for the fifteen- to nineteen-year-old age group in a regression where the omitted group is seventy years old and older, so it is typically a negative number measuring the difference in religiosity between the young and the old. The second column presents the same regressions for the coefficient on the female dummy in the same regression, a measure of how much more religious are women than men, controlling for age and education.

The first column provides some evidence in favor of the Azzi and Ehrenberg interpretation of religiosity and age and against the secularization story. On the latter, the age gap in religiosity is not related to past economic growth in the country, as it should be if it is growth in national income (or

Table 8.3   **Cross-country regressions of within-country age and sex effects**

	Age religiosity gap (Young relative to old)		Female religiosity gap	
	Coefficient	t-value	Coefficient	t-value
Constant	0.224	(2.6)	0.039	(1.3)
Low middle income	0.036	(0.9)	0.009	(0.7)
High middle income	0.011	(0.2)	0.039	(2.4)
High income	0.049	(0.9)	0.004	(0.2)
Majority other Christian	−0.001	(0.0)	−0.008	(0.7)
Majority Muslim	0.044	(1.3)	−0.066	(5.9)
Majority other	0.058	(1.5)	−0.040	(3.2)
Average GDP growth	−0.434	(0.6)	0.456	(2.0)
Life expectancy	−0.006	(3.7)	0.001	(1.3)

Notes: The dependent variable in the first regression is the estimated coefficient in the religiosity regression of the age dummy for fifteen- to nineteen-year-olds relative to those aged seventy and older. There are 130 countries in the regression. The F-statistics for the three income groups are 0.51, and for the three majority religion groups are 1.33. Average GDP growth comes from chained real GDP per capita in the Penn World Table, and is calculated over the longest span available for each country. The dependent variable in the second regression is the estimated coefficient in the religiosity regression of the female dummy. There are again 130 countries, and the F-statistics are 3.47 for the income groups and 14.22 for the majority religion groups.

more widely, modernization) that is driving the decline in religion. On the former, the age gap is negatively related to life expectancy, which is what would be expected if longer lives make it less important to become religious earlier. The contrast between the two findings is explored further in figures 8.3 and 8.4, which split up the results by income group. Figure 8.3 shows at least some evidence that, within the income groups, the age religiosity gap is larger where life expectancy is higher. It is only in the high income countries that this is not true, but even they, as a group, lie in the appropriate position on the general regression line. Figure 8.4 shows that there is no such pattern for the rate of economic growth; in particular it is not true that economic growth drives secularization in the richer countries but not in the poorer ones. These results are hardly conclusive, but the evidence leans toward the age-effects hypothesis, and is consistent with the accumulation of capital for the hereafter, and leans against the cohort-effects secularization hypothesis, at least if secularization is driven by modernization, as represented by increasing per capita GDP. Note also from the first column of table 8.3 that the patterns of aging and religiosity do not appear to be different across the different majority religions.

Table 8.3 also shows a regression of the female religiosity effect on income group, major religion, life expectancy, and growth. In contrast to the age regression, life expectancy has no effect on the differential religiosity of men and women. There is a mild and barely significant growth effect—economic

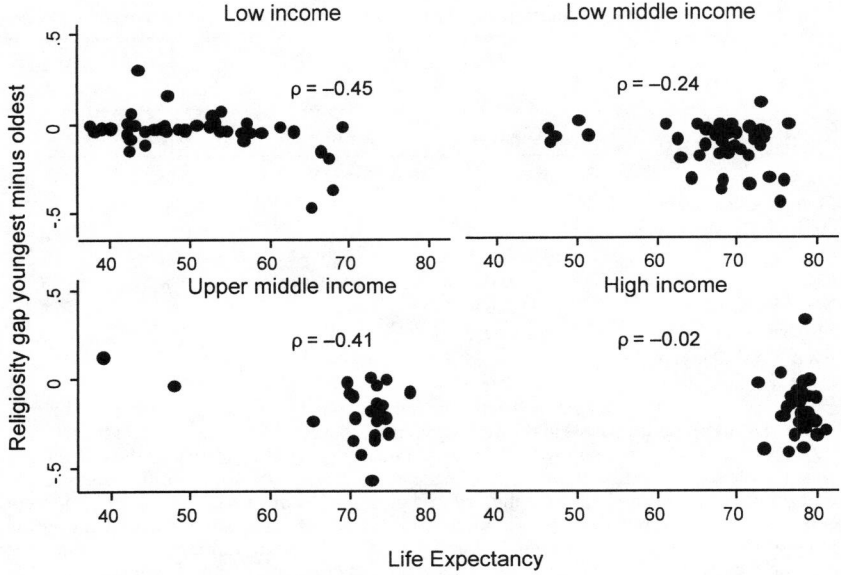

Fig. 8.3   Religiosity age gap and life expectancy

growth actually *widens* the gap between men and women—and a marginally significant effect of the income group dummies—the gap is widest in the upper-middle income countries. The major effect here is the one that we have already seen in figure 8.2, that the greater religiosity of women is most pronounced in the majority Christian countries and much less pronounced elsewhere, as picked up by the negative dummies.

I have also experimented with adding fertility rates to the regressions in table 8.3. The age gap in religiosity is strongly positively associated with fertility and fertility is now the *only* variable that is significant. Fertility is *negatively* associated with the gender age gap, so that conditional on income group (now not significant) and majority religion (significant), the gender gap is highest in the low fertility countries, which is inconsistent with the view that the greater religiosity of women is associated with childbearing, or that it occurs in societies where women's primary role is childbearing. The obvious issue here is reverse causality, that religiosity is driving fertility, not the other way around. Given the results in the literature (and those in the next section), that is also an issue for life expectancy, but surely a good deal less so. On a religion to fertility interpretation, fertility depends on the young being relatively religious, and on men being relatively religious. Further exploration of these issues is beyond the scope of this chapter.

Table 8.2 shows that, averaged over countries, the richer and better educated people within each country are less likely to be religious. If income and

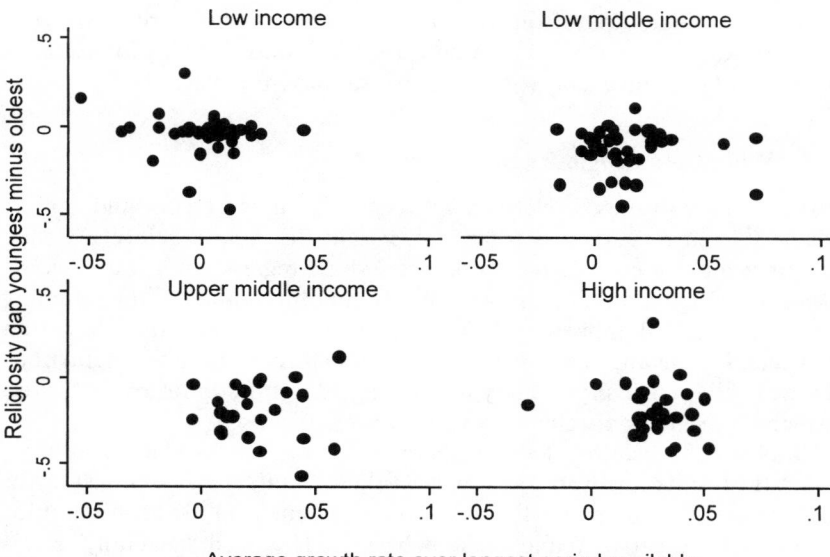

Fig. 8.4   Religiosity age gap and economic growth

education are essential ingredients in "development," these within-country results can help us understand secularization with development over time. They are also consistent with Hume's view of religion as a superstition that is dispelled by education, and Mill's argument that higher incomes induce substitution of present for future pleasures. But in contrast to the effects of sex and age, the signs of these income and education effects are far from uniform across countries. In Model 1, where income is excluded and there are 142 countries, in 58 the coefficient on high school *is positive;* and in Model 3, where both income and education are included for 132 countries, in 52 the coefficient on income is positive. Most of these are countries where average religiosity is high, but they also include (for education) Holland, New Zealand, Finland, and Ireland, and for income, India, Pakistan, Latvia, and Lithuania. In these data, unlike some reported in the literature, the United States shows (insignificant) negative effects of education and income on (this measure of) religiosity. The diversity of these results around the world speaks against any universal account of secularization through better education and rising incomes. It is also consistent with the relatively muted role of income and education in the cross-section of countries in table 8.1.

Heterogeneity also characterizes the results for whether rural people are more religious than urban people. In a diverse group of 43 of the 125 countries for which we have data, the coefficient on rural residence is negative, and significantly so, for Tanzania, Ghana, Benin, Georgia, Estonia, Guinea,

Latvia, and Togo. Apart from age and sex, the fundamental drivers of secularization are hardly well-understood, at least if we are looking for explanations that hold universally (or near universally) across the globe.

8.5   What Does Religiosity Do for Health?

I turn now to the correlations between religion and health and health-relevant behaviors. My procedure is essentially the same as before. For each country, and for each of ten outcomes, I run a regression of the outcome on a set of age dummies, on two education group dummies, on a dummy for female, on a dummy for religiosity, and on a dummy for the interaction between female and religiosity. At a second stage, I also add interactions between the religiosity dummy and the age dummies in order to explore whether the effects of religiosity vary by age.

Table 8.4, for health outcomes, and table 8.5, for health-related measures, show the results. An overall summary of these results is that, controlling for age, education, and sex, religion is generally beneficial for health and for health-related personal and social behaviors. The word "generally" refers to the average over the countries for which we have data, and that there are always exceptions, so that for some of the outcome measures, there are almost as many countries where the partial correlation with health is negative as there are countries where the partial correlation is positive. The results also show that "generally" holds more often for men than for women, for whom the health benefits of religion are often markedly smaller. Indeed, these are among the main results of this chapter, that the beneficial effects of religiosity on health are far from universally apparent. Even so, there are some patterns that are standard across many countries. Men who report that religion is important in their lives are consistently more likely to be married in 105 out of 142 countries. They are more likely to report that they were treated with respect all day yesterday in 112 out of 142 countries, and they are less likely to have smoked on the day before the interview in 70 out of 85 countries. They are more likely to trust the health and medical system in 101 out of 132 countries. Yet the increased prevalence of marriage, of being treated with respect, of being a nonsmoker, and of trusting the medical system are markedly less for women than for men. The average coefficient on the interaction of female and religiosity has the opposite sign to that coefficient on religiosity though it is smaller in absolute magnitude, so the differences between religious and nonreligious women (the sum of the religiosity and interaction coefficients) are smaller than the differences between religious and nonreligious men (the coefficient on religiosity.)

In more detail, table 8.4 shows that, averaged over countries, religious people report that they have more energy, and are more likely to be satisfied with their personal health. For both of these outcomes, there is a good deal of heterogeneity across countries; for energy and health satisfaction, the balance is about two-thirds favorable to one-third unfavorable.

Table 8.4   **Summary of within-country regressions on effects of religiosity on health outcomes**

	Mean coefficient	t-value of mean	Number of countries	Countries with coefficients same sign as mean (%)
Pain				
Religiosity	−0.017	(3.4)	142	53
Female	0.011	(1.5)	142	62
Female*religiosity	0.022	(2.9)	142	60
Energy				
Religiosity	0.042	(4.2)	92	72
Female	−0.036	(2.8)	92	72
Female*religiosity	0.004	(0.3)	92	52
Satisfied with health				
Religiosity	0.032	(7.6)	142	63
Female	−0.016	(2.7)	142	70
Female*religiosity	−0.030	(4.6)	142	64
Disabled				
Religiosity	0.001	(0.2)	142	54
Female	0.020	(2.9)	142	65
Female*religiosity	0.016	(2.3)	142	57

Notes: The four questions are: for pain, "did you experience the following feelings during a lot of the day yesterday? How about physical pain?"; for energy, "did you have enough energy to get things done yesterday?"; for satisfied with health, "are you satisfied or dissatisfied with your personal health?"; and for disabled, "do you have any health problems that prevent you from doing any of the things that people your age can normally do?" All are dichotomous, with yes coded 1, and no coded 0. The third column shows the number of countries for which the World Poll asked the question, and the fourth column the percentage of countries for which the estimated coefficient is the same sign as the mean shown in the first column. In each country with data, I ran a regression of each outcome on a set of six age group dummies, on dummies for educational status, and on religiosity, female, and the interaction of female and religiosity. The first column is the (unweighted) mean across countries of the last three coefficients. The t-value tests that this global mean is zero, and is calculated from the estimated variances of the individual regressions.

For pain and health satisfaction, men and women are different. As is often found in the literature, women are consistently more likely than men to report pain (by 1.1 percentage points), to report less energy (by 3.6 percentage points), to report dissatisfaction with their personal health (by 1.6 percentage points), and to report that they are disabled (by 2.0 percentage points). But although religious men are on average in better health than nonreligious men, the same is not true of women. To compare religious and nonreligious women, add the first and third coefficients in each cell of the first column, and this shows that there is no health benefit for religiosity for women in either pain or self-reported health status, while religious women are actually more likely than nonreligious women to report disability. Again, it should be emphasized that there is much international heterogeneity in these results.

Table 8.5 shows the results for outcomes or behaviors that affect health,

Table 8.5   **Summary of within-country regressions on effects of religiosity on health-related behaviors and outcomes**

	Mean coefficient	t-value of mean	Number of countries	Countries with coefficients same sign as mean (%)
Married				
Religiosity	0.042	(9.2)	142	74
Female	0.015	(2.2)	142	51
Female*religiosity	−0.038	(5.4)	142	66
Friend in need				
Religiosity	0.026	(5.6)	141	60
Female	0.005	(0.7)	141	70
Female*religiosity	0.007	(1.0)	141	50
Treated with respect				
Religiosity	0.056	(13.4)	142	79
Female	0.021	(3.4)	142	55
Female*religiosity	−0.016	(2.4)	142	55
Time with friends				
Religiosity	0.004	(0.1)	86	47
Female	−0.030	(0.4)	86	52
Female*religiosity	0.148	(1.8)	86	51
Smoker				
Religiosity	−0.080	(13.1)	85	82
Female	−0.225	(27.5)	85	95
Female*religiosity	0.025	(2.8)	85	56
Trust medical system				
Religiosity	0.063	(11.3)	132	77
Female	0.017	(2.1)	132	50
Female*religiosity	−0.017	(2.0)	132	47

Notes: See table 8.4 notes for procedures. The six outcomes analyzed here are defined as follows. Married refers to current marital status, and is defined as 1 if current status is married, and 0 for all other responses, including single, never married, separated, divorced, widowed, or domestic partner. Friend in need is 1 if the respondent answers yes to the question, "if you were in trouble, do you have relatives or friends you can count on to help you whenever you need them?" Treated with respect is yes if the respondent says he or she was treated with respect all day yesterday. Time with friends is the answer to, "Approximately, how many hours did you spend, socially, with friends or family yesterday?" The interview is instructed to include e-mail or telephone time. This is the only one of the left-hand side variables that is not dichotomous. Smoker is 1 if the respondent said yes to "did you smoke yesterday?" Trust medical system is 1 if the respondent says that he or she has confidence in or trusts the health care or medical system.

or have been frequently linked to health in the literature. They vary from clear examples like cigarette smoking, to somewhat less clear cases, such as marriage, which almost always appears as a positive correlate of health, to social capital variables, such as time spent socially with friends and relatives, whether there is a friend or relative who would help in time of need, and whether the respondent is treated with respect. I also include whether the respondent has confidence in the health or medical system; this is hardly a health outcome variable, though it is surely a positive factor in people's lives, and the religion-based provision of health care is one of the mechanisms through which religion can affect health.

There is no partial correlation between religiosity and social time, but religiosity is estimated to be a positive force for the other five categories. The benefits of religion are particularly significant and likely to be universal across countries for marriage, being treated with respect, smoking, and trusting the health care system. This last may well reflect the role of religious organizations in providing health care in much of the world. However, it is notable that these are benefits for religious over nonreligious men, and they are typically smaller—and sometimes even nonexistent—between religious and nonreligious women. Religious women are no more likely to be married than nonreligious women, which echoes the effect on health of marriage itself, where the literature often finds health benefits for men but not women (see, e.g., Elo and Preston 1996). For being treated with respect, trust in the health care system, and smoking, the coefficient on the interaction between female and religiosity is of the opposite sign to the coefficient on religiosity, so that the benefits of religiosity among women are smaller than those among men, but remain positive. Note the very large main effect of being female on smoking—over the eighty-five countries for which we have data, women are 23 percentage points less likely to smoke than men.

Figures 8.5 through 8.8 provide further disaggregation of these results, focusing on the cases where religiosity has an effect that varies by age or by income group. In the regressions underlying these graphs, religiosity is fully interacted with the age groups, so that I am allowing different age patterns for the religious and nonreligious. I then average the coefficients over the four World Bank income groups, and plot the outcome by age for religious and nonreligious people separately. Drawing the graphs this way may suggest that people are either religious or nonreligious throughout their lives, which will not be true if there is an age effect in religiosity, as I have argued in the previous section. Note also that the graphs are drawn for men; the curves for women are those for men displaced by a constant vertical amount. In some cases, such as pain, this will change the relative position of the religious and nonreligious groups.

Figures 8.5, 8.6, and 8.7 are broadly similar. Pain decreases and energy and health satisfaction increase as we move from the low income to the high income countries. In the low income group, religion is protective, but there is little or no effect in the other three groups. Religious people have more energy and more health satisfaction in the low income and lower-middle income groups, but do no better in the upper income or high income countries. Religious people are more likely to be treated with respect throughout the income regions of the world, however (see figure 8.8), and once again, the size of the effect is largest in the poorest countries. Remarkably, there is a steady increase in being treated with respect with country income; higher

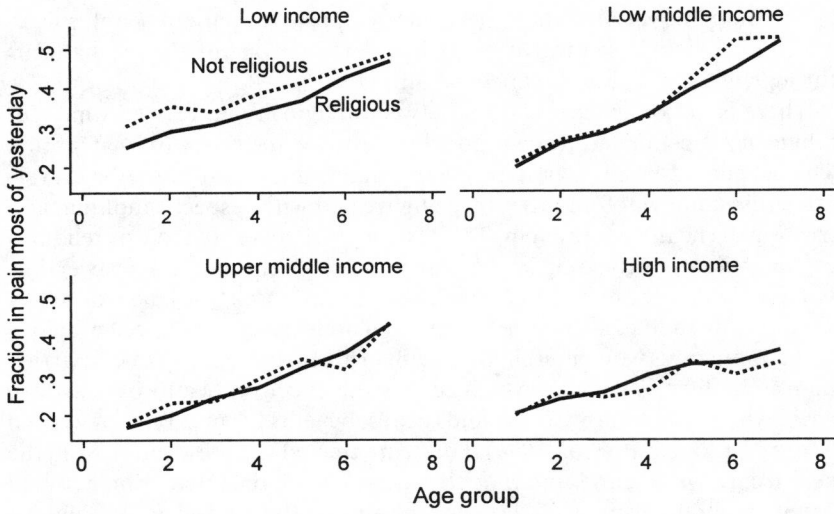

Fig. 8.5   Pain by religiosity, age, and country income level

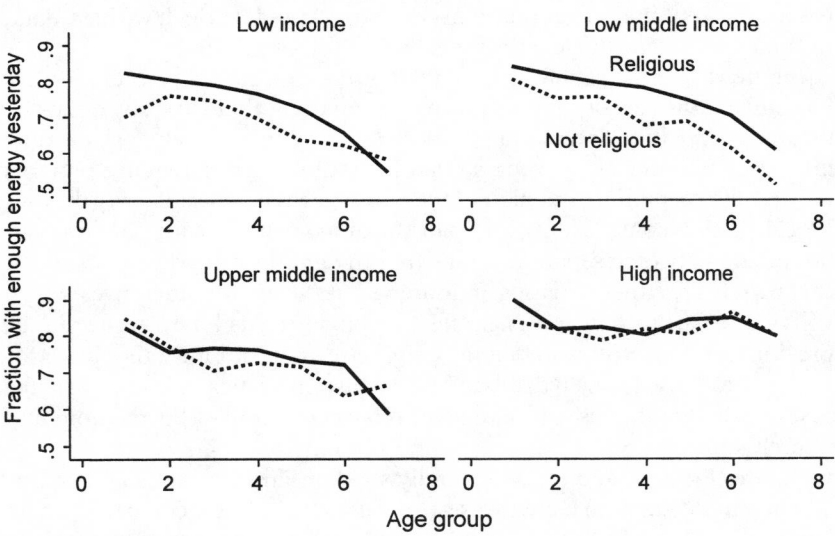

Fig. 8.6   Energy by religiosity, age, and country income level

income comes with better health and better relationships between people, an important aspect of greater freedom. Finally, figure 8.9 shows that religious people smoke less throughout the world, and at all ages. For smoking, rates are lowest in the rich world—presumably because people are more likely to understand the health risks—and highest in the middle income countries—

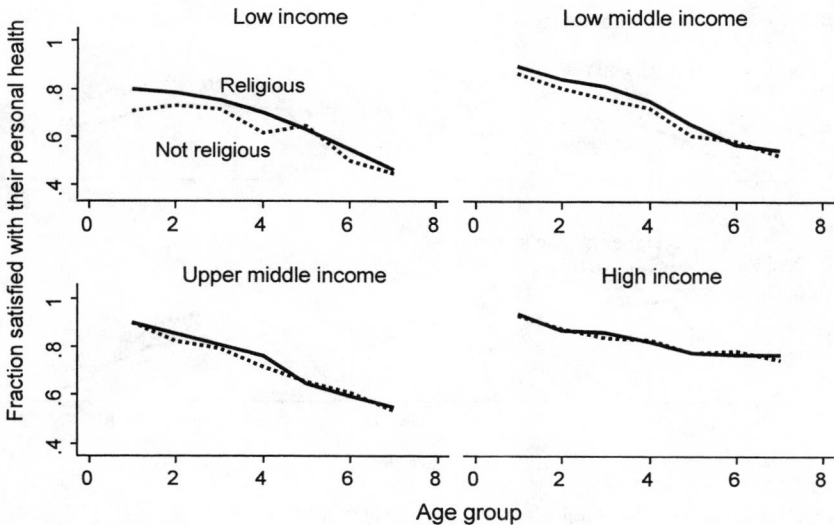

Fig. 8.7   Health satisfaction by religiosity, age, and country income level

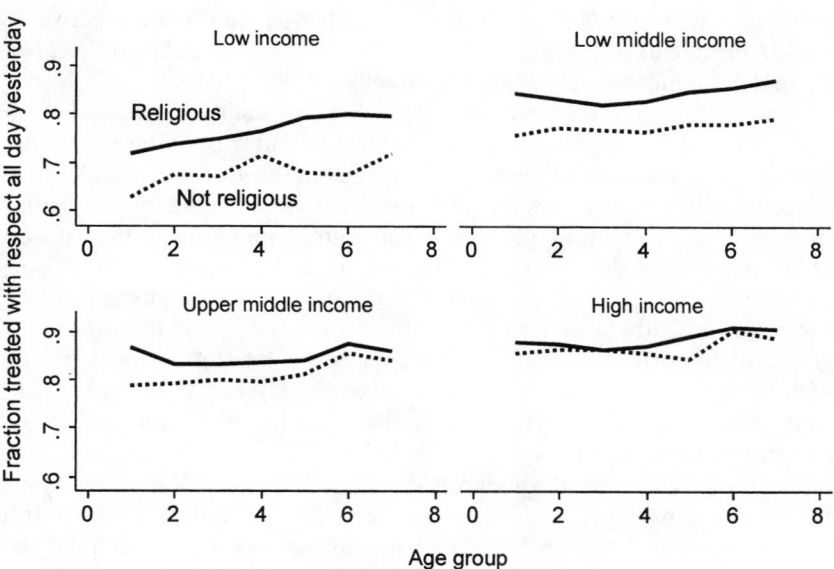

Fig. 8.8   Being treated with respect by religiosity, age, and country income level

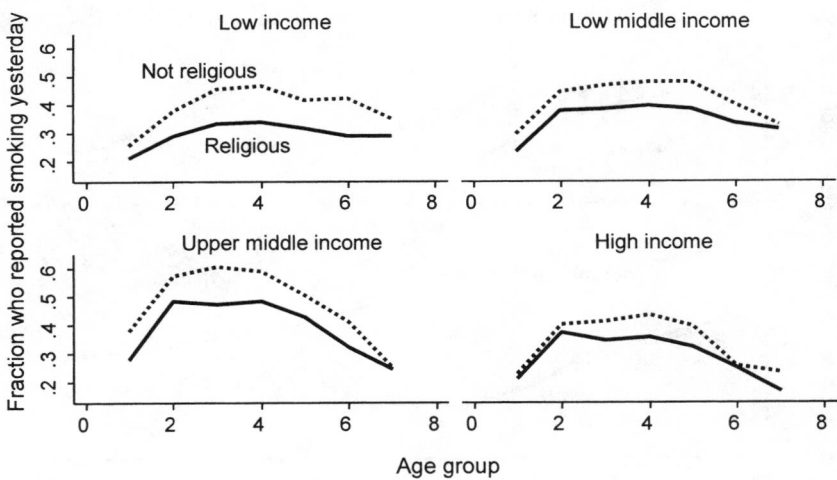

Fig. 8.9   Smoking by religiosity, age, and country income level

presumably because of the combination of relatively high income and still relatively low health awareness. But everywhere, religion is protective of health through its inhibiting the use of tobacco. This is perhaps the clearest example of a link between religion and self-control.

For the other outcomes in tables 8.4 and 8.5—disability, marriage, having a friend in time of need, time spent with friends, and trust in the health care or medical system—the disaggregation by income group and age adds nothing to what we already know because the effects are either absent or similar by age and income group. I have also run regressions of the coefficients on religiosity against dummies for country income group and for the majority religion in each country. In all but three cases, these add nothing to the results already presented. The three cases where there are significant effects of majority religion are self-reported health status, being treated with respect, and having a friend in time of need, all of which are significantly higher in majority Muslim countries than would be predicted by the country's income group.

None of figures 8.5 through 8.9 shows notable effects of interactions between religiosity and age. The estimated effects of religiosity on health and health-related outcomes are similar at all ages, at least as far as can be seen in these data. Of course, as shown in the previous section, religiosity itself rises with age so that the importance of the protective effects of religion also rises with age, simply because of its greater prevalence.

8.6 Conclusions

This chapter has presented a largely descriptive analysis of patterns of aging, gender, religiosity, and health throughout the world. In the vast majority of the countries of the world, women are more religious than men, and the elderly are more religious than the young. These two phenomena are related in that the difference in religiosity between men and women is strongly positively correlated with the difference in religiosity between the young and the old. It is difficult to separate out age from cohort effects, but at least some of the evidence is consistent with pure age effects that are roughly consistent with rational choice theory, that religion should be postponed until late in life, that lower wages promote religiosity, and that the acquisition of religion can be postponed when life is longer. There is no obvious link between long-term income growth and the gap in religiosity between young and old, which is contrary to income-driven secularization. The gap in religiosity between men and women is not easily explained, and remains controversial in the literature, but both the wage and risk-taking theories are consistent with at least some of the global evidence.

I also find that, at least on average, over all countries, and over countries sorted into income groups, religious people do better on a number of health and health-related indicators. These protective effects appear to be stronger the poorer is the country—as suggested by Inglehart (2008), religion is a route to a better life in poor countries, but not in rich ones—and to protect men more than women, though this hypothesis requires more extensive investigation.

None of the results show that the health benefits of religion can be obtained simply by joining a church, or even by undertaking a serious conversion. People who are religious are almost certainly different from nonreligious people in ways that go beyond their religiosity and beyond the basic educational and demographic controls that are used here. Even so, some of the correlations presented here are remarkably universal across the religions and countries of the world, and need to be explained and better understood.

References

Azzi, C., and R. Ehrenberg. 1975. Household allocation of time and church attendance. *Journal of Political Economy* 83 (1): 27–56.

Deaton, A. 2008. Income, health, and well-being around the world: Evidence from the Gallup World Poll. *Journal of Economic Perspectives* 22 (2): 53–72.

Elo, I., and S. H. Preston. 1996. Educational differences in mortality: United States, 1979–85. *Social Science and Medicine* 42 (1): 47–57.

Fox, J., and S. Sandler. 2004. The religion and state project. Available at: http://www.biu.ac.il/soc/po/ras/index.html.

Guiso, L., P. Sapienza, and L. Zingales. 2003. People's opium? Religion and economic attitudes. *Journal of Monetary Economics* 50:225–82.

Helliwell, J. F., and R. D. Putnam. 2004. The social context of well-being. *Philosophical Transactions of the Royal Society of London,* B 359:1435–46.

Hummer, R. A., R. G. Rogers, C. B. Nam, and C. G. Ellison. 1999. Religious involvement and U.S. adult mortality. *Demography* 36 (2): 273–85.

Idler, E. L., and S. V. Kasl. 1997. Religion among disabled and non-disabled persons I: Cross-sectional patterns in health practices, social activities, and well-being. *Journal of Gerontology Social Sciences* 52B (6): S294–305.

Inglehart, R. F. 2010. Faith and freedom: Traditional and modern ways to happiness. In *International differences in well-being,* ed. E. Diener, J. F. Helliwell, and D. Kahneman, 351–97.

Koenig, H. G., M. E. McCullough, and D. B. Larsen. 2000. *Handbook of religion and health.* Oxford: Oxford University Press.

McCleary, R. M., and R. J. Barro. 2006. Religion and economy. *Journal of Economic Perspectives* 20 (2): 49–72.

McCullough, M. E., and T. B. Smith. 2003. Religion and health: Depressive symptoms and mortality as case studies. In *Handbook of the sociology of religion,* ed. M. Dillon, 190–206. Cambridge, MA: Cambridge University Press.

McCullough, M. E., and B. L. B. Willoughby. 2009. Religion, self-regulation, and self-control: Associations, explanations, and implications. *Psychological Bulletin* 135 (1): 69–93.

Micklethwait, J., and A. Wooldridge. 2009. *God is back: How the global revival of faith is changing the world.* New York: Penguin Press.

Mill, J. S. 1878. Utility of religion. In *Three essays on religion,* 69–122. New York: Henry Holt.

Miller, A. S., and J. P. Hoffmann. 1995. Risk and religion: An explanation of gender differences in religiosity. *Journal for the Scientific Study of Religion* 34 (1): 63–75.

Miller, A. S., and R. Stark. 2002. Gender and religiousness: Can socialization explanations be saved? *American Journal of Sociology* 107 (6): 1399–423.

Norris, P., and R. F. Inglehart. 2004. *Sacred and secular: Religion and politics worldwide.* New York: Cambridge University Press.

Shah, T. S., and M. D. Toft. 2009. God is winning: Religion on global politics. In *Blind Spot: When journalists don't get religion,* ed. P. Marshall, L. Gilbert, and R. G. Adamson, 11–30. Oxford: Oxford University Press.

Tomes, N. 1985. Religion and the earnings function. *American Economic Review* 75 (2): 245–50.

Wilson, D. S. 2002. *Darwin's cathedral.* Chicago: Chicago University Press.

Comment   James P. Smith

Economics has a well-deserved reputation as an imperialistic discipline. There is little in human behavior that we seem unwilling to place under our

James P. Smith is a senior economist and holds the Distinguished Chair in Labor Markets and Demographic Studies at RAND Corporation.

These comments were written with the support of grants from the National Institute on Aging and were delivered at the NBER conference on the Economics of Aging, Carefree, Arizona, May 2009.

analytical microscope, using either its theoretical or statistical lens. With relatively few exceptions, the economic microscope has shied away from all things religious. This is unfortunate since religion is clearly one of the most fundamental and influential institutions affecting human behavior, an influence that transcends time and geography. We may see some of its more negative manifestations in today's newspaper headlines with religious wars still raging around the globe. The flip (and now quieter) side of religion in promoting better personal behaviors and interactions between people is often forgotten in the daily headlines but may be just as fundamental and influential.

Angus Deaton is not shy. He takes on religion with ambition and insight, subjecting it to economics straight and pure and no apologies, thank you very much. The World Gallup Poll that he uses is a terrific data source. One could quibble about the lack of depth and scope in the substantive content of the questions, but that would be missing the larger picture. The Gallup World Poll has no match in what it does well, covering 98 percent of the world's population in over 140 countries. Peoples in all regions of the world are represented. While variation in outcomes limited to those living within a particular country are significant, they pale next to the scope of variation observed around the world.

One of the expected, and in this case realized, pleasures in reading a paper by Angus Deaton, especially if you are the discussant, is that you know that the empirical findings will be fully transparent. After reading the chapter, I basically felt that I knew all there was to know about the principal empirical regularities about religion in the Gallup data. And Angus did all the work, which makes it a double pleasure for me. I have no comments, criticisms, or quibbles about the empirical methods that produced these results, having full trust in the master's voice that these are the principal empirical regularities surrounding religion. My main points center instead about how to interpret these findings.

The chapter is substantively written around two issues. The first concerns determinants of religiosity around the world and in particular how the degree of religiosity changes with economic development. The second takes religiosity as given and focuses on the impact of religiosity on a set of health outcomes. I will discuss each in turn.

There are two key empirical relationships about religiosity and a theory to match on which Angus focuses in this chapter. First, religiosity declines with income or level of development, with richer countries being on average less religious than poorer ones. Similarly, within countries poorer individuals—in the United States women, blacks, and the less educated, for example—will be more religious than their better off counterparts. Second, even without any cohort effects, with younger cohorts richer than older ones placing us right back in the poor-rich implications of the theory, religiosity increases with age. This is especially the case at older ages when one gets closer to the end of life on earth and presumably becomes more concerned with the nature and quality of any life that may lie beyond.

The theory represents a simple but powerful use of economics. On the first empirical regularity, the relationship between income levels and religiosity starts with a two-period problem—life on earth, which throughout most of human history and for most people even today is pretty harsh, and life in heaven, which by any standards and at any time is something to look very much forward to. With normal income effects, increases in income or standard of living in the earth life increases the value of earth life compared to the heavenly afterlife, which was pretty ideal to begin with, implying an income elasticity of zero.

Within countries, using very much the same type of reasoning, those with lower wages—women, blacks, and Latinos in the United States, for example—have poor earth lives compared to the quality of their prospective lives in heaven. In the Deaton theory, they will be more religious in their behaviors.

The theory on which Deaton relies is a theory for saints. In many religions, the promise of an eternal life is not just the heavenly version of eternal bliss, but also the hellish variant of eternal damnation. Depending on the type of life that has been led, the expected afterlife may be one of very low utility and not high utility. For those where the relevant odds of a very bad afterlife cannot be dismissed, increases in income would be devoted to reducing the prospects of such an event, which can be done by being a better person or being more religious rather than less.

A more comprehensive version of the theory may be that as economic development takes place, the good become less religious while the bad become more religious. If there are more good than bad, then the net effect is that religiosity will decline with economic development, as the data appear to be telling us. But so will heterogeneity in the extremes of behavior, with fewer saints and devils among us with moral behaviors becoming more commonplace but less extreme at both ends.

I also have some concerns with the use of this theory for within-country analysis, particularly for women. In most societies, women are much more religious than men. An interpretation within this theory is that women have lower wages than men do and therefore are poorer and more religious. But men and women typically live together and have pretty much the same household incomes and standard of living, even if their wages are quite different.

A more likely reason in my view starts with women's role as caretaker of children, largely in charge of the intergeneration transmission of past cultural values. One of the most important values to transmit to children is the religion of one's ancestors, if only to inculcate a set of moral beliefs that will help constrain their behavior. The more children one has the greater the value of this role for women using a simple scale effect argument. If my conjecture is correct, another relevant variable that may capture this is the cohort-specific fertility rate, which could be easily appended to the Gallup survey. As economic development proceeds, not only do incomes rise, but fertility rates typically fall. Declining fertility over time may even explain the much steeper rise in religiosity with age among women in the cross-section. This would not represent an age effect at all, but rather cohort effects where fertility of younger women is much lower than fertility of older women in the cross-section.

The theory underlying the increase in religiosity with age is even simpler. The closer one gets to the afterlife the more optimal it becomes to invest in behaviors that would improve one's prospects of a good hereafter even if the belief in its very existence is not assigned a probability of one. With any set of probability beliefs, there appears to be little to lose with deathbed conversions.

But hold on there. This is a one-sided model with a very naïve all-knowing God on the other side. In a two-person (or one-person, one God) game with full knowledge, one would like to believe that one's life's work in all things spiritual might be more relevant.

The next part of the chapter switches to the second question—what role does religiosity play in promoting better health? Deaton is justifiably cautious in not claiming causality in this relationship, but equally right in pointing out that establishing the correct associations is a useful beginning in our understanding. There are two complementary steps to the empirical arguments. The first involves a model regressing a set of health outcomes (pain, energy, being satisfied with health, and being disabled) on religiosity while the second regresses a set of behaviors known to improve health (married, having a friend in need, treated with respect, spending time with friends, smoking, and trusting the medical system) on religiosity. While the evidence that many of these outcomes, especially the social capital ones, actually improves health is very much in dispute, there is little left to dispute with smoking.

Table 8C.1 summarizes Deaton's results for the impact of religiosity on health. An up arrow indicates that religiosity increases the outcome listed in the first column while a down arrow means the outcome fell when religiosity increased. A star (*) symbolizes statistically significant. Separate columns are presented for the impact on male and female health. The final column

Table 8C.1   **Effects of religiosity on health**

	Male effect	Female effect	% of countries with wrong sign
Pain	↓*	0	47
Energy	↑*	↑*	28
Satisfied with health	↑*	0	36
Disabled	0	↑*	46

*Statistically significant.

Table 8C.2   Effects of religiosity on health behaviors

	Male effect	Female effect	% of countries with wrong sign
Married	↑*	0	3
Friend in need	↑*	↑*	40
Treated with respect	↑*	↑*	23
Time with friends	0	↑*	53
Smoker	↑*	↑*	18
Trust medical system	↑*	↑*	23

*Statistically significant.

contains a particularly useful and insightful Deaton innovation in the presentation of empirical findings. This column lists the percent of countries in which the sign of the coefficient is "wrong"—that is, religiosity is associated with worse health. Many of these wrong signs in individual countries are not, of course, statistically significant, but I still find this addition to the summary stats very helpful in assessing universality of results.

The results for men support the notion that religion is good for your health. Among men being more religious is associated with pain reduction, increased energy, and being more satisfied with one's health. There does not appear to be any association with male disability. But before you start running out to church, the results for women do not indicate any effect of religiosity on health at all. Religiosity does increase energy among women but neither pain nor, more importantly, satisfaction with health is affected by religious behavior. Disability actually works in the opposite direction. In my view, there is no evidence of any effects of religiosity on women's health.

Even the more male positive results have to be given a major caveat. The last column of table 8C.1 demonstrates that in a large fraction of countries estimated effects are in the opposite direction. Since an even larger fraction will not be statistically positive associated with good health, there may be relatively few countries driving the male health-enhancing impact of religion.

Additional pertinent evidence on the nature of these effects of religiosity on health is contained in Deaton's figures, separating these effects by income level. For all health outcomes except smoking these effects appear to be concentrated exclusively on the low income countries.

The format of table 8C.2 parallels that of table 8C.1 but now the summary pertains to the estimated impacts of religiosity on a set of health behaviors associated with better health. The rightmost column once again lists the percent of countries with the "wrong" sign. These pathway results to health-promoting behaviors from religiosity are actually much more consistent (the fraction of wrong country signs are smaller) and stronger than the health results themselves. Being married makes men more religious (but not women), and most of the social capital variables are associated with more religiosity for both men and women. One apparent benefit of religiosity is that it discourages smoking, a reliable pathway to better health. Resolving one small technical issue would help in interpreting these results. These are correlated pathway outcomes so it may be that there is only an effect through smoking and these other somewhat weaker outcomes are telling us that they are more or less correlated with smoking.

The strenth of these pathway results on health behaviors actually makes you wonder why the health effects of religiosity are not even larger. For example, the pathway effects are just as strong for women as for men, but Deaton finds essentially no health effects of religiosity for women. The question, then, is what about religion promotes better health since it seems far from a universal constant across place or across people? It has the opposite sign in as many as one-third of the countries in the Gallup survey, it affects men but not women, and appears only to be a force within low income households. Like religion itself, it is more than a bit of a mystery. Deepening the mystery only makes me want to learn more about the role and appeal of religion in the world. I can ask for no better guide to my learning than having Angus Deaton probe deeper in the future on this most important of topics.

Work Disability, Work, and Justification Bias in Europe and the United States

Arie Kapteyn, James P. Smith, and Arthur van Soest

9.1 Introduction

The fraction of workers on disability insurance (DI) is vastly different across Western European countries with similar levels of economic development and comparable access to modern medical technology and treatment (Eurostat 2001). Institutional differences in eligibility rules or generosity of benefits contribute to an explanation of differences in disability rolls (Boersch-Supan 2007). Recent survey data show, however, that significant differences between Western European countries and the United States are also found in self-reports of work-limiting disabilities. Table 9.1, taken from Kapteyn et al. (2009), illustrates the point.[1] We see considerable variation in both DI expenditures as a percentage of gross domestic product (GDP) and the percentage of males between forty and sixty-five reporting some form

Arie Kapteyn is a senior economist and director of the Labor and Population program at RAND Corporation. James P. Smith is a senior economist and holds the Distinguished Chair in Labor Markets and Demographic Studies at RAND Corporation. Arthur van Soest is professor of econometrics at Tilburg University, a research fellow at Netspar, and an affiliated researcher at RAND Corporation.

This research was supported by grants from the National Institute on Aging to RAND and the Social Security Administration through MRRC. It uses data from SHARE Wave 1, primarily funded by the European Commission through its 5th and 6th framework programmes (project numbers QLK6-CT-2001-00360; RII-CT-2006-062193; CIT5-CT-2005-028857) and from HRS, funded by NIA. We are grateful to Angus Deaton for useful comments on an earlier version.

1. Self-reports for the European countries are taken from the European Community Household Panel (ECHP). For the United States they are taken from the Panel Study of Income Dynamics (PSID). The exact question on work disability in ECHP is: "Are you hampered in your daily activities by any physical or mental health problem, illness or disability?" In the PSID, it is: "Do you have any physical or nervous condition that limits the type of work or the amount of work you can do?"

Table 9.1   Expenditures on disability insurance and self-reported male work disability, 2001

	DI expenditure as a % of GDP	Self-reported male work disability, 40–65, 2001 (%)
Germany	1.6	40.3
Denmark	2.7	22.0
Netherlands	4.0	24.5
Belgium	2.2	14.3
France	1.7	20.5
UK	2.2	13.1
Ireland	1.3	15.7
Italy	2.0	8.0
Greece	1.6	13.3
Spain	2.3	15.5
Portugal	2.4	22.9
Austria	2.3	17.8
Finland	3.1	29.0
U.S.	1.1	19.3

of work disability. Remarkably, the two columns are only weakly correlated: the correlation is 0.20.

Croda and Skinner (2009), using data from Survey of Health, Aging, and Retirement in Europe (SHARE) and Health and Retirement Study (HRS), find little or no evidence that in countries with a higher proportion of individuals on DI, the fraction of DI recipients with self-reported fair or poor health is lower. This is what one would expect if access to DI were largely driven by health considerations and if the distribution of health in different countries would be roughly the same. In that case a system with strict eligibility rules or less generous benefits would mainly select individuals with the worst health condition. The more generous benefits or eligibility rules become, the more likely it is that individuals in better health are drawn into the pool of DI recipients. One explanation for the weak relation between DI recipiency rates and self-reported health across countries may lie in differences in response scales used to answer subjective health questions adopted by residents of different countries.

This chapter applies the same vignette methodology as in Kapteyn, Smith, and van Soest (2007) to determine the extent to which differences in self-reported work-limiting disability between several European countries and the United States are due to differences in response scales. In addition, we also consider the effect of work disability on employment and the potential effect of justification bias on the estimate of this effect.

The remainder of the chapter is organized as follows. The second section describes the data collection efforts in HRS and SHARE that make this research possible. Section 9.3 outlines the vignette methodology and our statistical model that corrects for response scale differences across countries.

The fourth section briefly describes the vignettes used in this study and how respondents in different European countries and the United States respond to the same vignette scenarios. Section 9.5 presents the empirical results and their implications for interpreting observed differences in self-reported work disability. Section 9.6 extends the model developed in section 9.3 to include employment and justification bias. Section 9.7 presents the estimation results of that model and shows their economic importance by means of a number of simulations. Our principal conclusions are contained in the last section.

9.2 Data Sources

For the United States, we use the 2004 wave of the Health and Retirement Study (HRS), a biannual panel with a representative sample of the U.S. population over fifty. It has been conducted by the University of Michigan since 1992. Information collected includes physical and mental health, socioeconomic status (including measures of labor market status, income, education and wealth), social support, and so forth. The surveys use a mixture of modes with most new interviews conducted face-to-face and most reinterviews by phone. Wave-specific overall response rates for the HRS have improved from 81.7 percent in 1992 to close to 90 percent at later waves, specifically 87.8 percent in 2004. The survey has a complex sample design and oversamples blacks, Hispanics, and residents of Florida. Details on the HRS methodology and the 2004 Wave are available elsewhere (Heeringa and Connor 1995). For our analysis we use a subsample of respondents who first completed a face-to-face interview and later completed a leave-behind questionnaire. The leave-behind questionnaire consisted of a series of work disability vignettes and was targeted toward respondents less than seventy-five years of age.

The SHARE is a large-scale project that aims to collect interdisciplinary longitudinal data on European citizens age fifty and older and their spouses. The eleven participating countries in the baseline wave were Denmark, Sweden, Germany, Belgium, the Netherlands, Austria, Switzerland, Spain, Italy, Greece, and France.[2] Using a common instrument, SHARE includes information on physical and mental health, socioeconomic status including measures of income, education and wealth, and social support. The first wave of the main survey was fielded in 2004, with between 1,000 and 4,000 individuals in each country, adding up to about 29,000 individuals.

While containing many unique features, in order to facilitate additional comparisons with the United States and England, SHARE was purposely modeled after the HRS and the English Longitudinal Survey of Aging

2. The Czech Republic, Poland, Israel, and Ireland were added later. See www.share-project .org for exact sample sizes.

(ELSA) and follows a common set-up across all countries with the goal of facilitating cross-country research.

For a subset of countries that agreed to participate, SHARE included a set of self-assessments and vignette questions on general health status and on work-limiting disabilities as part of a drop-off questionnaire. The eight countries that participated in this vignette experiment were Germany, France, Spain, Belgium, Greece, Italy, the Netherlands, and Sweden. The work disability vignettes were identical to the work disability vignettes in the HRS leave-behind questionnaire. Both were taken from the surveys used by Kapteyn, Smith, and van Soest (2007).

The work disability vignettes deal with work-limiting health problems in the domains of pain, depression, and cardiovascular disease. An example of a vignette is the following one (the first vignette cited in appendix B, which contains the full set of vignettes):

[Eva] feels worried all the time. She gets depressed once a week at work for a couple of days in a row, thinking about what could go wrong and that her boss will disapprove of her condition. But she is able to come out of this mood if she concentrates on something else.

For each vignette, the respondent is asked: "Please give us your judgment on how limited these people are in the kind or amount of work they can do."[3]

1. Not at all limited
2. Mildly limited
3. Moderately limited
4. Severely limited
5. Cannot do any work

The names used in the vignettes (Eva in the example) vary by vignette and, moreover, to each vignette either a male or a female name was randomly assigned. (See appendix B for details.[4])

Preceding the vignette questions, a respondent is asked the self-assessment of work disability question: "To what extent are you limited in the kind or amount of work you can do because of an impairment or health problem?"[5] with the same answer categories as before. As explained in the next section, these vignettes make it possible to analyze cross-country differences in work-related health, corrected for international differences in response

3. This is the question wording in the HRS. The wording in SHARE is slightly different (and translated in each country's language). See www.share-project.org.
4. There we also describe some differences in the formulation of the self-reported disability questions and one vignette across the two surveys. In this version of the chapter we have ignored these differences.
5. Again, this is the wording in the HRS; the wording in SHARE is somewhat different: "Do you have any impairment or health problem that limits the kind or amount of work you can do?" with answer categories "None," "Mild," "Moderate," "Severe," and "Extreme."

scales. Moreover, the vignettes will also be used for comparisons of different socioeconomic groups.

9.3 The Theory of Vignettes

In this section, we first provide an intuitive description of the use of vignettes for identifying response scale differences and then sketch our statistical approach. The basic idea is illustrated in figure 9.1, which presents the distribution of health-related work limitations (work disability for short) in two hypothetical countries. The density of the continuous work disability variable in country A is to the left of that in country B, implying that on average, people in country A suffer less work disability than in country B. The people in the two countries, however, use very different response scales if asked to report their work limitations on a five-point scale (none-mild-moderate-severe-extreme). These differences may be caused by cultural differences, or simply be the result of inadequate translation; for instance, because there exist no exact one-to-one translations of concepts from one language to the other. In the example in the figure, people in country A have a much more negative view on their capacity for work than people in country B. Someone in country A with the health indicated by the dashed line would report to have a severe work disability, while a person in country B with the same actual work limitation would report only a mild work disability. The frequency distribution of the self-reports in the two countries would suggest that people in country A are more work disabled than those in country B—the opposite of the true

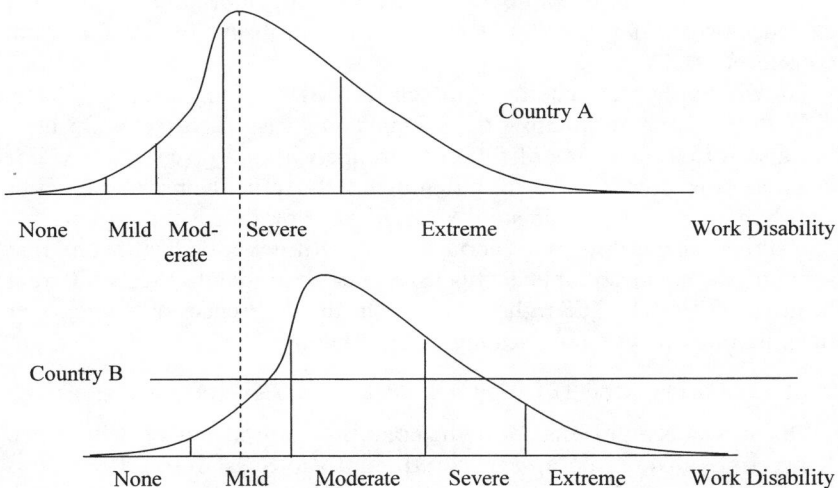

Fig. 9.1   Comparing self-reported health-related work limitations

disability distribution. Correcting for the differences in the response scales (DIF, or "differential item functioning," in the terminology of King et al. [2004]) is essential to compare the distributions of actual work limitations in the two countries.

Vignettes can be used to do the correction. A vignette question describes the work limitations of a hypothetical person and then asks the respondent to evaluate the work disability of that person on the same five-point scale that was used for the self-report of their own health. Since the vignette descriptions are the same in the two countries, the vignette persons in the two countries have the same actual work limitations. For example, respondents can be asked to evaluate the work limitation of a person whose disability is given by the dashed line. In country A, this will be evaluated as "severe." In country B, the evaluation would be "mild." Since the actual work disability is the same in the two countries, the difference in the country evaluations must be due to DIF.

Vignette evaluations thus help to identify differences between the response scales. Using the scales in one of the two countries as the benchmark, the distribution of evaluations in the other country can be adjusted by evaluating them on the benchmark scale. The corrected distribution of the evaluations can then be compared to that in the benchmark country—they are now on the same scale. In the example in the figure, this will lead to the correct conclusion that people in country B are more disabled than those in country A, on average. The main identifying assumption is *response consistency:* a given respondent uses the same scale for self-reports and vignette evaluations. King et al. (2004) provide evidence supporting this assumption by comparing self-reports and vignette evaluations of vision with an objective measure of vision. Van Soest et al. (2007) provide similar supporting evidence by comparing self-reported drinking problems to actual alcohol consumption.

We will apply the vignette approach to work-limiting disability, using vignettes not only to obtain international comparisons corrected for DIF, but also for comparisons of different groups within a given country. For example, it is often hypothesized that men self-report themselves in better health than objective circumstances would warrant, that as they age, people adjust their norms downward about what constitutes good health, and that some of the socioeconomic status (SES) health gradient reflects different health thresholds by SES rather than true health differences. Vignettes offer the potential for systematic testing of these hypotheses.

9.3.1   A Formal Model of Response Scales and Vignette Corrections

Our model is an extension of the conditional hopit model (Chopit, cf. King et al. 2004, and Kapteyn, Smith, and van Soest 2007). It explains respondents' self-reports on work limitations and their reports on work limitations of hypothetical vignette persons. The first of these is the answer Y_i (where i indicates respondent i) to the question

"Do you have any impairment or health problem that limits the kind or amount of paid work you can do?"

The questions on work limitations of the vignette persons use the same 5-point scale and are formulated in the same way ("Does Mr./Mrs. X have any impairment or health problem that limits the type or amount of paid work that he/she can do?"). The answers will be denoted by Y_{li} where each respondent i evaluates L vignettes $l = 1, \ldots, L$.

Self-reports are modeled as a function of respondent characteristics X_i and an error term ε_i by the following ordered response equation:

(1) $$Y_i^* = X_i\beta + \varepsilon_i; \varepsilon_i \sim N(0,1), \varepsilon_i \text{ independent of } X_i$$

(2) $$Y_i = j \text{ if } \tau_i^{j-1} < Y_i^* \leq \tau_i^j, j = 1, \ldots 5.$$

The thresholds τ_j^i between the categories are given by

(3) $$\tau_i^0 = -\infty, \tau_i^5 = \infty, \tau_i^1 = X_i\gamma^1 + u_i, \tau_i^j = \tau_i^{j-1} + \exp(X_i\gamma^j), j = 2,3,4$$

(4) $$u_i \sim N(0,\sigma_u^2), \text{ independent of } \varepsilon_i \text{ and } X_i.$$

The error term u_i reflects unobserved heterogeneity in the thresholds. The fact that different respondents can use different response scales τ_i^j is called "differential item functioning" (DIF).

Using the self-reports on own work disabilities only, the parameters β and γ^1 cannot be separately identified;[6] the reported outcome only depends on these parameters through their difference. For example, consider country dummies: two people (with the same characteristics) in two different countries can have systematically different work disability, but if the scales on which they report their work disability can also differ across countries, then self-reports alone are not enough to identify the work disability difference between the countries. This was illustrated in figure 9.1.

For our analysis we are using a common set of $L = 9$ vignette questions, three in each of three domains: affect, pain, and heart problems.[7] The evaluations of vignettes $l = 1, \ldots, L$ are modeled using similar ordered response equations:

(5) $$Y_{li}^* = \theta_l + \varepsilon_{li}$$

(6) $$Y_{li} = j \text{ if } \tau_i^{j-1} < Y_{li}^* \leq \tau_i^j, j = 1, \ldots 5$$

(7) $$\varepsilon_{li} \sim N(0,\sigma_v^2), \text{ independent of each other, of } \varepsilon_i \text{ and of } X_i.$$

The assumption of *"response consistency"* means that the thresholds τ_i^j are the same for the self-reports and the vignettes. The assumption of "vignette

---

6. The γ^j for $j > 1$ will still be identified.

7. Kapteyn, Smith, and van Soest (2007) also discuss a model in which thresholds are allowed to vary across the three domains of work disability. They find that the results for this more general model are very similar to the results for the model imposing equal thresholds across domains.

equivalence" implies that genuine work-related health of the vignette person Y_{li}^* does not depend on X_i; it only depends on the vignette description (l) and an idiosyncratic error term.[8]

Given these assumptions, it is clear how the vignette evaluations can be used to separately identify β and γ ($= \gamma^1, \ldots \gamma^4$): from the vignette evaluations alone, γ, $\theta_1, \ldots \theta_L$ can be identified (up to the usual normalization of scale and location). From the self-reports, β can then be identified in addition. Thus, the vignettes can be used to solve the identification problem due to DIF. The two-step procedure is sketched only to make intuitively clear why the model is identified. In practice, all parameters will be estimated simultaneously by maximum likelihood.[9]

Adjusting for DIF is straightforward in this model once the parameters are estimated. Define a benchmark respondent with characteristics $X_i = X(B)$. (For example, choose one of the countries as the benchmark country.) The DIF adjustment would now involve comparing Y_i^* to the thresholds τ_B^j rather than τ_i^j, where τ_B^j is obtained in the same way as τ_i^j, but using $X(B)$ instead of X_i. Thus, a respondent's work ability is computed using the benchmark scale instead of the respondent's own scale. This does not lead to an adjusted score for each individual respondent (since Y_i^* is not observed), but it can be used to simulate adjusted *distributions* of Y_i for the whole population or conditional on some of the characteristics in X_i. Of course, the adjusted distribution will depend upon the chosen benchmark.

9.4   Responses to Vignettes in Western Europe and the United States

Respondents in each of the eight European countries and the United States were given vignettes in three domains of work disability—pain, affect, and heart disease. In each of the three domains, three distinct vignettes are used to describe the conditions of a hypothetical person. The actual vignettes used are presented in appendix B.[10] Table 9A.1 in appendix A compares the responses for the pain domain, while tables 9A.2 and 9A.3 do the same for the affect and heart disease (CVD) domains, respectively. The numbering of vignettes corresponds to how vignettes are presented in

8. Allowing the vignette evaluations to depend upon gender of the vignette person (as was done in Kapteyn, Smith, and van Soest 2007) does not affect the results.
9. This is more efficient than the two-step procedure. Since all error terms are independent, the likelihood contribution is a product of univariate normal probabilities over all vignette evaluations and the self-report, which is relatively easy to compute.
10. The selection of vignettes is the result of simulation studies with the Dutch CentERpanel, where we administered five vignettes per domain and then estimated Chopit models that used subsets of these five. We found that the extreme vignettes (either describing someone who is healthy or someone who is clearly too sick to work) carried little information. We also looked at the effect of the number of vignettes per domain. Obviously, more vignettes will lead to more accuracy, but for practical reasons the number of vignettes per domain had to be limited. The simulation study led to the conclusion that three vignettes per domain strikes a reasonable balance between practical feasibility and statistical accuracy.

appendix B. For instance, pain1 is the first pain vignette shown in appendix B, pain2 is the second pain vignette, and so forth. Although the health conditions of the persons described in the vignettes are supposed to be the same in all countries, tables 9A.1 through 9A.3 show that there are large differences in the evaluation frequencies between the countries.

Some differences are striking. For instance, pain2 ("[Catherine] suffers from back pain that causes stiffness in her back, especially at work, but is relieved with low doses of medication. She does not have any pains other than this generalized discomfort") is said to provide no work limitation by almost 25 percent of the American respondents, while in the European countries that percentage is less than 4, with very little variation across European countries. Similarly for CVD2 ("[Tom] has been diagnosed with high blood pressure. His blood pressure goes up quickly if he feels under stress. Tom does not exercise much and is overweight") almost 29 percent of Americans consider this to be no or only a mild work disability, while the SHARE average is about 16 percent. The differences for the affect vignettes are most pronounced. For all three vignettes Americans are much more likely than Europeans to say that the health condition described in the vignette does not constitute a work disability.

Table 9.2 summarizes the responses to the work disability vignettes in the nine countries. The three vignettes per domain were selected to deliberately eliminate the extremes where individuals in all countries would tend to describe the vignette person as clearly work disabled or clearly not work disabled. As a result, the differences in the scenarios described in the vignettes are often not large (at least among the European countries) and there is noise in the ranking both within and across countries. Table 9.2 summarizes the vignette evaluations in two ways. First, the 5-point scale on work disability is collapsed into three groups, with "none and mild" combined into one group and "severe and extreme" into another group. The percentage of respondents reporting in two of these three groups ("none/mild" and "severe/extreme") is listed for each of the three vignettes in each of the three domains—pain, affect, and CVD.

The second way of arriving at a simple summary is contained in the rows labeled "Average rank" under each domain. This row is derived by ranking the countries in each of the three vignettes within a domain by which country is "hardest" on the vignette persons—that is, which country has the highest percentage of responses in the mild or no work disability category and the lowest percentage of responses in the severe or extreme category. The final row in table 9.2, labeled "Grand average rank," is just the average of these ranks across the three work disability domains.

Before we concentrate on the patterns in table 9.2, we first discuss some correlations summarized in table 9.3. The upper panel shows correlations between the average rankings of countries within domains. For example, the entry 0.44 in the upper left corner is the correlation of the average ranking

Table 9.2   Responses to work disability vignettes

	Germany	Spain	Greece	Italy	Netherlands	Sweden	France	Belgium	U.S.	Total EU
Pain										
pain 1										
none, mild	10.9	5.5	12.1	13.4	6.6	6.0	10.7	7.7	10.1	10.1
severe, extreme	54.1	72.0	61.9	56.4	64.8	80.0	48.6	60.7	55.0	58.7
pain 2										
none, mild	29.0	18.2	31.6	38.1	58.9	10.4	38.6	47.7	77.9	32.8
severe, extreme	16.0	36.9	20.4	13.9	11.2	54.0	8.7	10.5	3.4	18.7
pain 3										
none, mild	7.5	1.9	7.8	14.4	4.9	11.4	5.8	7.2	4.9	7.9
severe, extreme	70.4	72.7	68.4	51.9	59.3	51.5	68.5	59.9	74.1	64.5
Average rank	4.8	8.3	4.8	3.0	5.0	6.3	3.8	4.3	4.3	
Affect										
Affect 1										
none, mild	23.9	23.7	20.6	39.2	29.3	34.0	26.9	35.0	53.3	28.7
severe, extreme	27.5	30.3	35.7	17.6	24.2	16.5	23.0	23.5	14.5	24.6
Affect 2										
none, mild	28.2	21.0	22.4	35.6	18.7	14.6	26.2	22.4	55.5	26.9
severe, extreme	22.7	30.6	33.2	16.9	30.4	52.8	24.5	25.7	12.2	25.1
Affect 3										
none, mild	54.8	39.3	43.9	57.2	74.8	9.9	52.9	67.6	80.6	52.0
severe, extreme	4.5	17.4	15.9	10.7	6.5	57.8	5.8	4.4	3.6	10.8
Average rank	4.7	7.7	7.5	3.2	5.3	7.0	4.7	3.8	1.0	
CVD										
CVD 1										
none, mild	15.9	5.7	14.9	23.7	33.6	1.7	16.0	22.2	43.3	16.7
severe, extreme	37.5	63.8	51.9	30.0	27.5	88.5	47.7	31.9	19.0	43.4
CVD 2										
none, mild	14.6	4.4	5.8	26.2	30.5	26.2	13.6	21.3	28.6	16.6
severe, extreme	41.8	65.9	77.0	33.7	26.6	26.1	46.9	33.1	30.5	44.5
CVD 3										
none, mild	7.2	3.8	5.1	16.1	18.2	2.3	6.9	10.8	10.7	9.1
severe, extreme	71.3	81.8	85.9	62.4	46.7	86.3	75.8	59.6	64.3	71.1
Average rank	5.5	8.0	7.7	3.2	1.5	6.7	6.2	3.7	2.5	
Grand average rank	5.0	8.0	6.7	3.1	3.9	6.7	4.9	3.9	2.6	

Table 9.3   **Correlations between rankings**

	Pain	Affect	CVD
Vignettes 1 and 2	0.44	0.43	0.51
Vignettes 1 and 3	0.06	0.45	0.89
Vignettes 2 and 3	−0.33	0.72	0.47
Correlations of average rankings across domains			
Correlation between rank averages of pain and affect			0.69
Correlation between rank averages of pain and CVD			0.57
Correlation between rank averages of affect and CVD			0.76

of countries obtained by calculating the average ranking for vignette 1 and for vignette 2 in the pain domain. One would expect that if countries differ strongly in how "soft" or "tough" they are in their vignette evaluations, the ranking of countries would be pretty much the same for each vignette. Table 9.3 indeed shows that all correlations but one are positive, but often the correlations are not particularly high. The correlations appear lowest for pain and highest for CVD. Thus, in particular for pain, there may be a fair amount of noise in the vignette evaluations.

The bottom panel shows the correlation of rank averages across domains. For example, the entry 0.69 is the correlation between the average ranking of countries for pain and for affect, as shown in table 9.3. We observe that the correlation of rank averages across domains is much higher than within domains (the average of the three correlations in the bottom panel is 0.67, while the average of the nine correlations in the top panel equals 0.40). This supports the notion that the sometimes weak correlations in the top panel of table 9.3 are at least partly the result of noise. Aggregating across vignettes leads to a considerable reduction of noise and thus to higher correlations in rankings of countries based on different vignettes.

Table 9.2 indicates several salient patterns. First, residents of the eight European countries do not share a common view on what constitutes a work disability. For example, while a third of the Dutch respondents state that the first CVD vignette constitutes no or only a mild work disability, the comparable fraction for Spaniards is one-in-twenty and for Swedes one-in-fifty. Yet, the variation within Europe is less striking than the difference between Europe and the United States. Comparing the last two columns, which present the United States and the SHARE averages, we see that with the exception of pain3 ("[Mark] has pain in his back and legs, and the pain is present almost all the time. It gets worse while he is working. Although medication helps, he feels uncomfortable when moving around, holding, and lifting things at work") European respondents are always more likely to call a vignette person work disabled than Americans.

Second, the ranking among the European countries depends to some extent on the specific domain chosen. For example, the Italians are quite

Table 9.4   National norms about work disability and employment protection

	Rank	OECD employment protection indicator	
		Version 1	Version 2
Italy	3.1	3.1	3.1
Belgium	3.9	2.2	2.5
Netherlands	3.9	2.1	2.3
France	4.9	3.0	2.9
Germany	5.0	2.2	2.5
Greece	6.7	2.8	2.9
Sweden	6.7	2.2	2.6
Spain	8.0	3.1	3.1
U.S.	2.6	0.2	0.7
Correlation with rank	1.00	0.52	0.56

demanding ("tough") in the affect domain, but the Dutch are the toughest on CVD. Yet the differences in ranking across domains are not dramatic, consistent with the earlier observed high correlations across domains. The Americans are the toughest overall, followed by the Italians, the Belgians, the Dutch, and the French. At the other end of the spectrum, the Greeks, Swedes, and Spaniards appear most inclined to call a health condition work limiting. The Germans are in the middle.

It is of interest to relate national norms about work disability to institutional arrangements. Table 9.4 provides a very simple way of doing so. The first column reproduces the grand average ranks from table 9.2. Columns (2) and (3) show two indicators of employment protection published by the Organization for Economic Cooperation and Development (OECD 2004). Both indicators aggregate in some fashion three main domains that make it difficult for an employer to dismiss an employee. These domains are (see OECD 2004, 65):

1. Difficulty of dismissal; that is, legislative provisions setting conditions under which a dismissal is "justified" or "fair."
2. Procedural inconveniences that the employer may face when starting the dismissal process.
3. Notice and severance pay provisions.

Version 2 is somewhat broader than version 1.

There is a fairly strong positive correlation between the strength of employment protection and a country's rank in the vignette distribution. People in countries with more employment protection are on average "softer" on work disability (i.e., more inclined to see a given health condition as work limiting). Naturally, there are various alternative explanations for this positive correlation. One would be "culture." In a country with a tough culture, citizens are tough on work disability and do not find employment protection very important. This is then reflected in laws with little protection. The United States would be a case in point.

9.5   Model Estimates for Response Scales and Self-Reported Work Disability

In this section, we present our parameter estimates for predicting work disability in the nine countries. Our models incorporate a number of standard demographic covariates—age dummies (less than fifty-eight, fifty-eight to sixty-four, sixty-five to seventy-one, seventy-two or more), years of education, dummies for being female, and for currently married. In addition, a series of health indicators are included: heart problems, lung disease, high blood pressure, diabetes, pain, arthritis, cancer, and the Center for Epidemiologic Studies Depression Scale (CES-D) score—for the European countries, the Euro-D scale. The benchmark country is the United States. We include a full set of interactions with an EU dummy. Furthermore, we include country dummies for the separate EU countries. Table 9.5 lists the means of the explanatory variables and self-reported work disability by country.

Panel A of the table shows large differences in years of education, with low means in the southern European countries. There are also substantial differences in the age composition, with, for example, relatively few sixty-five to seventy-one-year-olds in Sweden. Most chronic conditions are much more prevalent in the United States than in most European countries. This applies in particular to obesity, high blood pressure, diabetes, arthritis, and heart problems. Still, self-reported work disability in the United States seems well in line with that in the European countries. Only Greek, and to a lesser extent Dutch, respondents seem to face fewer work-related health impairments. The vignette evaluations suggest that, compared to Europeans, U.S. respondents underemphasize work-related health impairments, so that their actual work-related health limitations may be larger than those suggested by the means in panel B. Simulations based upon the estimates of the econometric model will look at this in detail.[11]

Table 9A.4 in appendix A presents estimation results for the complete model, allowing for DIF. Table 9A.5 presents the work disability equation in a model without DIF. The latter model is a standard ordered probit explaining the self-reported work disability on a 5-point scale. The differences between the two models illustrate the effects of allowing for differences in response scales. The model not allowing for response scale variation is strongly rejected by the data, as is immediately apparent from a comparison of the log-likelihoods.

---

11. The difference in wording between the work disability self-assessment in the United States and Europe might also play a role.

Table 9.5   **Sample means by country**

A Demographics

Country	female	marrlt	educyrs	age 58–64	age 65–71	age 72+
U.S.	0.543	0.693	13.026	0.204	0.227	0.151
Germany	0.558	0.632	13.409	0.229	0.234	0.241
Sweden	0.510	0.669	10.674	0.267	0.147	0.267
Netherlands	0.509	0.726	11.974	0.236	0.193	0.214
Spain	0.545	0.632	6.682	0.226	0.181	0.288
Italy	0.549	0.615	7.239	0.266	0.184	0.261
France	0.558	0.702	9.559	0.221	0.191	0.300
Greece	0.534	0.685	9.205	0.237	0.246	0.241
Belgium	0.535	0.737	10.594	0.202	0.216	0.265

B Health Conditions

Country	heart	lung	hbp	diabetes	pain	arthritis
U.S.	0.192	0.083	0.492	0.160	0.373	0.511
Germany	0.113	0.069	0.343	0.102	0.567	0.131
Sweden	0.121	0.095	0.303	0.081	0.552	0.096
Netherlands	0.099	0.100	0.239	0.081	0.355	0.093
Spain	0.101	0.080	0.343	0.119	0.479	0.239
Italy	0.118	0.131	0.366	0.087	0.591	0.364
France	0.144	0.087	0.288	0.101	0.531	0.311
Greece	0.154	0.050	0.326	0.120	0.503	0.195
Belgium	0.141	0.063	0.286	0.074	0.504	0.256

Country	cancer	obese	cesd	sdis
U.S.	0.107	0.300	1.302	1.967
Germany	0.063	0.175	0.992	1.994
Sweden	0.085	0.155	0.964	1.983
Netherlands	0.052	0.126	0.909	1.764
Spain	0.058	0.212	1.327	2.028
Italy	0.054	0.152	1.446	1.967
France	0.064	0.158	1.353	1.906
Greece	0.027	0.168	1.166	1.624
Belgium	0.067	0.196	1.128	2.026

Notes: female: dummy female; marrlt: dummy married or living together (benchmark: single, divorced, separated, or widowed); educyrs: years of education; age 58–64, age 65–71, age 72+: dummies age groups 58–64, 65–71, and 72 and older, respectively (benchmark: 50–57). All sample means are weighted. Heart, . . . cancer: dummies for chronic conditions based upon answers to survey questions "has the doctor ever told you that you have . . ."; heart: heart problems; lung: lung disease; hbp: high blood pressure; pain: 1 if answer is "yes" to "do you often have pain?"; obese: BMI > 30 (based upon self-reported weight and height); cesd: Center for Epidemiological Studies depression score in HRS; 0.5*EURO-D depression score in SHARE; a higher value indicates more depression related symptoms; sdis: self-reported work disability on a scale from 1 (none) to 5 (extreme). All means are weighted.

The estimated coefficients for the demographic attributes yield few surprises. Work disability increases with age, decreases with schooling, and is lower for married respondents. Having any of the health conditions that are included in the model makes it more likely that one reports a work disability. The interactions with the dummy for Europe show that in particular the effects of cancer and depression on work disability are stronger in the European countries than in the United States. No such effects are found in the model that does not correct for DIF (table 9A.5). The country dummies in table 9A.4 demonstrate that, once we correct for response scale differences and control for health conditions, the Europeans are considerably less likely to be work disabled than the Americans (the United States is the reference category). The effects are similar, but smaller, in the model without DIF, in accordance with the fact that U.S. respondents less easily classify someone as work disabled (compare to table 9.2). Both the models with and without DIF show that the effect of education or being married on work disability is less in Europe than in the United States.

The significant estimates of the effect of covariates on the thresholds explain why the effects of demographics and health conditions on self-reported work disability change once we take response scale differences into account. Comparing effects of country dummies on the first threshold across the European countries suggests that Italians are toughest and Spaniards softest, consistent with the raw data summarized in table 9.2. Compared to country dummies, effects of health conditions and demographics on the first threshold are modest. More educated respondents tend to be softer, albeit less so in the European Union than in the United States. Females are harder in the United States, but not in the European Union. Older respondents are softer in the United States, but not in the European Union.

The interpretation of the estimated parameters for the remaining thresholds is not very straightforward since these parameters reflect shifts of the second threshold relative to the first one (compare to equation [3]). Rather than extensively discussing these parameters, we turn to some simulations that are easier to interpret.

9.5.1 Simulation Results

Figure 9.2 provides a first impression of the effects of using different scales. The first column presents the distribution of self-reported work disability for the United States, using U.S. data and U.S. parameters. This simply predicts sample observations for the United States. Similarly, the last column predicts the distribution of work disability using EU (SHARE) data and EU parameters. Comparing the first and last column suggests relatively minor differences in work disability prevalence between the European Union and the United States. For instance, the percentage saying that they have no work disability is predicted to be about 51 percent in the United States and 49 percent in the European Union. On the other hand, the percentage

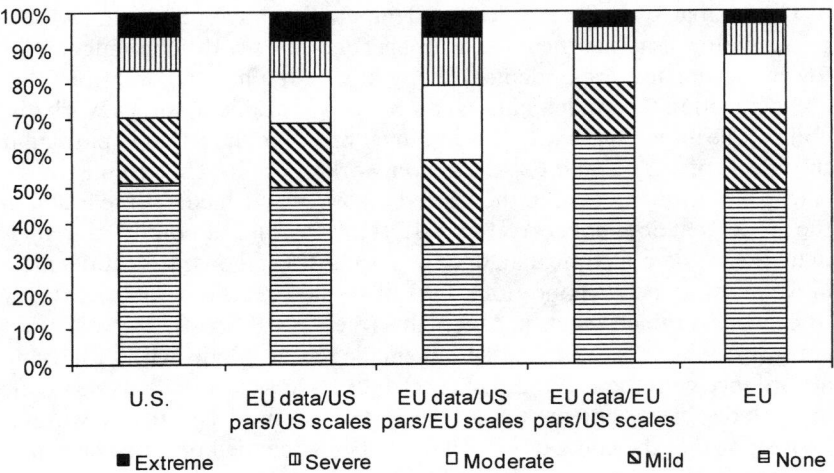

Fig. 9.2   Simulated work limitations according to different scenarios

of Americans with severe or extreme work disabilities is predicted to be about 16 percent in the United States and only 12 percent in the European Union. These seemingly modest differences are the result of two counteracting effects: Americans use response scales that are "harder" while Europeans appear to suffer from less work disability. This is illustrated by the remaining three columns in figure 9.2.

The second column uses EU data, but U.S. scales and U.S. parameter estimates to predict EU disability. The distributions in columns (1) and (2) are virtually identical, with a slight shift in the direction of more work disability in the EU. This implies that distributional differences in demographics and health have only a minor effect on differences in observed work disability prevalence in the United States and the European countries.

The middle column is based on EU data, U.S. parameters of the work disability equation, and EU response scales. Compared to the first and second column, we now see a dramatic shift in the distribution in the direction of increased work disability. The shift is due to the fact that Europeans use softer response scales and more easily call someone disabled. It is also instructive to make a comparison with the fifth column (both EU data and EU parameters). Since the only difference between the third and fifth column is the use of U.S. parameters in the work disability equation, this comparison suggests that, for given demographics and health conditions, the risk to face an actual work disability is substantially higher in the United States than in Europe. For instance, column (3) implies that 34 percent has no work limitation, while column (5) implies that 49 percent has no work limitation.

Finally, a comparison of columns (4) and (5) isolates the effect of response scales on observed work disability distributions in the European countries.

Table 9.6   **Work disability by country**

	None	Mild	Moderate	Severe	Extreme	None/ mild	Severe/ extreme
Germany							
U.S.	51.4	19.1	13.2	9.9	6.5	70.4	16.4
EU, U.S. scales	61.2	17.7	11.0	6.9	3.2	78.8	10.1
EU	45.4	23.5	18.7	9.8	2.6	68.8	12.5
Sweden							
U.S.	51.4	19.1	13.2	9.9	6.5	70.4	16.4
EU, U.S. scales	68.6	15.1	8.7	5.2	2.5	83.6	7.7
EU	52.2	19.3	14.0	10.5	4.1	71.4	14.6
Netherlands							
U.S.	51.4	19.1	13.2	9.9	6.5	70.4	16.4
EU, U.S. scales	69.6	15.3	8.3	4.8	2.1	84.8	6.8
EU	53.2	29.0	11.3	4.4	2.1	82.2	6.5
Spain							
U.S.	51.4	19.1	13.2	9.9	6.5	70.4	16.4
EU, U.S. scales	68.6	12.8	8.1	5.7	4.8	81.4	10.5
EU	45.6	22.9	16.9	11.1	3.5	68.5	14.6
Italy							
U.S.	51.4	19.1	13.2	9.9	6.5	70.4	16.4
EU, U.S. scales	60.0	15.1	10.3	7.8	6.7	75.1	14.5
EU	47.6	22.9	16.4	7.7	5.4	70.5	13.1
France							
US	51.4	19.1	13.2	9.9	6.5	70.4	16.4
EU, U.S. scales	65.8	15.4	9.2	6.0	3.6	81.2	9.6
EU	52.0	20.6	16.7	8.4	2.2	72.7	10.6
Greece							
U.S.	51.4	19.1	13.2	9.9	6.5	70.4	16.4
EU, U.S. scales	81.5	9.5	4.9	2.7	1.4	91.1	4.1
EU	68.9	15.1	9.4	4.5	2.1	84.0	6.6
Belgium							
U.S.	51.4	19.1	13.2	9.9	6.5	70.4	16.4
EU, U.S. scales	59.0	17.0	11.3	7.9	4.8	76.0	12.7
EU	43.4	26.7	16.7	8.9	4.4	70.1	13.2

When we assign U.S. scales to EU respondents, we observe a dramatic fall in reported work disability. For instance, the percentage of respondents without a work disability goes up from 49 percent to 64 percent, while the percentage with severe or extreme work limitations falls from 12 percent to about 10.5 percent. Again, this is a consequence of the fact that Americans less easily classify someone with a given impairment as work disabled.

Table 9.6 presents simulated work disability by country. The first row in each panel presents work disability for the United States; the second row presents work disability in the country, but using U.S. scales, and the third row presents work disability simulated using the response scale of that country.

As was observed for the set of all European countries, using U.S. scales has dramatic effects on the distribution of disability within each European country. It is worth noting that generally most of the changes take place in the categories "none" and "mild." The percentage of respondents in the EU country whose work disability falls in the severe/extreme range is not affected as much. This is as one would expect; there is probably less scope for disagreement about whether a serious health condition constitutes a work disability than whether a mild condition should be seen as work limiting. The biggest reduction in the "severe/extreme" category takes place in Sweden (from 14.6 percent to 7.7 percent) and Spain (from 14.6 percent to 10.5 percent). In other countries the changes are much less dramatic and in some cases the adoption of the U.S. scales leads to an increase in the percentage of respondents with severe or extreme work disabilities. This happens for Italy (an increase by 1.4 percentage points) and the Netherlands (an increase by .3 percentage points).

When considering the changes in the categories none and mild we see the biggest decrease in Spain (by 12.8 percentage points) and Sweden (12.2 percentage points). The smallest decrease is seen in the Netherlands (2.6 percentage points) and Italy (4.6 percentage points).

We have seen earlier that the use of U.S. scales actually increases the difference in work disability between the U.S. and the EU countries we are considering here. It is also of interest to investigate if the use of vignettes reduces the differences between the EU countries. A simple measure is the variance of the percent none/mild and of the percent severe/extreme across European countries. We find that the variance of the percentage none/mild is 36.9 if we use the own country scales and 26.5 if we use the common (U.S.) scale. For the percentage severe/extreme, the use of a common scale has virtually no effect. Using the own scale the variance is equal to 11.0 and when using the common scale the variance equals 10.8.

Next we consider a number of socioeconomic categories. Table 9.7 shows results by age. The scale effects appear to be fairly uniform by age. For instance, the effect of going from European scales to U.S. scales on the percentage severe/extreme varies from 1.2 in the fifty-eight to sixty-four category to 1.8 in the seventy-two-plus category. Similarly, the effect on the percentage none/mild varies from −7.5 in the fifty-eight to sixty-four category to −9.9 in the seventy-two-plus category.

9.6 Work Disability, Work, and Response Scales

We now extend the model presented in section 9.3 by adding an equation explaining employment status, while allowing for justification bias. Justification bias has been introduced by Bound (1991) as a possible effect of nonemployment on self-reported work disability, where respondents may exaggerate their work limitations to justify that they do not work. The em-

Table 9.7   Work disability by age in the European Union and the United States

	50–57			58–64			65–71			72+			All		
	U.S.	EU	EU U.S. scale	U.S.	EU	EU U.S. scale	U.S.	EU	EU U.S. scale	U.S.	EU	EU U.S. scale	U.S.	EU	EU U.S. scale
None	59.8	59.4	75.5	49.8	55.5	71.4	48.4	45.9	61.4	34.7	32.9	48.2	51.4	48.8	64.5
Mild	17.7	20.8	12.7	19.6	22.5	14.2	19.5	23.7	16.2	21.2	24.0	18.6	19.1	22.6	15.3
Moderate	10.7	12.5	6.4	13.3	14.0	7.7	14.2	17.4	10.6	18.4	22.5	14.3	13.2	16.4	9.6
Severe	7.3	5.5	3.7	10.3	6.1	4.6	10.8	9.3	7.3	14.9	14.4	10.5	9.9	8.7	6.4
Extreme	4.5	1.8	1.9	7.0	1.9	2.2	7.1	3.7	4.6	10.9	6.3	8.4	6.5	3.4	4.2
None/mild	77.5	80.3	88.1	69.4	78.1	85.6	67.9	69.6	77.6	55.9	56.9	66.8	70.4	71.4	79.8
Sev/extr.	11.8	7.2	5.5	17.3	8.0	6.8	17.9	13.0	11.8	25.8	20.7	18.9	16.4	12.1	10.6

pirical evidence for the existence of justification bias appears to be mixed (see, for instance, Kreider and Pepper [2007] or Jones [2007] and references therein). The use of vignettes provides a novel approach to the estimation of justification bias.

As before, Y_i denotes the answer of respondent i to the 5-point scale self-assessed work disability question while the answers to the work limitations of the vignette persons on the same 5-point scale are denoted by Y_{li}, where each respondent i evaluates L vignettes $l = 1, \ldots, L$.

For employment status, we use a binary variable E, with $E_i = 1$ if respondent i does some paid work, and $E_i = 0$ otherwise. In principle we could distinguish more than two categories here (unemployed, on disability benefits, retired, homemaker, etc.) but the numbers of observations in some of these employment states are quite small in some countries, making estimation of a richer model difficult.

The equation for self-reported work disability is the same as before (compare equations [1] and [2]). To keep the model manageable by limiting the number of parameters to be estimated and to facilitate interpretation of the results, we replace the threshold equations (3) and (4) by:

(8) $\qquad \tau_i^0 = -\infty, \tau_i^5 = \infty, \tau_i^1 = X_i\gamma + \delta E_i + u_i, \tau_i^j = \tau_i^{j-1} + \gamma^j, j = 2,3,4$

(9) $\qquad\qquad u_i \sim N(0,\sigma_u^2)$, independent of ε_i and X_i.

This is a more parsimonious specification than the one used in equation (3). All threshold shifts are the same. The error term u_i again reflects unobserved heterogeneity in thresholds. The effect of employment status E_i on the response scales reflects justification bias: depending on their employment status, respondents may use different response scales. The advantage of the more parsimonious specification is that in this model, justification bias is captured by a single parameter δ (which will be allowed to be different for U.S. and European respondents in the empirical work) instead of a set of parameters affecting several thresholds differently. We expect a positive estimate of δ if employed respondents are less likely to evaluate a given (vignette) person as work disabled than nonemployed respondents.

The evaluations of vignettes $l = 1, \ldots, L$ are also modeled as before (compare equations [5] through [7]). Employment status is modeled using a probit-like equation:

(10) $\qquad\qquad\qquad E_i^* = X_i\varphi + \pi Y_i^* + \eta_i$

$\eta_i \sim N(0,1)$, η_i independent of $X_i, u_i, \varepsilon_{ri}, \varepsilon_{1i}, \ldots, \varepsilon_{Li}$

$E_i = 1$ if $E_i^* > 0$; $E_i = 0$ if $E_i^* \leq 0$.

The coefficient π represents the effect of work disability on employment status, which is the main coefficient of interest in many studies of the effect of work-related health on employment (cf., e.g., Kreider and Pepper 2007).

In this model, error terms are all independent of each other, and no exclusion restrictions are needed for identification. The intuitive argument for this is as follows: equations (5) and (8) are identified from the vignette evaluations alone, since employment status is exogenous to the errors in (5) and (8). Equation (1) is then identified as well, just like in the model of section 9.3. Since the error term ε_i in (1) is independent of the error term in (10), the variation in Y_i^* induced by the variation in ε_i is sufficient to identify equation (10) (although estimation of [10] is complicated by the categorical nature of Y_i).

As a sensitivity check, we will also present results for an overidentified version of the model, where we impose the exclusion restriction in the employment equation that health conditions affect employment status through work disability only and not directly (maintaining the assumption that all errors are independent of each other).

Figure 9.3 presents the model, including work and justification bias, in graphical form. Actual work disability affects employment status (the parameter π in [10]), but we assume there is no reverse effect of employment

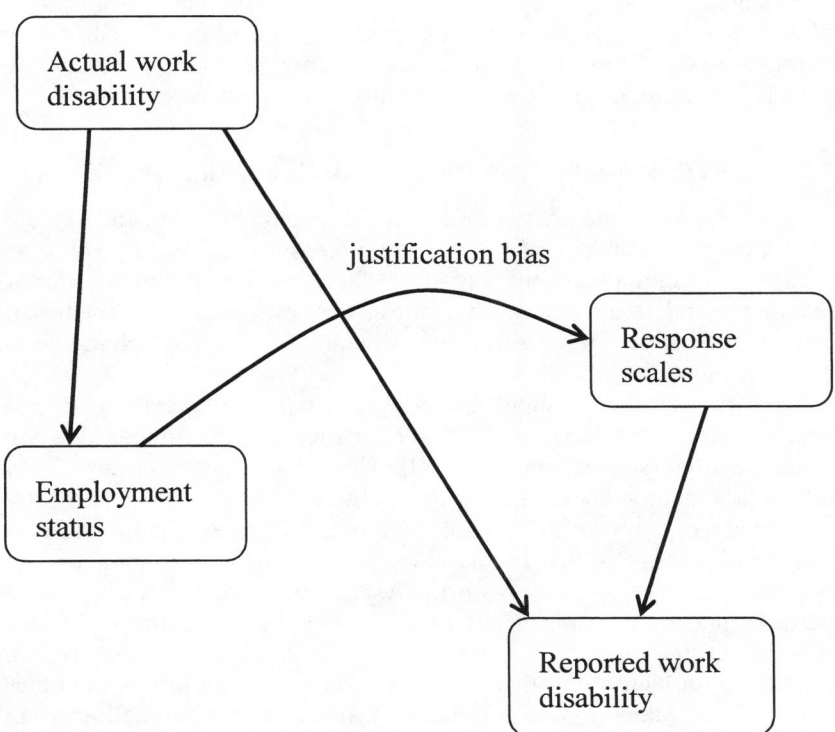

Fig. 9.3   Work, work disability, response scales, and justification bias

status on actual work disability, in line with, for example, the results of a recent panel data study of Böckerman and Ilmakkunnas (2009). We could in principle allow for a reverse effect if appropriate exclusion restrictions were available. In our model, employment status affects *reported* work disability through the justification bias effect on response scales (the parameter δ).

The figure does not show the vignette evaluations. We maintain the assumptions underlying the vignette approach discussed in section 9.3, in particular vignette equivalence and response consistency. The first now also implies that workers and nonworkers do not interpret the genuine work-related health of the vignette persons in systematically different ways, and we see no reason not to find this assumption plausible. Response consistency now also implies that justification bias plays the same role in vignette evaluations as in self-assessments. This is an identifying assumption that cannot be tested with the current data. Thus, if nonworkers evaluate themselves as more work limited than workers with the same actual work-related health, they are assumed to also do this with the vignette persons. One might argue that they will be less inclined to exaggerate the vignette person's health problems than their own impairment, which would imply that the effect of employment status on the vignette evaluations is an underestimate of justification bias in self-assessments. Since our estimate of justification bias is driven by the effect on vignette evaluations, this would imply that with our method, we get a lower bound on the "true" justification bias in self-assessments.

9.7 Model Estimates for Work Disability, Work, and Threshold Equations

Tables 9A.6 through 9A.10 present the model estimates with and without DIF. Comparing table 9A.6 with the estimates for the disability equation in table 9A.4 shows that generally the coefficients are of a similar order of magnitude and have the same sign. One notable difference is the coefficient on gender, which is significantly negative in table 9A.6, and which was completely insignificant in table 9A.4.

The results for the threshold equation given in table 9A.7 cannot be compared directly to table 9A.4, as the specification is much simpler. We will use simulations (shown later) to see if the simpler specification leads to very different outcomes. The country dummies (with the United States as the reference category) appear to be smaller, although Greece maintains its status as somewhat of an outlier. The parameter of primary interest in table 9A.7 is the coefficient on the dummy work. The coefficient is significantly positive in the United States, while the interaction with the EU dummy makes clear that the effect of employment status on the thresholds is essentially zero in the European Union. In other words, we find significant justification bias in the United States and no evidence of justification bias in the European Union. It suggests that not working is much more accepted in the European Union (for whatever reason) than in the United States. Even if our estimate of justification bias is an underestimate of the true justification bias since it does not affect vignette evaluations as much as self-assessments (see the end of the previous section), we still believe this conclusion is justified, since we see no reason why the violation of response consistency would apply in Europe but not in the United States. It might mean that justification bias is present in Europe as well as the United States, but then it is still much bigger in the United States than in Europe.

The estimates of the vignette equation are presented in table 9A.8. The estimated coefficients on the vignette dummies are similar to those in table 9A.4, although they do not show exactly the same ranking across vignettes. Still, the correlation between the dummy estimates in the two tables is 0.97.

The employment equation estimates are shown in table 9A.9. Since the model without DIF is soundly rejected, we concentrate on the estimates for the model with DIF. Since (genuine) work disability is controlled for, the effects of the health dummies indicate the effect of a specific condition on employment *keeping work disability constant*. The negative effects of mental health (measured through the CES-D score) and, in the United States, diabetes on employment therefore imply that the negative effects of these health conditions on employment are larger than their effect through work disability would suggest. On the other hand, the effect of obesity on employment in the United States is smaller than its effect through work disability. The insignificant effects of other health conditions simply mean that the effects of conditions are well-captured by the effect of work disability. The estimated age dummies show the expected pattern that employment falls with age. This pattern is much stronger in the European Union than in the United States. Similarly, females are less likely to be employed than males and also this difference is stronger in the European Union than in the United States.

The parameter of main interest in the employment equation is the coefficient of work disability. It is more than twice as large in absolute terms in the United States than in the European Union (−.464 in the United States and −.192 in the European Union). This result remains essentially unchanged when we specify the employment equations more parsimoniously by omitting the health conditions (table 9A.10). One possible interpretation of this is that individuals in the United States are more likely to work for pay and that health is one of the main impediments for doing so. In the European Union on the other hand, also individuals in relatively good health are often not working, for instance as a result of more generous income replacement schemes. Following, we will present simulations that shed more light on this (and other) interpretations.

Comparing the coefficient of work disability with the estimate of the same coefficient in a model without DIF shows the effect of controlling for justification bias when estimating the effect of work disability on employment. For the European countries, there is virtually no difference between the DIF corrected and not DIF corrected estimates in table 9A.9 (−.192 and −.197, respectively), which corresponds to the finding that there is no evidence of justification bias for these countries. For the United States the difference is larger (−.464 versus −.516) and, as expected, we find that the size of the effect of work disability on employment is overestimated if justification bias is not corrected for—part of the negative correlation between work disability and employment is due to the fact that the nonemployed tend to overreport their work disability. But the size of the bias is modest. (But then again, our estimate might be seen as a lower bound on the bias, if justification bias plays less of a role in vignette evaluations than in self-assessments; see the discussion at the end of section 9.6).

9.7.1   Simulation Results

Figure 9.4 is analogous to figure 9.2, but now based on the extended model, including an employment equation and allowing for justification bias. Compared to the model underlying figure 9.2, the current model has one extra equation (the employment equation) so that there are more possible combinations of data and parameters that can be used in simulating counterfactuals. The first three bars in figure 9.4 are most comparable to those in figure 9.2, while the last two bars in figure 9.4 correspond to the last two bars in figure 9.2. Qualitatively the patterns appear to be similar. If we move from U.S. data to EU data (but retaining U.S. scales and parameters)—that is, from the first column to the second—we see again a slight shift in the direction of more work disability in the European Union than in the United States.

When we move from the second to the third column (EU data, U.S. parameters, EU scales) we see an increase in work disability, but the shift is not as dramatic as in figure 9.2. Finally, a comparison of the last two columns shows again that if we move from EU data and EU parameters, but U.S. scales to all data, parameters and scales European, then work disability increases substantially (but not as much as in figure 9.2). This illustrates once again the difference in response scales used in the EU countries and in the United States. The reason that the changes are less dramatic than in figure 9.2 is probably the fact that we have imposed that all threshold shifts are parallel to obtain a parsimonious model (see section 9.6).

Comparing columns (4) (EU-data, U.S.-disability equation, EU-work equation, U.S.-scale) and (8) (EU-data, EU-disability equation, EU-work equation, U.S.-scale) shows a substantial fall in the prevalence of work disability. Since the only difference between the two columns is the difference in disability parameters, it illustrates once more the finding that Europeans are less work disabled than the Americans, although the reported work disability levels are similar.

The only difference between columns (6) (EU-data, EU-disability equation, U.S.-work equation, U.S.-scale) and (8) (EU-data, EU-disability

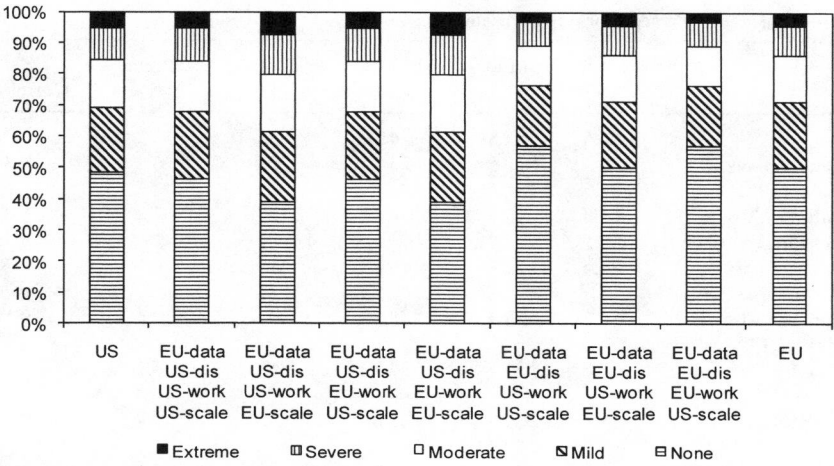

Fig. 9.4   Simulated work limitations; model including employment equation

equation, EU-work equation, U.S.-scale) is that in the former the U.S. employment parameters have been used, while in the latter we use the EU employment parameters. These differences in parameters appear to have minimal impact on the distribution of observed work disability, even though observed work disability does depend on employment status through its (justification bias) effect on the response scales.

Table 9.8 and figure 9.5 show the percentage of people working for each of the five levels of work disability (the last column of table 9.8 is discussed later). As could be expected on the basis of the raw data, a comparison of the first and last row of table 9.8 shows that Europeans work less than Americans for any work disability category. A comparison across the rows of table 9.8 (or the columns of figure 9.5) shows that a major source of differences lies in the parameters of the employment equation. Whenever we simulate labor market outcomes using the U.S. employment parameters, we find considerably higher employment rates than when we use EU parameters. This is particularly true for the less severe work disability categories, in line with the larger effect of work disability on employment in the United States than in Europe. Once we move to extreme work disabilities the differences become small; with an extreme work disability neither Americans nor Europeans are likely to work.

Figure 9.6 shows total employment rates in the United States and the European Union. Consistent with table 9.8 and figure 9.5, we see that employment is about twice as large when a U.S. employment equation is used than when we use the EU parameters in the employment equation. Whether the EU or the U.S. disability parameters are used has very little impact.

Finally, we return to the issue of justification bias. The last column of table

Table 9.8   **Percent working by disability category**

	None (%)	Mild (%)	Moderate (%)	Severe (%)	Extreme (%)	Correlations
U.S.	66.6	45.8	34.3	23.5	12.2	0.32
EU-data U.S.-dis U.S.-work U.S.-scale	59.5	36.5	25.0	15.1	6.3	0.34
EU-data U.S.-dis U.S.-work EU-scale	61.8	40.5	28.6	18.0	7.8	0.33
EU-data U.S.-dis EU-work U.S.-scale	34.4	22.3	16.7	11.5	6.1	0.20
EU-data U.S.-dis EU-work EU-scale	35.3	24.4	18.8	13.4	7.4	0.19
EU-data EU-dis U.S.-work U.S.-scale	59.8	35.3	24.3	15.0	6.7	0.33
EU-data EU-dis U.S.-work EU-scale	61.8	39.3	27.8	17.7	8.2	0.33
EU-data EU-dis EU-work U.S.-scale	33.6	20.7	15.4	10.8	6.1	0.20
EU	34.5	22.9	17.4	12.4	7.3	0.19

9.8 shows simulated correlations between the binary outcomes employment (employment = 1 and nonemployment = 0) and not having a work-limiting health condition (none = 1, mild or worse = 0). Other things equal, one would expect a stronger correlation between work and self-reported disability if U.S. scales are used, because of justification bias, which is significant in the United States and absent in the European Union. We see a small effect of justification bias. For instance, comparing the second and third row we see the correlation decrease from .34 to .33. Other comparisons show similar small effects. However, using the U.S. employment parameters rather than the EU ones has a much bigger effect. This confirms once again the much weaker relation between disability and employment in the European Union than in the United States.

9.8   Conclusions

We have provided several pieces of evidence on differences in work disability between older Europeans and Americans. The descriptive vignette analyses suggest that opinions about what constitutes a health-related work limitation are related to the generosity of earnings replacement schemes and employment protection in different countries. We also find that the differences in self-reported disabilities across European countries fall substantially when we use common reporting scales (i.e., if we use vignette corrections to make scales comparable). Consistent with earlier research, we find that Americans are less likely to call themselves work disabled than Europeans.

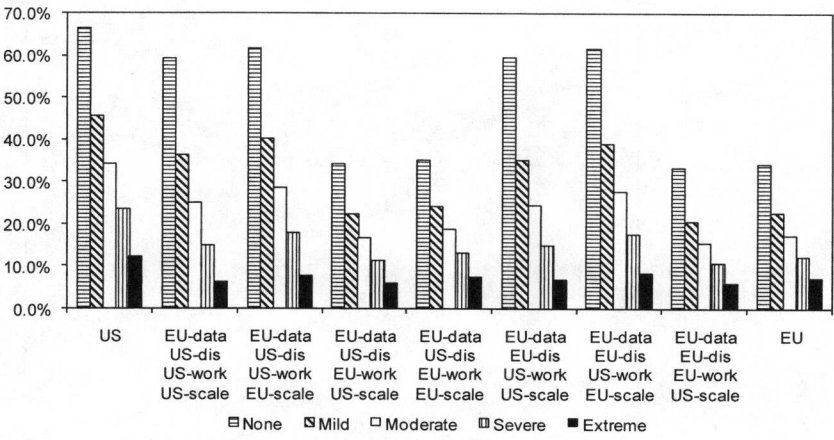

Fig. 9.5   Percent working by disability category

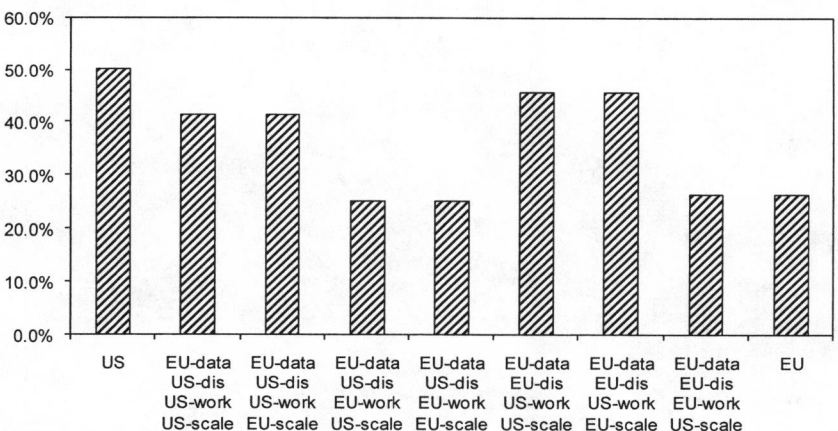

Fig. 9.6   Employment rates

The extended model with employment included suggests that justification bias plays a role in the United States, but not in the European Union. Americans use health as a justification for not working, whereas Europeans do not feel the need to do so. The effect of health limitations on employment is about twice as large in the United States than in the European Union. Our simulations suggest that this mainly reflects the fact that in the European Union even healthy individuals are less likely to be working than in the United States.

Appendix A

Tables

Table 9A.1   Responses to pain work disability vignettes

	Germany	Spain	Greece	Italy	Netherlands	Sweden	France	Belgium	Total EU	U.S.
Pain 1										
None	1.96	0.65	0.41	4.03	2.12	1.51	1.56	1.28	2.05	1.53
Mild	8.91	4.80	11.65	9.33	4.48	4.50	9.14	6.41	8.02	8.54
Moderate	35.08	22.56	26.00	30.27	28.55	13.98	40.68	31.64	31.25	34.99
Severe	47.77	62.20	41.12	43.47	36.49	53.16	43.83	42.00	47.45	48.32
Extreme	6.29	9.79	20.82	12.89	28.35	26.85	4.78	18.67	11.24	6.63
Total	100	100	100	100	100	100	100	100	100	100
Pain 2										
None	2.28	1.81	3.40	6.58	2.63	0.94	5.29	2.90	3.72	24.97
Mild	26.77	16.38	28.18	31.47	56.23	9.48	33.31	44.83	29.04	52.90
Moderate	54.94	44.95	48.07	48.06	29.92	35.53	52.75	41.81	48.51	18.78
Severe	13.85	34.78	17.22	11.73	10.72	47.59	7.67	9.59	16.71	2.25
Extreme	2.15	2.09	3.13	2.16	0.50	6.46	0.98	0.87	2.02	1.11
Total	100	100	100	100	100	100	100	100	100	100
Pain 3										
None	1.22	0	0.41	2.62	1.47	0.45	1.15	1.35	1.28	1.16
Mild	6.29	1.94	7.39	11.78	3.46	10.93	4.70	5.86	6.62	3.72
Moderate	22.06	25.41	23.77	33.73	35.78	37.14	25.70	32.88	27.61	21.06
Severe	57.57	63.15	48.03	34.96	36.75	43.78	61.77	47.86	51.59	50.43
Extreme	12.85	9.50	20.41	16.91	22.53	7.69	6.68	12.05	12.90	23.62
Total	100	100	100	100	100	100	100	100	100	100

Table 9A.2   Responses to affect disability vignettes

	Germany	Spain	Greece	Italy	Netherlands	Sweden	France	Belgium	Total EU	U.S.
Affect 1										
None	3.78	1.12	3.78	6.27	3.94	5.32	5.28	5.54	4.30	22.12
Mild	20.07	22.62	16.77	32.91	25.37	28.69	21.59	29.44	24.40	31.15
Moderate	48.64	45.91	43.70	43.25	46.54	49.47	50.15	41.55	46.68	32.21
Severe	24.78	28.72	25.68	15.33	20.26	15.49	21.70	22.56	22.12	13.26
Extreme	2.71	1.62	10.07	2.25	3.89	1.03	1.28	0.91	2.50	1.26
Total	100	100	100	100	100	100	100	100	100	100
Affect 2										
None	3.38	1.88	2.93	5.93	2.41	1.41	4.84	3.66	3.82	18.33
Mild	24.81	19.08	19.48	29.67	16.26	13.19	21.35	18.73	23.05	37.12
Moderate	49.11	48.43	44.40	47.51	50.92	32.57	49.35	51.87	48.04	32.35
Severe	21.62	27.21	27.15	14.86	25.29	45.02	22.52	22.21	22.48	10.74
Extreme	1.08	3.40	6.04	2.03	5.13	7.80	1.94	3.52	2.60	1.46
Total	100	100	100	100	100	100	100	100	100	100
Affect 3										
None	8.58	3.41	10.81	8.87	5.90	0.91	13.09	10.87	8.33	39.54
Mild	46.20	35.90	33.06	48.36	68.90	8.94	39.77	56.78	43.66	41.02
Moderate	40.69	43.28	40.22	32.11	18.69	32.32	41.38	27.99	37.23	15.86
Severe	4.53	16.98	11.87	8.96	6.51	47.38	5.02	4.15	9.61	2.71
Extreme	0	0.44	4.04	1.70	0	10.45	0.74	0.22	1.16	0.87
Total	100	100	100	100	100	100	100	100	100	100

Table 9A.3   Responses to heart disease work disability vignettes

	Germany	Spain	Greece	Italy	Netherlands	Sweden	France	Belgium	Total EU	U.S.
CVD1										
None	3.10	0.63	1.41	4.08	2.47	0.15	4.11	3.30	2.88	7.84
Mild	12.78	5.10	13.44	19.61	31.10	1.52	11.88	18.86	13.85	35.41
Moderate	46.57	30.52	33.26	46.33	38.96	9.78	36.27	45.97	39.82	37.76
Severe	34.47	57.95	40.42	23.96	22.37	60.56	43.69	26.32	37.60	16.12
Extreme	3.08	5.81	11.46	6.02	5.09	27.99	4.06	5.55	5.85	2.87
Total	100	100	100	100	100	100	100	100	100	100
CVD2										
None	3.31	0.30	0.60	4.47	3.76	1.95	3.62	2.46	2.98	8.16
Mild	11.27	4.09	5.16	20.73	26.70	24.30	9.95	18.89	13.47	20.46
Moderate	43.46	29.74	17.20	38.65	42.90	47.68	39.50	45.51	38.50	40.88
Severe	39.15	54.30	49.30	24.12	21.15	22.22	41.95	30.44	37.01	26.93
Extreme	2.45	11.57	27.74	8.31	5.49	3.85	4.98	2.70	7.08	3.57
Missing	0.36	0	0	3.72	0	0	0	0	0.96	
Total	100	100	100	100	100	100	100	100	100	100
CVD3										
None	3.99	0.45	1.86	5.31	3.04	0.15	2.14	3.83	3.12	3.10
Mild	3.20	3.39	3.25	10.75	15.15	2.12	4.77	6.93	5.99	7.55
Moderate	21.55	14.35	8.96	21.55	35.13	11.40	17.34	29.66	19.80	24.99
Severe	53.39	57.53	33.63	36.62	32.80	54.02	55.52	42.04	48.11	48.61
Extreme	17.87	24.28	52.29	25.77	13.89	32.32	20.23	17.54	22.99	15.74
Total	100	100	100	100	100	100	100	100	100	100

Table 9A.4   **Parameter estimates; model with DIF**

		Parameter	Standard error	*t*-value
		Disability equation		
U.S.				
	constant	−0.457*	0.131	3.490
	Female	−0.020	0.049	0.416
	Married/LT	−0.136*	0.052	2.645
	Educyrs	−0.043*	0.008	5.563
	Heart prob	0.437*	0.054	8.129
	Lung dis	0.391*	0.077	5.072
	High blood	0.114*	0.049	2.355
	Diabetes	0.241*	0.061	3.942
	Pain	0.384*	0.050	7.635
	Arthritis	0.342*	0.049	6.969
	Cancer	0.185*	0.069	2.674
	Cesd score	0.139*	0.013	11.147
	Obese	0.130*	0.053	2.434
	Age 58–64	0.141*	0.065	2.177
	Age 65–71	0.112+	0.063	1.766
	Age 72+	0.372*	0.072	5.157
Interaction EU				
	Female*EU	−0.090	0.062	1.451
	Marr/LT*EU	0.084	0.068	1.245
	Educyrs*EU	0.036*	0.008	4.574
	Heart*EU	0.013	0.075	0.172
	Lung*EU	−0.044	0.097	0.449
	Highbl*EU	−0.047	0.063	0.744
	Diabetes*EU	−0.011	0.087	0.122
	Pain*EU	0.067	0.064	1.052
	Arthr*EU	0.008	0.069	0.120
	Cancer*EU	0.235*	0.102	2.315
	Cesd*EU	0.148*	0.021	7.137
	Obese*EU	0.035	0.072	0.481
	Age 58–64*EU	−0.002	0.082	0.026
	Age 65–71*EU	0.170*	0.083	2.054
	Age 72+*EU	0.116	0.090	1.289
Country dummies				
	Germany	−0.913*	0.153	5.949
	Sweden	−1.130*	0.152	7.441
	Netherlands	−0.993*	0.151	6.573
	Spain	−1.279*	0.149	8.608
	Italy	−1.112*	0.152	7.292
	France	−1.244*	0.145	8.560
	Greece	−1.767*	0.149	11.875
	Belgium	−0.891*	0.150	5.955
		Threshold 1		
U.S.				
	const thrh	0	0	0
	Female	0.070*	0.016	4.315
	Married/LT	−0.011	0.017	0.684

(continued)

Table 9A.4 (continued)

		Parameter	Standard error	t-value
	Educyrs	−0.012*	0.003	4.651
	Heart prob	−0.023	0.020	1.174
	Lung dis	−0.004	0.030	0.136
	High blood	−0.014	0.017	0.863
	Diabetes	−0.068*	0.019	3.585
	Pain	−0.053*	0.018	2.889
	Arthritis	−0.017	0.017	0.995
	Cancer	0.044+	0.025	1.763
	Cesd score	−0.013*	0.005	2.751
	Obese	−0.008	0.017	0.489
	Age 58–64	−0.021	0.024	0.883
	Age 65–71	−0.037+	0.021	1.797
	Age 72+	−0.108*	0.024	4.418
Interaction EU				
	Female*EU	−0.077*	0.022	3.514
	Marr/LT*EU	0.021	0.024	0.907
	Educyrs*EU	0.007*	0.003	2.502
	Heart*EU	0.012	0.030	0.404
	Lung*EU	0.052	0.039	1.343
	Highbl*EU	−0.013	0.023	0.559
	Diabetes*EU	0.156*	0.029	5.376
	Pain*EU	0.014	0.025	0.577
	Arthr*EU	0.023	0.027	0.838
	Cancer*EU	−0.085*	0.038	2.254
	Cesd*EU	−0.005	0.009	0.508
	Obese*EU	0.061*	0.027	2.273
	Age 58–64*EU	0.033	0.031	1.080
	Age 65–71*EU	0.061*	0.029	2.126
	Age 72+*EU	0.093*	0.033	2.856
Country dummies				
	Germany	−0.639*	0.054	11.797
	Sweden	−0.657*	0.062	10.586
	Netherlands	−0.659*	0.051	12.993
	Spain	−0.915*	0.059	15.412
	Italy	−0.527*	0.051	10.332
	France	−0.575*	0.051	11.304
	Greece	−0.662*	0.057	11.715
	Belgium	−0.630*	0.054	11.695

$$\log(threshold\ 2 - threshold\ 1)$$

U.S.				
	const thrh	−0.726*	0.048	15.162
	Female	0.040*	0.018	2.206
	Married/LT	0.071*	0.020	3.629
	Educyrs	0.017*	0.003	6.313
	Heart prob	0.017	0.022	0.751
	Lung dis	−0.030	0.032	0.928
	High blood	−0.008	0.018	0.464
	Diabetes	−0.002	0.024	0.101

Table 9A.4   (continued)

		Parameter	Standard error	*t*-value
	Pain	0.020	0.019	1.091
	Arthritis	0.021	0.019	1.122
	Cancer	0.014	0.026	0.547
	Cesd score	−0.008	0.005	1.586
	Obese	−0.021	0.020	1.078
	Age 58–64	0.016	0.025	0.640
	Age 65–71	−0.010	0.024	0.402
	Age 72+	0.048+	0.028	1.680
Interaction EU				
	Female*EU	0.009	0.025	0.369
	Marr/LT*EU	−0.061*	0.028	2.184
	Educyrs*EU	−0.013*	0.003	4.333
	Heart*EU	−0.041	0.035	1.184
	Lung*EU	0.045	0.044	1.036
	Highbl*EU	0.025	0.026	0.944
	Diabetes*EU	−0.098*	0.038	2.549
	Pain*EU	0.013	0.026	0.486
	Arthr*EU	−0.023	0.029	0.775
	Cancer*EU	0.043	0.043	1.005
	Cesd*EU	−0.001	0.010	0.072
	Obese*EU	−0.055+	0.030	1.796
	Age 58–64*EU	0.020	0.033	0.596
	Age 65–71*EU	0.048	0.034	1.440
	Age 72+*EU	−0.012	0.038	0.329
Country dummies				
	Germany	0.338*	0.062	5.435
	Sweden	0.180*	0.069	2.598
	Netherlands	0.665*	0.058	11.478
	Spain	0.447*	0.063	7.140
	Italy	0.441*	0.058	7.539
	France	0.289*	0.058	5.012
	Greece	0.238*	0.060	3.943
	Belgium	0.523*	0.059	8.926

$$log(threshold\ 3 - threshold\ 2)$$

U.S.				
	const thrh	−0.836*	0.049	17.019
	Female	0.012	0.019	0.627
	Married/LT	0.062*	0.020	3.028
	Educyrs	0.019*	0.003	6.497
	Heart prob	−0.008	0.022	0.380
	Lung dis	0.026	0.031	0.840
	High blood	−0.003	0.019	0.149
	Diabetes	0.027	0.024	1.137
	Pain	0.036+	0.019	1.916
	Arthritis	0	0.020	0.012
	Cancer	0.014	0.028	0.505
	Cesd score	−0.014*	0.005	2.800
	Obese	−0.022	0.021	1.068

(continued)

Table 9A.4 (continued)

		Parameter	Standard error	*t*-value
	Age 58–64	0.019	0.027	0.717
	Age 65–71	0.039	0.025	1.559
	Age 72+	0.126*	0.028	4.489
Interaction EU				
	Female*EU	−0.039+	0.022	1.742
	Marr/LT*EU	−0.060*	0.025	2.390
	Educyrs*EU	−0.018*	0.003	6.112
	Heart*EU	0.005	0.029	0.188
	Lung*EU	−0.047	0.037	1.281
	Highbl*EU	0.046*	0.023	1.965
	Diabetes*EU	−0.065*	0.032	2.069
	Pain*EU	0.023	0.023	1.010
	Arthr*EU	−0.039	0.025	1.543
	Cancer*EU	0.007	0.037	0.175
	Cesd*EU	0.026*	0.007	3.526
	Obese*EU	−0.014	0.027	0.528
	Age 58–64*E	0.012	0.031	0.379
	Age 65–71*E	−0.023	0.030	0.779
	Age 72+*EU	−0.066*	0.033	1.992
Country dummies				
	Germany	0.586*	0.055	10.590
	Sweden	0.285*	0.057	5.031
	Netherlands	0.478*	0.055	8.708
	Spain	0.550*	0.055	10.085
	Italy	0.558*	0.054	10.336
	France	0.589*	0.053	11.021
	Greece	0.395*	0.054	7.268
	Belgium	0.521*	0.054	9.577

$$log(\ threshold\ 4 - threshold\ 3\ )$$

		Parameter	Standard error	*t*-value
U.S.				
	const thrh	−0.584*	0.052	11.278
	Female	−0.072*	0.020	3.597
	Married/LT	0.043*	0.021	2.020
	Educyrs	0.024*	0.003	7.703
	Heart prob	0.004	0.023	0.185
	Lung dis	0.001	0.035	0.030
	High blood	−0.011	0.020	0.554
	Diabetes	−0.055*	0.026	2.142
	Pain	0.002	0.022	0.104
	Arthritis	0.030	0.021	1.397
	Cancer	0.051+	0.031	1.661
	Cesd score	−0.016*	0.005	3.038
	Obese	−0.018	0.022	0.799
	Age 58–64	0.050+	0.028	1.742
	Age 65–71	0.051+	0.027	1.899
	Age 72+	0.080*	0.030	2.704
Interaction EU				
	Female*EU	0.047+	0.024	1.928
	Marr/LT*EU	−0.042	0.026	1.583

Table 9A.4 (continued)

		Parameter	Standard error	*t*-value
	Educyrs*EU	−0.022*	0.003	7.002
	Heart*EU	−0.009	0.031	0.293
	Lung*EU	−0.017	0.043	0.385
	Highbl*EU	−0.012	0.025	0.482
	Diabetes*EU	0.047	0.034	1.377
	Pain*EU	−0.021	0.026	0.806
	Arthr*EU	−0.026	0.028	0.929
	Cancer*EU	−0.004	0.043	0.098
	Cesd*EU	0.027*	0.008	3.398
	Obese*EU	−0.058*	0.028	2.039
	Age 58–64*EU	−0.001	0.034	0.023
	Age 65–71*EU	−0.016	0.033	0.492
	Age 72+*EU	0.017	0.035	0.472
Country dummies				
	Germany	0.560*	0.059	9.510
	Sweden	0.419*	0.058	7.171
	Netherlands	0.134*	0.059	2.261
	Spain	0.637*	0.056	11.288
	Italy	0.160*	0.059	2.683
	France	0.551*	0.057	9.741
	Greece	0.217*	0.057	3.821
	Belgium	0.313*	0.058	5.381
	Vignette dummies			
	d vig pain	1.003*	0.044	22.666
	d vig pain	0.202*	0.042	4.769
	d vig pain	1.145*	0.045	25.561
	d vig aff	0.372*	0.042	8.780
	d vig aff	0.424*	0.043	9.926
	d vig aff	0.019	0.042	0.454
	d vig cvd	0.641*	0.043	14.904
	d vig cvd	0.720*	0.043	16.620
	d vig cvd	1.167*	0.045	25.986
	Standard deviations of errors / unobserved heterogeneity			
	sig selfr	1	(Normalization)	
	sig thres	0.423*	0.007	63.621
	sig vignet	0.513*	0.007	69.770

Note: * = significant at two-sided 5 percent level; + = significant at two-sided 10 percent level.

Table 9A.5   **Parameter estimates; model without DIF**

		Parameter	Standard error	*t*-value
	Disability equation			
U.S.				
	constant	−0.135	0.107	1.261
	Female	−0.103*	0.043	2.377
	Married/LT	−0.179*	0.045	4.003
	Educyrs	−0.046*	0.007	6.957
	Heart prob	0.487*	0.048	10.232
	Lung dis	0.421*	0.068	6.175
	High blood	0.145*	0.044	3.312
	Diabetes	0.325*	0.052	6.238
	Pain	0.431*	0.045	9.625
	Arthritis	0.352*	0.044	8.073
	Cancer	0.142*	0.061	2.321
	Cesd score	0.171*	0.011	15.952
	Obese	0.163*	0.047	3.464
	Age 58–64	0.154*	0.058	2.636
	Age 65–71	0.130*	0.056	2.315
	Age 72+	0.461*	0.064	7.194
Interaction EU				
	Female*EU	−0.014	0.058	0.245
	Marr/LT*EU	0.113+	0.063	1.810
	Educyrs*EU	0.041*	0.007	6.052
	Heart*EU	−0.032	0.070	0.453
	Lung*EU	−0.139	0.090	1.543
	Highbl*EU	−0.068	0.059	1.152
	Diabetes*EU	−0.115	0.079	1.456
	Pain*EU	0.005	0.060	0.076
	Arthr*EU	−0.019	0.065	0.292
	Cancer*EU	0.260*	0.098	2.643
	Cesd*EU	0.114*	0.020	5.815
	Obese*EU	0.008	0.067	0.114
	Age 58–64*EU	−0.015	0.077	0.197
	Age 65–71*E	0.132+	0.077	1.709
	Age 72+*EU	0.012	0.083	0.150
Country dummies				
	Germany	−0.497*	0.139	3.571
	Sweden	−0.600*	0.135	4.433
	Netherlands	−0.609*	0.137	4.445
	Spain	−0.642*	0.134	4.791
	Italy	−0.790*	0.137	5.768
	France	−0.840*	0.130	6.449
	Greece	−1.254*	0.133	9.449
	Belgium	−0.535*	0.135	3.969
Threshold parameters				
	const thrh	0	0	0
	const thrh	−0.299*	0.013	22.472
	const thrh	−0.290*	0.013	21.482
	const thrh	−0.109*	0.013	8.164

Table 9A.5 (continued)

	Parameter	Standard error	*t*-value
Vignette dummies			
d vig pain	1.621*	0.024	68.127
d vig pain	0.747*	0.015	48.776
d vig pain	1.779*	0.025	70.588
d vig aff	0.928*	0.017	55.996
d vig aff	0.982*	0.018	55.413
d vig aff	0.563*	0.014	39.134
d vig cvd	1.217*	0.019	63.722
d vig cvd	1.309*	0.020	65.060
d vig cvd	1.798*	0.025	70.885
Standard deviations of error terms			
sig selfr	1	(normalization)	
sig vignet	0.728*	0.009	77.316
log-likelihood	−96584.3457		

Note: * = significant at two-sided 5 percent level; + = significant at two-sided 10 percent level.

Table 9A.6 **Parameter estimates for work disability equation**

	Model without DIF		Model with DIF	
	Coeff.	St. error	Coeff.	St. error
constant	−0.126	0.107	−0.189	0.118
Female	−0.106*	0.043	−0.017	0.045
Married/LT	−0.175*	0.045	−0.118*	0.047
Educyrs	−0.046*	0.007	−0.039*	0.007
Heart prob	0.484*	0.048	0.463*	0.050
Lung dis	0.423*	0.068	0.421*	0.071
High blood	0.139*	0.044	0.112*	0.045
Diabetes	0.321*	0.052	0.256*	0.056
Pain	0.426*	0.045	0.411*	0.047
Arthritis	0.354*	0.044	0.364*	0.046
Cancer	0.142*	0.061	0.206*	0.064
Cesd score	0.170*	0.011	0.148*	0.011
Obese	0.167*	0.047	0.137*	0.049
Age 58–64	0.157*	0.058	0.166*	0.061
Age 65–71	0.138*	0.056	0.135*	0.059
Age 72+	0.463*	0.064	0.426*	0.068
Female*EU	−0.007	0.058	−0.075	0.060
Marr/LT*EU	0.110+	0.063	0.078	0.065
Educyrs*EU	0.042*	0.007	0.034*	0.007
Heart*EU	−0.027	0.070	−0.033	0.073
Lung*EU	−0.141	0.090	−0.098	0.094
Highbl*EU	−0.065	0.059	−0.028	0.061
Diabetes*EU	−0.110	0.079	−0.076	0.083
Pain*EU	0.006	0.060	0.048	0.062
Arthr*EU	−0.019	0.065	−0.038	0.067

(*continued*)

Table 9A.6 (continued)

	Model without DIF		Model with DIF	
	Coeff.	St. error	Coeff.	St. error
Cancer*EU	0.262*	0.098	0.209*	0.102
Cesd*EU	0.114*	0.020	0.126*	0.020
Obese*EU	0.004	0.067	−0.020	0.069
Age 58–64*EU	−0.018	0.077	0.004	0.079
Age 65–71*EU	0.122	0.077	0.161*	0.080
Age 72+*EU	0.010	0.083	0.087	0.087
Germany	−0.503*	0.139	−0.689*	0.145
Sweden	−0.612*	0.136	−1.066*	0.142
Netherlands	−0.615*	0.137	−0.699*	0.142
Spain	−0.646*	0.134	−0.999*	0.140
Italy	−0.798*	0.137	−0.895*	0.142
France	−0.848*	0.130	−1.023*	0.136
Greece	−1.260*	0.133	−1.690*	0.139
Belgium	−0.542*	0.135	−0.654*	0.141

Note: * = significant at two-sided 5 percent level; + = significant at two-sided 10 percent level.

Table 9A.7   **Thresholds equation (model with DIF)**

	Coeff.	St. error		Coeff.	St. error
Work	0.097*	0.015	Work*EU	−0.104*	0.023
Female	0.096*	0.013	Female*EU	−0.082*	0.019
Married/LT	0.051*	0.013	Marr/LT*EU	−0.031	0.020
Educyrs	0.003	0.002	Educyrs*EU	−0.004+	0.002
Heart prob	−0.016	0.016	Heart*EU	−0.014	0.027
Lung dis	−0.002	0.022	Lung*EU	0.037	0.033
High blood	−0.024+	0.013	Highbl*EU	0.028	0.020
Diabetes	−0.065*	0.014	Diabetes*E	0.069*	0.025
Pain	−0.038*	0.015	Pain*EU	0.046*	0.022
Arthritis	−0.005	0.014	Arthr*EU	−0.008	0.024
Cancer	0.066*	0.020	Cancer*EU	−0.048	0.036
Cesd score	−0.022*	0.004	Cesd*EU	0.008	0.008
Obese	−0.039*	0.014	Obese*EU	0.014	0.023
Age 58–64	0.021	0.020	Age 58–64*EU	0.034	0.028
Age 65–71	0.020	0.016	Age 65–71*EU	0.039	0.027
Age 72+	0.021	0.020	Age 72+*EU	0.026	0.030
			Germany	−0.187*	0.047
const thrh 1	0	0	Sweden	−0.452*	0.051
thr2–thr1	0.722*	0.010	Netherlands	−0.074+	0.043
thr3–thr2	0.704*	0.010	Spain	−0.356*	0.049
thr4–thr3	0.822*	0.012	Italy	−0.083*	0.042
			France	−0.147*	0.043
sigma u	0.426*	0.007	Greece	−0.417*	0.046
			Belgium	−0.114*	0.046

Note: * = significant at two-sided 5 percent level; + = significant at two-sided 10 percent level.

Table 9A.8   **Vignette equation (model with DIF)**

	Coeff.	St. error
dvigpain1	1.453*	0.038
dvigpain2	0.631*	0.034
dvigpain3	1.598*	0.039
dvigaff1	0.803*	0.034
dvigaff2	0.853*	0.035
dvigaff3	0.455*	0.034
dvigcvd1	1.075*	0.036
dvigcvd2	1.161*	0.036
dvigcvd3	1.615*	0.039
Sigmav	0.527*	0.007

Note: * = significant at two-sided 5 percent level; + = significant at two-sided 10 percent level.

Table 9A.9   **Employment equation**

	Model without DIF		Model with DIF	
	Coeff.	St. error	Coeff.	St. error
Disability	−0.516*	0.038	−0.464*	0.036
Disability*EU	0.319*	0.049	0.272*	0.049
Constant	0.473*	0.151	0.440*	0.135
Female	−0.289*	0.059	−0.246*	0.057
Married/LT	−0.069	0.065	−0.034	0.062
Educyrs	0.030*	0.009	0.034*	0.009
Heart prob	0.015	0.076	−0.015	0.074
Lung dis	−0.102	0.109	−0.125	0.107
High blood	0.016	0.059	−0.001	0.057
Diabetes	−0.189*	0.079	−0.228*	0.076
Pain	0.131*	0.064	0.102+	0.061
Arthritis	0.041	0.062	0.031	0.060
Cancer	−0.023	0.084	0.004	0.085
Cesd score	−0.035*	0.017	−0.051*	0.016
Obese	0.223*	0.064	0.204*	0.059
Age 58–64	−0.633*	0.079	−0.620*	0.078
Age 65–71	−1.285*	0.077	−1.268*	0.073
Age 72+	−1.815*	0.101	−1.813*	0.100
Female*EU	−0.282*	0.081	−0.319*	0.079
Marr/LT*EU	−0.096	0.094	−0.125	0.092
Educyrs*EU	−0.015	0.010	−0.020*	0.009
Heart*EU	−0.021	0.128	−0.002	0.127
Lung*EU	−0.032	0.161	0.002	0.160
Highbl*EU	0.034	0.085	0.051	0.084
Diabetes*EU	0.122	0.128	0.152	0.127
Pain*EU	−0.058	0.086	−0.025	0.085
Arthr*EU	−0.066	0.101	−0.058	0.100
Cancer*EU	0.058	0.155	0.034	0.155
Cesd*EU	−0.039	0.032	−0.026	0.031

(*continued*)

Table 9A.9   (continued)

	Model without DIF		Model with DIF	
	Coeff.	St. error	Coeff.	St. error
Obese*EU	−0.296*	0.097	−0.284*	0.094
Age 58–64*EU	−0.399*	0.098	−0.406*	0.097
Age 65–71*E	−1.288*	0.133	−1.296*	0.130
Age 72+*EU	−1.407*	0.211	−1.402*	0.211
Germany	0.310	0.196	0.291	0.184
Sweden	0.852*	0.206	0.784*	0.196
Netherlands	0.239	0.195	0.241	0.183
Spain	0.252	0.192	0.208	0.181
Italy	−0.129	0.197	−0.126	0.186
France	0.310+	0.189	0.300+	0.177
Greece	0.215	0.191	0.157	0.183
Belgium	0.044	0.191	0.041	0.178
Log-likelihood (of complete model)	−99650.54		−90792.80	

Note: * = significant at two-sided 5 percent level; + = significant at two-sided 10 percent level.

Table 9A.10   **Employment equation without objective health conditions**

	Model without DIF		Model with DIF	
	Coeff.	St. error	Coeff.	St. error
Health	−0.506*	0.032	−0.477*	0.031
Health*EU	0.282*	0.041	0.257*	0.040
Constant	0.505*	0.142	0.399*	0.141
Female	−0.280*	0.057	−0.239*	0.057
Married/LT	−0.038	0.064	0.000	0.063
Educyrs	0.030*	0.009	0.036*	0.009
Age 58–64	−0.627*	0.075	−0.614*	0.075
Age 65–71	−1.280*	0.070	−1.261*	0.070
Age 72+	−1.830*	0.097	−1.825*	0.096
Female*EU	−0.313*	0.079	−0.347*	0.078
Marr/LT*EU	−0.103	0.093	−0.134	0.088
Educyrs*EU	−0.015+	0.009	−0.021*	0.009
Age 58–64*EU	−0.391*	0.094	−0.398*	0.092
Age 65–71*EU	−1.277*	0.125	−1.287*	0.125
Age 72+*EU	−1.366*	0.205	−1.365*	0.204
Germany	0.218	0.182	0.260	0.181
Sweden	0.760*	0.194	0.748*	0.193
Netherlands	0.132	0.183	0.199	0.182
Spain	0.129	0.180	0.142	0.179
Italy	−0.255	0.183	−0.188	0.181
France	0.175	0.174	0.226	0.172
Greece	0.084	0.174	0.080	0.165
Belgium	−0.067	0.178	−0.006	0.177
log likelihood (of complete model)	−99670.88		−90815.50	

Note: * = significant at two-sided 5 percent level; + = significant at two-sided 10 percent level.

Appendix B

The SHARE and HRS Work Disability Vignettes and Self-Reports SHARE

Work-Limiting Disabilities

Three domains: affect, pain, cardiovascular disease.
One overall self-report on work-limiting disabilities.
Three vignettes per domain.

Response Categories (for All Questions; Same As for Health Domains):

1. None
2. Mild
3. Moderate
4. Severe
5. Extreme/Cannot Do

Self-Report:

Do you have any impairment or health problem that limits the kind or amount of work you can do?

Introduction to Vignettes:

We would now like to give you a number of examples of persons with some health problems. We would like you to indicate the extent to which you think these people would be limited in the kind or amount of work they can do. In terms of their age, their education, and their work histories, you should imagine that these men or women are similar to yourself. Other than the conditions explicitly mentioned, you should imagine the individual is in reasonably good health.

General Form of Vignette Questions:

How much was [name of person] limited in the kind or amount of work he/she could do?

Affect Vignettes:

1. [Eva] feels worried all the time. She gets depressed once a week at work for a couple of days in a row, thinking about what could go wrong and that her boss will disapprove of her condition. But she is able to come out of this mood if she concentrates on something else.

2. [Tamara] has mood swings on the job. When she gets depressed, everything she does at work is an effort for her and she no longer enjoys her usual activities at work. These mood swings are not predictable and occur two or three times during a month.

3. [Henriette] generally enjoys her work. She gets depressed every three weeks for a day or two and loses interest in what she usually enjoys but is able to carry on with her day-to-day activities on the job.

Pain Vignettes:

1. [Yvonne] has almost constant pain in her back and this sometimes prevents her from doing her work.

2. [Catherine] suffers from back pain that causes stiffness in her back, especially at work, but is relieved with low doses of medication. She does not have any pains other than this generalized discomfort.

3. [Mark] has pain in his back and legs, and the pain is present almost all the time. It gets worse while he is working. Although medication helps, he feels uncomfortable when moving around, holding, and lifting things at work.

CVD Vignettes:

1. [Norbert] has had heart problems in the past and he has been told to watch his cholesterol level. Sometimes if he feels stressed at work he feels pain in his chest and occasionally in his arms.

2. [Tom] has been diagnosed with high blood pressure. His blood pressure goes up quickly if he feels under stress. Tom does not exercise much and is overweight.

3. [Dan] has undergone triple bypass heart surgery. He is a heavy smoker and still experiences severe chest pain sometimes.

Randomization

All vignette questions are asked to all respondents. The only randomization concerns the names of the vignette persons and the order of the vignette questions. The SHARE questionnaire had two versions. Each has alternating male and female names on the vignettes, but where version 1 has a male name, version 2 has a female name, and so forth. Version 1 has the order of the questions as just given. Version 2 reverses things: first work disability, then health; domains in reverse order; vignettes in each domain in reverse order. The self-report always comes before the vignettes.

HRS

Although the vignettes and self-reports in HRS are very similar to those in SHARE, there are a few noticeable differences.

Self-Report in 2004 Leave-Behind Questionnaire:

1a. To what extent are you limited in the kind or amount of work you can do because of an impairment or health problem?
Not at all limited, Mildly limited, Moderately limited, Severely limited, Cannot do any work

Vignettes

The HRS fielded the same vignettes as used in Kapteyn et al. (2007), with some slight changes in formulation. The SHARE vignettes are a subset of these. Comparing the vignettes that are common between HRS and SHARE, we find one difference. The SHARE vignette CVD-2 in the HRS version reads:

Diane has been diagnosed with high blood pressure. Her blood pressure goes up quickly if she feels under stress. Diane does not exercise much and is overweight. Life can sometimes be hectic for her. She does not get along with her boss very well.

References

Böckerman, P., and P. Ilmakunnas. 2009. Unemployment and self-assessed health: Evidence from panel data. *Health Economics* 18 (2): 161–79.

Boersch-Supan, A. 2007. Work disability, health, and incentive effects. Mannheim Research Institute for the Economics of Aging (MEA), University of Mannheim. Working Paper.

Bound, J. 1991. Self-reported versus objective measures of health in retirement models. *Journal of Human Resources* 26 (1): 106–38.

Croda, E., and J. Skinner. 2009. Disability Insurance and health in Europe and the U.S. Paper presented at Netspar 2009 Annual Conference, The Hague, April. Available at: http://www.netspar.nl/events/2009/annual/paperskinner.pdf.

Eurostat. 2001. *Disability and social participation in Europe.* Luxembourg: Office for Official Publications of the European Communities.

Heeringa, S. G., and J. Connor. 1995. *Technical description of the Health and Retirement Study sample design.* Online version at www.hrsonline.isr.umich.edu (originally published as *HRS/AHEAD Documentation Report* DR-002).

Jones, M. K. 2007. How accurate are estimates of the impact of disability on labour market participation? Evidence from the Health Survey for England. Swansea University, School of Business. Working Paper.

Kapteyn, A., J. P. Smith, and A. van Soest. 2007. Vignettes and self-reported work disability in the U.S. and the Netherlands. *American Economic Review* 97 (1): 461–73.

Kapteyn, A., J. P. Smith, A. van Soest, and J. Banks. 2009. Labor market status and transitions during the pre-retirement years: Learning from international differences. In *Research findings in the economics of aging,* ed. D. Wise, 63–92. Chicago: University of Chicago Press.

King, G., C. Murray, J. Salomon, and A. Tandon. 2004. Enhancing the validity and cross-cultural comparability of measurement in survey research. *American Political Science Review* 98 (1): 567–83.

Kreider, B., and J. V. Pepper. 2007. Disability and employment: Reevaluating the evidence in light of reporting errors. *Journal of the American Statistical Association* 102 (478): 432–41.

Organization for Economic Cooperation and Development. 2004. *OECD employment outlook.* OECD: Paris.

Van Soest, A., L. Delaney, C. Harmon, A. Kapteyn, and J. P. Smith. 2007. Validating the use of vignettes for subjective threshold scales. RAND, Labor and Population Working Paper. Available at: http://www.rand.org/pubs/working_papers/WR501/.

Comment   Angus Deaton

I organize my comments around two facts or sets of facts that are at the core of this chapter:

- Fact 1: In matching surveys in Europe and the United States, people are asked to rate their own disability into five categories. The distribution of reports over those categories is very similar in Europe and the United States.
- Fact 2: In matching surveys in Europe and the United States, people are asked to rate other people's disability (using vignettes) into five categories. The distribution of reports over those categories is quite different in the two places; in particular, people in the United States are "tougher" in that they are less willing to admit that some conditions are disabling.

Kapteyn, Smith, and van Soest (henceforward KSvS) argue that fact 2 shows that Americans and Europeans use different scales to rank all disabilities, whether others or their own, a behavior that is known in the literature as "differential item functioning," or DIF for short. Once DIF is recognized, and the vignettes used to reinterpret the original responses in fact 1, we come to the conclusion that, in fact, the distribution of disability is worse in the United States than in Europe. I call this interpretation 1:

- Interpretation 1: Disability is worse in the United States than in Europe, but Americans have tougher standards, and so report the same levels as Europeans.

Fact 1 is misleading because Americans are tougher on themselves than are Europeans. The chapter makes a further contribution by allowing the extent of DIF to depend on whether or not someone is out of work—people might be less tough on themselves if they are not working, in effect a "justification bias." Their estimates suggest that this effect is present in the United States, but not in Europe. They conclude that "Americans use health as a justification for not working, whereas Europeans do not feel the need to do so."

Angus Deaton is the Dwight D. Eisenhower Professor of International Affairs and professor of economics and international affairs at the Woodrow Wilson School of Public and International Affairs and the Economics Department at Princeton University, and a research associate of the National Bureau of Economic Research.

As the authors note, this use of vignettes rests on two assumptions: "response consistency," which means you rank other people's conditions as you would your own, and "vignette equivalence," that respondents are equally "tough" or "lax" over all the vignettes that they are asked to rank. It is not obvious that either of these assumptions is correct, although the chapter lists two studies that provide some support for response consistency. The assumption is in principle testable; for example, by asking people to rate other people who have exactly the same conditions that they have themselves.

What we are talking about here is the extent to which people can feel each other's pain, whether they do it well, whether they want to do it, and whether they feel it as if it were their own. It is clear that people do not always care to do so, as demonstrated by my Scottish schoolmasters who, when administering corporal punishment to their pupils, and in visible pleasurable anticipation of the experience, would utter the ritual words, "This is going to hurt me more than it is going to hurt you." History is littered with more extreme examples. I know from my own experience that I am much more sympathetic to joint pain in others than I was before I had my own hip replaced, which would rule out vignette equivalence. I also know from my experience before the surgery that other people, even those who were trying hard, had little appreciation for the extent of my disability. There is also good scientific evidence that people have great difficulty in recalling even their own feelings or level of disability about previous conditions that have now been reversed; see in particular Smith et al. (2006) on the misremembering of colostomies. It is not clear that these examples are exactly relevant to the way that vignettes are used here, but they should certainly give us cause for concern.

We can think of response consistency as depending on the degree of empathy, whether respondents rank *other people's* conditions in the same way that they would rank their own if they were to have those conditions. For the vignettes to work for international comparisons, we require that there be no international variation in empathy, that Europeans are just as good or bad as empathizing with others as are Americans. There is a literature on whether women are more empathetic than men (Hoffman 1977; Eisenberg and Lennon 1983), but I know of know of no findings on international differences. However, my main point is not the factual one, but the logic of the vignettes. The use of vignettes *rejects* the assumption that people's self-reports of disabilities are internationally comparable, and *replaces* it with an assumption that their capacity for empathy is internationally comparable. Since the two assumptions are very similar, and similarly plausible or implausible, I do not see that anything is gained by replacing one by the other. The validity of vignettes depends on an assumption that is much the same as the assumption that they are designed to replace and I see no basis for accepting one and rejecting the other.

To see how this argument applies to the facts with which I began, I would propose an alternative interpretation of facts 1 and 2.

- Interpretation 2: The self-reports of own disability are accurate in the first place, and the distribution of disabilities in the United States and Europe is the same. The ratings of the vignettes are different because Americans are tougher on other people, without being tougher on themselves.

It seems to me that interpretation 1 and interpretation 2 are equally plausible—they provide contradictory views of the evidence, and I do not know how to choose between them. The correlation that KSvS report between differential responses to vignettes and national institutions for dealing with disability could just as well be due to differences in empathy as to differences in perceptions of own disability. Perhaps we need to add vignettes for empathy to the surveys, but then we would need vignettes for those vignettes, and so on ad infinitum.

For reasons already explained, I think that there must also be doubts about the assumption of vignette equivalence, that people are not differentially tough over different vignettes; for example, being more sympathetic to those where they have personal experience, or because different cultures recognize different disabilities. (Depression is a permanent condition in Scotland, but it is applied to the weather, not to people.) Vignette equivalence is also especially hostage to difficulties of translation; the problem is well-illustrated in the happiness literature by the fact that the English "happy," and the French "heureux," although exact translations, have different meanings and patterns of use in the two countries (see Wierzbicka 2004). It would seem relatively easy to relax vignette equivalence, at least in part, because there are always more vignettes than are needed to identify the model. Indeed, the model that is estimated in the chapter is clearly overidentified as written, and it would be a useful exercise to try to relax and test some of the assumptions. What I do not know is whether, if my main objections are met, identification will remain.

References

Eisenberg, N., and R. Lennon. 1983. Sex differences in empathy and related capacities. *Psychological Bulletin* 94 (1): 100–31.

Hoffman, M. L. 1977. Sex differences in empathy and related behaviors. *Psychological Bulletin* 84 (4): 12–22.

Smith, D. M., R. L. Sherriff, L. J. Damschroder, G. Loewenstein, and P. A. Ubel. 2006. Misremembering colostomies? Former patients give lower utility ratings than do current patients. *Health Psychology* 25 (6): 688–95.

Wierzbicka, A. 2004. Happiness in cross-linguistic and cross-cultural perspectives. *Daedulus* Spring: 34–43.

IV

Aging in Less Developed Countries

Is Decentralized Iron Fortification a Feasible Option to Fight Anemia among the Poorest?

Abhijit Banerjee, Esther Duflo, and Rachel Glennerster

10.1   Introduction

Iron deficiency is believed to be the most common nutrient deficiency in the world today. While estimating the number of anemic people is difficult, the World Health Organization (WHO) estimates that two billion people are anemic worldwide, and that about half of these cases can be traced to iron deficiency (WHO 2001). Iron deficiency anemia is more common among

Abhijit Banerjee is the Ford Foundation International Professor of Economics and a director of the Abdul Latif Jameel Poverty Action Lab at the Massachusetts Institute of Technology, and a research associate of the National Bureau of Economic Research. Esther Duflo is the Abdul Latif Jameel Professor of Poverty Alleviation and Development Economics and a director of the Abdul Latif Jameel Poverty Action Lab at the Massachusetts Institute of Technology, and a research associate of the National Bureau of Economic Research. Rachel Glennerster is executive director of the Abdul Latif Jameel Poverty Action Lab at the Massachusetts Institute of Technology.

Funding for the evaluation is graciously acknowledged from the Center for Health and Wellbeing at Princeton University (for the baseline survey), the MacArthur Foundation, and the National Institute of Aging. Funding for the intervention was provided by the MacArthur Foundation and the R. D. Tata Trust. We thank Angus Deaton, whose collaboration on the baseline was instrumental in getting this project started, and Amitabh Chandra for useful comments. This project is a collaborative effort involving many people. We particularly thank the team at Seva Mandir, especially Neelima Khetan, CEO, Dr. Sanjana Mohan (the head of the health unit when this project was started, and who was instrumental in designing this project), Bhagirath Gop (coordinator for the fortification project), and Priyanka Singh (head of the health unit when the project was finished). Bruce Daviau played a key role in the design of this program. Specifically, we owe him the design of the mixing machine, but his contribution does not stop there. We thank Hardy Dewan (organisation secretary), Tushita Lodha (project in charge for the health study), and Pramod Tiwari (field coordinator) from Vidya Bhawan for directing and coordinating the data collection. Several research assistants have done spectacular work on the field over the years: Callie Scott, Danielle Li, Vanessa Valentino, Cindy Palladines, Andrew Fraker, Anuja Singh, Payal Sinha, Neil Shah, Dhruva Kothari, and Michael Eddy. Eric Lewis provided expert and incredibly timely data analysis.

populations with a diet low in animal proteins and high in rice or in whole wheat with high phitates content (phitates reduce absorption). It is therefore a particularly serious issue in Asia and in South Asia. In Indonesia, a large-scale study of iron supplements found that 50 percent of women aged fifteen and above and 40 percent of men sampled were anemic at baseline (Thomas et al. 2003) (using thresholds of 12g/dL and 13g/dL for women and men, respectively).

In our study area, tribal villages in the district of Udaipur in Rajasthan, 80 percent of adult women and 27 percent of adult men out of a sample of 2,519 adults had hemoglobin levels below 12 g/dL (Banerjee, Deaton, and Duflo 2004). Fifty one percent of men had hemoglobin levels below 13 g/dL, the WHO cutoff for anemia for men. Older women were at least as likely to be anemic as younger women, and nutrition was likely a key factor in these high levels of anemia.

Iron deficiency anemia (IDA) has been linked to low productivity in adults and slowing of cognitive and physical growth among children. It increases susceptibility to infection, and increases the likelihood of experiencing weakness or fatigue symptoms (see Haas and Brownlie [2001] for a review of the medical evidence). Among pregnant women, severe anemia can result in low birth weight and child mortality (Stoltzfuz 2001). The medical literature establishes a relationship between iron supplementation and productivity. Iron deficiency affects physical activity by reducing aerobic capacity and by reducing endurance. Few randomized evaluations have looked at the impact of IDA on actual output. Basta et al. (1979) found a large effect of iron supplementation on sugar tree tappers in Indonesia (but the study suffered from fairly large attrition). Li et al. (1994) and Edgerton et al. (1979) found a much smaller effect on productivity, but increased time spent on voluntary activities. The largest and most comprehensive study to date is Thomas et al. (2003), which found a large effect of an iron supplementation program on the labor supply of males who were anemic at baseline, and an increase in the earnings of self-employed males. This study also found reduced anemia, and improved health (including mental health).

While iron deficiency anemia has been recognized as a serious public health problem in developing countries for several years, not much progress has been made against it. Possible interventions to address it include iron supplements (in the form of pills) and supplementation of food. On a large scale, iron supplements are commonly distributed to pregnant women and young children, but males and nonpregnant women are not the focus of regular distribution. Systematic distribution of iron supplements appears to be an unpractical policy in resource poor settings, where the public health systems do not have the capacity to distribute these supplements reliably on a large scale.

Iron supplementation of foods is one alternative: it requires no additional effort on the part of the consumer, and can be done relatively cheaply in centralized locations. Foods that can be fortified with iron include flour, milk products, fish sauce, and (recently) salt. The number of countries routinely adding iron to flour increased from two in 1990 to almost fifty in 2004, including countries of Central and South America and the Middle East, plus Indonesia, Nigeria, and South Africa.[1] Several states in India are now promoting wheat fortification. Gujarat is the leading state for this program. Thirty-five mills produce 40,000 metric tons a month (enough to feed 6.7 million people). Fortifying mills are private, and they receive 50 percent subsidy for iron and folic acid from the state government, and then sell the flour on the open market. West Bengal, Tamil Nadu, Punjab, Andhra Pradesh, and Haryana have smaller, but growing programs. Distribution of fortified flour through the Public Distribution Shops (where those who have a means-test ration card are entitled to buy food at a subsidized price), is now authorized, and Gujarat is piloting it in Ahmadabad, Sabarkantha, and Valsad districts. The government is planning further distribution though school meals programs, hospitals, and other government schemes.

However, for very poor and isolated populations, such as the population in the tribal district of Udaipur where this study was conducted, centralized food fortification is not a practical solution: most households consume their own grain, and do not purchase any goods that could easily be fortified.[2] Even households who obtain wheat or maize from the Public Distribution system obtain whole grain, which cannot be fortified. Fortification of commercialized food would thus leave marginalized households behind, which would be particularly unfortunate given that they are likely to be the most at risk for IDA.

The only way to reach these households through flour fortification is to fortify flour at the village level. In our study area, households get their grain (maize or wheat) milled once or twice a month by a local miller, or *chakki*. At this point, the flour can be fortified by mixing it with a preblend of flour and elemental iron, plus vitamin A or folic acid to facilitate absorption. This is a simple operation, which the miller can do immediately after having milled the grain. Community-level fortification is supported by the Micronutrient Initiative (2007), but we were not able to find documentation on other examples. It requires managing considerable logistics, including supplying, training, and monitoring millers in each of the villages. However, the decision to fortify has minimal impact on villagers' behavior. Villagers only have to decide to fortify once, and the nature of milled wheat and maize does not change with fortification. If they experience improvements in their health or in their work capacity, villagers may in turn be willing to pay for

1. According to the Micronutrient Initiative website: http://www.micronutrient.org/english/view.asp?x=579.

2. With the recent exception of salt. Double fortified salt has recently become available (Micronutrient Initiative 2008) and has shown promising results in field-based randomized control trials.

such a program. Thus, despite the logistical challenges, community-level (or decentralized) iron fortification is potentially a promising channel to increase iron bio-availability in a consistent and sustained way for the poorest populations. There are, however, many open questions on whether this can be done in a sustainable way: are millers able to fortify regularly, will households demand the service, and how willing are they to pay for it?

This chapter reports on the evaluation of a novel community-level iron supplementation program designed and implemented by Seva Mandir, a nongovernmental organization (NGO) that has worked for over fifty years in tribal areas in the district of Udaipur, Rajasthan. The intervention was implemented in sixty-eight villages, randomly chosen out of 134, where there is a team led by Vidya Bhawan (a local consortium of schools and colleges) and the Abdul Latif Jameel Poverty Action Lab (J-PAL).

A first objective of the evaluation was to assess the logistical feasibility of the intervention: is it possible to recruit, train, and monitor millers and to keep them regularly supplied? Will the population accept the program? A second objective was to determine the impact of the program on anemia. To this end, we collected data on hemoglobin levels at baseline, midline, and end line. The third objective was to determine whether the program had any health effect, beyond a possible reduction in anemia. To achieve this, we collected rich data on health at baseline and end line and a unique monthly health survey, where individuals reported every month on symptoms, self-reported health, and schedule during the past week. The final objective was to assess whether there would be any economic impacts of the program (e.g., increase in work capacity, schooling attendance, etc.).

The results suggest that community-level iron supplementation, when adopted by a substantially large number of people, has the potential to lead to a significant decline of anemia, larger for men than for women (most likely because the dose of iron provided by the program is a lower fraction of the recommended amount for women than for men). However, a troubling finding is that after a rapid ramp up, the take up of the program declined over time in all the regions. In two blocks that took up the program particularly intensively, over 60 percent of the surveyed households were fortifying at the peak and this fell to about 40 percent after the program had been in place for more than a year. In the other three blocks, it fell to about 20 percent at the end of the study period. The consequence is that, in the entire sample, there is no impact of the program on anemia by end line. There is, however, a positive impact of the program on anemia in a midline survey conducted in the two first blocks to start the program after six months and at the end line survey for the two blocks that still had high fortification rates by the end of the program.

Our monthly health monitoring reveals a similar pattern for one of the health symptoms, weakness. Symptoms of weakness declined in the treatment group, relative to the control group in the first six months of the program (when take up was increasing), yet increased again from this low point forward as take-up declined. Other symptoms (diarrhea, vomiting, cough) do not appear to be affected, but it is on weakness that we would expect to see an effect of iron, so this is not surprising. By the end line survey, there appears to be no effect on health (except for self-reported health, happiness, and symptoms of depression for women, but as we argue later there is a good chance that those are reporting or placebo effects).

Finally, there seems to be no impact on the program on the ability to work or the number of days worked. At the end line, the activities of daily living (ADL) scores are similar in treatment and control groups in all blocks, and the ability to do strenuous activities (carry something heavy, climb a hill, walk five kilometers) is no higher, even in the groups with the higher take up. In the continuous monitoring survey, we do not see an increase in days of work, either on average over the period, or concomitant with the ramp up of the program. Of course, they may have been more productive during these days or worked and made more money. Unfortunately we do not have data on this, (collecting income data on a monthly frequency would be impossible), and there is no prima facie evidence that decentralized iron fortification has helped create wealth by improving health. This may explain why the household's willingness to pay for the program, even in the form of a minor inconvenience of walking further to find a chakki that fortifies, is quite low.

The rest of the chapter is organized as follows: section 10.2 describes the context and the detail of the decentralized fortification program. Section 10.3 discusses the identification strategy. Section 10.4 describes the result, and section 10.5 concludes.

10.2   The Context and Program Details

10.2.1   Baseline Descriptive Statistics

This program took place in Udaipur District, Rajasthan. At the baseline (2002 to 2003), their average per capita household expenditure was 470 rupees, and more than 40 percent of the respondents live in households below the official poverty line (compared with only 13 percent in rural Rajasthan in the latest official counts for 1999 to 2000). Only 46 percent of adult (fourteen and older) males and 11 percent of adult females report themselves as literate. Of the 27 percent of adults with any education, three-quarters completed standard eight or less.

The surveyed households have little in the way of household durable goods and only 21 percent have electricity.

In terms of measures of health, 80 percent of adult women and 27 percent of the adult men had hemoglobin levels below 12 grams by deciliters. Fifty-one percent of adult men had hemoglobin levels below 13, the threshold the

WHO recommends for men. Five percent of adult women and 1 percent of adult men have hemoglobin levels below 8 grams by deciliters. Using a standard cutoff for anemia (12 g/dL for women, and 13 g/dL for men) 80 percent of adult women and 51 percent of men are anemic. The fact that the rate of anemia is high among men and among older women suggests that diet is a key factor. Indeed, the average body mass index (BMI) is 17.8 among adult men and 18.1 among adult women, which is very low by any standard.

Symptoms of disease are widespread, and adults (self) report a wide range of symptoms: a third reported cold symptoms in the last thirty days, and 12 percent say the condition was serious. Thirty three percent reported fever (14 percent serious); 42 (20) percent reported "body ache"; 23 (7) percent reported fatigue; 14 (3) percent problems with vision; 42 (15) percent headaches; 33 (10) percent back aches; 23 (9) percent upper abdominal pain; 11 (4) percent had chest pains; and 11 (2) percent had experienced weight loss. Few people reported difficulties with personal care, such as bathing, dressing, or eating, but many reported difficulty with the physical activities that are required to earn a living in agriculture. Thirty percent or more would have difficulty walking 5 kilometers, drawing water from a well, or working unaided in the fields. Eighteen to 20 percent have difficulty squatting or standing up from a sitting position.

The baseline data suggest a correlation between anemia status and other measures of health and ability to perform activities of daily living. Those who are anemic have higher ADL scores (indicating more difficulty to perform those difficulties), and lower reported self-reported health, for example. There is also a correlation between anemia and economic well-being. Furthermore, the correlation between anemia and household wealth is stronger for individuals who are earning an income, suggesting that the correlation may go in part from health to earning. However, these correlations remain difficult to interpret without exogenous variations in anemia status. The iron supplementation program provides such exogenous variation.

10.2.2   Community Iron Fortification Program

Most of the households in our sample rely on their own production or on whole grain purchased by the Public Distribution System (PDS) for their daily consumption of staples. Specifically, 76 percent of the households never mill their grain at home, and never purchase floor (12 percent sometimes mill at home, and sometimes purchase flour). Wheat and Maize are the main staple foods and they are consumed seasonally in the form of rotis (flat bread made of maize or wheat flour).

The community-level iron program was designed to increase bioavailability of iron for families who do not buy commercial food. The program was designed by Seva Mandir's health unit, headed by Dr. Sanajana Mohan, assisted by Baghirath Mop, in consultation with the Micronutrient Initiative.

On average, each hamlet has four chakkis (this is also the median number). Three percent of the villages have one chakki, and 20 percent have two. When there was more than one chakki in a hamlet, Seva Mandir chose two participating chakki (thus, not all chakkis participate). Chakkis were offered a flat monthly payment to participate (subsequently the payment was changed to reflect the quantity milled, with bigger chakki getting a large compensation). Chakkis were not chosen randomly, but to serve a maximum number of households. Involving only one chakki per month was a cost-minimizing measure for Seva Mandir (given the fixed cost involved in working with each chakki). It will also give us the opportunity to examine the willingness of households to switch to (or away from) a participating chakki.

This fortification program had two objectives: to supply a sufficient quantity of iron in the diet, and to avoid supplying too much iron. Safety was also a concern, as the process was not as tightly monitored as it would have been in a factory. It was important that the program was robust to accidental over fortification.

The technology for fortification begins with a premix, a dry powdered mix with specific concentrations of one or more micronutrients. This premix is diluted into a preblend (because premix is too concentrated to be properly hand-mixed into the flour) and then added to flour either (a) during the milling process, or (b) after the grain has been milled.

Elemental iron is available in different forms (reduced iron, ferrous sulphate, or ferrous fumerate). After consultations with micronutrient initiatives and various experts, Seva Mandir chose to use ferrous sulfate ($FeSO_4$) and folic acid (which helps with iron absorption). This premix was then mixed with flour at Seva Mandir (16.66 g of premix is added in 1 kg of flour), to produce a preblend that had 3300 ppm (or milligram per kilo) of elemental iron (as ferrous sulfate). This quantity is sufficiently diluted, so that if someone were to eat the preblend without mixing, there would be no health risk.

This preblend was then mixed with the ground grain (maize of wheat) using the following procedure. Customers bring their whole grains to the chakki in bags, boxes, or baskets. First, the chakki empties this into his own milling machine, which grinds the grains into flour, and weighs the resulting flour (chakki charge by weight, so they all have scales for weighing flours). Second, he transfers the flour into a separate mixing machine (see appendix, figure 10A.1 for a picture of the milling machine, which was designed for Seva Mandir by Canadian engineer Bruce Daviau), and adds the required amount of preblends using a 30 g scoop that was provided by Seva Mandir. A scoop thus contains 100 mg of iron. The number of scoops to be added corresponds to table 10.1. He then turns the handle of the mixing machine ten times in one direction, and ten times in the other, and gives the fortified flour to the customer. He does not charge the customer for the extra supplement.

Table 10.1   **Amount of preblends**

Kg of flours	Number of scoops
3–5.99	1
6–8.99	2
9–11.99	3
12–14.99	4
15–18	5

The final concentration of iron in the flour thus ranges from about 20 to 33 mg per kilogram (except for the top of the first bin). A pilot survey on the kilograms of flour milled showed that the average adult eats .3 kg of flour per day. This implies that the average adult would get an extra 6 to 12 mg from the fortified flour. The WHO provides recommended iron intakes for populations with very low dietary intake of iron. For adult males the WHO recommends 27.4 mg/day. For adult, nonmenopausal females, this number is 58.8 mg/day. Thus, the program provides between 20 and 40 percent of the Recommended Daily Intake (RDI) in iron for males, and 10 to 20 percent for females. We should thus expect a larger effect on reduction in anemia for males, especially as they presumably eat more than women and thus absorb more than the average. In practice, intervention monitoring suggests that households consume on average 400 g of flour per day, which increases slightly the anticipated iron intake of a fortifying family.

The participating chakkis, their employees, and all their family members involved in their business, were trained by Seva Mandir in these procedures. Chakkis were initially given a flat fee to participate in the program, independent of the volume of their business or the number of households who fortified.[3] Chakkis were instructed to keep logbooks where they indicated how much grain had been milled, and whether or not they had fortified.

Seva Mandir put in place a system of monitoring of the chakki, which was implemented by the research team at Vidya Bhawan. About once a month, a field officer visited each chakki, inspected the log book, performed a spot test of fortified flour at the chakki, and randomly visited a few families who had fortified recently to perform a spot test at their house. The spot test is semiquantitative: it indicates the presence of iron in the flour, but it cannot indicate how much there was.

Before the program was started in a village, a village meeting took place, where the cause and consequences of iron deficiency anemia were discussed, as well as what households could do to prevent it (changes in diet, etc.). The program was then explained to the village, and the village collectively agreed to participate (all villages agreed). To avoid creating spurious effects due to

---

3. Later on, the payment was made contingent on the chakki's size, to compensate him for the large amount of extra work involved.

the information regarding anemia, Seva Mandir held a village meeting in control villages as well, where the discussion was the same (except that the program was not discussed). Each village had participating and nonparticipating chakkis. At the individual level, a household had to initially agree to be a participant. Once a household had accepted the program once, the chakki were to consider them to be participating households, unless they explicitly declined fortification. However, in spite of the initial decision to fortify, many households did not regularly fortify, either because the chakki did not always fortify the grain, or because households switched to nonparticipating chakkis.

Monitoring revealed some implementation challenges. Chakkis did not keep good records (many are illiterate), and seem to not have followed the instruction to continue to fortify flour for a household if they had initially decided to participate. On one key dimension, the program appears to have been consistently well-implemented, however: most of the spot checks do reveal the presence of iron among households chosen among those who had fortified. The household visit was also the occasion to collect information on any possible side effects or issue. There were essentially no side effects or complaints, except for a few complaints that the roti (flat bread) sometimes became black when on the fire. To our knowledge, this occasionally happens, and the fact that the flour is fortified does not increase the likelihood of this event.

10.3   Evaluation Design and Data Collection

This research is a collaborative undertaking of Seva Mandir (the organization that designed and implemented the decentralized iron fortification program), Vidya Bhawan (a consortium of schools and colleges who undertook the data collection), and a team from MIT led by the authors of this chapter.

Ethical approval for this project and the study was obtained from MIT, the human subject committee at Vidya Bhawan, Udaipur, and the Indian Council of Medical Research.

One hundred and thirty four "hamlets" were part of the study. The sample was stratified according to access to a road (out of the 134 hamlets, half of them are at least 500 meters away from a road). Hamlets within each stratum were selected randomly, with a probability of being selected proportional to the hamlet population. A baseline survey of ten households in each of 100 hamlets was conducted in 2002 and 2003. In 2004 and 2005, twenty additional households were surveyed in each hamlet, and thirty-four hamlets were added to the sample.

Out of these 134 hamlets, 65 were randomly selected (by the research team, using the random generator in Stata) to received the iron fortification program. The randomization was done after stratification by block (a block is an administrative area, below the district, and also an administrative unit for Seva Mandir), and by the randomization status for two other interventions that were conducted and evaluated in the same villages (a nurse absenteeism study, and an immunization incentive program). The program started in a staggered fashion by block: after an initial pilot in four villages, it started in the first two blocks (Bargaon and Girwa) in January 2006. It then was introduced in Jadhol in June 2006, in Kotra in October 2006, and in Kherwara in November 2006.

An end line survey was conducted between July 2007 and March 2009. All the individuals surveyed at baseline in all the households were attempted to be surveyed at end line. Almost all households (96 percent) were found. At the individual level, the attrition is 19 percent. Attrition is mainly due to seasonal migrants, who could not be traced back to the village.

The baseline and end line survey data include a detailed household module (including information about consumption, assets, etc.). For households in treatment villages, we also have information specific to fortification (which chakki they normally use, whether the chakki they use fortifies flour, whether they choose to fortify, and if not, why not), and an individual module, which includes, among other things, information about working hours for the past week, and a detailed interview on health-seeking behavior. The individual module also includes health and mental health information: self-reported conditions experienced in the past thirty days, self-reported health status, self-reported happiness, and a depression module. Finally, basic health measurements are obtained: health, weight, blood pressure, peak flow meter, and hemoglobin.

Hemoglobin was measured using hemocue machines. The respondent's finger is pricked with a lancet, and the second drop of blood is put in a cuvette, which is inserted in the machine, which provides an immediate reading. In what follows, we adopt the following threshold from the World Health Organization[4] to determine "anemia": a hemoglobin level below 12 is considered to be anemic for nonpregnant women (11 for pregnant women), and a hemoglobin level below 13 is considered to be anemic for men.

In addition to the baseline and end line survey, several other data sets were collected for the analysis. First, we have data from the spot checks conducted to monitor program implementation (availability of iron in the flour at the chakki, and availability of iron in the flour of the households who were reported to have recently fortified their flour). We also have information on the location of all the chakkis in the village.

Second, we have collected a unique data set: the continuous household survey (CHS). This data set is a short survey, performed every month. One local person (a paraworker) was hired to conduct this survey every month among the thirty households in the villages. The survey included questions

4. See http://whqlibdoc.who.int/publications/2008/9789241596657_eng.pdf.

on symptoms experienced by household members over the last thirty days (including vomiting, diarrhea, and weakness), days spent doing different activities (work for pay, work in the field, tending the animals, school, etc.) over the last week, and visits to different health facilities over the last month. The individual questions were to be asked directly to the individual. A few months after the program started in the first two blocks, a question was added asking how many times the household had milled grain in the past month, and whether or not they had fortified the flour.

A monitor visited the paraworker regularly (about once a month) to check that the surveys were properly filled, and accompanied the paraworker during the household visit that day for on-the-job training. There are 841,057 observations (individual-month) for a panel of about 4,000 households, spanning over two years. While the data is certainly not as good as a panel collected by a professional supervisor may be (and we still need to more work to validate it), it is a useful data source for other purposes.

10.4   Results

10.4.1   Program Take up

Figure 10.1 shows the fraction of households fortifying their flour at least once in the past month (according to their self-report in the continuous household surveys, which introduced the question a few months after the program started in the first regions), and figure 10.2 shows the fraction of times when they were fortifying their flour in the past month (out of the num-

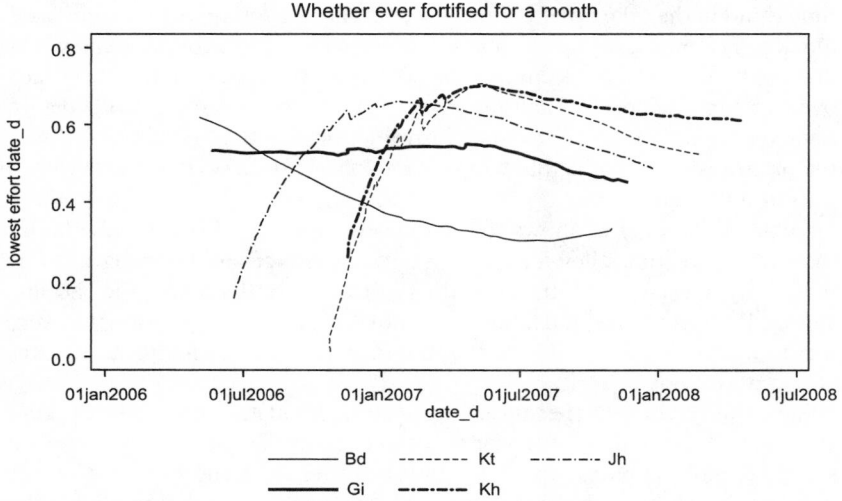

Fig. 10.1   Whether ever fortified for month

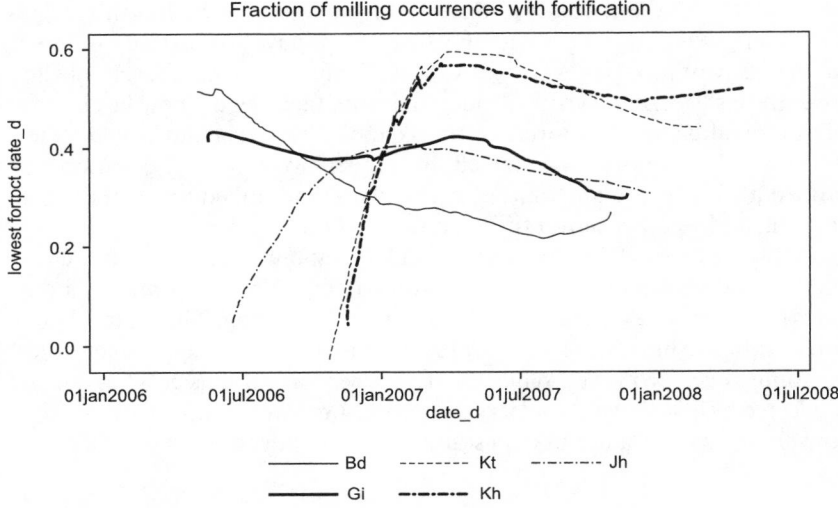

Fig. 10.2   Fraction of milling occurrences with fortification

ber of times they actually milled flour), in the different administrative blocks where Seva Mandir is operating. Unfortunately, the fortification question was introduced with some delay in the CHS: we do not have the beginning of the program for the first two blocks to start (Girwa and Bagdaon).

Both figures show that take up varied across regions, with the two blocks that started later having consistently higher take up. They show very sharp time trend in the take up of the program: at the beginning, take up increases quickly. Following a peak about six months after the program was introduced, there is a strong decline in the take up of the program by households over time in all regions. Table 10.2, panel A, shows a regression of take up on a spline function of date since introduction, for the first six months of the program, and for the following six months, and shows that those trends are strongly significant.

Table 10.2, panel B, shows the fraction of household that fortified, and the fraction of time they fortified, over the entire period the program was in activity in the region, and over the last three months before the end line survey. By the time the end line survey took place, very few households were fortifying their flour in three of the blocks, while two had fortification rates above 50 percent.

Some insight on why the take up declined is provided by figure 10.3. Figure 10.3 plots the take up of the program as a function of the date the program started for all the blocks together, and separates the households into three groups: those for whom the closest chakki fortifies; those who do not fortify, but have a fortifying chakki nearby (within 1.5 kilometers for this specifica-

Table 10.2   **Take up of the program**

	A Take up over time	
	no. of households who fortify	
Spline: Slope all months	0.0645	0.0694
	(0.0081)	(0.0087)
Spline: Slope for months 7–end	–0.0854	–0.0863
	(0.0095)	(0.0096)
Average take up first 6 months	0.5639	
Block fixed effects	N	Y

	B Average take up			
	Entire period		Last 3 months before end line	
	Fortified last month	% time fortified	Fortified last month	% time fortified
Badgaon	0.31	0.39	0.20	0.28
Kotra	0.47	0.58	0.42	0.54
Girwa	0.41	0.57	0.30	0.48
Kherwara	0.50	0.64	0.43	0.56
Jhadol	0.35	0.52	0.29	0.43
All blocks	0.41	0.54	0.33	0.45

tion, but the findings are robust to other distance); and those who do not have a fortifying chakki within 1.5 kilometers (which does happen, given that Udaipur district is very sparsely populated). Take up initially increases in all three groups, but does not reach the same peak for those who do not have a chakki nearby. All those who have a chakki nearby reach the same peak, but take up falls down more quickly for those for whom it is not the closest one, presumably because households switched back to their normal chakki after a while.

10.4.2   Impact on Anemia and Hemoglobin Levels

Attrition

One unfortunate limitation in our ability to detect any impact of the program on anemia is that while overall attrition in the survey is fairly low, attrition in hemoglobin measurement is much higher, and is significantly different in treatment and control groups (see table 10.3).

This is primarily due to a combination of dysfunctional hemocue machines (about two-thirds of the cases among adults) and refusals (about one-third among adults). While the interviewing team spent considerable time

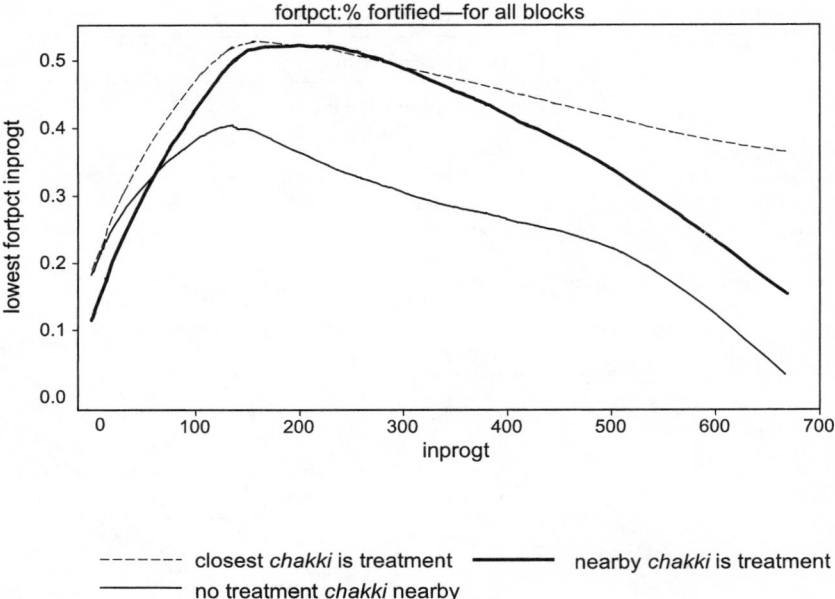

Fig. 10.3   **Percentage fortified for all blocks**

tracking down households and individuals, for ethical reasons, interviewers were instructed to address any concerns over safety, use of the blood, or confidentiality, but not to insist beyond this if individuals still refused the blood prick.[5] Refusals are particularly high among children: in the control group, only 20 percent of the children age zero to five who are in the end line survey have a valid hemocue measurement, and only 55 percent of the children aged five to fourteen have a valid hemocue measurement. Among adults, in the control group, 36 percent of those who are otherwise present in the end line do not have valid hemoglobin data.

Attrition does not appear to be random. First, it is lower in the treatment group than in the control group by about 6 percentage points for adults. Second, those for whom we have end line data on other variables but no anemia data tend to be older, skinnier, and more likely to be anemic at baseline (table 10.4). Since the anemia test involved a blood prick, refusals are more frequent when people are weak (or for young children), often because respondents feared that the test might make them even weaker. In villages where iron was distributed, it appears that interviewers were more likely to be able to convince respondents to be subject themselves to the blood prick,

5. Interviewers generally come from a much higher social background than respondents, and the line between persuasion and undue influence could have been quite fine if interviewers were requested to insist on the test.

Table 10.3   **Attrition**

A	% observations in baseline with valid anemia data at end line			% individual with individual interview at end line, but no anemia test		
	Treatment (1)	Control (2)	Difference (3)	Treatment (4)	Control (5)	Difference (6)
Adults (14+)	0.707	0.660	0.047	0.215	0.276	−0.061**
Men	0.721	0.680	0.041	0.217	0.270	−0.053**
Women	0.695	0.646	0.050	0.215	0.281	−0.066**
Children 6–13	0.664	0.607	0.057	0.347	0.421	−0.075**
Children 0–5	X	X	X	0.737	0.812	−0.075***

B	Reason for no anemia test for people in end line		
	Technical issues	Refuse or cannot do it	Invalid hemo reading
Adults (14+)	0.599	0.398	0.003
Men	0.757	0.241	0.002
Women	0.460	0.536	0.004
Children 6–13	0.349	0.648	0.003
Children 0–5	0.208	0.792	0.001

Note: X indicates not surveyed.

perhaps because respondents were grateful for the program, and happy to cooperate to its evaluation. The likely effect of attrition is to lead to underestimate the impact of the program on anemia, since the extra observations in the treatment groups are drawn from a weaker group.

Impacts: Reduced Forms

Despite this shortcoming of the hemoglobin data, we examine the impact of the program on hemoglobin level and anemia. Given the very high rates of attrition among children, we focus on adults.

The analysis is conducted with a simple linear regression, in the sample of individuals aged fourteen or higher at the end line, and who are present in the baseline:

(1) $$y_{ij} = \alpha + \beta T_j + X\gamma + \varepsilon_{ij},$$

where y is the outcome of interest, T is a dummy indicating whether the household was in a treated village, and X are control variables. The standard errors are adjusted for heteroskedasticity and clustering at the village level using White standard errors. All the regressions are weighted by the inverse of the probability of selection of the village in the overall sample.

Table 10.4   **Attrition: Difference between attritors and nonattritors for selected characteristics**

	Age			BMI		
	Treatment (1)	Control (2)	Difference (3)	Treatment (4)	Control (5)	Difference (6)
In end line survey	36.6	36.7	−0.125 (0.661)	17.999	18.044	−0.045 (0.181)
Not in end line survey	37.2	36.0	1.109 (5.867)	17.917	17.296	0.621 (0.674)
In end line survey with anemia data	36.7	36.7	−0.063 (0.694)	18.025	18.019	0.006 (0.191)
In end line survey no anemia data	36.2	36.6	−0.310 (1.310)	17.932	18.099	−0.167 (0.245)

	Hemocue at baseline			Self-reported health		
	Treatment (7)	Control (8)	Difference (9)	Treatment (10)	Control (11)	Difference (12)
In end line survey	11.702	11.605	0.097 (0.123)	5.929	5.858	0.071 (0.144)
Not in end line survey	11.362	11.883	−0.521 (0.438)	5.972	6.332	−0.359 (0.682)
In end line survey with anemia data	11.709	11.721	−0.011 (0.123)	5.855	5.803	0.052 (0.156)
In end line survey no anemia data	11.681	11.348	0.332 (0.209)	6.121	5.980	0.141 (0.236)

In the basic specification, X only contains dummies for blocks' age, age squared, and gender (unless the analysis is separated by gender). We also include a specification where we control for baseline hemoglobin level (observations without hemoglobin status are included, as well as a dummy for "missing hemoglobin status").

The results are presented in table 10.5, panel A, for the overall sample. There appears to be no detectable difference in hemoglobin or in the prevalence of anemia between the treated and the control groups for women. For men, there is a 4 percentage point reduction in anemia, significant at the 10 percent level when we control for baseline anemia. (However, surprisingly the reduction in anemia between treatment and control groups is no higher for those who were anemic at baseline.)

While these estimates are indicative of the (lack of) effect of the fortification program in the entire sample after eighteen months to two years of existence, they may reflect in part the very low take up of the program toward its end, at least in three of the blocks where it had been operating for a long time. The question of whether the fortification program *could* reduce anemia if take up were higher is therefore of independent interest.

Table 10.5 Effect on hemoglobin level and anemia indicator (all blocks)

	Adult females				Adult males			
	Hemoglobin level		Anemia status		Hemoglobin level		Anemia status	
	OLS Reduced form	IV Average: Last 3 months	OLS Reduced form	IV Average: Last 3 months	OLS Reduced form	IV Average: Last 3 months	OLS Reduced form	IV Average: Last 3 months
	(1)	(2)	(3)	(4)	(5)	(6)	(7)	(8)
Means in the control group	10.888	10.882	0.732	0.734	12.805	12.771	0.507	0.512
A Basic control (Age, Age2, block dummies)								
Iron treatment / take up	−0.031	−0.100	0.016	0.050	0.129	0.301	−0.039	−0.088
	(0.077)	(0.189)	(0.020)	(0.049)	(0.086)	(0.207)	(0.024)	(0.057)
N	3,890	3,362	3,890	3,362	3,527	3,154	3,527	3,154
B Controlling for baseline anemia (including missing values)								
Iron treatment / take up	−0.024	−0.087	0.014	0.046	0.132	0.309	−0.040*	−0.091*
	(0.074)	(0.183)	(0.020)	(0.049)	(0.082)	(0.196)	(0.023)	(0.055)
Baseline anemia	−0.836**	−0.817**	0.173**	0.179***	−0.861***	−0.893***	0.199***	0.215***
	(0.062)	(0.069)	(0.019)	(0.020)	(0.072)	(0.075)	(0.020)	(0.021)
Missing baseline anemia	−0.627**	−0.656**	0.101**	0.121***	−0.422***	−0.396***	0.071***	0.077***
	(0.087)	(0.088)	(0.025)	(0.027)	(0.090)	(0.095)	(0.027)	(0.027)
N	3,890	3,362	3,890	3,362	3,527	3,154	3,527	3,154

Notes: Average take up in the last three months and during the treatment period is taken from the monthly CHS survey. All IV regressions in panels A and B use original treatment status as the instrument. Standard errors (corrected for clustering at the village level) are shown in parentheses.

***Significant at the 1 percent level.

**Significant at the 5 percent level.

*Significant at the 10 percent level.

Table 10.6   **Midline effect on hemoglobin level and anemia indice (Girwa and Bargaon)**

	Adults only					
	Hemoglobin level			Anemic		
	All	Female		All	Female	
	(1)	(2)	Male	(3)	(4)	Male
Means in the control group	11.466	10.717	12.416	0.706	0.789	0.601
	Basic control (Age, Age2, block dummies)					
Iron treatment	0.299	0.308**	0.298	–0.071*	–0.077**	–0.065
	(0.183)	(0.149)	(0.288)	(0.040)	(0.037)	(0.059)
N	2,253	1,324	929	2,253	1,324	929
	Basic controls plus control for baseline anemia status					
Iron treatment	0.274	0.233	0.335	–0.068**	–0.075**	–0.059
	(0.179)	(0.154)	(0.292)	(0.034)	(0.031)	(0.056)
N	1,439	851	588	1,439	851	588

**Significant at the 5 percent level.
*Significant at the 10 percent level.

A midline survey, which was realized in two blocks that started the program first (Girwa and Bargaon) sheds more light on this question: the midline was conducted there a year after the program started, when the take up in those blocks was still high. Table 10.6 shows the impact of the treatment on anemia in these two blocks at midline. It shows a significant difference in anemia rate of about 7 percentage points between treatment and control villages. The effects are larger than at the end line, are are now similar for men and for women. The difference is due to the timing of the survey (when the take up was high) and not to the fact that the program effects are somehow larger in Girwa and Bargaon: to the contrary, when we separate the results by blocks, the endline anemia differences are highest in Kotra and Kerwara, the two blocks where take up was highest by the end line (results omitted to save space).

To sum up, flour fortification appears to be associated with a decline in the rate of anemia as long as a sufficient number of people take it up. But take up of the program was not sustained, which eventually made it largely ineffective. This suggests a potentially large impact of the iron supplementation itself on anemia, combined with a relatively low take up.

Impacts of Iron Supplementation on Anemia
Status Instrumental Variable Specification

To estimate the effect of the supplementation program, we estimate an instrumental variable specification. In equation (1), T_{ij} is replaced by variables indicating the fraction of times in the last three months that a household has fortified their flour (F_{ij}). This equation is then estimated with two-stage least squares, T_i, serving as the instrument for F_{ij}.

The results are presented in the even columns in table 10.5. Not surprisingly, since the first stage is the same for men and women (since it is defined as the household basis), we find the same conclusion that, at the end line, iron supplementation seems to have significant impacts only for men. The implied effects are fairly large: regular iron supplementation over the last three months would lead to a reduction of 9 percentage points in the incidence of anemia among men, a 17 percent decrease. It should be noted that the instrumental variable (IV) estimate gives us the effect for those who chose to fortify, and thus who may have experienced the largest effect.

10.4.3   Impacts on Health and Work Outcomes

Table 10.7 shows the impact on health at the end line survey. In the entire sample, women in villages that received the program have significantly higher BMI, higher self-reported health, higher self-reported happiness, and are less likely to be depressed. There is no impact on symptoms reported, ADL score, or their ability to carry strenuous activity. The results go in the same direction for men (with the exception of the ability to climb a hill, which appears to be lower in the treatment group), but are all insignificant. When we look at the results separately for the high fortification and low fortification blocks, the results (omitted to save space) are very similar in both types of blocks.

The fact that the results are higher for women than for men, and high in all blocks irrespective of the take up by end line (and thus the effect on anemia by end line), suggests that there may be a reporting bias in the self-reported measures, with women ready to report themselves in better health to be polite to the investigators.

The continuous household survey is the ideal data set to look at the impact of the program on conditions experienced by each individual, self-reported health, and activities, since we have one data point per household every month. We can look at the impact of the program during the entire time it was in place (rather than just at the very end, when take up was low), as well as look at how the impact varies over time. It is also less likely that households would differentially report their health in treated and control villages, since they are reporting this information to a village member, not to an outside surveyor, and they are reporting every week. The symptoms reported in the continuous household survey are diarrhea, vomiting, weakness, and "other." Anemia should primarily affect weakness, which is therefore our main symptom of interest. Diarrhea and vomiting are also of interest, since they are possible side effects of iron supplementation. We also examine the impact of the project on self-reported health and days of work activity over the last week (these aggregate several possible work activities: work in the field, work for a wage, tending animals, etc.).

For each outcome y_{ijt}, we present the following specifications:

Table 10.7   **Effect on health outcomes (all blocks)**

	Females		Males	
	OLS Reduced form (5)	IV Average: Last 3 months (7)	OLS Reduced form (9)	IV Average: Last 3 months (11)
BMI	0.241*	0.521	0.172	0.391
	(0.132)	(0.317)	(0.113)	(0.267)
Self-reported health	0.165*	0.450**	0.088	0.192
	(0.097)	(0.223)	(0.094)	(0.222)
Cold	−0.004	−0.006	0.005	0.006
	(0.018)	(0.042)	(0.019)	(0.043)
Any kind of cough	−0.010	−0.009	−0.017	−0.046
	(0.017)	(0.040)	(0.017)	(0.039)
Fever	−0.019	−0.038	0.014	0.032
	(0.017)	(0.038)	(0.016)	(0.039)
Weakness	−0.028	−0.054	0.011	0.015
	(0.018)	(0.042)	(0.016)	(0.038)
Body ache	0.000	0.013	0.022	0.045
	(0.014)	(0.033)	(0.015)	(0.034)
Vomiting	−0.010	−0.015	0.019***	0.039**
	(0.009)	(0.022)	(0.007)	(0.018)
Diarrhea	−0.001	0.000	0.007	0.018
	(0.010)	(0.024)	(0.009)	(0.024)
Self-reported happiness	0.076*	0.139	0.032	0.075
	(0.042)	(0.095)	(0.041)	(0.093)
Depression index (higher = less depressed)	0.112**	0.245*	−0.020	−0.047
	(0.055)	(0.128)	(0.033)	(0.078)
ADL score (z) (higher = less difficulty)	−0.048	−0.169	0.193	0.412
	(0.220)	(0.492)	(0.157)	(0.387)
Walk 5 km	0.005	0.018	−0.023	−0.044
	(0.024)	(0.055)	(0.018)	(0.045)
Draw water	−0.003	−0.013	−0.015	−0.026
	(0.020)	(0.044)	(0.012)	(0.030)
Carry object	0.003	0.003	−0.011	−0.021
	(0.012)	(0.027)	(0.009)	(0.023)
Work in a field	−0.012	−0.031	−0.007	−0.007
	(0.028)	(0.062)	(0.019)	(0.045)
Climb a hill	0.010	0.003	−0.020**	−0.046*
	(0.016)	(0.037)	(0.010)	(0.026)

Notes: Each row gives the coefficient of a separate regression, where the outcome is regressed on a dummy for whether the village is a treatment village. The standard errors (corrected for clustering at the village level) are in parentheses below the coefficient.

***Significant at the 1 percent level.

**Significant at the 5 percent level.

*Significant at the 10 percent level.

The first specification is:

(2) $$y_{ijt} = \alpha + \beta T_j + \gamma TP_{tj} + \delta T_j * TP_{tj} + X_{ijt} \lambda + \varepsilon_{ijt},$$

where T_j is a dummy for whether the village was selected for the iron program, and TP_{jt} is a dummy for whether the program was in operation in this block at that date (irrespective of treatment status). The coefficient of interest in this specification is δ.

The second specification accounts for the pattern of take up of the program, as shown in figure 10.1 and table 10.2: we reproduce

(3) $$y_{ijt} = \alpha + \beta T_j + \gamma TP_{tj} + \gamma_1 S_{1\,tj} + \gamma_2 S_{2\,tj} + \delta T_j * TP_{tj}$$
$$+ \delta_1 T_j * S_{1\,tj} + \delta_2 T_j * S_{2\,tj} + X_{ijt} \lambda + \varepsilon_{ijt},$$

where the notation is as before, and in addition, S_1 is a spline for the first six months of the program, and S_2 is a spline for the second seven months of the program. This specification will tell us if the impact on health closely follows the take up pattern.

The results of both specifications are presented in table 10.8: panel A for the entire sample, panel B for males only, and panel C for females only. Over its entire duration, the program does not appear to have any significant impact on self-reported health, any symptoms, or days of work, for either men or women (cutting the sample by high and low take up blocks gives very similar results).

However, the spline specification shows that "weakness", the one condition that we expect should be affected by the program, seems to follow a time pattern that corresponds closely with the evolution of the take-up of the program: the number of occurrences of weakness declines over time in the first six months after the program is introduced, and the trend is reversed afterwards. Figure 10.4 illustrates this: it is a line that represents the difference between treatment and control in a nonparametric regression of weakness on the number of days since the program started. It shows that the occurrence of the weakness symptoms initially declined, and then increased again, following the same time pattern as the take up of the program.

This pattern is similar for men and women, though it is stronger for women (recall that, by the midline, women also experienced positive effects on anemia). A similar shape is observed by women for occurrence of vomiting (note that vomiting *improved,* rather than worsened, as would be expected if iron had strong side effects on stomach functions) and a combined indicator for the reporting of any symptom. This suggests that the iron fortification program may indeed have improved stamina as long as it was taken up at a high rate. At the peak usage, this suggests that the rate at which people experienced weakness was 5 percentage points (27 percent) lower in treatment group than in control.

Even if it did improve stamina, however, the program did not increase the number of days of work, neither for men nor for women. The number of days worked was not higher during the treated period in treated villages,

Table 10.8   Effect on health and work outcomes: continuous household survey

	Any symptom (1)	Diarrhea (2)	Vomiting (3)	Weakness/fatigue (4)	Other symptoms (5)	Self-reported health (6)	Days of work activity (any work) (7)
			A All adults				
Treatment village	−0.003	−0.028*	−0.010	0.018	0.016	0.067	0.045
	(0.035)	(0.015)	(0.010)	(0.030)	(0.032)	(0.156)	(0.104)
Treatment village*treated period	−0.029	−0.012	−0.006	−0.027	−0.023	0.123	−0.036
	(0.026)	(0.013)	(0.011)	(0.027)	(0.022)	(0.118)	(0.085)
Treated period	−0.051***	−0.054***	−0.036***	−0.032	−0.021	0.097	0.185***
	(0.019)	(0.009)	(0.007)	(0.022)	(0.017)	(0.086)	(0.054)
N	399,050	398,883	398,750	398,573	398,664	395,885	398,925
Treatment village	−0.004	−0.028*	−0.010	0.018	0.016	0.070	0.044
	(0.035)	(0.015)	(0.010)	(0.030)	(0.032)	(0.155)	(0.104)
Treatment village*treated period	0.016	−0.012	0.003	0.025	−0.003	0.001	0.002
	(0.032)	(0.022)	(0.012)	(0.030)	(0.024)	(0.131)	(0.107)
Treatment village*slope all months (spline)	−0.010*	−0.001	−0.003	−0.012**	−0.004	0.031	0.001
	(0.006)	(0.004)	(0.002)	(0.006)	(0.005)	(0.020)	(0.018)
Treatment village*slope month 7 to end (spline)	0.012	0.002	0.004	0.013*	0.005	−0.039	−0.009
	(0.009)	(0.005)	(0.003)	(0.007)	(0.007)	(0.029)	(0.024)
Treated period	−0.051**	−0.040*	−0.041***	−0.038*	−0.013	0.017	0.200**
	(0.024)	(0.021)	(0.008)	(0.023)	(0.018)	(0.099)	(0.089)
Slope all months (spline)	0.000	−0.002	0.001	0.002	−0.002	0.009	−0.018
	(0.004)	(0.004)	(0.001)	(0.004)	(0.004)	(0.014)	(0.012)
Slope month 7 to end (spline)	0.000	0.002	−0.001	−0.003	0.002	−0.001	0.034**
	(0.005)	(0.004)	(0.002)	(0.005)	(0.005)	(0.019)	(0.016)
N	398,310	398,144	398,010	397,834	397,926	395,189	398,176
Mean control group	0.419	0.120	0.072	0.206	0.304	6.140	5.840

B Male adults

Treatment village	-0.006	-0.022	-0.009	0.017	0.011	0.097	-0.029
	(0.033)	(0.014)	(0.009)	(0.027)	(0.030)	(0.164)	(0.138)
Treatment village*treated period	-0.027	-0.010	-0.005	-0.028	-0.015	0.131	0.007
	(0.026)	(0.012)	(0.010)	(0.026)	(0.022)	(0.118)	(0.112)
Treated period	-0.052***	-0.052***	-0.029***	-0.028	-0.027	0.106	0.230***
	(0.020)	(0.009)	(0.007)	(0.022)	(0.017)	(0.087)	(0.080)
N	188,307	188,248	188,194	188,106	188,121	187,183	188,253
Treatment village	-0.006	-0.022	-0.009	0.016	0.011	0.100	-0.031
	(0.033)	(0.014)	(0.009)	(0.027)	(0.030)	(0.164)	(0.138)
Treatment village*treated period	0.002	-0.011	-0.002	0.009	-0.008	0.055	0.061
	(0.031)	(0.021)	(0.011)	(0.028)	(0.025)	(0.138)	(0.143)
Treatment village*slope all months (spline)	-0.007	-0.002	-0.001	-0.008	-0.002	0.019	0.000
	(0.006)	(0.003)	(0.002)	(0.005)	(0.005)	(0.022)	(0.023)
Treatment village*slope month 7 to end (spline)	0.008	0.003	0.002	0.010	0.002	-0.024	-0.010
	(0.009)	(0.004)	(0.003)	(0.007)	(0.007)	(0.031)	(0.031)
Treated period	-0.043*	-0.036*	-0.034***	-0.026	-0.014	0.025	0.279**
	(0.025)	(0.020)	(0.008)	(0.023)	(0.019)	(0.104)	(0.114)
Slope all months (spline)	-0.001	-0.002	0.001	0.000	-0.002	0.010	-0.024
	(0.004)	(0.003)	(0.001)	(0.004)	(0.004)	(0.016)	(0.015)
Slope month 7 to end (spline)	0.001	0.001	-0.001	0.000	0.002	-0.003	0.039**
	(0.005)	(0.003)	(0.002)	(0.005)	(0.005)	(0.020)	(0.020)
N	188,025	187,967	187,912	187,824	187,839	186,917	187,962
Mean control group	0.372	0.103	0.056	0.180	0.268	6.454	5.553

(continued)

Table 10.8 (continued)

	Any symptom (1)	Diarrhea (2)	Vomiting (3)	Weakness/fatigue (4)	Other symptoms (5)	Self-reported health (6)	Days of work activity (any work) (7)
			C Female adults				
Treatment village	-0.001	-0.032**	-0.011	0.020	0.021	0.043	0.119
	(0.037)	(0.016)	(0.012)	(0.033)	(0.034)	(0.153)	(0.103)
Treatment village*treated period	-0.030	-0.012	-0.007	-0.025	-0.031	0.114	-0.077
	(0.028)	(0.015)	(0.012)	(0.029)	(0.023)	(0.124)	(0.078)
Treated period	-0.049**	-0.056***	-0.042***	-0.035	-0.015	0.073	0.162***
	(0.020)	(0.011)	(0.008)	(0.023)	(0.017)	(0.089)	(0.043)
N	209,351	209,243	209,166	209,077	209,152	207,314	209,279
Treatment village	-0.001	-0.033**	-0.012	0.020	0.021	0.046	0.119
	(0.037)	(0.015)	(0.012)	(0.033)	(0.034)	(0.153)	(0.103)
Treatment village*treated period	0.031	-0.013	0.008	0.041	0.002	-0.058	-0.050
	(0.035)	(0.024)	(0.014)	(0.035)	(0.026)	(0.135)	(0.095)
Treatment village*slope all months (spline)	-0.014**	0.000	-0.004	-0.015**	-0.007	0.043**	0.002
	(0.007)	(0.005)	(0.002)	(0.007)	(0.006)	(0.021)	(0.020)
Treatment village*slope month 7 to end (spline)	0.016*	0.000	0.005	0.017**	0.008	-0.053*	-0.008
	(0.009)	(0.006)	(0.003)	(0.009)	(0.008)	(0.030)	(0.026)
Treated period	-0.058**	-0.043**	-0.046***	-0.049***	-0.013	0.011	0.134*
	(0.025)	(0.022)	(0.009)	(0.024)	(0.019)	(0.102)	(0.079)
Slope all months (spline)	0.002	-0.003	0.001	0.004	-0.001	0.005	-0.010
	(0.004)	(0.004)	(0.002)	(0.005)	(0.003)	(0.015)	(0.013)
Slope month 7 to end (spline)	-0.002	0.003	-0.001	-0.006	0.002	0.004	0.027
	(0.006)	(0.005)	(0.002)	(0.006)	(0.005)	(0.019)	(0.017)
N	208,894	208,786	208,709	208,621	208,697	206,885	208,822
Mean control group	0.461	0.136	0.087	0.229	0.338	5.855	6.094

Notes: Each column presents the results of a separate regression. Standard errors (corrected for clustering at the village level) are presented in parentheses.

***Significant at the 1 percent level.

**Significant at the 5 percent level.

*Significant at the 10 percent level.

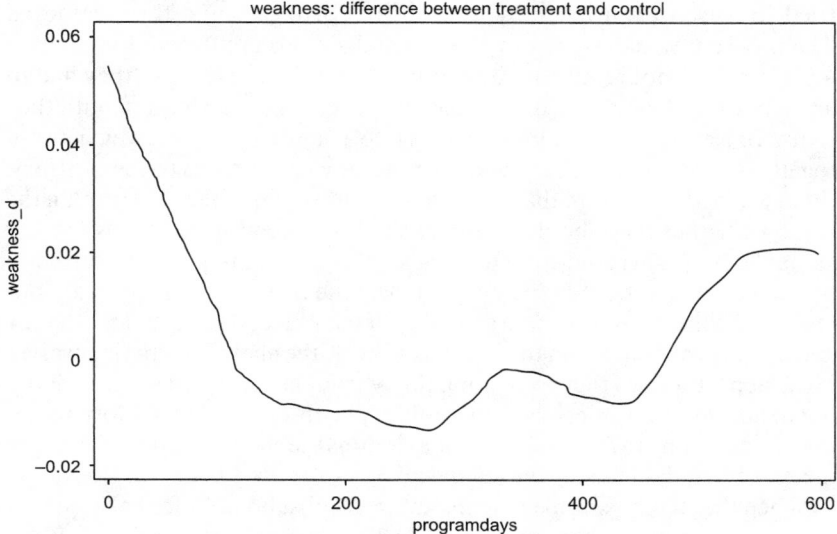

Fig. 10.4   Weakness: Difference between treatment and control

and days of work did not increase and decrease in treatment villages with the take up of the program. Thus, even though people felt less weak, they did not use this energy to work more (or the effects were too low to be detected). This lack of effect is consistent with Edgerton et al. (1979), who found very small effects of iron supplementation on productivity of tea pickers in Indonesia; and Li et al. (1994), who found small increases in output of female cotton mill workers in China. In the latter case, energy efficiency among these workers did increase significantly, but technology impeded productivity improvements at the cotton mills. It is also possible that, in this case as well, the ability to work at any given time is primarily a function of the environment (they have to be able to find work). Another possibility is that the effect would be small.

10.5   Conclusion

Iron deficiency anemia affects millions of people worldwide, affecting their health and productivity. While field trials have shown that iron supplementation through pills can reduce anemia, improve strength, and, in some cases, lead to increase in labor supply and productivity, the systematic distribution of iron supplementation pills to the entire population is not a practical solution. Food fortification is an alternative, but centralized fortification will leave out the poorest, who are not purchasing fortified foods.

This innovative program, developed from the ground up by an NGO, tried to solve this problem by introducing fortification at the local level. The program was designed to be easy and safe to implement by illiterate millers, and to not require many extra steps for the consumers (they had to agree once, and would then be considered as part of the program until they refused). Nevertheless, the program ran into a number of issues, which, taken together, reduced its effectiveness: first, despite instructions to the contrary, they switched away from the initial fortification default decision, asking the person whether they should fortify each visit; second, households did not value the program sufficiently to walk slightly further to get fortification.

These two factors combined explain why the take up of the program faltered over time. We interviewed a number of chakkis and households after the end of the program. From the point of view of the chakki, fortifying was an extra step, and since they were not paid by the quantity fortified, they chose not to take this step unless the household explicitly demanded it. Most households were happy to fortify their flour as long as the chakki did it for them, but in most cases, did not stay during the milling to check whether he was doing it. When the chakkis stopped mixing the iron, most households believed that the program must have stopped, and few bothered insisting on fortification. Ultimately, low demand from the households seems to be at the root of the decay of the program. This is despite some positive impact on symptoms of weakness in the program's initial phase, and impacts on self-reported health and happiness by the end line (which may have been placebo or reporting effects, however). It is possible that the low demand stems from the lack of any life-changing effect: the extra stamina did not allow those individuals to work more days (there may not be that much more work to be had), and it is not clear that being slightly less likely to experience weakness symptoms was enough to be convinced to do anything different than the usual.

From a policy perspective, this experience thus suggests that iron fortification may need to be even less painful for the individuals for them to take it up consistently: fortification of salt (which even poor households do purchase) seems to be a promising avenue. An alternative, which we are currently exploring in Udaipur, is to make the fortification process even easier, for example, by mixing the iron premix with the grain at the moment it is milled, thus removing the extra step. This raises the issue of whether and why such a policy is justified if households' willingness to pay for the program is so low that they will not bother to ask the chakki to do something free for them. Unlike immunization, bed nets, or TB pills, there are no obvious externalities to iron deficiency anemia, so one could argue that individuals should be left alone to deal with this problem. This question leads to a more speculative, and possibly more interesting, economic argument: individuals may have little interest in any action, however small, that brings about incremental changes to their lives, perhaps because they do not really see the point today of feeling just slightly better tomorrow (Banerjee and Mullainathan 2008). Even if the action is just to ask for a service, or to walk a little further, the simple fact to consider is that it still requires the individual to project themselves into this future, which is rather depressing to consider: a future where, whether with iron fortification or not, they will still be sick often and not have much work to do. This may be why people give up so easily.

Despite this, ex post, the individual would still enjoy being a little stronger, if this was just offered to him. This underscores the importance of the status quo, or default (Madrian and Shea 2001; Choi et al.; Rabin and Thaler; Kahneman, Knetsch, and Thaler 1991). This program was meant to be in part a "default" program, but this would have relied on the cooperation of the chakkis, who prefer, like everyone, to do a little less extra work. Selling fortified salt in PDS would address this issue, but the question that will arise is the following: should the only double fortified salt be available? This would curtail the individual's freedom (some people may not *want* to get their salt fortified), but having both kinds of salt reintroduces a choice. Perhaps the best option is to have both types available, but to sell the double fortified salt at a small discount over the regular price. Take up may then be high, since comparing prices and taking the cheaper good is easy to do and to justify to oneself without considering the future.

Appendix

Fig. 10A.1   The fortification machine is on the left, and the milling machine is on the right

References

Banerjee, A., A. Deaton, and E. Duflo. 2004. Wealth, health, and health services in rural Rajasthan. Poverty Action Lab Paper no. 8, May.

Banerjee, A., and S. Mullainathan. 2008. Limited attention and income distribution. *American Economic Review* 98 (2): 489–93.

Basta, S., S. Soekirman, D. Karyadi, and N. Scrimshaw. 1979. Iron deficiency anemia and the productivity of adult males in Indonesia. *American Journal of Clinical Nutrition* 32 (4): 916–25.

Choi, J. J., D. Laibson, B. C. Madrian, and A. Metrick. 2002. Defined contribution pensions: Plan rules, participant decisions, and the path of least resistance. In *Tax policy and the economy,* ed. J. M. Poterba, 67–114. Cambridge, MA: MIT Press.

Edgerton, V., G. Gardner, Y. Ohira, K. Gunawardena, and B. Senewiratne. 1979. Iron-deficiency and its effect on worker productivity and activity patterns. *British Medical Journal* 2:1546–9.

Haas, J., and T. Brownlie. 2001. Iron deficiency and reduced work capacity: A critical review of the research to determine a causal relationship. *Journal of Nutrition* (Supplement) 131: 676S–88S.

Kahneman, D., J. Knetsch, and R. Thaler. 1991. Anomalies: The endowment effect, loss aversion, and status quo bias. *Journal of Economic Perspectives* 5 (1): 193–206.

Li, R., X. Chen, H. Yan, P. Deurenberg, L. Garby, and J. Hautvast. 1994. Functional consequences of iron supplementation in iron-deficient female cotton workers in Beijing China. *American Journal of Clinical Nutrition* 59:908–13.

Madrian, B., and D. Shea. 2001. The power of suggestion: Inertia in 401(k) participation and savings behavior. *The Quarterly Journal of Economics* 116 (4): 1149–87.

Micronutrient Initiative. 2007. Building the capacity of small millers: Training manual developed, September. Available at http://www.micronutrient.org/CMFiles/News%20Room/Announcements/Training-Manual-Capacity-Building-Small-Millers-KL-_2_.pdf.

———. 2008. Micronutrient Initiative: Five year strategic plan. Available at http://www.micronutrient.org/CMFiles/News%20Room/Announcements/MI-StratPlan-08-13.pdf.

Rabin, M., and R. H. Thaler. 2001. Anomalies: Risk aversion. *Journal of Economic Perspectives* 15 (1): 219–32.

Stolfzfus, R. 2001. Iron-deficiency anaemia: Reexamining the nature and magnitude of the public health problem. Summary: Implications for research and programs. *Journal of Nutrition* 131 (Suppl. 2): 697S–701S.

Thomas, D., E. Frankenberg, J. Friedman, J. Habicht, M. Hakimi, N. Jones, C. McKelvey, et al. 2003. Iron deficiency and the well-being of older adults: Early results from a randomized nutrition intervention. Paper presented at the Population Association of America Annual Meetings. April, Minneapolis, MN.

World Health Organization (WHO)/UNICEF/UNU. 2001. *Iron deficiency anaemia: Assessment, prevention, and control.* Geneva, WHO. Available at: http://www.who.int/nut/documents/ida_assessment_prevention_control.pdf.

Comment   Amitabh Chandra and Heidi Williams

Morbidity and mortality from preventable diseases represent substantial global health burdens. For example, the World Health Organization (WHO) estimated that in 2002 there were over 1.5 million deaths globally from diseases for which vaccination is part of most national immunization schedules (that is, diseases such as measles and tetanus).[1] On one hand, it is admirable that despite the many challenges facing health systems in most low-income countries, approximately three-quarters of the world's children receive a standard package of childhood vaccines; on the other hand, these vaccine-preventable deaths represent some of the tremendous costs of *not* expanding immunization to remaining groups of children. The morbidity costs of these diseases—both in terms of direct health costs and other costs, such as lost work productivity—would only add to the already large burdens of these vaccine-preventable diseases.

In this innovative chapter, Banerjee, Duflo, and Glennerster evaluate a novel program designed to address iron deficiency anemia—another preventable disease. Iron deficiency is thought to be the most prevalent nutrient deficiency globally, and to generate large costs in terms of poor health and lost work productivity. Traditional public health mechanisms to target anemia include pill-form iron supplements and food fortification (such as for flour and salt), neither of which reaches very isolated populations such as those in the tribal district of Udaipur, which is the focus of this study. For example, most households in this district consume their own grain, which makes centralized food fortification interventions infeasible. In this chapter, Banerjee, Duflo, and Glennerster report results from a randomized evaluation of a novel community-level fortification program that aimed to deliver iron supplementation to this population through giving households the choice to have free ferrous sulphate added to their flour at the point of milling. The basic findings of the evaluation are that the program was effective at reducing anemia and fatigue when take up of the program was sufficiently high, but did not lead to other health improvements or increases in labor supply. Moreover, willingness to pay for the program appeared to be low, and take up decreased over time from 60 percent to 20 percent.

Amitabh Chandra is professor of public policy at the John F. Kennedy School of Government, Harvard University, and a faculty research fellow of the National Bureau of Economic Research. Heidi Williams is a visiting fellow in aging research at the National Bureau of Economic Research.

Chandra acknowledges support from the National Institute on Aging (NIA P01AG19783-02), and Williams gratefully acknowledges financial support from the National Institute on Aging (T32-AG000186) to the National Bureau of Economic Research.

1. See http://www.who.int/immunization_monitoring/burden/estimates_burden/en/index .html.

A natural question is, given the observed improvements in health and low private costs of the program, why did take up drop off? The authors focus on a "low demand" interpretation of their results—arguing that, absent jobs and other opportunities, incremental improvements in health may not be valued and that it is only in the presence of large-scale "structural" interventions that aid will be effective. We certainly agree that this is a reasonable conjecture consistent with the results of the study. Although not extensively discussed in the chapter, this argument is related to poverty-trap-style models in which it is necessary for countries or individuals to get over a certain threshold before being able to "take off" economically; at a microeconomic level, the case for poverty traps typically involves nonconvexities in returns to investments, such as health and human capital investments. An alternative hypothesis would be that poverty is due as much to poor government policies as to poverty traps, and that small interventions that fill holes not currently being filled by government policies (such as increasing access to clean water, or increasing access to childhood vaccines, or decreasing iron deficiency) could in fact have high returns. This latter view is more in line with the authors' extensive previous work evaluating small-scale development interventions in low-income countries, but it does raise the puzzle of why this potentially cost-effective intervention was not as effective as we may have expected ex ante.

In this discussion we offer several thoughts (some more speculative than others) on potential explanations for the observed results of the program.

Demand-Side Explanations

Our first point is to argue that demand for health and health care may operate differently from demand for health inputs. Health is produced from a variety of factors—biological processes such as aging, predetermined factors such as genes, health care inputs given in an acute setting (such as rescue angioplasty or admission to a neonatal intensive care unit), and health inputs (ranging from medicines for chronic diseases to diet and exercise). The distinction between health care inputs given in an acute setting and other health inputs may seem artificial, but we argue this distinction is conceptually useful. Whereas the effects of rapid acting interventions are often quite clear to consumers, the effects of health inputs can be more difficult to quantify. The benefits of health inputs may be realized with a (potentially long) time lag, whereas any financial costs or short-term side effects are likely to be realized immediately, introducing two potential issues: first, hyperbolic consumers may overvalue short-term costs relative to long-term benefits; and second, particularly in environments where there are high levels of communicable diseases and frequent health shocks, it may be difficult for consumers (however rational) to separate the gains from health inputs from other determinants of health. Both issues are likely relevant in explaining why patients all over the world struggle with compliance to medicines for chronic diseases.

These issues are likely to be exacerbated if the health inputs cause side effects that are experienced immediately. According to the U.S. Centers for Disease Control (CDC), iron supplementation can sometimes cause side effects such as nausea, vomiting, constipation, and diarrhea; Murray et al. (1978) and Gera and Sachdev (2002) discuss potential side effects for children. In theory, such short-term side effects could have been overvalued by consumers relative to longer-term health benefits of the supplementation. However, in the case of the Banerjee, Duflo, and Glennerster experiment, the authors took care to monitor potential side effects for adults in their study, and received few reports of side effects.[2] While possible that individuals may not have reported side effects that are common for other reasons in this population, presumably surveyed individuals should have been aware of any side effects that would have affected compliance behavior. Thus, although appearing not to be relevant in the case of this study, this type of issue could be important in other contexts.

One way to address the challenge that consumers may overvalue short-term costs relative to long-term benefits would be to try to inform consumers of the benefits of health inputs in the short term, through providing patients with information on quantifiable health indicators for the duration of the intervention. In the United States, many medical treatments are set up such that patients get direct feedback on at least some effects of the treatments. Consider cholesterol-lowering statins as one example—consumers have their cholesterol level measured before initiation of statin therapy, and frequently continue to monitor their (hopefully, declining) cholesterol level after statin therapy is initiated. A natural question is whether observing changes in health metrics (here, cholesterol level) makes people believe that statins are more effective than they would believe in the absence of seeing such data—and indeed, whether seeing such data affects compliance behavior. Even if reductions in an individual's cholesterol level are an imperfect proxy for long-term health impacts, if such metrics have strong benefits in terms of improving compliance behavior it may be very worthwhile to invest in technologies to monitor such health metrics for a broader set of conditions. In the case of anemia, consumers could be shown data on their hemoglobin level and one could measure potential impacts on take up behavior.

Finally, key to understanding take up in this context may be to understand the etiology of anemia. Specifically, recent work in medicine (Calis et al. 2008) suggests that iron deficiency is inversely associated with bacteremia (bacteria in the blood), consistent with the idea that iron deficiency

---

2. The exceptions were a few reports that roti—a flat bread—sometimes became black when fired, although realistically the probability of such blackening may not increase when fortified flour is used.

protects against opportunistic bacteria by creating an unfavorable environment for their growth. This may be one reason why Murray et al. (1978) and Sazawal et al. (2006) noted worsening health outcomes after iron supplementation in areas with prevalent anemia. While speculative, this suggests that if Banerjee and colleagues had monitored side effects among children as well as among adults, adverse effects may have been detected.

Supply-Side Explanations

One interpretation of the experimental results is that the chakkis (local millers) did not seem to have sufficient incentives to participate in the program, which in turn made them switch out of the "fortification default," which in turn produced lower take up. This suggests either changing the incentives facing chakkis, or placing incentives on consumers in a way that somehow circumvents the chakkis.

On the first point, one natural "next step" would be to try a chakki payment scheme that gives chakkis a small mark-up for each unit sold. Obviously one would not want the chakkis to have an incentive to pressure households into purchasing the fortified grain, but it seems that at the moment the marginal payment to the chakki is not covering their marginal cost, hence the problems with them wanting to switch consumers out of the "fortification default."

On the second point, assuming that villagers pay chakkis a small amount for grain milling, it might be possible to give a small price subsidy on fortified units to make those units more attractive to consumers relative to nonfortified units (similar to the suggestion in the chapter's conclusions of giving small price subsidies for fortified salt), or even to put in a negative price subsidy for fortified units.

Optimism

There are three reasons why we are optimistic about the intervention studied in this chapter. First, the intervention is cheap, and consequently, even very small improvements in health or fatigue would make it cost-effective. This interpretation makes the simple point that interventions that cost (for example) ten dollars per person only have to generate 10/100,000 of a quality-adjusted life year in order to be considered cost-effective at conventional thresholds. To put that number into perspective, if an intervention only operates on the dimension of reducing mortality, then a ten dollar intervention only has to generate an additional hour of survival to be deemed cost-effective. It is also possible that this intervention generated improvements in health too small to be measured by the survey metrics, but commensurate with the low costs of the program.

Second, Banerjee, Duflo, and Glennerster report an intent-to-treat analysis. This is the relevant parameter for determining the overall cost-effectiveness of a public policy. However, if this is a treatment whose benefits exhibit wide variation across the population (perhaps because of how side-effects are valued), an equally interesting parameter is the treatment-on-the-treated, or the improvement in health for those who chose to continue in the program. To obtain this parameter it is necessary to scale the reported estimates by the take up rates (because take up rates are less than 100 percent, this will increase the measured effect of the program). Assuming that take up was at 50 percent in the villages of Kotra and Kherwara, this would double the estimates for these villages. These are large effects and suggest that there is more work to be done in precisely understanding the role of supply and demand explanations in affecting program take up.

Finally, the presence of externalities suggests that the study may not have fully captured the benefits of reducing anemia. Banerjee, Duflo, and Glennerster are more circumspect about drawing such conclusions and write ". . . there are no obvious externalities to iron deficiency anemia, so one could argue that individuals should be left alone to deal with this problem." Yet there may be two types of "externalities": first, there may be within-person "internalities" where hyperbolic consumers may not take actions today that would have future benefits (even if the actions today are zero cost), and that there are externalities on future "selves"; and second, if parents make decisions about fortification for their children but do not fully internalize benefits realized by the children (for example, in the form of increased birth weight for yet-unborn children of pregnant women), parental decisions may have externalities on their children.

The authors discuss potential concerns over curtailment of freedom from only offering fortified salt, but there are a number of precedents suggesting we take similar actions in other situations—iodizing salt, fluoridating water, putting vitamin D in milk, and so forth. Presumably such policies were justified based on a desire to reduce public expenditures on treatments (which could be less relevant in countries without large public insurance programs such as Medicare and Medicaid), or based on the existence of relatively large fixed costs that need to be absorbed, or based on more paternalistic motivations that connect to our point about discounting future benefits. Understanding the rationale for these precedents will help us think about whether we should be designing centralized policies for improving certain dimensions of health versus policies that allow patients to select their treatment.

References

Calis, J. C. J., K. S. Phiri, E. B. Faragher, B. J. Brabin, I. Bates, L. E. Cuevas, R. J. de Haan, et al. 2008. Severe anemia in Malawian children. *New England Journal of Medicine* 358 (9): 888–99.

Gera, T., and H. P. S. Sachdev. 2002. Effect of iron supplementation on incidence of infectious illness in children: Systematic review. *British Medical Journal* 325 (7373): 1142–44.

Murray, M. J., A. B. Murray, M. B. Murray, and C. J. Murray. 1978. The adverse effect of iron repletion on the course of certain infections. *British Medical Journal* 2 (6145): 1113–5.

Sazawal, S., R. E. Black, M. Ramsan, H. M. Chwaya, R. J. Stolzfus, A. Dutta, U. Dhingra, et al. 2006. Effects of routine prophylactic supplementation with iron and folic acid on admission to hospital and mortality in preschool children in a high malaria transmission setting: Community-based, randomised, placebo-controlled trial. *Lancet* 367 (9505): 133–43.

Requiescat in Pace?
The Consequences of High-Priced Funerals in South Africa

Anne Case and Alicia Menendez

11.1 Introduction

Funerals can serve several purposes, including honoring the dead, comforting those who grieve, and knitting social fabric for extended families and communities. In Southern Africa, funerals are generally considered an individual's most important rite of passage. As a result, they tend to be more elaborate and expensive than weddings, graduations, or naming ceremonies for children. Households may spend the equivalent of a year's income for an adult's funeral, borrowing from money lenders if need be to have a funeral that befits the status of the household and of the person who died (Case et al. 2008).

Social norms surrounding funerals were set at a time when people died largely in early childhood or in old age. Neither type of death would be apt to put financial strain on the household: young children's funerals are simple, and older person's funerals are largely protected by funeral insurance. The AIDS crisis has changed the mortality patterns observed in Southern Africa, with the greatest increase in mortality rates found for adults aged twenty to

Anne Case is the Alexander Stewart 1886 Professor of Economics and Public Affairs and professor of economics and public affairs at the Woodrow Wilson School of Public and International Affairs and the Economics Department at Princeton University, and a research associate of the National Bureau of Economic Research. Alicia Menendez is a research associate (associate professor) in the Harris School of Public Policy and a lecturer in the Department of Economics at the University of Chicago.

We have benefited from the help of the Agincourt Health and Population Unit under the leadership of Stephen Tollman and Kathy Kahn. We thank Mark Collinson and Martin Wittenberg for help in drawing a sample, Merton Dagut for survey management, Alice Muehlhof for expert data assistance, Karla Hoff for many useful conversations, Esther Duflo for helpful comments on an earlier draft, and the NIH for financial support under grants from the National Institute on Aging (R01 AG20275-01, P01 AG05842-14, and P30 AG024361).

thirty-four years old (Kahn, Garenne, et al. 2007). This increase in mortality in middle age can lead to economic hardship for households that experience a death, if those who die do not have burial policies and if norms of what constitutes an appropriate funeral do not change to reflect the change in mortality patterns.

In this chapter, we use data we collected on 2,922 individuals in 473 households in the Agincourt Demographic Surveillance Site in South Africa in 2004 to examine funeral spending and the impact of the death and funeral spending on household functioning. We find that, on average, funeral expenses total 3,400 rand when an adult dies—equivalent to 40 percent of average annual total household expenditure. We find households that experienced a death in the past five years have significantly lower expenditure per person than do other households. Adults in households that experienced a death report significantly more symptoms of depression and anxiety, and significantly more problems in their households. Children in households that experienced a death in the past five years are significantly less likely to be enrolled in school than are other children their age. Many of these difficulties can be explained by the amount of money that the household spent on the funeral.

Section 11.2 introduces the Agincourt Demographic Surveillance Site and presents summary statistics on the sample drawn for analysis. Section 11.3 examines funeral costs, and reports contributions made toward funeral expenses by household members and others. Section 11.4 looks at the association between death in the household in the past five years and outcomes for members on a variety of dimensions. Section 11.5 discusses alternative explanations for our findings, and section 11.6 concludes.

11.2   The Agincourt Demographic Surveillance Site

The Agincourt Health and Population Unit (AHPU) is an educational and research unit located within the School of Public Health at the University of the Witwatersrand, South Africa. Since 1992, AHPU has been collecting information on birth, death, and migration for all individuals identified as members of the approximately 11,700 households under surveillance in a rural subdistrict in (what is now) Mpumalanga Province, South Africa.[1] The area is home to South Africans and Mozambicans, the latter group settling here legally during the civil war in Mozambique. Most Mozambicans here have permanent residency status which, according to the South African Constitutional Court, allows them access to government transfers. However, it is more difficult for Mozambicans to access government grants, largely because they lack the documents necessary to do so (Case and Menendez 2007).

---

1. For more information on the Agincourt Unit, see http://web.wits.ac.za/Academic/Health/PublicHealth/Agincourt/. See also Kahn, Tollman et al. (2007).

11.2.1   Sample Design

In January 2004, using this census information, we drew a stratified random sample of 475 households, with stratification on both citizenship (South African versus Mozambican) and on whether the household had lost a member to death in the period from June 1, 2002 to May 31, 2003. We chose this window in order to reach households soon enough after the death that memories of funeral spending would still be fresh, but not so soon that we would offend grieving members. Our sample was drawn in such a way that refusals could be replaced by a household in the same (nationality-death status) stratum. Our sample design and the actual number of households interviewed in each stratum is shown in table 11.1. The sample was designed to be 60 percent South African and 40 percent Mozambican. In execution, slightly fewer South African households without a death were interviewed (187 instead of 190), and one extra South African household with a death was interviewed (96 instead of 95).

These discrepancies were the result of confusion over which households were considered to have a "complete" interview in cases where the head of household refused to be interviewed. The survey is composed of a household module, to be completed by a knowledgeable household member; an adult module, to be completed by each member aged eighteen or older; and a child module, to be completed for each child aged twelve or younger. Some adult household members were migrants who were not in the field site to be interviewed (although the field team made a great effort to make appointments with the household to return at month end, or at Easter, to interview returning migrants). In addition, some adult members refused to be interviewed. We decided that if the household module was completed, and at least one adult was interviewed, the household had a "complete" interview.

In the South African-Death Stratum, an extra household was interviewed because the household head came home for Easter, after the rest of the household had been interviewed, and refused to participate. The field team then interviewed a replacement household, but need not have: we had made a decision that if the head refused to participate, but did not stop other members from doing so, then that household's information would be used.

Table 11.1   **Sample design for Agincourt field work**

	Number of households	South African households	Mozambican households
No death in household	Design	190	127
	Actual	187	127
Death in household	Design	95	63
	Actual	96	63

However, if a returning head refused to let any members participate (even if they had already been interviewed), we did not use that household in our analysis.

11.2.2   Data Collected

Households were interviewed between January and July 2004. A knowledgeable household member was asked to provide information about all other members, including their ages, educational attainment, incomes from a variety of sources and, for younger members, whether they were currently enrolled in school. In addition, this person was asked about household assets and household spending on various types of food, phones, fuel, rent, rates, children's schooling, and hire purchase payments. We included a battery of questions on death in the household module. We began by asking about all deaths in the last five years, and went on to ask a set of questions about the funeral of the person who had died most recently.

Every adult in the household was interviewed separately, and was asked about personal expenses (such as their clothing and transport) and about their sources of income. We also asked each about his or her health, mental health, and problems observed in the household.

Summary statistics for the households are presented in table 11.2. On average, households in the sample have just over six members. Mozambican households are significantly larger than South African households, with

Table 11.2   **Summary statistics on the households drawn into the sample**

	All households	South African households	Mozambican households
Household size	6.18	5.79	6.75***
Number of members aged 0–5	0.76	0.64	0.93***
Number of members aged 6–17	2.06	1.90	2.30**
Number of members aged 18+	3.29	3.21	3.40
Percent female	0.52	0.52	0.52
Total monthly expenditure per member	161	199	103***
Total monthly expenditure	782	896	611***
Number of assets owned	5.94	6.06	3.76***
Number of deaths in past 5 years	0.49	0.46	0.54
Number of deaths for members aged 0–5	0.11	0.07	0.15**
Number of deaths for members aged 6–17	0.03	0.03	0.04
Number of deaths for members aged 18+	0.36	0.36	0.36
Number of households	473	283	190

Notes: Sample means presented. Expenditures are reported in rands. Asterisks in column 3 denote that the difference between South African households and Mozambican households is significant at the 10 percent (*), 5 percent (**) or 1 percent (***) level. Monthly expenditure is the sum of household spending on mealie meal, bread, milk, cold drinks, sweets, fruit and vegetables, meat, chicken and fish, groceries, rent or bond payment, electricity, rates, fuel, telephone, cell phone, hire purchase, and children's school uniforms, books, and fees.

Table 11.3   **Summary statistics on the deceased**

	All	SA All	MZ All	SA (18 and older)	MZ (18 and older)
Female	0.428	0.421	0.438	0.451	0.483
Age at death	37.1	42.1	30.1***	51.3	42.3***
Indicator: pension aged at death	0.212	0.274	0.125***	0.341	0.182**
Years of education	2.36	2.95	1.61**	3.51	2.18*
Financial contribution was important when healthy	0.490	0.526	0.438	0.648	0.636
Deceased was the household head	0.428	0.474	0.363	0.582	0.527
Number of observations	194	114	80	91	55

Notes: Sample means presented. Asterisks in column (3) denote that the difference between South Africans (SA) in column (2) and Mozambicans (MZ) in column (3) is significant at the 10 percent (*), 5 percent (**), or 1 percent (***) level. Asterisks in column (5) compare results between South Africans in column (4) and Mozambicans in column (5).

fully one additional member—generally a child under the age of eighteen. South African households are more affluent than their Mozambican counterparts, with expenditure per member on food and other household goods twice as high in South African households, and with a significantly greater number of assets reported. On average, total monthly household spending is approximately equal in value to that of the state old-age pension at this time (which was R740), underscoring the fact that the region is poor.

Mozambicans report a greater number of deaths of children age five or younger in the last five years, but equal numbers of deaths of members aged five to seventeen, and deaths of adult members (eighteen and above).

Summary statistics for the *most recent* death in the household are presented in table 11.3, where results are presented for all such deaths, and separately for deaths of adult members (eighteen and older). Mozambicans are significantly younger on average at death, and significantly less likely to be of pension age (sixty years old for women, sixty-five for men). They are also reported to have completed fewer years of schooling—although educational attainment among the deceased is very low in general, with fewer than three years reported for South Africans also. For adult deaths, approximately two-thirds of households report that the most recently deceased's member made an important financial contribution to the household while they were healthy.

Seventy-five percent of households reporting a death came from the strata targeted for a recent death. (We also use information on a death in the past five years if that death fell before or after the window June 1, 2002 to May 31, 2003.) We turn now to the funerals of the most recent death in each household.

Table 11.4   **Purchases for the most recent funeral**

	Fraction reporting expenditure on this category	Amount spent, conditional on reporting positive expenditure	Amount spent, unconditional on reporting positive expenditure
Coffin	0.65	2,221	1,392
Meat	0.85	1,099	924
Groceries	0.76	693	512
Cemetery costs	0.17	343	50
Clothing	0.58	188	105
Flowers	0.22	112	21
Transport	0.30	205	47
Food for prayer service	0.61	190	100
Other	0.16	337	52
Total spending on funeral	—	—	2,877 ($n = 165$)
Total, South African household	—	—	3,710 ($n = 99$)
Total, Mozambican household	—	—	1,629 ($n = 66$)
Total, knowledgeable household member	—	—	3,195 ($n = 140$)

Notes: Sample means presented. Expenditures are reported in rands. The sample used in the final row is restricted to deaths for which the knowledgeable household member knows the expenditure for meat, or reports that no meat was purchased. Dashed cells = not applicable (through table 11.6).

11.3   Funeral Expenses

For the most recent funeral in the past five years, we asked whether the household spent money for a coffin, meat, groceries, additional cemetery costs, burial and mourning clothing, flowers, transport for mourners, food for a prefuneral prayer service, and other expenses.[2] If the respondent reported spending on these categories, we asked the rand amount for this item. Results of these reports are presented in table 11.4. The largest outlays are for a coffin, meat for the meal following the funeral, and groceries both for the meal and to feed mourners who come to pay respects (some of whom stay with the mourning household for several days). Sixty-five percent of households report purchasing a coffin and, conditional upon this purchase, report spending 2,200 rand. The vast majority (85 percent) report buying meat, and among those who purchased meat, 1,100 rand were spent. Three-quarters bought groceries, and those who did spent 700 rand. The average

2. In four cases, no information about the funeral was provided by the knowledgeable household member. In two of these, the funeral was held elsewhere and the respondent did not know what was spent. In two other cases, the respondent was not willing to answer these questions.

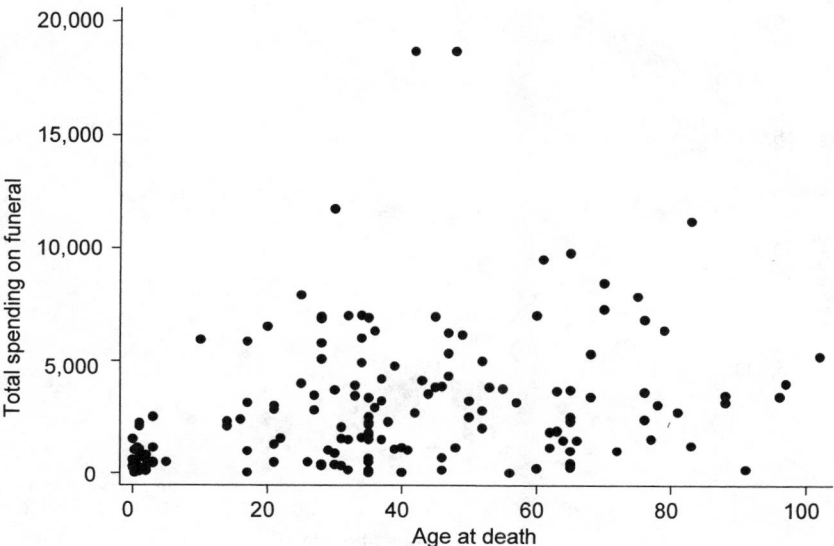

Fig. 11.1   Total spending on funerals by age of death

funeral expenses totaled 2,900 rand, with the relatively wealthier South Africans spending 3,700 rand on average and Mozambicans, 1,600 rand. These totals are presented for all funerals in which any spending was reported. If we restrict the sample to a (possibly more reliable) sample of respondents who remember what was spent on meat, funeral spending totaled 3,195 rand on average.

Significantly less is spent on the funerals of small children. Figure 11.1 presents total spending on funerals by the age of the deceased. It is clear that, for those younger than age six, funerals are much more modest. On average, for the funerals of children aged zero to five, 682 rand were spent. For the funerals of household members older than age five, on average 3,415 rand were spent. As seen in figure 11.2, when we restrict the sample to those who were older than age five at their death, there is no relationship between age and funeral spending.[3] This is true even if large outliers (e.g., two funerals where more than 18,000 rand are reported) are removed from the sample. In what follows, we will use the fact that the funerals for household members ages six to seventeen are as expensive as funerals for adult members (many of whom had been contributing to household income before their deaths) to argue that it is the death of a member greater than age five, or spending on funerals for members greater than age five, that is

3. It is interesting to contrast this with the age-funeral spending profile found among the Zulus, where funeral spending increases with age through age seventy (Case et al. 2008).

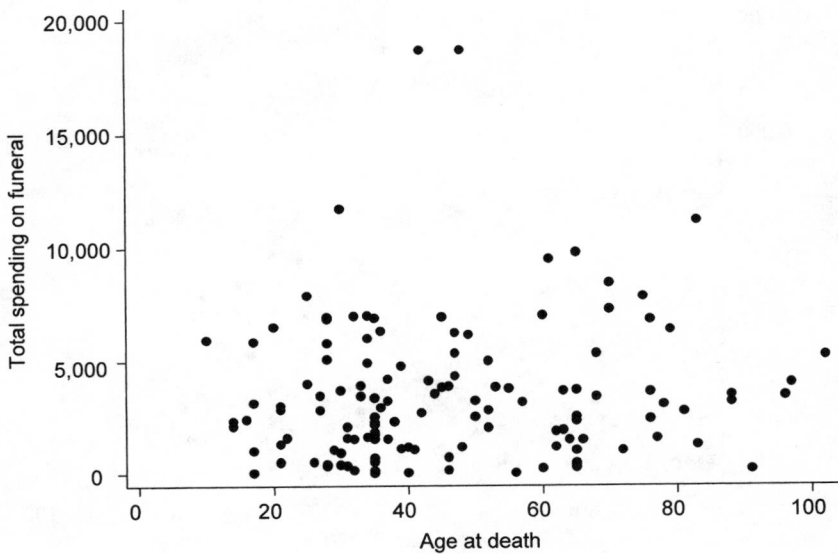

Fig. 11.2   **Total spending on funerals for members above age five**

responsible for the hardships that households report after the death of a household member.

Table 11.5 presents information on who paid for the funeral in the Demographic Surveillance Site. In 81 percent of funerals, household members contributed money and, when they did, on average they contributed almost 2,500 rand. This includes any money that the household received from a burial society or funeral policy for the deceased. Extended family, not in the household, is reported to contribute to 73 percent of all funerals. They contribute a smaller but still substantial sum (1,358 rand on average). The community is reported to contribute in 72 percent of all funerals, and the church in more than half of all funerals, although in both cases substantially less is contributed. Employers contribute to only one in ten funerals, but when they do contribute the amount is substantial (2,900 rand on average). The knowledgeable household member, reporting on the funeral, can remember 3,200 rand of contributions on average, which is close to what was reported on funeral spending (2,900 rand). This adding up need not have happened—questions on what was spent are asked in a separate section from questions on who contributed what—so this provides a check on the quality of the data.

Mechanisms have evolved in South Africa to help individuals save for funerals. These include membership in a burial society, or the purchase of a funeral policy with a funeral parlor or an insurance company. Money paid into a funeral policy can only be drawn upon at death. For approximately 20 to 30 rand per month (more, if one is insuring additional household

Table 11.5   **Contributions for the most recent funeral**

	Percent of group reported to have contributed to the most recent funeral	Amount contributed, conditional on reporting positive contribution	Amount contributed, unconditional on reporting positive contribution
Household members	0.81	2,478	1,819
Other family not in the household	0.73	1,358	882
Community	0.72	344	209
Church	0.53	282	121
Employer	0.12	2,889	220
Other	0.07	1,165	61
Total spending on funeral	—	—	3,182 ($n = 153$)
Total, South African household	—	—	4,225 ($n = 93$)
Total, Mozambican household	—	—	1,564 ($n = 60$)

Notes: Sample means presented. Contributions are reported in rands.

members), individuals are guaranteed that some expenses incurred for their funerals will be paid for by the insurer.

Table 11.6 presents information on whether the deceased was covered by a burial society or funeral policy and, if so, whether that fund paid money or contributed a coffin, food, or transport for the funeral. In a third of all cases, the deceased was covered by a funeral policy or burial society. In a quarter of all deaths, the policy paid money (4,750 rand on average). In 20 percent of cases, the policy contributed a coffin—which would have saved the household approximately 2,200 rand in funeral costs on average.

Ownership of a funeral policy is highly correlated with being of pension age. Each month, after receiving their pension, pensioners can pay into their burial account at the *pension pay point*. (Funeral parlors and insurance companies are the only private firms allowed to conduct business inside pension pay points, which are generally surrounded by a fence or barrier of some sort.) Seventy percent of pension-aged people who died had a funeral policy, in contrast to 27 percent of those not yet of pension age. Why would younger adults not belong to a burial society? We can only speculate, but one possibility, suggested to us by Karla Hoff, "is the same reason that Duflo, Kremer, and Robinson (2008) find that farmers aren't keen on buying fertilizer when they need it (at the beginning of the season) but are very responsive to the option to buy fertilizer immediately after their harvest. It might be that people don't like to plan, but if they have money in hand, and a seller is strategically positioned when they receive cash, then they will buy what they know they will need later on" (Karla Hoff, personal correspondence). A noncompeting hypothesis is that planning for one's own death is painful, and more so for the young than for the old.

Table 11.6   Burial society and funeral policy contributions

	Fraction reporting	Conditional on reporting money, amount transferred
Indicator: Deceased covered by a funeral policy or burial society	0.36	—
Indicator: Policy paid money	0.26	mean = 4,750 median = 2,250
Indicator: Policy contributed a coffin	0.21	—
Indicator: Policy contributed food	0.12	—
Indicator: Policy contributed transport	0.19	—

Notes: Sample means presented. The number of observations is 194 for the indicator of having a policy; 193 for indicators that a coffin, food, or transport were part of the policy; and 192 for reports of whether money was part of the policy.

In what follows, we will focus primarily on the number of deaths and the ages of those who died in the household in the past five years. We will not use information on whether a burial policy paid out, in order to sidestep the issue of whether people who have burial policies know how to plan, which may then be a marker that their households are better organized. We turn to the consequences of deaths in the household in the next section.

11.4   Household and Individual Outcomes

Our identification strategy in quantifying the impact of death and funeral expenses is to assume, by nationality, that households that had experienced a death would be similar in measures of well-being to those that did not, if the death had not occurred. We will return in section 11.5 to discuss alternative explanations for our findings.

11.4.1   Expenditure per Member in 2004

A knowledgeable household member reported expenditures on all household goods, the sum of which we use to construct a marker of current household economic status. Table 11.7 presents results from ordinary least squares (OLS) regressions in which we regress the log of monthly expenditure per member in 2004 on deaths in the household in the past five years, together with other controls, in order to characterize the impact of the death and funeral.[4]

---

4. All regressions include an index for the number of spending categories for which the knowledgeable household member knew something was spent, but did not know the amount.

Table 11.7   Household deaths in the past 5 years and log (expenditure per member)

	(1)	(2)	(3)	(4)	(5)	(6)
Number of deaths ages 18 or older in the past 5 years	-0.222*** (0.066)	—	—	—	—	—
Number of deaths ages 6–17 in the past 5 years	-0.177 (0.189)	—	—	—	—	—
Number of deaths ages 0–5 in the past 5 years	-0.022 (0.114)	—	—	—	—	—
Number of deaths ages 6 or older in the past 5 years	—	-0.216*** (0.063)	—	-0.159* (0.082)	-0.187** (0.085)	-0.278*** (0.090)
Any deaths ages 6 or older in the past 5 years	—	—	-0.197** (0.090)	—	—	—
Deceased was of pension age (latest death)	—	—	0.015 (0.150)	—	—	—
Deceased's income was financially important (latest death)	—	—	—	-0.134 (0.124)	—	—
Number of deaths ages 6 or older interacted with Mozambican	—	—	—	—	-0.065 (0.126)	—
Indicator: Most recent death was 2002–2004	—	—	—	—	—	0.109 (0.114)
Indicator: Household is Mozambican	-0.582*** (0.077)	-0.584*** (0.077)	-0.589*** (0.078)	-0.588*** (0.077)	-0.559*** (0.091)	-0.586*** (0.077)

Notes: Dependent variable = log(monthly expenditure per member on household goods). OLS regressions coefficients are presented, with standard errors in parentheses. Asterisks note that the coefficient is significant at the 10 percent (*), 5 percent (**) or 1 percent (***) level. Regressions are run at the household level for 467 households who answered questions on household expenditures. All regressions include an index for the number of spending categories for which the knowledgeable household member knows something was spent, but does not know the amount. The mean of the dependent variable is 4.729. Dashed cells = the variable listed in the first column is not included in the regression reported in any given column (through table 11.9; also includes table 11.11).

Column (1) controls separately for the number of deaths of members aged eighteen and older, aged six to seventeen, and aged zero to five years old. All regressions include a control for whether the head of household was Mozambican. Consistent with the information presented in table 11.2, expenditure per member is approximately twice as high in South African households than in Mozambican households.

We find spending in households that lost an adult in the past five years is approximately 20 percent lower than in households that did not. The point-estimate on the number of deaths of members aged six to seventeen, although imprecisely estimated, also suggests approximately 20 percent lower spending in households who lost members in that age range. An F-test does not reject that the impact of an adult death and that of a member aged six to seventeen are the same. Spending on the death of a child aged zero to five appears to be orthogonal to current log expenditure per member: the point estimate is small (−0.02) and not significantly different from zero.

In order to present some interaction terms in a parsimonious way, we combine the number of deaths of members ages six to seventeen and those ages eighteen and older, and present results in column (2). As in column (1), each death in this age group is associated with a 20 percent reduction in household spending per person. Perhaps because only 8 percent of households had multiple deaths in this period, results are very similar if we use an indicator for *any* deaths of members aged six or above (column [3] of table 11.7). We continue to find that expenditure per member in households with a death is approximately 20 percent lower. We find no difference between deaths of members ages six to pension age and those above pension age, which can also be seen in column (3) of table 11.7: an indicator that the deceased was of pension age has no significant association with log expenditure per member.

The inclusion of a control that the deceased's income was "financially important when healthy," in column (4), reduces the coefficient on the number of deaths aged six or above, from 22 to 16 percent. The coefficient on number of deaths is still negatively and significantly associated with current household spending, while the indicator that the deceased's income was financially important is not.

In both South African and Mozambican households, death of a member is associated with a 20 percent reduction in spending per person. Column (5) includes an interaction term between the number of deaths of members above the age of five with an indicator that the household was Mozambican. The coefficient on this interaction term is small and insignificantly different from zero.

We also tested whether the impact of a more recent death was larger than that of a death that occurred more than two years ago, to see whether households appear to rebound after a funeral. The regression in column (6) includes an indicator that the most recent death was in 2002, 2003, or 2004 (as opposed to 1999, 2000, or 2001). The coefficient is small, insignificant, and of a counterintuitive sign.

The large sums of money spent on funerals must come from somewhere. Results in table 11.7 are consistent with households—whatever their financing mechanism—having to reduce future expenditures per member to pay for funerals. These findings are qualitatively similar to those of other studies reviewed in Naidu and Harris (2005).

11.4.2   Problems in the Household

Each adult was asked questions about whether he or she was currently experiencing certain problems. Specifically, the question was asked, "Is _____ a problem for you right now?" We present the association between reports of having problems and death in the household in table 11.8, where all regressions control for age, sex, years of education, and nationality. We find that reports of "not having enough money" and "unemployment of family members" are positively, but insignificantly, associated with recent death. We find a significant association between death and reports of "not having enough food," "quarrels in the household," and "safety in the neighborhood." All are approximately 5 percentage points higher with each death of a member aged six or older. For "food" and "quarrels," the association between death in the household and these problems can be explained by the lower socioeconomic status of households in which someone died: when a control for expenditure per member is added to each regression, the associations between food and death, and between quarrels and death, become smaller and insignificant.

11.4.3   Investments in Children

The household module asked whether each member aged five to twenty-five was enrolled in school. We use this as a measure of current investments made in children. (We chose not to use educational attainment, because it may reflect school-going during the period when the deceased was in need of care.) All regressions include controls for sex, age, age squared, the number of assets the household owns, and the log expenditure per member.

The first two columns of table 11.9 present OLS regression results on the association between enrollment and the number of deaths of members by age group (eighteen and above, six to seventeen, and age five and younger). The last three columns present results on the number of deaths of members aged six or older. Beginning with results by age group, we find each adult death reduces the probability of enrollment by 4 percentage points, and the death of a six- to seventeen-year-old reduces the probability by 5 percentage points (although the latter is just shy of being statistically significant). An F-test shows that the difference in the effect of an adult death and that of a six- to seventeen-year-old are not statistically different (F-test $= 0.08$, p-value $= 0.772$). Results in column (3), where all deaths above age five are

Table 11.8   Household deaths in the past 5 years and reports of problems currently facing respondents

	Dependent variable									
	Not having enough money [0.791]		Not having enough food [0.697]		Unemployment of family members [0.730]		Quarrels in the household [0.287]		Safety in the neighborhood [0.249]	
Number of deaths ages 6 or older in the past 5 years	0.021 (0.018)	0.010 (0.018)	0.051** (0.021)	0.032 (0.020)	0.029 (0.020)	0.010 (0.019)	0.038* (0.020)	0.029 (0.021)	0.045** (0.020)	0.039* (0.20)
Log expenditure per member	—	-0.097*** (0.016)	—	-0.153*** (0.0180)	—	-0.152*** (0.016)	—	-0.064*** (0.018)	—	-0.039** (0.017)
Number of observations	1,240	1,231	1,239	1,230	1,239	1,230	1,239	1,230	1,239	1,230

Notes: Standard errors are presented in parentheses. The sample is restricted to adults ages 18 and older. All regressions include controls for age, sex, years of education, and nationality.

***Significant at the 1 percent level.

**Significant at the 5 percent level.

*Significant at the 10 percent level.

Table 11.9   Household deaths in the past 5 years and children's outcomes

	(1)	(2)	(3)	(4)	(5)
Number of deaths ages 18 or older in the past 5 years	-0.038**	0.011	—	—	—
	(0.015)	(0.020)	—	—	—
Number of deaths ages 6–17 in the past 5 years	-0.048	-0.058	—	—	—
	(0.031)	(0.036)	—	—	—
Number of deaths ages 0–5 in the past 5 years	0.010	0.024	—	—	—
	(0.022)	(0.027)	—	—	—
Number of deaths ages 6 or older in the past 5 years	—	—	-0.040***	-0.030*	-0.004
	—	—	(0.014)	(0.015)	(0.019)
Amount household members paid for most recent funeral (1,000 R)	—	-0.027**	—	—	-0.025*
	—	(0.014)	—	—	(0.014)
Amount household members paid squared	—	0.001	—	—	0.001
	—	(0.001)	—	—	(0.001)
F-test: Joint sig of death variables (*p*-value)	3.02	1.20	—	—	—
	(0.029)	(0.308)	—	—	—
F-test: Number deaths 18 plus = number deaths 6–17 (*p*-value)	0.08	3.19	—	—	—
	(0.772)	(0.074)	—	—	—
Number of observations	1,533	1,301	1,533	1,301	1,301

Notes: Dependent variable = 1 if individual is enrolled, ages 5 to 25 [0.723]. OLS regression results reported, with standard errors presented in parentheses. All regressions include controls for sex, age, age squared, number of assets the household owns, log expenditure per member, and nationality.

***Significant at the 1 percent level.

**Significant at the 5 percent level.

*Significant at the 10 percent level.

combined, show a similar result. Results in columns (1) and (3) are changed by the inclusion of controls for the amount of money spent by the household on the most recent funeral in the past five years. (This is zero if the household did not experience a death.)[5] Adding the household's expenditure on the funeral and that expenditure squared, the impact of the number of deaths in the past five years becomes statistically insignificant, whether these deaths are expressed by age category (column [2]), or as the number of deaths above the age of five (column [5]). The household's funeral spending variables are jointly significantly different from zero, whether deaths are expressed by age category (F-test $= 3.27$, p-value $= 0.038$) or as deaths above the age of five (F-test $= 2.76$, p-value $= 0.064$). The household's funeral spending variables suggest that each 1,000 rand that the household puts toward the funeral reduces the probability that a member of school-going age will be enrolled by approximately 3 percentage points.

11.4.4   Depression and Anxiety

Table 11.10 presents results on adults reporting symptoms of depression, using questions from an abbreviated Center for Epidemiologic Studies Depression Scale (CES-D) that asked how often the respondent felt the following:

- I felt I could not stop feeling miserable, even with help from my family and friends.
- I felt depressed.
- I felt sad.
- I cried a lot.
- I did not feel like eating. My appetite was poor.
- I felt everything I did was an effort.
- My sleep was restless.
- I could not get "going."

Respondents were asked to report whether, in the last week, they felt these symptoms hardly ever, some of the time, or most of the time. Table 11.10 presents mean responses for these indicators in square brackets for each depression symptom. Approximately a third of all respondents report having felt miserable, depressed, sad, and having had restless sleep. A quarter report having a poor appetite and an inability to get going. We regress these indicators on age, sex, nationality, years of education, and the number of deaths in the household in the past five years. Women are significantly more likely to report many of these symptoms. Controlling for age, sex, and nationality, education appears to be protective against depression. The number of deaths in the household is significantly associated with reports of feeling

---

5. Results on the impact of household funeral spending are very similar if we restrict the sample to only households that experienced a death in the past five years.

Table 11.10   Household deaths in the past 5 years and markers for depression

	Dependent variable						
	Felt miserable [0.317]	Felt depressed [0.400]	Felt sad [0.316]	Cried a lot [0.106]	Poor appetite [0.288]	Restless sleep [0.417]	Could not get going [0.269]
Number of deaths ages 6 or older in the past 5 years	0.035* (0.021)	0.036* (0.021)	0.007 (0.021)	0.041*** (0.014)	0.027 (0.020)	0.044** (0.021)	0.054*** (0.019)
Indicator: Female	0.041 (0.027)	0.044 (0.028)	0.077*** (0.028)	0.115*** (0.018)	0.076*** (0.026)	0.082*** (0.028)	0.066*** (0.025)
Years of education	-0.015*** (0.005)	-0.024*** (0.005)	-0.020*** (0.005)	-0.008** (0.003)	-0.017*** (0.005)	-0.019*** (0.005)	-0.008* (0.004)
Number of observations	1,236	1,235	1,235	1,234	1,235	1,235	1,236

Notes: OLS regression coefficients reported, with standard errors presented in parentheses. The sample is restricted to adults ages 18 and older. All regressions also include controls for age and nationality.

***Significant at the 1 percent level.

**Significant at the 5 percent level.

*Significant at the 10 percent level.

miserable, feeling depressed, crying a lot, having restless sleep, and reporting an inability to get going.

We aggregate the eight indicators together into an index, and regress that index on the number of deaths in the household of members aged six or older, in the first set of columns of table 11.11.[6] We find each death increases the depression index by a quarter of a point, on average. In results estimated but not reported in table 11.11, we find that women report a significantly larger number of symptoms, all else held constant. We find education, household asset holdings, and expenditure per member negatively and significantly associated with depression.

In column (2), we restrict the sample to respondents for whom household spending on the funeral is not missing, to make sure the results are not driven by a change is sample composition, and in column (3) we add to this regression the amount of money that household members contributed to the most recent funeral, and that amount squared. We find the depression index increases with the amount spent on the funeral through a spending level of 7,200 rand—well beyond the ninety-fifth percentile of household spending on funerals. Moreover, the inclusion of the household's financial contribution to the funeral reduces the impact of deaths from 0.20 to –0.02, and leaves it insignificantly different from zero.[7] Coefficients on several other factors associated with depression (sex, education, assets, expenditure per member) are largely unchanged. (These results were estimated but are not reported in table 11.11.)

The last three columns in table 11.11 investigate the association between death in the household and reports of anxiety. Specifically, we asked respondents whether "during the past 12 months, did [they] ever have a period lasting one month or longer when most of the time [they] felt worried, tense, or anxious." On average, 39 percent of respondents reported that they had. Deaths above age five are associated with a 5.5 percentage point increase in the probability of reporting a period of anxiety lasting a month or longer. However, including controls for the household's financial contribution to the most recent funeral, which is significantly associated with reports of anxiety, reduces the coefficient on the death variable to 0.001 and leaves it insignificantly different from zero.

11.5   Discussion

Results in section 11.4 suggest that death in the household and household spending on funerals leave household members vulnerable: spending in their

6. Results are qualitatively similar if we score a report of "most" of the time as a 2, and "some" of the time as a 1 before aggregating the responses into an index.

7. Results on the impact of household funeral spending on depression and anxiety are very similar if we restrict the sample to only households that experienced a death in the past five years.

Table 11.11   Household deaths in the past 5 years and reports of depression and anxiety

	Dependent variable			
	Depression index [2.46]		= 1 if reported a month of worry [0.390]	
Number of deaths ages 6 or older in the past five years	0.262*** (0.107)	0.202* (0.122)	0.055** (0.022)	0.065*** (0.025)
Amount household members paid for most recent funeral (1,000 R)	—	0.245*** (0.100)	—	0.076*** (0.020)
Amount household members paid squared	—	−0.017* (0.009)	—	−0.006*** (0.002)
Number of observations	1,225	1,079	1,226	1,079

Notes: OLS regression coefficients reported, with standard errors presented in parentheses. The sample is restricted to adults ages 18 and older. The depression index is the sum of self-reports that some or most of the time in the past week the respondent felt miserable; felt depressed; felt sad; cried a lot; did not feel like eating; felt everything was an effort; had trouble sleeping; and could not get "going." Also included in each regression are controls for age, age squared, sex, education, number of assets owned, log expenditure per member, and nationality.

***Significant at the 1 percent level.

**Significant at the 5 percent level.

*Significant at the 10 percent level.

households is significantly lower following the funeral, relative to other households; children in households that experienced a death are significantly less likely to be enrolled in school; and adults are significantly more likely to report problems in the household, symptoms of depression, and periods of anxiety.

Children's lower rates of enrollment and adults' reports of depression and anxiety following the death of a member aged six or older can be "explained" by the household's financial contribution to the funeral. The larger the contribution, the less likely it is that children are enrolled in school, and the more likely it is that adults are depressed and anxious. There are, however, alternative explanations for these findings.

We did not observe households prior to the deaths reported in 2004, so we do not know what was true in households before a member passed away. Perhaps spending in these households was always lower than in other households. Children in these households may always have been less likely to be enrolled in school, and adults in these households always more prone to depression and anxiety.

To explore whether households that experienced a death are different from other households in observable ways, we looked in the data for (relatively stable) markers of household socioeconomic status (SES). At the household level, we looked at the association between death in the households and the number of assets the household owned, maximum education of any member, whether the household has access to any kind of toilet facility or latrine, and whether the household lived in a formal dwelling. We present results on these measures of SES in table 11.12, where the first four regressions are run at the household level. We find no association between the death of members aged six or older and assets holdings, maximum education of a member, or an indicator that the household lived in a formal dwelling. Households that experienced a death might have been asset-poor before the death or may have sold off assets to pay for the funeral, but we find no evidence to support either of these ideas.[8] To the extent we find any significant relationships between deaths and markers of SES, we find that the deaths of infants and children under the age of six are significantly associated with larger asset holdings, and greater education of the most educated member in the household. In addition, deaths above the age of five are associated with an increased probability of reporting access to any type of toilet facility. Again, these do not strengthen the case that households that had deaths were poorer prior to the death, and we are only picking up that fact in our current data.[9]

---

8. In field work in Zululand we rarely observed households selling assets to pay funeral expenses (Case et al. 2008). This is consistent with findings of Roth (1999), who argues that this is largely because the time between the sale of the asset and the receipt of cash is too long for households who need immediate cash to pay for funeral-related items.

9. Having a better educated member may be correlated with the age structure of the household. The lack of association between death in the household and maximum education of a member continues to be observed in regressions that also control for the age structure of the household.

Table 11.12   Correlates of death in the households in the past five years

			Dependent variable		
	Number of assets [5.14]	Maximum education of a member [7.42]	Access to any type of toilet or latrine [0.793]	Formal dwelling [0.867]	Education of adults (21+) [4.85]
Number of deaths ages 6 or older in the past 5 years	−0.021 (0.201)	0.165 (0.243)	0.073** (0.029)	0.034 (0.025)	0.036 (0.130)
Number of deaths ages 0–5	0.738** (0.366)	0.934** (0.442)	0.003 (0.054)	0.015 (0.043)	0.255 (0.218)
Number of observations	473	472	473	472	1,284

Notes: OLS regression coefficients reported, with standard errors presented in parentheses. All regressions also include a control for nationality. The final column also includes controls for age and sex.

***Significant at the 1 percent level.

**Significant at the 5 percent level.

*Significant at the 10 percent level.

We also regress the educational attainment of all adults in the household aged twenty-one or higher on deaths in the household, with controls for nationality, sex, and age. These results, in the last column of table 11.12, are also consistent with households that experienced a death being much like other households in the demographic surveillance area.

There are other possible explanations for our findings. For example, the size of the funeral might be larger, the higher the status of the person who died. The loss of a high status member might lead to depression and anxiety among adults left behind. Although we cannot rule this out, we can report that household spending on funerals, for those who died above the age of five, does not correlate with the age of the person who died, or whether the deceased was the head of household, or whether the deceased's financial contribution to the household was important when he or she was healthy. Funeral spending is significantly correlated with the education of the deceased, but only marginally so. Thus, while this is a possible explanation, we find little evidence to support it. (That said, we have made very little progress in understanding the determinants of funeral spending in the field site. If we were able to identify why some funerals were larger than others in the Agincourt Demographic Surveillance Area, we might be in a better position to evaluate the argument that the funeral is a marker for status, and it is the loss of a high status member that leads to future misfortune in the household.)

11.6   Conclusion

A household that experiences the death of a member is at risk for poorer outcomes on a number of dimensions following the funeral, and the risk appears to be greater, the more the household spent to bury their dead. The South African Council of Churches has called repeatedly for "appropriate and affordable" funerals. (See, for example, http://www.sacc.org.za/docs/AnRept05.pdf.) Our results suggest that reining in the size of funerals may improve households' long-run prospects.

References

Case, A., A. Garrib, A. Menendez, and A. Olgiati. 2008. Paying the piper: The high cost of funerals in South Africa. NBER Working Paper no. 14456. Cambridge, MA: National Bureau of Economic Research, October.
Case, A. and A. Menendez. 2007. Does money empower the elderly? Evidence from the Agincourt Demographic Surveillance Area. *Scandinavian Journal of Public Health* 35 (3): 157–64.
Duflo, E., M. Kremer, and J. Robinson. 2008. How high are rates of return to fertil-

izer? Evidence from field experiments in Kenya. *American Economic Review: Papers and Proceedings* 98 (2): 482–88.

Kahn, K., M. L. Garenne, M. A. Collinson, and S. M. Tollman. 2007. Mortality trends in a new South Africa: Hard to make a fresh start 1. *Scandinavian Journal of Public Health* 35 (S69): 26–34.

Kahn, K., S. M. Tollman, M. A. Collinson, S. J. Clark, R. Twine, B. D. Clark, M. Shabangu, F. X. Gómez-Olivé, O. Mokoena, and M. L. Garenne. 2007. Research into health, population and social transitions in rural South Africa: Data and methods of the Agincourt Health and Demographic Surveillance System. *Scandinavian Journal of Public Health Suppl.* 69:8–20.

Naidu, V., and G. Harris. 2005. The impact of HIV/AIDS morbidity and mortality on households—a review of household studies. *South African Journal of Economics* 73:533–44.

Roth, J. 1999. Informal micro-finance schemes: The case of funeral insurance in South Africa. Social Finance Unit Working Paper no. 22, International Labour Office. International Labour Organization, Geneva.

Comment   Esther Duflo

During the presentation of this article at the Boulders conference, Anne Case mentioned that the king of Swaziland had sought to ban funeral expenditures. Indeed, in 2002, the king issued a decree banning lavish funerals.[1] And some rural communities imposed a high tax on funeral expenditures: any family that slaughters a cow for a funeral has to give up another cow, to be added to the local chief's herd.

The king of Swaziland is not alone in his concern with runaway funeral expenditure. The South African Council of Churches (SACC) was also concerned about the "high cost and increasing ostentation associated with Christian funerals." The SACC was concerned enough to have called a special conference of all the stakeholders "to help to identify the factors that often prevent South Africans from commemorating their loved ones in appropriate, dignified, meaningful and affordable ways." Discussion revealed that "undertakers and funeral directors, state officials, insurance companies and churches all engage in practices that impose unnecessary burdens on the bereaved and compromise their ability to honor the deceased in a dignified manner."[2] As for policy, the SACC, favoring the same solution as the king

Esther Duflo is the Abdul Latif Jameel Professor of Poverty Alleviation and Development Economics and a director of the Abdul Latif Jameel Poverty Action Lab at the Massachusetts Institute of Technology, and a research associate of the National Bureau of Economic Research.

1. "Funeral Feasts Off the Swazi Menu," BBC News, 2002. Available at: http://news.bbc.co.uk/2/hi/africa/2082281.stm.
2. The South African Council of Churches, Annual Report, 2005, 7 (quotes). Available at: http://sacc.org.za/docs/AnRept05.pdf.

but working within different institutions, issued a call for the regulation of the funeral industry.

Why the concern? Why do both the king and the SACC feel obligated to abrogate the rights of a family to spend as much as seems proper to the family on the funeral of a loved one? Is theirs a legitimate concern? Is it rooted in ulterior motives or in the welfare of the bereaved family? This article sheds some light on this question.

First, the evidence is that families are not properly insured for the cost of the funerals of the prime-age adults (funerals for young children are not too expensive and those of the elderly are covered by burial policies). An expensive funeral—and most of them are very expensive, at about 40 percent of average annual *total* expenditure—leads to significant reduction of expenditures in the future as well as an increased probability of children dropping out of school. The chapter presents some evidence that this loss can be largely attributed to the funeral itself, not to the loss of breadwinners. The most convincing piece of evidence on this point is that the funerals of pre-teenage and teenage children, who are not contributing to the family earnings, have as large an effect on future expenditure as those of adults, an effect much larger than that of young children.

Second, on balance, spending that much money leaves the household unhappy. Households that have had a funeral are more likely to report stress and worries, or problems in the family, problems that are very likely to be related to money. This suggests that large funeral expenditures lead to a real loss in welfare. The large ceremonies may certainly not be worth the painful losses that follow. One can speculate that, weighed down the loss of a loved one, members of the bereaved household could not enjoy the ceremony.

This evidence lends some support to the view, shared by king and the SACC, that families are compelled by social norms or misled by unscrupulous funeral agents to spend more than they would rather. Indeed there are anecdotes in the press: in August 2003, the *Sunday Times* of Johannesburg carried an interview with one Sepata, who reported having spent R16,000 on his mothers' funeral, though he had planned to spend only a quarter of that. He said, "All this spending was imposed on me by family elders, when I would have been happy to spend 500 bucks on a coffin for my mom, and maybe get a nice tombstone that her great grandchildren can visit every day. Instead, it's money wasted."[3]

These "social expenditures" take a huge toll on the household. No individual is in a position to refuse to spend some money on these social expenditures. Nevertheless, it would be socially efficient if society as a whole could switch to a different equilibrium, one where the norm is the subdued funeral

---

3. "Funerals spell financial suicide: Township families go deep into debt by hosting lavish burials," *Sunday Times* (Johannesburg), August 31, 2003.

and where high funeral expenses are frowned upon as squandering the baby's milk money.

Regulation could help, by providing a focal point. Both the king and the SACC also make appeals to culture, and try to recast the values. The king argued that expensive funerals are not part of Swazi culture, while SACC argued that they are neither "African" nor "Christian" nor "dignified."

But neither argument has had much traction. A report by the BBC on the decree says, some people, "while agreeing with the 'bring your own bottle funeral party' idea in principle, feared that even the poorest families would feel embarrassed about not feeding the mourners."[4] A 2004 study by the Joint Economics, AIDS, and Poverty Program of the University of Kwa-Zulu Natal in Durban found the decree notwithstanding, funeral expenditures in Swaziland were still very high, even higher to what people spent in Agincourt, South Africa (about 7,000 rand or twice what was found in Agincourt).[5]

Funerals are not the only example of large expenditures that are potentially socially determined. In a survey of very poor households in Udaipur districts, Rajasthan, India, I found that households living under a dollar a day spend on average 14 percent of their annual income on various festivals, including weddings (Banerjee and Duflo 2007). Social pressure to spend on such events could partly explain why households do not spend more on food or education for their children. More generally, the need to "keep up with the Joneses" seem to play an important role in terms of determining people's sense of the adequacy of their own consumption (Fafchamps and Shilpi 2008), and therefore presumably their choices of what to spend money on. These social obligations need to be a part of how economists consider household consumption choices, and this chapter is a striking example of why it matters.

The chapter makes a second point of general relevance. There are burial societies in South Africa. In fact, the funeral insurance they provide covers most of the expenses for the elderly. But younger people are generally not covered. Why don't the young buy funeral insurance?

Presumably, despite the prevalence of HIV-AIDS, prime-age adults could get the policy for a bargain (in the same way that the premium for life insurance is low for prime-age adults) and it would help their family cope with their own death. The chapter cites an explanation proposed by Karla Hoff. He attributes the lack of planning to a general difficulty of saving and planning ahead of the future.

I have every reason to like the Kenyan fertilizer example, for I have devoted

---

4. "Funeral Feasts Off the Swazi Menu," BBC News, 2002.
5. Kristin Palitza, "Health-Southern Africa: AIDS Puts Funeral Traditions Under Pressure," Inter Press Service, 17 February 2006. Available at: http://www.ips.org/africa/2006/02/health-southern-africa-aids-puts-funeral-traditions-under-pressure/.

a good part of my life to it. Nevertheless, I do think that the problem of planning for funeral for a prime-age adult not only potentially different but substantially harder than that of planning to buy fertilizer. In South Africa, burial insurance societies set up shop next to the old-age pension pay point. (In fact they the only business allowed to set up inside the enclosure where the old-age pensions are distributed.) Most of the pensioners go straight from the pay point to the burial society counter to pay their contribution. Young adults, who are not getting a pension, would need to take initiative to contribute. If we assume that the young do worry about the burden that funeral costs could impose on their relatives, then one possible explanation is that planning for one's own death when one is young and hale is simply too painful. More generally, insurance against catastrophic events—be it a death, a big health shock, or a drought—may be psychologically very difficult to plan for. The payout would be made, not just in the distant future, but in a future where one's world is in particularly bad shape. So, it may be to protect one's psychological well-being that one does not spend too much time anticipating these events; one must after all have one's sanity. This may explain why the poor households are unlikely to have formal insurance against catastrophic health events or weather disasters, and that even when that insurance is available and offered to them, the take up rates remain extremely low (Cole et al. 2009).

References

Banerjee, A., and E. Duflo. 2007. The economic lives of the poor. *Journal of Economic Perspectives* 21 (1): 141–67.

Cole, S. X. Gine, J. Tobacman, P. Topalova, R. Townsend, and J. Vickery. 2009. Barriers to household risk management: Evidence from India. Harvard Business School Working Paper no. 09-116, April.

Fafchamps, M., and F. Shilpi. 2008. Subjective welfare, isolation, and relative consumption. *Journal of Development Economics* 86:43–60.

Contributors

Abhijit Banerjee
Department of Economics, E52-252d
Massachusetts Institute of Technology
50 Memorial Drive
Cambridge, MA 02142-1347

John Beshears
Graduate School of Business
Stanford University
518 Memorial Way
Stanford, CA 94305

Anne Case
Department of Economics and
    Woodrow Wilson School
367 Wallace Hall
Princeton University
Princeton, NJ 08544

Amitabh Chandra
John F. Kennedy School of
    Government
Harvard University
79 John F. Kennedy Street
Cambridge, MA 02138

James J. Choi
Yale School of Management
135 Prospect Street
P.O. Box 208200
New Haven, CT 06520-8200

Angus Deaton
Woodrow Wilson School
328 Wallace Hall
Princeton University
Princeton, NJ 08544-1013

Esther Duflo
Department of Economics
Massachusetts Institute of Technology,
    E52-252G
50 Memorial Drive
Cambridge, MA 02142

Amy Finkelstein
Department of Economics
Massachusetts Institute of Technology,
    E52-274C
50 Memorial Drive
Cambridge, MA 02142

Rachel Glennerster
Abdul Latif Jameel Poverty Action Lab
Massachusetts Institute of Technology
30 Wadsworth Street, E53-320
Cambridge, MA 02142

Gopi Shah Goda
Stanford Institute for Economic Policy
    Research (SIEPR)
Stanford University
366 Galvez Street
Stanford, CA 94305

Florian Heiss
Department of Statistics and
  Econometrics
Johannes Gutenberg-Universität
  Mainz
Haus Recht und Wirtschaft II
D-55099 Mainz, Germany

Michael D. Hurd
RAND Corporation
1776 Main Street
Santa Monica, CA 90407

Arie Kapteyn
RAND Corporation
1776 Main Street
Santa Monica, CA 90407

David Laibson
Department of Economics
Littauer M-12
Harvard University
Cambridge, MA 02138

Brigitte C. Madrian
John F. Kennedy School of
  Government
Harvard University
79 John F. Kennedy Street
Cambridge, MA 02138

Samuel Marshall
Dartmouth College
Hanover, NH 03755

John J. McArdle
Department of Psychology
University of Southern California
3620 South McClintock Avenue
Los Angeles, CA 90089-1061

Daniel McFadden
University of California, Berkeley
Department of Economics
549 Evans Hall #3880
Berkeley, CA 94720-3880

Kathleen McGarry
Department of Economics
Bunche Hall 9359
University of California, Los Angeles
Los Angeles, CA 90095

Alicia Menendez
Harris School of Public Policy
University of Chicago
1155 East 60th Street, Suite 148
Chicago, IL 60637

James M. Poterba
Massachusetts Institute of Technology
  and National Bureau of Economic
  Research
1050 Massachusetts Avenue
Cambridge, MA 02138

Lindsay Sabik
Department of Health Care Policy
Harvard Medical School
180 Longwood Avenue
Boston, MA 02215

John B. Shoven
Department of Economics
Stanford University
579 Serra Mall at Galvez Street
Stanford, CA 94305-6015

Jonathan S. Skinner
Department of Economics
Dartmouth College
6106 Rockefeller Hall
Hanover, NH 03755

Sita Nataraj Slavov
Department of Economics
Occidental College
1600 Campus Road
Los Angeles, CA 90041

James P. Smith
RAND Corporation
1776 Main Street
Santa Monica, CA 90406

Arthur van Soest
Tilburg University
Department of Econometrics & OR
Office K 609
P.O. Box 90153
5000 LE Tilburg, Netherlands

Steven F. Venti
Department of Economics
Dartmouth College
6106 Rockefeller Center
Hanover, NH 03755

David R. Weir
Institute for Social Research
University of Michigan
426 Thompson Street
Ann Arbor, MI 48104

Finis Welch
Welch Consulting
1716 Briarcrest Drive, Suite 700
Bryan, TX 77802

Heidi Williams
National Bureau of Economic
    Research
1050 Massachusetts Avenue
Cambridge, MA 02138

Robert Willis
Health and Retirement Study,
    3048 ISR
University of Michigan
426 Thompson Street
Ann Arbor, MI 48104

Joachim Winter
Department of Economics
University of Munich
Ludwigstr. 28 (RG)
D-80539 Munich, Germany

David A. Wise
Harvard University and National
    Bureau of Economic Research
1050 Massachusetts Avenue
Cambridge, MA 02138-5398

Richard Woodbury
National Bureau of Economic
    Research
1050 Massachusetts Avenue
Cambridge, MA 02138

Author Index

Subject Index

DATE DUE

BRODART, CO.

Cat. No. 23-221